MW00946932

To Charlie Dyon,

I hope you enjoy these tales from a friend and a fellow Marine.

Semper fidelis,
Chuck

NO KIDS,
NO MONEY
AND A CHEVY

NO KIDS,
NO MONEY
AND A CHEVY

A POLITICALLY
INCORRECT MEMOIR

CHUCK MANSFIELD

To order additional copies of this book, contact:
Xlibris Corporation
1-888-795-4274
www.Xlibris.com
Orders@Xlibris.com
18404

CONTENTS

PART I
The Early Years

PART II
The Vietnam Era

PART III
Back in The World

PART IV
The Warp and Woof of Religion, Culture and Politics in Early Twenty-First Century America

PART V
End Papers

For Mame, the love of my life;
for Chas, John and Kate, our children and pride;
for Tim, Marissa, Kevin and Justin, joys all;
for Mike, my brother and counsel;
and for Mary and Charlie, who made me what I am.

Poems

Time Cannot Kill
Ode to the World of Light
Vietnam Valentine: Reflections on Leaving You and Coming Home
Ode to Joy, Also Known As Mame

Essays

An Approach to Evaluating Foreign Bank Credit Risk
Another Vote for Export Trading Firms
Contemporary Commercial Bank Credit Policy:
Economic Rationale and Ramifications
Credit Policy and Risk Acceptability for
International Financial Institutions
The Function of Credit Analysis in a U.S. Commercial Bank
Giving the Best Its Due
It Wasn't Mere Flaw That Led to Tragedy
Letters of Credit: Promises to Keep
Lessons from a Legend
Too Many Hats
Vietnam Memory: Acts of Good Faith

PREFACE

Try to keep your soul young and quivering right up to old age, and to imagine right up to the brink of death that life is only beginning. I think that is the only way to keep adding to one's talent, and one's inner happiness.

—George Sand

In 1991 I wrote a letter to someone who had asserted that my family and I weren't "living in the real world." My reply may be instructive to anyone who wonders about this. Coincidentally, it provides a synopsis of my adult life.

"If 'the real world' is spending a year of one's life at war in Vietnam," I wrote, "then I live in it. If it's living with my wife and children in a happy home, then I live in it. If it's being unemployed for almost a year, then I live in it. If it's finding comfort and strength in my family, my faith and my friends, then I live in it. If I write poems for my family, then I live in it. If I do everything I can every day of my life to help someone else, then I live in it. If I am responsible for my actions and words, then I live in it. If it's working as hard as I can up to the best of my God-given ability, then I live in it."

Were one to read this essay, it is possible that he or she might finish and still wonder about the meaning of its title. By way of explanation, therefore, perhaps the best place to start is in October 1992 when my wife and I drove to Cambridge, Massachusetts, to attend Parents' Weekend festivities at Harvard University.

Still on the rebound from a corporate downsizing nearly two years earlier, I was then scraping my way back to an adequate income level, this time as a self-employed management consultant. For us, things were hardly strong financially. We had also just become empty nesters, with our youngest child Kate a freshman at Harvard. I needed a car for business but I could not at the time afford anything but a basic, functional vehicle. Accordingly, I leased a 1992 Chevrolet *Lumina*, which had neither a tape player nor power windows. (Since someone recently asked, I should clarify that it *did* have heat and air conditioning.)

These facts—no children at home, a tenuous financial position and a very basic automobile—led my daughter to observe that, for my wife and me, life had come full circle. As Kate put it so well and with affectionate humor, "Mom and Dad, today things are the same as they were when you were first married: You have no kids, no money and a Chevy." Thus, the title of this work was born.

I suppose my overall message is that life's road is neither straight nor smooth. In fact, there is a mathematical model that conveys this clearly. It states that in any closed interval there are high points and low points, or *relative extrema*. (*Extrema* is the Latin plural for 'extremes.') Like all human lives, mine is a closed interval, and it has had many highs and lows. For me—who once lived life as if someday, if he worked hard and did the right thing, life would be perfect—the lesson of living fully and enjoying each day and every opportunity God provides is crucial, but I had been, at least temporarily, distracted from it.

One of the consistent—and longest—threads in this tale is my service in the United States Marine Corps in the late nineteen-sixties, especially my time in Vietnam, a defining moment in the lives of many Americans and their families in those days. Commissioned an officer at my college graduation, I was an unremarkable Marine but still one proud to serve in what he perceived (and still perceives) as the best of America's armed forces. Indeed, this pride has only grown over time. Ironically, Vietnam represented the greatest—and most fulfilling—management challenge I have ever had, and my experience there was both a high and a low. In other words, Vietnam was a *relative extremum* (the singular of *extrema*).

Tim O'Brien, in his 1990 book *The Things They Carried*, which is about the Vietnam War, wrote: "In any war story but especially a true one, it's difficult to separate what happened from what seemed to happen. What seems to happen becomes its own happening and has to be told that way." O'Brien continues, "By telling stories, you objectify your own experience. You separate it from yourself. You pin down certain truths." I believe this to be true, as it is of much in life. After all, what I have experienced can be revisited only by telling it.

My story is not intended to be an autobiography, although much of it is autobiographical. It is more accurately a collection of stories that took place on my journey through life so far. Moreover, it is an attempt to, in the words of my friend and mentor Hank Mueller, "give substance to why life has unfolded as it has." I write not only because it gives me pleasure but also because I wish to leave primarily for my children and grandchildren a life-writing and a compendium of values I hope they will some day read.

Since I first sat at my computer to begin this undertaking, the September 11, 2001 terrorist attacks on the United States forever changed the lives of all Americans. As Vice President Dick Cheney, a former Secretary of Defense, put it, "many of the steps we have now been forced to take will become permanent in American life. They represent an understanding of the world as it is, and dangers we must guard against perhaps for decades to come."

Because no other event in my lifetime has been so monumental, it is a significant and recurring topic herein. As I have said often to family and friends since that terrible day, we must now learn to live like the Israelis. Indeed, as Benjamin Netanyahu, former prime minister of Israel, has reminded us, "Israel (is) a nation that has been fighting terrorism since the day it was born."

Despite all its relative extrema, my life's journey has been blessed in many ways. Among these blessings have been wonderful parents, membership in a great family, an upbringing that formed me well, epic friendships and unconditional love.

Deo gratias!

Charles F. Mansfield, Jr.

Well, right now, I'm not dead. But when I am, it's like . . . I don't know, I guess it's like being inside a book that nobody's reading. . . . An old one. It's up on the library shelf, so you're safe and everything, but the book hasn't been checked out for a long, long time. All you can do is wait. Just hope somebody'll pick it up and start reading.

—Tim O'Brien in *The Things They Carried*

ACKNOWLEDGMENTS

The motto of the United States Marine Corps is *Semper fidelis*, which is Latin for "Always faithful." To the men and women whose names are listed below, and to others not named here, I am deeply grateful for their time, effort, patience and affection throughout this endeavor. They have been and are *Semper fidelis*.

Walter Anderson
William J. Basel
O.J. Betz III
James L. Blackstock
Joanne Squazzo Blackstock
Michael F. Carey
Major General Matthew P. Caulfield, USMC (Ret.)
Brother Thomas Cleary, S.M.
Henry Clifford
Brian Dennehy
William A. Donohue, Ph.D.
Richard B. Fisher
Captain A. Norman Gandia, USN (Ret.)
Vincent P. Garbitelli, M.D.
Rear Admiral Paul T. Gillcrist, USN (Ret.)
Gregory A. Greenfield
Fran Greiner
Joanne Heap Hunt
W. Rogers Hunt, Jr.
Matthew P. Kaplan
Thomas P. Kiley, Jr.
Earl P. Kirmser, Jr.

John R. Lenz

Carl T. LoGalbo

Patricia Byron Lund

Robert E. Lund

Alan S. MacKenzie, Jr.

Eugene F. Maloney, Esq.

Charles F. Mansfield, III

John C. Mansfield

Kathryn M. Mansfield

Mary Ann Mansfield

Mary C. Mansfield

Michael L. Mansfield

Lieutenant Colonel Michael P. Manzer, USMCR (Ret.)

Major Hector E. Marcayda, USMC

Lieutenant Colonel Peter G. McCarthy, USMC

William McGurn

Craig Middleton

Joseph C. Moosbrugger, Jr.

Charles H. Morin, Esq.

P. Henry Mueller

Denis M. Murphy, M.D.

John E. Murray, Jr., J.D.

James C. Norwood, Jr.

Marilyn O'Grady, M.D.

Cynthia Ozick

Patricia Mansfield Phelan

Judy Rodriguez

Francis X. Schroeder, Esq.

Jack Scovil

Marjorie P. Smuts

Christopher P. Sweeny

Brother Lawrence W. Syriac, S.M.

Francis J. Teague, Esq.

Joseph F. Thomas

John E. Wehrum, Jr., Esq.

Reverend James C. Williams, S.M.

Part I
THE EARLY YEARS

Born today you have an exceptionally adaptable versatility which makes it easy for you to do a lot of things better than average. You also have an affable personality and you get along with all types of people. You can usually influence them to do as you wish. Hence it is important that you keep your ideals high so that you are always doing something constructive, since you could as easily become a wrong influence as a good one! You have an indomitable will and can overcome obstacles more easily than many. You have considerable energy but the chances are that you need to live in a whirlwind of excitement to keep going at your top speed of production.

—Stella, *Brooklyn Daily Eagle*, April 10, 1945

1

A BROOKLYN BOY

Mary seems to have nicknamed the baby "Chuck."
I like it and hope it sticks.

—2nd Lieutenant Charles F. Mansfield,
U.S. Army Air Corps [May 1, 1945]

President Franklin Delano Roosevelt died suddenly of a cerebral hemorrhage on Thursday, April 12, 1945, two days after I was born in Midwood Hospital in Brooklyn, New York. German Nazi dictator Adolf Hitler reputedly committed suicide on the thirtieth of that month, rather than face defeat during the final months of World War II, as our Russian allies were about to overrun his underground bunker in Berlin.

This war was the largest and most violent armed conflict in human history. A protracted, total war fought for unlimited aims, it was a global struggle between two powerful coalitions, the United States and its allies on one side, and the so-called Axis powers, which consisted of Nazi Germany, Italy and the Empire of Japan, on the other.

On December 7, 1941, Japanese Navy and air forces struck a devastating blow in a surprise attack against the backbone of the American naval fleet at Pearl Harbor, Hawaii, in the Pacific. Eighteen of our ships, including four battleships and approximately 2,300 of our men, were destroyed in a single day. Hitler's Germany, then unbeaten in Europe, declared war on the United States just four days later.

According to my parents, I was conceived in Fresno, California, on or about the Fourth of July, 1944. *Made in California, born in New York.*

> *The destiny of mankind is not decided by material computation. When great causes are on the move in the world . . . we learn that we are spirits, not animals, and that something is going on in space and time, which, whether we like it or not, spells duty.*

> —Winston Churchill [June 16, 1941]

My Dad, Charles F. Mansfield (October 26, 1921–July 26, 1999), known throughout his life as Charlie, was not present at the time of my birth. He was serving our country as an officer in the U.S. Army Air Corps in the South Pacific, as the U.S. was preparing for a possible invasion of Japan, which did not take place.

In a letter from the Soutwwest Pacific dated Sunday, April 8, 1945, two days before my birth, Dad wrote:

> The Japs are at the end of their rope now—and recent events seem to prove that they realize it . . . I wouldn't be at all surprised to see Japan fold up before Germany! . . . Their Air Force is so depleted that now they don't even take a chance on sending over nuisance raiders at night. The lifeline of their empire—the Philippines and the China Sea—are under Uncle Sam's watchful eyes all the time now—so their shipping is shot to hell. Soon we'll control China—I think— and then they'll definitely be finished, that is, if we don't go right to Tokyo first.

When I read these words of his, the thought occurred to me that Dad should have been a journalist.

On May 25, 1945, U.S. Army General George C. Kenney, Commander, Headquarters of Allied Air Forces in the Southwest Pacific, wrote to my mother that

your husband . . . was decorated with the Air Medal. It
was made in recognition of courageous service to his combat
organization, his fellow American airmen, his country, his
home and to you.

Your husband was cited for meritorious achievement
while participation *(sic)* in sustained operational flight
missions in the Southwest Pacific Area from December 19,
1944 to April 15, 1945.

I would like to tell you how genuinely proud I am to
have such men as your husband in my command . . .

Instead of an invasion of the Japanese homeland, on August 6,
1945, an American Boeing B-29 bomber nicknamed "Enola Gay"
dropped an atomic bomb nicknamed "Little Boy" on the Japanese
city of Hiroshima. Three days later another American bomber
dropped another atomic bomb on Nagasaki, another city in Japan.
These were the first atomic bombs used in warfare, and both cities
were destroyed.

Before the raid, Hiroshima had a population of 255,000,
about the size of Dallas, Texas, or Providence, Rhode Island.
Of these, 66,000 were killed and 69,000 injured. By
comparison, Nagasaki had a pre-raid population of 195,000,
of whom 39,000 were killed and 25,000 injured. Thus, total
casualties from the two bombing raids aggregated 199,000.
This was far less than an estimate in advance of the raids that
an invasion of Japan might cost as much as a million lives on
the American side alone, with an equal number of the enemy.

There are some people who consider America's use of nuclear
weapons against the Empire of Japan a "crime against
humanity." I happen to side with those, including, incidentally,
many Japanese, who believe that our use of such weapons then
hastened the end of the war and saved countless thousands of
both Japanese and American lives that would undeniably have
been lost in an invasion of the Japanese mainland.

At the beginning of the war, which lasted from 1939 to 1945, the bombing of civilians was regarded as a barbaric act. As the war progressed, however, all sides abandoned their prior restraints. Indeed, the bombing of the Japanese mainland brought the war to a swift conclusion. On September 2, 1945, the Japanese formally and unconditionally surrendered to U.S. Army General Douglas MacArthur aboard the American battleship *U.S.S. Missouri*, which was anchored in Tokyo Bay.

In his radio broadcast on the evening of September 1, 1945 (it was already the 2nd in Tokyo), President Harry S. Truman said of this great warship and the surrender:

> There on that small piece of American soil anchored in Tokyo Harbor the Japanese have just officially laid down their arms.

> Four years ago the thoughts and fears of the whole civilized world were centered on another piece of American soil— Pearl Harbor. The mighty threat to civilization which began there is now laid at rest. It was a long road to Tokyo—and a bloody one.

> We shall not forget Pearl Harbor.

> The Japanese militarists will not forget the *U.S.S. Missouri*.

> The evil done by the Japanese war lords can never be repaired or forgotten. But their power to destroy and kill has been taken from them. Their armies and what is left of their Navy are now impotent.

> To all of us there comes first a sense of gratitude to Almighty God who sustained us and our Allies in the dark days of grave danger, Who made us to grow from weakness into the strongest fighting force in history, and Who now has seen us overcome the forces of tyranny that sought to destroy His civilization.

As I first read President Truman's words I was struck by how uncannily they parallel the challenge the United States faces sixty-one years after Pearl Harbor. I refer, of course, to the eradication of terrorism from the planet in the wake of the surprise terrorist attacks on the "Twin Towers" of the World Trade Center in New York and on the Pentagon in Washington, D.C. on September 11, 2001, or "9/11," now spoken as "nine eleven." Given a recent survey that showed that 52% of the American people "now think that religion's effect is in decline," I was also impressed by his ready reference to "Almighty God who sustained us." As mentioned above, at Pearl Harbor, 2,300 of our military people were killed; at the Trade Center and the Pentagon, nearly 3,000 innocent men, women and children were murdered.

World War II had begun with the appalling failure of American intelligence to predict the Japanese attack on Pearl Harbor. Similarly, the attacks of September 11, 2001 were also a huge surprise and, according to author Thomas Powers, for mostly the same reasons. These included "too much information, processed too casually, and, above all, a failure to take seriously an opponent's ability and determination to strike on American territory."

As the French say, "Plus ça change, plus c'est la même chose."

⧖

In Tom Brokaw's book *The Greatest Generation*, he has captured well what life was like for my parents, especially my Dad, at the beginning of their life together during World War II:

> At a time in their lives when their days and nights should have been filled with innocent adventure, love, and the lessons of the workaday world, they were fighting in the most primitive conditions possible across the bloodied landscapes of France, Belgium, Italy, Austria, and the coral islands of the Pacific. They answered the call to save the world from the two most powerful and ruthless military

machines ever assembled, instruments of conquest in the
hands of fascist maniacs. They faced great odds and a late
start, but they did not protest. They succeeded on every
front. They won the war; they saved the world. They came
home to joyous and short-lived celebrations and immediately
began the task of rebuilding their lives and the world they
wanted. They married in record numbers and gave birth to
another distinctive generation, the Baby Boomers . . . They
(were) exceptionally modest . . . In a deep sense they didn't
think that what they were doing was that special, because
everyone else was doing it too.

Shortly before her marriage to my father on April 27, 1944 in
Our Lady Help of Christians (OLHC) Roman Catholic Church
on East Twenty-eighth Street in the Flatbush section of Brooklyn,
my mother, Mary, had an appendectomy. Thus, after the wedding
she lived for a brief period of convalescence with her parents at
1227 East Twenty-ninth Street, later my neonatal home. My
maternal grandparents were Angelica Theresa (Stewart) and
Lawrence Jules Charrot (a French-Swiss name pronounced
"sharrow"), whom their grandchildren called Mimi and Poppa.
("Mimi" is my corruption of 'grandma,' which, I have been told, I
was unable to pronounce in my earliest attempts at speech.) Many
years later, thanks to the genealogical diligence of my sister Patricia
(Pat) Phelan, we would come to know our Charrot cousins in both
England and Switzerland.

Shortly after my father's return from the war in the autumn of
1945, he purchased a home at 1337 East Twenty-ninth Street,
just a block away from Mimi and Poppa's. Our house was directly
across the street from the front steps of OLHC grammar school,
which I attended from 1950 to 1952. My classmates' names are
now mostly fuzzy, but I still remember adorable little white-blonde
Barbara Francis; Joe Hart, whom I would see occasionally through
the years; Joe and Mike Logan, the latter with whom I became
reacquainted many years later when we both lived in Garden City,
New York; Frankie Wilpret, a mildly handicapped but highly

enthusiastic lad; and Dick DeVita, later also a high-school classmate, who passed away suddenly some years ago while working out in a gym. There were also lovely pig-tailed twin girls whose family name, if memory serves, was Lee. Another classmate was Ed Rush, whom I was to meet again forty-six years later in Southampton, Long Island; believe it or not, he insisted that he remembered me! Indeed, Ed extended his right hand and exclaimed "Hi, classmate!"

My friends in the neighborhood included Billy Coyle, now deceased, his sister Kathy and brothers Larry and Johnny; Tommy and Marty Dugan and their sister Eileen; the Logan boys and their sister Rosemary; Felicia Fitzpatrick, Jackie Daly, Steve Buckley, later a U.S. Marine, Dickie Gelston, whose family moved to Saudi Arabia, and Tony Longobato.

The Coyle kids had an Aunt Mae, an elderly Irish woman, who lived with them and their parents. Said she in her brogue to my mother about me, then age five: "Mary, he's been in the world before." Sadly, soon after she made this memorable utterance Aunt Mae passed away.

Ours was an all-white neighborhood of Irish and Italian, Catholic and Jew. It was also, in those days, all Brooklyn Dodgers baseball. After suffering through five consecutive World Series victories by the New York Yankees from 1949 through 1953, Dodger fans finally saw "dem Bums" win their first Series in 1955 when the boys of summer, in a so called subway series, beat the Bronx Bombers in seven games.

East Twenty-ninth Street was a marvelous little world in which all children roller-skated, girls in dresses—never blue jeans—hop-scotched in sidewalk chalk-drawn boxes, and boys played stickball in the street. A fire hydrant, known as a "johnny pump," was a base or a hit or home run marker. As far as we kids knew, our neighborhood was a fun-filled, nonviolent world.

It also meant a quick walk to Mimi and Poppa's house, as well as a bicycle ride to Mimi Mansfield's. This second "Mimi" was Alice Kirkwood Mansfield, my father's stepmother, who later in life asked to be called "Grandma." She lived at 1739 Burnett Street with her daughter Alice Mary, Dad's half-sister, whose nickname is "Feedie" or, simply, "Fee." Dad's natural parents, Anna (Lowndes) and Charles F. Mansfield, died prematurely in, respectively, August 1930 and April 1935. Fee and her husband Jim Lissemore and their family of four daughters and two sons, not to mention now many grandchildren, are great people. Jim is a former Marine and a Korean War veteran whom I affectionately call "Gunny" (for Gunnery Sergeant); he calls me "Captain," with perhaps slightly less affection.

Joseph F. Mansfield is Dad's first cousin and my godfather. Joe has been a close friend and mentor throughout my life.

Likewise, A. Jeanne Peters, my mother's sister and my godmother, has been a wonderful, caring aunt and friend.

I received First Holy Communion on Saturday, May 24, 1952, at 8:00 a.m. Mass in OLHC Church. It was a beautiful, sunny day. All the girls wore traditional white dresses, and the boys, unlike today, wore all white as well—white jackets, shirts, shorts and ties, plus white shoes with white knee-length socks.

After the ceremony, Mom and Dad had a sumptuous brunch for the family, at which I was showered with gifts, mostly congratulatory cards containing cash. At a time when a nickel actually had purchasing power, at least from a kid's perspective, the cash gifts I received totaled $14.00.

Now, that may not sound like much but to me then it was a staggering sum. My newly acquired wealth in hand, the next day I convened my friends and distributed the money among them, keeping maybe two dollars for myself. When my father learned of my largesse, I thought he would kill me.

Also while living in Brooklyn I made my television debut, at age five, appearing as a guest in the "Peanut Gallery" on *The Howdy Doody Show*. Actually I appeared twice, in 1950 and 1951. Truth be told, Clarabelle the Clown squirted me, inadvertently I'm sure, with his infamous seltzer bottle! By the way, Buffalo Bob Smith was a very nice man; Princess Summer Fall Winter Spring was, alas, a shrew.

My comfortable little world seemed almost to come undone on June 24, 1952 when my parents moved my siblings and me from East Twenty-ninth Street to a brand new home in Garden City (hereinafter called GC), about twenty miles to the east in Nassau County, New York. At that time Mom and Dad had four children, of whom I was the eldest. Next came Michael Lawrence, born March 20, 1947; Patricia Anne (Phelan), on June 29, 1949; and Margaret Mary, called Peggy, on November 9, 1951. Two more girls were to join the brood: Elisabeth Anne, also my goddaughter, born April 7, 1956; and Mary Kathryn, now known as Kate, who arrived on January 12, 1958.

The real voyage of discovery consists not in seeking new landscapes, but in having new eyes.

—Marcel Proust

2

Garden City, New York

The great affair is to move.

—Robert Louis Stevenson in *Travels with a Donkey*

Just after our move to GC at the beginning of the summer of 1952, my brother Mike and I, ages five and seven, respectively, would tell people that we had moved to "the country." To modern-day GC residents, such a comment might seem ludicrous. Nonetheless, to a couple of street urchins from the gritty streets of Flatbush, it was a nearly bucolic change.

Our new home was located at 62 Fairmount Boulevard in GC, a lovely, upscale suburb of New York City, which *The New York Times* once described as "an oasis." (Dad later told me that he paid $19,000 for it; at this writing, its value has recently been estimated at approximately $800,000.) Five of us children (all but Kate) graduated from St. Anne's Catholic grammar school, just one block and an easy walk from home.

St. Anne's and GC proved to be rich with new friends and opportunities.

Next-door to the west at 60 Fairmount was the McMackin family: Frank, Mary Ann and their children Joe, Holly and Megan. Next-door to the east at No. 64 was the Zukas family: Vito, Joan and their four daughters, JoAnn, Mary (Jane), Annie and Patty. In my teenage years, I was very fond of Mary. Down the street at No. 56 were the Kellys, Jim and Irene, and their kids, Jimmy, Kevin and Valerie. Jimmy was my best friend in the new neighborhood and later preceded me by a year at Chaminade High School. At No. 54 were Joe and Marie Irwin and their seven children, Stephen, Michael, Joanne, Susan, Mary, Laura and John. Across the street were the families of the brothers William and James Scully, as well as the Leonards. On Dartmouth Street, parallel to and a block south of Fairmount, were the Wallace, Strain, Quinn and Schultz families. The Reillys later bought the Schultz house and fit seamlessly into a neighborhood that all of us still cherish.

St. Anne's offered membership in Cub Scout Pack No. 166, of which Rudolph Giuliani, former Mayor of New York City and a 9/11 hero, was then also a member. I was an altar boy, which, in those days, provided my first exposure to the Latin language, thanks to Father Thomas Colgan. On December 9, 1954 I received the sacrament of Confirmation from Bishop Kearney, Bishop of the Diocese of Brooklyn.

It was at my new school that I met many lifelong friends, especially Tom Greene (Greenie), who was once a Marine and is today a retired bank credit officer; Larry Hennessy, a businessman; Denis Murphy (Murph), who served as an Air Force officer and is an acclaimed gastroenterologist; and Jim Norwood (Jimmy), a former Navy man, a businessman and an entrepreneur. All of these men later served as ushers in my wedding party. Jimmy is my son Chas's godfather, and always signed his letters to me "Your best buddy." Murph, whom my Mom calls her "third son," was later my college roommate. We are all the closest of friends even to this day. Then there are other wonderful, generous men, such as Don Franz (a.k.a. Chowderhead, a tag his father gave him), the late Terry Mahony, Brian Maxwell (Maxie or Max), Brian Tart and Jeff Zabler, each of whom would also graduate from high school with me.

When I graduated from St. Anne's in June 1958 I was awarded the English medal for excellence in that subject. Earlier I had won a typewriter, first prize in a Catholic-school essay contest sponsored by *The Tablet*, the newspaper of the Diocese of Brooklyn. (My topic was "Vocations, Our Urgent Need.") I used it throughout high school and college, and still have it. Someone told me it's now an antique and possibly worth something.

Mother James, a nun of the Religious of the Sacred Heart of Mary, was my seventh- and, surprisingly, eighth-grade teacher. Irish-born, she did not use her family name but, later, after a modernization of her religious order, she became Sister James Brennan, RSHM. James was her father's name.

When seventh grade ended in June 1957, everyone was very happy for it was presumed that our class had seen the last of Mother James. On the first day of school the following September, however, she breezed into our classroom, perhaps, we guessed, to say hello. Instead, she announced, flashing her bright, broad Irish smile, that, since she had come to love us so much as seventh-graders, she had requested and obtained the principal's approval to teach us again in eighth grade. To say that the groans from her astonished students were audible is an understatement.

This lady was a tough, no-nonsense sort of person. In fact, her legendary reputation as a disciplinarian caused many of her young students to complain about her methods, which did *not* include corporal punishment. It should be borne in mind that, in those days, the teacher was always right, and parents would invariably side with the teacher in virtually any matter, but especially in a case that involved a breach of discipline.

> *When I was a boy of 14 my father was so ignorant I could hardly stand to have the old man around. But when I got to be twenty-one I was astonished at how much the old man had learned in seven years.*

—Mark Twain

Even I complained to my parents about "Jamesie" or "Jesse," Mother James's two most common nicknames. My complaints, however, were in the end ignored. You see, when my parents met with her at a school function, all she told them about me was that "Charles is a darlin' boy." Talk about a trump and, yes, one of those relative extrema.

Over the years I managed to keep up what became a strong friendship with Mother James, who retired to a convent at Marymount College in Tarrytown, New York. My last visit with her was in early December 1993, and she passed away about eighteen months later. I believe she was ninety.

⌛

Without a doubt the most embarrassing and, thus, most unforgettable episode from this era occurred on the last school day before October 12, 1957, Columbus Day, which was a school holiday. There were we, eighth-graders, along with younger classes, sitting quietly in the St. Anne's School basement auditorium awaiting the start of a student assembly. When the guests of honor—Fathers Ambrose Gilmartin (our pastor), David Farley and Thomas O'Donnell, as well as Mothers James, Nicholas (the other eighth-grade teacher) and Patricia (our principal)—were seated in the front row of the audience, I, then twelve and a half years old, ascended the steps of the stage to stand alone and deliver my brief address.

No doubt boring to some of those present, my speech was about—what else—Christopher Columbus, the Niña, the Pinta and the Santa Maria, the discovery of America, etc. It was probably no longer than seven or eight minutes. Still, I was nervous and speaking from memory—no index cards or papers of any kind. Despite its actual brevity, what happened next made my oration's duration seem like eternity.

Around the midpoint of my effort, someone in the audience broke wind that almost blew the roof off. Considering the fact that we were in the basement, that's saying a lot. For some reason, I looked, perhaps even glared, at my buddies seated centrally about six rows deep. From my vantage point I could easily spot them— Tom Greene, Larry Hennessy, Denis Murphy, Jimmy Norwood and others—all bending over in their seats and apparently huddled together, their bodies shaking in mini-spasms of stifled laughter. I remember this with utmost clarity. Then I cast a quick glance at the dignitaries in the front row, suddenly realizing that the untimely and untoward blast, no matter whose, had distracted and caused me, if only momentarily, to stop speaking. Mortified, I got back to the business at hand. I finished the speech and got off the stage as quickly as I could. I remember feeling embarrassed and angry.

When the assembly concluded, I joined my impudent friends as we returned together to our classrooms. Laughing freely, some offered "Attaboys" while others mischievously inquired if I had heard any unusual noises while on stage. It was then that a grinning Jackie Fitzmaurice emerged, put his arm around me and asked, "So, how did you like that beauty, Charlie?" I wanted to tell him that I wished he had decided in that puerile and sophomoric moment to control himself. Not possessing such vocabulary at the time, however, I believe I said "Drop dead, Jack."

⌛

As for "The Village," as many GC residents call it, it had outstanding recreation programs, including Little League Baseball; the GC Pool, an exciting aquatic complex that opened in 1957; and the GC Rams, a "midget" football team that belonged to a "Pop Warner"-type league. At age 12, I pitched a perfect game for the GC Eagles, striking out twelve of the eighteen batters I faced; a few months later I was named the Rams' "Best Lineman." I remember being very happy. Life was good.

In a little over five years, then more than two-fifths of my life, the old Brooklyn neighborhood had become only a distant memory.

⌛

Jimmy Norwood's were my second set of parents. His Dad was also named James, whom my Dad dubbed "Big Jim," who in turn called my father "Big Charlie." Jim's mother was Dorothy. His sisters were Jean, Joan, Janice and Jane.

As a rule, every Friday evening at 7:15 in my high-school years I would walk to the Norwoods' home at 221 Elton Road in Stewart

Manor, a fifteen-minute hike from mine. I would reverse the trip at 9:45 in order to be home by ten, my normal curfew. At Jim's we would usually watch television or simply sit around and "shoot the bull." Invariably, Greenie, Larry, Maxie and Murph would also be on hand; Louie Lorenz and Brandon Fullam frequently joined our group as well. While our weekend gatherings occasionally took us elsewhere, Jimmy's was centrally located and generally the meeting place of choice.

Beginning in the summer of 1958, the Norwoods would invite me and one or two of the other guys to their beach house on West Meadow Beach in Setauket, New York, on Long Island Sound. There water skiing, fishing and clamming, as well as meals fit for kings, were the wonders of those days. I recall two or three trips a summer up to that classic beach house on the Island's north shore.

In college years, our get-togethers tended to move to my parents' basement due in large part to the fact that we had a pool table. Over time we migrated to The Garden Chop House where Budweiser, live music and lovely young ladies were featured.

The bonds among us were and still are extraordinary. Except for Max, who went to the same high school as I, all of us went our separate ways after St. Anne's. We all went to different colleges, except for Murph, who went to the same school as I—Holy Cross. We shared our new friends from high school and college, naturally, but the relationships formed among us as boys have remained not only intact but also vibrant after fifty years.

Growing up, most of us, as well as our fathers and brothers, had our hair cut at the same barbershop.

⟨⟨⟨⟩⟩⟩

Now, some who read this essay may wonder who Mike Paulino is; others who knew him may wonder why I give him so much ink. Maybe the best answer to both queries is that I am not related to Mike, except by love. He is also one of my most enduring early memories of GC.

When I visited Mike alongside his hospital bed shortly before

Christmas in 1996, he was a restless, mentally impaired man who was valiantly fighting the dreadful demons of Parkinson's disease. It was the last time I would see him alive.

One of the least aggressive and totally non-violent men I have ever known, Mike fought and fought and fought those demons to the end. Perhaps that is why he looked so peaceful, even serene, in death sixteen months later. After all, he had fought the good fight and finished the race, despite the wretched physical condition he endured.

I first met Mike, or "Uncle" Mike, as he was known to so many of his family members and customers, in the summer of 1952. For those of you who have done the arithmetic, that means I met Mike when I was seven. More of that part of the story later.

As a former Marine, I am keenly aware of the Marines' advertising campaign of yesteryear about the Marines wanting, or consisting of, "a few good men." As I age, I also become more sharply aware of the quality of goodness in people—and especially in men, in whom it often seems so curiously rare. Consequently, I find myself taking special note of those men who seem to be genuinely good in every sense of the word. Mike Paulino was just such a man.

Some people who knew Mike reminded me at his wake that he was "uneducated." Upon reflection, all I can say is that, if only educated men were as good and honest and caring as Mike, we humans might actually achieve peace on earth. I believe that Mike's life was a model for all of us, indeed for me personally, because he was so kind, so gentle, so loving.

Mike always made me feel good about myself. He always took an interest in what was going on in my life. In sum, to me Mike was not just one of a few good men, he was one of the finest I have ever known, and I miss him.

Mike Paulino was a family man, but not in the traditional sense. Yes, he married his beloved Kathleen, albeit late in life; I believe he was fifty-four. But, no, he never had any children of his own. Still, Mike did more for his nieces and nephews than many parents ever do for their own children. Mike lived and cared, gave and shared.

Today, most folks in GC know the name Ben Paulino, Mike's nephew, not to be confused with Ben's cousin of the same name. Ben's "Beauty Enterprises" on New Hyde Park Road has become an institution in the world of western Nassau County beauty care. In fact, I first made Ben's acquaintance back in the fifties in what was then called the "Modern Barber Shop."

As previously mentioned, I first met Mike Paulino in the summer of 1952 when my brother Mike and I first set foot in that barber shop that came to feel so much like home. My brother was five; I, seven. Mike Paulino, his late brother Vince and a mustachioed third barber called John practiced their art there.

After our haircuts that day, and for years thereafter, Mike, The Great Barber, would see that my brother and I crossed busy New Hyde Park Road safely as we began our block-and-a-half walk or bike-ride home. Mike Paulino held our small hands as he led us.

I am happy that my memories of Mike are still vivid.

⧗

On Saturday, September 5, 1992, I settled into Mike's comfortable barber chair fully expecting at any moment his customary 7:30 a.m. greeting.

"So what's your excuse today, Chuck?" he would ask. "How come you're so late?"

As an aside, I now wonder if Mike's chair was really by itself as comfortable as I remember, or if The Great Barber just managed to make it so. Even Mike himself found it comfortable enough for a nap when business was slow.

That day was different for, as I sat there waiting for my friend The Great Barber, I noticed a gold sign that said "Happy Retirement" strung across the mirror directly opposite Mike's barber chair. There was also a neatly handwritten note that read simply, "Saturday September 5th will be my last day . . ." As I began to realize that this, perhaps my five hundredth haircut from my friend The Great Barber, was to be my last by him, the maestro appeared on the scene, uncharacteristically sheepish.

"So, Mike, what am I supposed to do now?" I asked, feigning annoyance. "Would you consider a few private sittings at my house from time to time?" I joked.

My friend The Great Barber replied with a hearty laugh, "If I do that, my wife will shoot me—and you too! Tell ya', Chuck, my legs and back are killin' me, so I think it's time to take it easy." There was pain in his eyes.

"That's good," I replied.

He was right. He deserved a rest. Nearly seventy-nine when he retired, my friend The Great Barber had been plying his trade in at least three different buildings on both sides of New Hyde Park Road for about sixty years. Furthermore, he had been for a long time the only barber in his nephew Ben's fine establishment.

Strange as it may seem to some, that final haircut by my friend The Great Barber was one I didn't want to end. After all, here was a man who, probably unwittingly, had witnessed change and maybe even growth in my life and perhaps his own. Mike Paulino had cut my hair the day before I graduated from St. Anne's and, four years later, Chaminade High School. He followed my schoolboy and young-man "careers" in football and baseball, and he would chide me about my girlfriends.

When I was in college and in need of extra cash, my friend The Great Barber actually put *me* in the barbering business by personally teaching me his craft after business hours, and arranging for me the purchase of the best equipment at, no doubt, the best price.

He cut my hair again and made sure I would pass muster on June 10, 1967, my wedding day.

A year later, my friend The Great Barber was one of the last friends I visited before I left for my tour of duty with the Marines in Vietnam. To be sure, that visit was not just for a haircut, for my friend The Great Barber was then, as always, one of the great constants in my life. He had served in the Army during World War II and he knew what I was feeling. For a man who had no children of his own, his words and approach to me were unmistakably paternal.

While I was in Vietnam, my wife took Chas, our first son, to Mike for his first haircut. That event made three generations of my family who were Mike's customers.

So, Mike, can I do anything, or get something for you, now that you're retiring?" I asked, feeling woefully inadequate.

"No, Chuck," he said with the same tug in his voice that I would feel a moment later, "your comin' in here these past forty years is more than I could have asked for."

With that, I found it difficult to speak.

"Thanks, Mike, I'll miss you . . . Mike, I'll call you, okay?" I was fighting the "chokes."

"Yeah, sure, that'll be great. Thanks, Chuck," he said.

Then my friend The Great Barber and I hugged each other briefly. He kissed me on the cheek, a first, and I reciprocated with deepest affection.

"Good luck, Chuck."

"Same to you, Mike. I'll call you soon."

"Yeah, that's good. Thanks. See ya'."

"So long, Mike."

I was honored by Mike's family to give his eulogy in St. Anne's Church in GC on April 15, 1998. Like Mike's niece Loretta at that time, I found it appropriate but not surprising that my friend The Great Barber had left us on Easter Sunday, as I believe we shall all see Mike again, some sooner, some later, with the Resurrection our hope.

Of Mike Paulino I believe that to have known him was to have loved him.

Requiescat in pace.

In GC I also met and came to know well both Bob Gargiula and Craig Middleton, whose brother Todd was my Rams' teammate, as well as a buddy and high-school teammate of Bob Healy, now my close friend and brother-in-law. They are great men and faithful friends with wonderful wives and daughters. (Craig's essay, "The Sentinel," appears at the end of the chapter entitled **Captain Cancer**.)

All these relationships are friendships I treasure deeply. Nevertheless, GC's greatest and most unforgettable contribution to my life is that on or about July 14, 1959, at the GC Pool, I was introduced to a person who would become my best friend. Indeed, she was the girl I would marry, and whose beauty Mimi Charrot would characterize seven years hence as "stunning."

She and I would raise our family in The Village.

But innovation is more than a new method. It is a new view of the universe, as one of risk rather than of chance or of certainty. It is a new view of man's role in the universe; he creates order by taking risks. And this means that innovation, rather than being an assertion of human power, is an acceptance of human responsibility.

—Peter Drucker

3

MAME

What will it take 'til you believe in me
the way that I believe in you?

—Billy Joel

Her full name is Mary Ann Emilia Locasto. Emilia, her
Confirmation name, derives from that of her uncle, Emil
Sarlo, who died in the Philippines during World War II
and was married to Aunt Grace, her father's sister. She was born
two days after Christmas in 1944. Like me, she was born in
Brooklyn. Just as with my Dad at my birth, hers was not present
at hers. Like mine, he was also serving as an Army officer in the
South Pacific during the war against Japan. His name was Camillo
Benedicto Locasto (August 7, 1911-November 9, 1969), and he
was known as Cam.

The third of the five lovely Locasto sisters, Mary Ann has two
elder sisters, twins named Rosina and Camille; her younger sisters
are Bernice and Catherine. As little girls, Mary Ann's sisters called
her Mamie Ane, which was eventually shortened to Mame and
became her nickname, although her parents usually called her Mary.
Their mother, Bernice Mary (Bonner, July 27, 1917-August 7,
2001), gave birth to her five daughters in just four years.

The Locasto family lived on Linden Street in the Ridgewood
section of Brooklyn where the girls attended St. Brigid's Roman
Catholic School. In February 1959, like the Mansfield family seven
years earlier, the Locastos moved to GC.

That summer, in which Santo and Johnny's instrumental *Sleep Walk* was a hit song, Mary Ann and I met at the GC Pool. She wore a one-piece, slightly faded red bathing suit, a hand-me-down from one of her twin sisters. I could not believe how beautiful she looked. To be candid, the bathing suit was slightly tight but in all the right places. (In other words, her shapeliness was obvious.)

I had never seen or imagined anyone so fine, so graceful, so exquisite. Her face was simply magnificent, perfectly proportioned, radiant and elegant, fresh and rare. She was, and is, as bright as sunshine. She had poise and presence.

And her eyes! They were so sparkling and flawless; her eyelashes, the longest I had ever seen.

To me, hers was the face of an angel. As her face was to my eyes, so her voice delighted my ears.

Both of us only fourteen, Mary Ann was nonetheless mature, friendly, energetic and incredibly effervescent. Throughout her life, countless people would use the word "bubbly" to describe her.

At first she seemed a mirage but it became a tour de force in almost no time. I honestly didn't know what to make of her for I had never before had the feelings that attended me while in her presence.

Not long after our first meeting I realized that I had fallen instantaneously in love with her. Although I knew nothing about falling in love, I knew it had to be the only explanation for what I was feeling.

Love at first sight? How could this be? It was something I could hardly fathom, let alone discuss with anyone. Still, I knew in my heart it was true.

Well, I think I'm goin' out of my head over you.

—Little Anthony

Although I would think of her often, I don't believe I saw her again until the new school year began in September. I distinctly remember hearing her name mentioned frequently by friends and former classmates of mine who were now her classmates at GC High School, where she was in tenth grade. Everyone who knew her had only the most favorable and positive things to say about Mary Ann Locasto, and all I could think of was how *I* felt about her. *She's my girl*, my heart would shout silently within me.

As Chaminade, my high school, was not far away, I would often walk to GC High on Saturday afternoons to watch a football game, following my own football practices. There I would sometimes run into Mary Ann and ask if I could walk her home after the game. Those Saturday afternoon walks are some of the fondest memories I have of my youth. She was so wonderful, so perfect!

Both of us would usually attend high-school dances held at St. Anne's and St. Joseph's, the two Catholic parishes in GC. We would also go to "sock hops" at Chaminade. These dances were crucial from my point of view since Mary Ann's parents would not permit their daughters to date. Only church and school dances were permitted, as well as an occasional party at a private home, provided Dr. and Mrs. Locasto knew the other parents personally. Still, these were good times with good friends. Mary Ann's girlfriends would usually be there, as would my buddies.

A watershed came on December 26, 1960, the day before Mary Ann's sixteenth birthday. Prior to that Christmas vacation, I had stopped by GC High and asked her to be my 'date' at the St. Joseph's Christmas dance. She agreed, and I was, as the British say, "over the moon."

Now, there was a slightly surreptitious aspect to our plan to meet at the dance because of the No-date Rule. We understood this. What her parents didn't know couldn't hurt them, right? The secret was ours alone.

For me, love turned to pain and anger at that dance. When I arrived, Denis Murphy, after an early reconnaissance, reported that he had seen Mary Ann. Then, in an early ego exercise, I shared with him the plan she and I, presuming impunity, had devised to meet that evening. Next, Murph gave me the unvarnished, hurtful truth: Mary Ann was there with another guy, and *holding hands* with him, no less! (Today's young people, often sexually active early, may laugh but, in my day, holding hands was a meaningful, intimate act. In 1964 even the Beatles seemed to acknowledge this in their first U.S. smash hit "I Want to Hold Your Hand.") In a fit of immaturity, I was crushed—and angry. Was I being punished for partaking in a 'surreptitious' plan?

At the end of the evening, Mary Ann and I met by chance near the cloakroom.

Effervescent as ever, she expressed surprise at seeing me and said, "Hi, Chuck, how *are* you?"

In a paroxysm of macho pique I responded, "Go to hell!"

The look on her face was one of shock.

It didn't take me long to feel pretty stupid about what I had done. I could and should have said something polite to get my point across, and perhaps have thereby won a few points with her. After all, that's what Chaminade guys are supposed to do. Of course, I could just as soon have let the whole matter drop. But not me.

On the same evening I met a young woman named Barbara Goble, a classmate and friend of Mary Ann. She told me that she would "fix things up" between Mary Ann and me. As it turned out, I dated Barbara for more than a year after that evening. She was also "bubbly," warm and great fun, but Mary Ann was, in the words of the Willie Nelson song, "always on my mind." Anyway, about two weeks after telling me she wanted to marry me, Barbara announced that she would enter a convent in Wilton, Connecticut, where she remained for the next twelve years.

Mary Ann came back into my life in June 1962, the month she and I graduated from high school. Barbara had already decided not to go to the Chaminade senior prom with me although she did choose to attend with one of my classmates. I then invited Mary Ann but she was committed to attending the GC High prom the same evening with her beau, a young man named Bruce Corbridge, another former Rams teammate of mine. However, Mary Ann surprised me by asking if I would be her escort for her graduation and the formal dance that followed.

Ever consistent, Mary Ann's parents would not permit her to have Bruce as her date (sorry, I should say escort) for *both* the prom and the graduation dance, which I had a very strong suspicion she would have preferred. Thus, I knew I was only a stand-in for Corbridge but I was secretly thrilled that she even considered me. At least I was still *somewhere* on her list, if not in her heart.

Mary Ann graduated at the top of her class and won a New York State Regents scholarship, which she chose to use at Marymount College in Tarrytown, New York, about an hour's ride northwest of GC. I went off to the College of the Holy Cross in Worcester, Massachusetts.

⧗

In 1962 and '63 Mary Ann and I saw each other only occasionally. Where she was concerned, my attitude had become decidedly negative and pessimistic for, while I loved her deeply, I truly believed I was not good enough for her, nor could I ever be.

⧗

In the summer of 1963 I worked three jobs. From 7:30 a.m. to 12:30 p.m. I served on the maintenance crew at Chaminade. There Earl Kirmser (a Chaminade and Holy Cross College classmate and teammate and a lifelong friend), Bob Delfoe (Chaminade '61 and later a Citibank colleague) and I were responsible for painting the wooden bleachers on the north and south sides of the old football field, now called Ott Field, after Alexander Ott, Chaminade's founder. From 1 to 6 p.m. I stocked shelves at the old A&P supermarket on Seventh Street in GC. Then from 7 to 10 p.m. I worked behind the counter, serving Cokes, ice cream sodas and the like, at "Dolly's" on New Hyde Park Road on GC's west side, a short walk from home and directly opposite Mike Paulino's barber shop. Thanks to this work, I usually had more than a few bucks in my pocket.

Despite my chronic negative feelings vis-à-vis my relationship with Mary Ann, I extended, and she accepted, my invitation to see the Kingston Trio, a popular folk group from the late fifties and early sixties, perform at Long Island's Westbury Music Fair. It was a perfect summer evening. We double-dated with Gay O'Brien and Jim Norwood, who drove his Dad's business car (the first vehicle I had ever ridden in that had electric windows). The concert was "fabulous," as GC girls in those days would describe anything that was good.

Sitting in the back seat with Mary Ann on the way home from the concert, I took a huge risk, although I didn't think of it in such terms then. With only the street light on GC's Chestnut Street momentarily illuminating her magnificent face, I kissed her, nervously and quickly. Though she did not object, I did not push my luck.

Besides, I was on cloud nine.

Never felt like this until I kissed ya!
How did I exist until I kissed ya?

—The Everly Brothers

The following summer was more eventful, although we didn't see each other much.

On June 15, 1964 I began a new job, thanks to my great uncle John J. Hagerty, Jr., known to the family as Uncle Johnny, at the A&P meat warehouse on GC's eastern outskirts. I was a "lugger," which meant I carried hind quarters and fore quarters of beef, many weighing well over 200 pounds, as well as whole carcasses of freshly slaughtered and refrigerated lamb and veal. The meat was shipped in by rail and tractor-trailer. Earl Kirmser was my partner.

Believe it or not, there were two men working at this meat warehouse who had surprisingly eponymous names. They were called by everyone, and even introduced themselves as, Joe Hamburger and Joe Salami. (Never mind that their surnames were actually spelled Hemburger and Salemi, respectively.)

What a great job it was! The nature of the work helped keep both Earl and me, then athletes, in good physical condition, and the pay was, in a word, fantastic. The base salary was $125 a week but, with frequent overtime at time-and-a-half, we frequently took home $200 or more a week. One's pay was distributed every Friday morning in *cash* in a small brown envelope. Today such a sum may not sound like a lot but, keep in mind, it was 1964. I earned and saved so much money that summer that, once back at school, I got into the lending business, making loans to less prosperous classmates and friends.

Thanks to Mike Paulino, my late friend "The Great Barber," I also learned to cut hair and parlayed that into a nice business too when I returned to college.

His clothes are dirty but his hands are clean
And you're the best thing that he's ever seen

—Bob Dylan

For her part, Mary Ann had decided to exercise her new-found independence by defying her folks and violating her midnight curfew. Not surprisingly, her parents "grounded" her for, as I recall, six weeks, which was half the summer.

I also remember telephoning her on a Sunday afternoon when I was tending bar at a garden party my parents were hosting at their home. My purpose was to ask her for a date. She told me of her grounding but, significantly, allowed that her first day of new freedom would be Thursday, August 12, 1964. With uncharacteristic confidence, I nailed down our next date for that seemingly far-off evening.

On the evening of August 12th, I found myself at home in my room studying for an exam (I was taking an English course at Adelphi University that summer). As I happened to gaze at the big calendar—a perennial Christmas gift from my Mom—which hung on the wall in Mike's and my bedroom, I saw the words "Mary Ann" written in the August 12th box.

Oh, my God! I had completely forgotten about the date I had made with Mary Ann weeks before. Immediately I called the Locasto home, only to be told that, since I had failed to show up, she had gone bowling with her sisters. I was mortified and, most of all, disgusted with myself. I apologized and requested that my message be conveyed to Mary Ann. How could I be *soooo* stupid???!!!

Despite my faux pas, I recall that Mary Ann and I managed to squeeze in a date before we returned to college. We went to the aforementioned Garden Chop House, a college hang-out with a great band known as "The Fortunes." We drank Budweiser beer and danced. She is a phenomenal dancer.

I was concerned about a rumor circulating in GC, but said nothing about it until it came time to drive Mary Ann home. I stopped on the way there in the GC High parking lot. She told me she wondered why I was stopping in such a place (perhaps because I hadn't kissed her in more than a year? Whom am I kidding?).

This rumor had it that she was "going steady" with a West Point cadet, one Jim Carson; indeed, people were saying that she was about to be engaged. Jealousy and fear of losing *my* girl consumed me; I had become possessive, perhaps too much so. As François de La Rochefoucauld put it so well, "Jealousy is always born together with love, but it does not always die when love dies."

Why wait any longer for the one you love
When he's standing in front of you

—Bob Dylan

I had the temerity but not the resistance to ask her about this relationship. In no uncertain terms, she made it clear that it was none of my business. Though feeling wounded and weakened, I believed this might be the last opportunity I'd have to say what had been in my aching heart for the preceding five years.

Sincere but, alas, foolish, I said words I had never before said to anyone: "Mary Ann, I love you."

She moved closer to me, took my hand and, despite the darkness, save for the nearby parking lot light stanchion, seemed to look into my soul. In this surreal moment, I didn't know what to expect.

Then she spoke softly but with great conviction, "Chuck, you will always be one of my best friends, but I could never love you."

There was nothing more to say. I started the car and drove her home.

Things have changed. She doesn't love me now.
She's made it clear enough. It ain't no good to pine.

—Herman's Hermits

I doubt there was any communication between us from that evening until December 19th, on the afternoon of which something motivated me to call her, now home for the Christmas holidays. I called to wish her and her family, all of whom I had come to know over the years, a Merry Christmas. During the conversation, despite lingering painful thoughts of the previous summer's debacle, I asked her if she had any plans for the evening. She told me she had a date, her fifty-second of the year (!), she said, but kindly encouraged me to call her during the following week.

At this time, the Righteous Brothers' smash hit *You've Lost That Lovin' Feelin'* could be heard at least a dozen times a day on the radio, and it would tear me up every time.

Once more the pessimist, I told myself that I was the biggest fool on earth to keep trying to see this brilliant and precious Mary Ann Locasto. I think I even hated myself for not having more courage where she was concerned. In a strange way, I felt that my love for her was killing me. Still, she was the most beautiful person I had ever known, and I knew in my heart I would love her forever, no matter what.

Well I keep on thinkin' 'bout you Sister golden hair surprise
And I just can't live without you Can't you see it in my eyes?

—America

Late on the afternoon of December 26, 1964, I telephoned her again. While dialing, I told myself that it was futile to continue this pursuit. As the phone rang, I thought briefly of hanging up. I knew I should have called her sooner, as she had suggested in our conversation a week earlier. Then someone answered the phone; it was Mary Ann.

She raved about her wonderful Christmas with her family, and I don't remember what else. Feeling downright inadequate, I somehow mustered enough nerve to ask her if she would be interested in going out that evening.

"I'd love to," she replied. My spirit soared.

Our evening together was low key fun. I kept the conversation light. Again, we drank Budweiser and danced. At the end of the evening I made sure I got her home before curfew. (And, no, I did not stop in the high school parking lot.)

On this Boxing Day, I felt I was at peace with Mary Ann— and with myself.

⌛

Mary Ann and I returned to our respective colleges for the final semesters of our junior years. The outlook for us would soon become more serious, in more ways than one. In the summer of 1965 I would travel to Quantico, Virginia, for Marine Corps Officer Candidates School (OCS). She would again work in GC for the summer, and was already looking ahead to graduate school. For both of us, major decisions were in the offing.

We corresponded and occasionally spoke on the phone. (In those days, there were very few public telephones in each college dormitory, and they were constantly in use. There were no private phones in dorm rooms, either.)

I asked Mary Ann to come to Holy Cross for "Winter Weekend" in February 1965, an invitation she readily accepted. I was thrilled; I also relished the prospect of introducing her to my friends, for I knew they would love her. Indeed, when my classmate and friend Bob Meikle first made her acquaintance, he turned to me and said, with obvious reference to Mary Ann, "Charle," as he still sometimes calls me, "you're really smoothin' it."

Winter Weekend included the annual Military Ball, a formal dinner dance for all Holy Cross military personnel, including R.O.T.C. (Reserve Officer Training Corps) students. Mary Ann and I doubledated this time with my classmate and friend Bob Lund and his date, Paula Mulligan, who came from his hometown of Pawtucket, Rhode Island. Both girls were spectacular in their gowns. Keeping in mind the old saw that 'You can't make a silk purse out of a sow's ear,' I would still say that even Bob and I looked pretty "spiffy" in our uniforms. Like Jim Norwood nearly two years before, Bob had his father's car for the evening, and once again Mary Ann and I found ourselves in the back seat.

On the way to the ball, something extraordinary happened.

Holding my arm and sitting closer to me than she had at any time I could remember, Mary Ann whispered in my ear. "From now on, I don't plan to go out with anyone but you." Virtually disbelieving what I had heard her say, and sorely wanting to hear it again, I asked her to repeat herself. She smiled faintly and told me once more. Next I turned toward her to take in her whole countenance amidst a New England winter's evening darkness broken only by the headlights of oncoming automobiles. She was radiantly beautiful and, yes, "stunning," as my grandmother would describe Mary Ann the following year.

I had never been happier in my life.

> *In his younger days a man dreams of possessing the heart of a woman whom he loves; later, the feeling that he possesses the heart of a woman may be enough to make him fall in love with her.*
>
> —Marcel Proust

In the spring of 1965, America's involvement in the Vietnam war escalated substantially. Like many of my friends, I came to understand then the inevitability of going there some day soon. That summer I went off to the Marine Corps Base in Quantico, Virginia, for OCS.

In one of her daily letters to me while I was in Quantico, Mary Ann wrote that she wanted to spend the rest of her life with me. Although OCS was hardly fun, I thought I had died and gone to heaven.

How could I have been so blessed? My soul ached to be with her. I had never felt anything like it. Think about it: I had been in love with this wonderful young woman for six years, and now she wanted to be my wife!

I was mad with joy.

⧗

In the spring of 1966 I wrote my first poem. It was for and about Mary Ann, but she knew nothing of it until it was published in *The Purple*, Holy Cross's literary magazine, in May of that year. Since it's part of the story, here it is. (The "friend" in the first line is West Pointer Jim Carson, a man I have never met; this is something I have never before disclosed.)

Time Cannot Kill

Travel on, friend tho' you be
For unkindness is not your lot
Nor is it mine to dispense.
Yet follow my advice: it is best.
(Have you been ill-directed
before on my account?)
My words are neither enigmatic
Nor meaningless;
Nor are they the empty sounds of
'A tale told by an idiot,
Full of sound and fury,
Signifying nothing.'

You appear and you are remembered;
You have returned from obscurity.
But, more than yourself,
Your words are memorable;
More than yourself,
Those words were intolerable
And the echo of bitter words
Never fades.
Indeed, you must think them unfelt—
Well, not so: Heartfelt—
In her heart so unexploitable: yet,
Such innocence you dared to delude.

For the future: (since you failed then)
Never pick the rose

Before its beauty unfolds.
Do not be impatient for its
Perfume in the spring.
A man once said that 'A rose
By any other name
Would smell as sweet.'
Now that rose will bear my name
And that rose cannot wait
For spring.

Love is a memory
That time cannot kill.
Is this the reason why you return?
Indeed, time cannot deal the blow—
But an empty heart hurled the memory
Into oblivion
And parched
The thirsty rose
Which withered
And died.

Yet, you live and you return.
Do you intend to resurrect
What is now dead, torn, worm-eaten?
Or would you rescue that rose
About to be cast into the fire?
What's this? You would die for—
Her?
Then die and be damned!
What a misery you are to me;
But what a pestilence to that rose!

The only rose I know has only now
Unfurled its inner beauty.
No, mine is not arrogance;
Rather, mine is the fragrance
And the rose itself, forever new.

My life's love is the cushion
Of sunglow about that rose;
My love's life is the cushion
Of velvet on which
I rest my head
And gather strength.

Thanks to the Internet, I have learned that the diamond ring has been a symbol of love and romance since 1477, when Archduke Maximilian of Austria gave Mary of Burgundy a gold ring set with a diamond as a token of his love. I also learned that 82% of all brides-to-be receive one.

On the last day of May 1966 I paid a visit to the "Diamond District" on New York's West Forty-seventh Street. By arrangement, I met with a diamond merchant with whom my father did business. In fact, I believe he was the same man from whose firm Dad had purchased my mother's diamond engagement ring some twenty-three years earlier. Suffice it to say that I was treated like family.

I selected and left the jewelry shop with not one but three rings. Each contained a round, well cut diamond in a platinum setting on a gold ring. The stones were of different sizes, and the merchant advised me to take all three to my bride-to-be and allow her to choose one, inasmuch as it was she who must ultimately be pleased with how a particular ring looks on her hand. Good advice, I thought.

On June 1, 1966 I presented Mary Ann the three ring selections. She chose neither the largest nor the smallest, and seemed very happy at the prospect of our engagement, as did I. Obviously, we had already decided that we wanted to be married, and spoke of the prospect increasingly. Thus, the ring was an important formality, but my presenting it to her would not occasion my first request for her hand. That understanding between us was already *fait accompli*.

Around this time, as it turned out, I unconsciously joined her sisters in their custom of calling her Mame instead of the more formal Mary Ann.

On that day she also graduated from Marymount College, *magna cum laude* and second in her class. Her Mom, Bernice, attended. Cam, her Dad, did not because he was angry with me and, derivatively, Mame. For deliberately absenting himself from her graduation, I thought he was incredibly "thick," in the Irish sense of the word. It was sad.

Following the era of arranged marriages when the groom would specify the exact payment he offered for his future wife, the formality of a groom asking the bride-to-be's father for her hand in marriage was said to preserve a trace of history. Moreover, it would often serve to cement the relationship between the groom-to-be and his future father-in-law. That was certainly Dr. and Mrs. Locasto's preferred approach, which I wasn't buying.

For weeks before our impending engagement, Mame, at her mother's urging, had been encouraging me to call on her father to formally ask for her hand in marriage. Flatly and arrogantly insisting that such a practice was antedeluvian, I refused. As I reflect on my resistance so long ago, I must now admit that I was perhaps unconsciously afraid that Dr. Locasto may very well have refused Mary Ann's hand.

A dermatologist-syphilologist and a 100% first-generation Sicilian-American, Dr. Locasto was highly respected in the medical and GC communities. A real bootstrap kind of guy, he put himself through school—both St. John's University and the University of Chicago School of Medicine. He was a good and serious man.

"The Doc," as many of us once called him, also inspired awe in young men because of his reputation as protector of his five fine daughters. A friend of mine from The Village once mused that The Doc was going to build a moat around his beautiful brick colonial home in GC just to keep riff-raff like us away from his girls. Strong, dedicated, generous and deeply loving, The Doc would practice his profession, and spend his free time with his wife and daughters, except for the occasional trip to the track, where he was never more than a two-dollar bettor. Although few of the young men who dreaded him had ever seen him, his image was a fierce one. In fact, The Doc was only 5'6", slender and relatively undaunting. Size aside, however, he was honorable and tough in the very best sense of the word.

At lunch on the day of Mame's Marymount graduation, her Mom, who would later become not only my mother-in-law but also one of my best friends, offered to drive me from the campus to the Tarrytown railroad station for my return trip to Manhattan and the jeweler's. Why Mame didn't accompany us I didn't know at the time but would soon find out.

Mrs. Locasto requested in the most pleasant way that I meet with her husband as soon as possible to formally ask for her daughter's hand in marriage. Actually, her words conveyed insistence, a rare behavior for her. A little annoyed, I first thought that mother and daughter had conspired to pressure me into doing what I had erstwhile rejected. For Mame's Mom it was a strong plea, although she deftly made me feel comfortable, and impressed upon me the critical importance, if only to her husband, of my derisively described antedeluvian message. I acquiesced and, with some trepidation, reported to 24 Locust Street at 8:00 p.m. on that same June first. In the final analysis, despite my limited military background, I recognized a direct order when I heard one.

Oh, yes, Mame did a smart thing in not returning to GC after graduation. Instead, she traveled to Cherry Hill, New Jersey, near Philadelphia, to visit one of her classmates, Kathy McShea, for she understood only too well what she was likely to miss at home that evening.

Twenty-four Locust Street was a special place for the Locasto family: Not only was it home; Dr. and Mrs. had bought the lot, and designed and built the house. Although I had visited their magnificent home on prior occasions, I had never done so under these unique circumstances.

Buona sera. Italian was Dr. Locasto's mother tongue, although he was also fluent in several other European languages.

In 1966 I spoke even less Italian than now, so I said "Good evening" when Mrs. Locasto greeted me at the front door of her home and directed me to its spacious and splendid living room. The Doc was sitting in an ample easy chair ostensibly reading a newspaper. "Good evening, Dr. Locasto," I said politely. Without putting his newspaper fully aside, he gestured to a lone wooden kitchen chair, exquisitely bereft of the plush comfort of the room's other furniture and tactically positioned in the center of the room on the elegant 32-foot oriental rug that graced its floor.

"Sit there," he intoned coldly, pointing to the chair.

I sat.

The Doc resumed reading the newspaper. I asked myself if he was really reading or merely trying to intimidate or irritate me. In truth, he was accomplishing both with this ploy.

I cleared my throat, probably through sheer nervousness, which I believe might have distracted or irked him, maybe both. At last he put down the paper and focused on me across the seven-foot chasm between us. His face was stern.

"I understand you want to marry my daughter" was The Doc's opening gambit. I thought of saying *I assume you are referring to Mary Ann* but thought better of it; any attempt at humor by me at this moment would have been ill received.

"Yes, sir, that's right." (It had long been my practice to call older men and cops "Sir.")

The Doc seemed perturbed. He then asked me why I wanted to marry Mame.

Not having a plausible response to such an inquiry, I replied simply, "I love her."

"Define love," he insisted.

Good God, help me! Suddenly, I felt I was in quicksand; it was a place, or at least a situation, I did not know. I was terrified. It was fight or flight but I was not prepared to do either. I prayed.

My mind groped lamely for some compelling chestnut gleaned from my college philosophy courses. *Holy Cross, don't fail me now! Teilhard de Chardin, where are you?* "It is not our heads or our bodies which we must bring together," wrote the French Jesuit philosopher, "but our hearts."

I learned belatedly from Mrs. Locasto, that The Doc actually liked me a lot, although during this visit he could have fooled me.

As an aside, one of my favorite stories about him is that he had trained his little black mutt, Nero, to urinate on the trouser leg of any young man whom he disliked. As a fellow Marine once said (in a tale told later herein), "It's better to be pissed off than pissed on." Suffice it to say that Nero behaved himself when I was around.

Dr. Locasto's profound reservations about Mame and me marrying grew out of the unfortunate story of Mame's namesake, the aforementioned Uncle Emil, who died tragically in the Philippines only a day or so *after* World War II had ended there. The Doc foresaw me going to Vietnam and possibly suffering the same fate. Moreover, he harbored a fear that his daughter, as a result of my untimely demise, would end up widowed with a child or two, as was the case with Emil's wife, The Doc's own sister, Grace. (Interestingly, Mame's Mom, who once confided that she became pregnant with Mame on her husband's last night before shipping out, gave birth to her while he was overseas.)

I don't recall how, if at all, I may have attempted to allay his fear. Nor do I recollect how much time may have elapsed since this impossible conversation began. Regardless, The Doc suddenly picked up his newspaper and held it up again in front of his face. I had the feeling he wasn't actually reading; rather, he had simply had his fill of looking at and listening to me. As the moments passed, I was tempted to conclude that our meeting was over. To this day, I don't remember asking him for Mame's hand, which was, of course, my commitment to his wife earlier that day and the primary purpose of this ghastly session. Even if I did ask, I am certain that he did not grant me his blessing.

I waited, my heart pounding. There was no way I was going to excuse myself prematurely. Were I to have done that, I suspect I would have given him perhaps more than enough incentive to declare "I'm not finished with you yet, young man!" So I just sat and waited.

After a while—I know not how long—he excused me with a "You may go," spoken in the same disaffected tone with which he had initially directed me where to sit. He resumed holding the newspaper in front of his face.

I said "Good night." He didn't.

I learned years later that Mrs. Locasto and two of her daughters had been eavesdropping from the kitchen on the exchange taking place in the living room that evening. I was struck by the consensus they reached, which they shared with me: Both The Doc and I were "thick."

Until that meeting, I had always thought that diamond was the hardest substance known.

> *Once you have found her,*
> *Never let her go.*

> —From "Some Enchanted Evening"
> in *South Pacific*

Mame and I next saw each other two days later at Boston's Logan Airport where I met her flight from Philadelphia on a warm, sunny morning. From there we were driven to Cape Cod by my Holy Cross classmate Chick Walsh. On the Cape we would rendezvous with Roger Hunt and Bob Lund, as well as Joanne Heap and Patty Byron, then their respective girlfriends and now their wives of more than three decades, for a long weekend of revelry with other friends leading up to Holy Cross graduation on June 8th, the following Wednesday.

The day was now beautiful and bright, as was Mame. It's embarrassing, as she has reminded me more than once over the years, but I couldn't wait to give her the engagement ring. Surely it would have been far more romantic to wait until, say, that evening, and give it to her in the moonlight while looking out on Cape Cod Bay, or walking along a beach, which we've often done. But it was not to be, for I was, in a way, like a little kid. Finding myself once again with her in the back seat of someone else's car, Chick's now top-down convertible, I rather unceremoniously, I'm afraid, gave Mame the ring. With the wind in her hair and the sunlight on her face, she accepted this token of my love, smiled and became my fiancée. More to the point, Mame and I were ecstatic.

Over the next several months we made our wedding plans. We decided to be married even without her parents' approval. She was studying for a Master of Arts in Teaching (M.A.T.) in Mathematics at Johns Hopkins University in Baltimore, Maryland. Then a Marine Corps second lieutenant, I was stationed in Quantico, Virginia, about an hour and a half by car south of Baltimore.

On December 30, 1966 I reported, along with Roger Hunt and Bob Lund, to the Naval Air Station at Pensacola, Florida, for training.

Our wedding day was to be February 11, 1967, and we planned to be married in the chapel on the base. About six weeks earlier, Mame decided to travel from Hopkins to GC to tell her parents that we would be married. Her Mom asked if she were pregnant, which she was not. For the record, there was no chance of that.

Knowing her daughter and husband well, Mrs. Locasto went into action. In a remarkably swift and effective negotiation, she got an agreement from both. If Mame and I would simply wait until June (to allow for appropriate planning and preparation time, etc.), her father would both bless our marriage and host a reception for family and friends.

Mame called and told me of the new plan successfully developed and negotiated by her mother. In a flashback to the "Define love" session with The Doc seven months earlier, I rejected it outright and, in a moment of anger and frustration, told my fiancée to come to Pensacola so that we could be married as planned. I even had the temerity to tell her that, if she did not come, all bets were off. Born of my fear that I would lose Mame anyway, this rash moment was witnessed by Roger and Bob, then my roommates. Having unavoidably overheard my side of the conversation with Mame on the only telephone in our house, they were incredulous. They also told me I had made a huge mistake. "Charlie, you're an asshole" was how Bob put it.

Early that evening my father telephoned. He related that Mame had walked the 3.2 miles across GC on a freezing afternoon from her parents' home to that of mine. She had arrived with suitcase in hand, and asked my Mom and Dad for a ride to the airport. She was coming to Pensacola after all.

Dad told me that, if Mame and I were to go ahead with our wedding plans, he, Mom and my five siblings would be there. He also assured me that he and Mom would support and respect whatever decision Mame and I would ultimately make. Having said all the right things, he had calmed me down somewhat. Then he took the opportunity to encourage me to consider my future in-laws' proposal carefully. Dad knew that this was an emotional time for Mame and me, as well as for her folks. He also reminded me of Mame's first visit to my parents' home in 1965, after which he told me, referring to her, "Don't let that one get away."

My father's intervention at that critical moment proved important and truly beneficial. He brought me gradually around to an acceptance of the Locastos' wholly reasonable approach. Knowing me as he had then for nearly twenty-two years, he saved me from doing a disservice to some very fine people. He spoke of the long run and how doing something precipitous at a time like this could have a way of becoming a deep regret later in life. He was right.

Mame and I were married in St. Joseph's Roman Catholic Church in GC on Saturday, June 10, 1967 at one o'clock in the afternoon. It was a glorious warm sunny day, and she was stunning!

When I think about this dream-come-true outcome, all that comes to mind are the beautiful words from *The Sound of Music*: "Somewhere in my youth or childhood I must have done something good."

All I ask of you is forever to remember me as loving you.

—Gregory Norbert, OSB

Ode to Joy, Also Known As Mame

I

On the day we first met back in fifty-nine
I could hardly imagine you'd ever be mine.
So warm were you, so bright, so friendly but, alas,
flirtatious;
And you couldn't hide even then that you were also
curvaceous!

All during our very naïve high-school years
I often wondered if ever, despite my fears,
You could one day come to feel about me
As deeply as I did then about thee.

Our dates as teenagers, infrequent tho' they were,
To me were filled always with excitement and wonder.
I felt then, as I do now, fierce pride being with you—
Despite in those days your too-early curfew!

Will you ever forget the night we went out
And I was convinced beyond a shadow of doubt
By rumors in town that you were nearly engaged
To that West Point cadet who seemingly wanted you
caged?

II

Then suddenly in the year nineteen-sixty-five
You gave me a message that brought me alive;
On a New England winter's night so deep
You told me I'd be the only company you'd keep!

For thirty-years now you've been the best part of my life:
Through high school, college, war and twenty-two years
my wife.
Indeed, for me personally life itself are you;
To tell the truth, you are my dream come true.

To me you are ever both marvel and delight,
As well as the sweetest with whom to spend the night!
But as is well known to our offspring and others,
Truly extraordinary, Mame, are you among mothers.

Your epic love for your children has simply no rival,
And you've always made clear that life's more than
survival.
You have consistently shown that your love's
unconditional,
And, as for forgiveness, you've made it traditional.

III
Your fairness and concern even family transcend
As you care for your students as mentor and friend.
To be sure, the quintessential math teacher are you:
In advanced statistics who else could have gotten me
through?

More than a score of years have passed
Since I penned for you my verses last.
My young-poet dreams then you do more than fulfill,
For your love is a memory that time cannot kill.

As often as I endeavor to communicate
To you and our family that I think you're great,
I am for words at a loss almost always;
Still, you are the joy and the light of my days.

Whatever otherwise my own life may be,
Nothing compares with or matters as much to me
As living with and loving you all my days.
Indeed, as your husband, you I cannot enough praise.

IV

Our past is prologue to the rest of our life
And I cannot imagine it without my first wife!
As the song goes, "You're my lover, you're my best friend,"
So please keep being both from now to the end.

And speaking of the end, it's high time I close
With some lines you may think that everyone knows.
Look back once again to a time ago long
When in the mid-sixties we called this one our song:

If they gave me a fortune, my treasure would be small;
I could lose it all tomorrow and never mind at all.
But if I should lose your love, dear, I don't know what I'd
do,
For I know I'd never find another you!

While you reflect on these lines from around sixty-five,
I look at you now and see how you thrive.
And now as I finish, I'd like simply to say:
My sweet Mame, I love you, and Happy Birthday!

December 27, 1989   *Chuck*

4

CHAMINADE HIGH SCHOOL: "A COMMUNITY OF FAITH, A COMMITMENT TO EXCELLENCE"

If we can't live our dreams, we can still lead a life that makes a difference. It's useful for us all to take a long view of things and try to grasp the big picture, while realizing that success is in the details. Thinking positively, having faith, and living by the Golden Rule all help too. What counts most are not the laurels or the nuts we gather along the way but the kind of human beings we are.

—P. Henry Mueller

After my St. Anne's graduation in June 1958, I went on to Chaminade High School in nearby Mineola, New York, a village adjacent to and just north of GC. Today, Mame and I have a small apartment there, in which I maintain an office.

Almost from the time my family moved to GC, I had wanted to go to Chaminade. A major reason was that I wanted most of all to play football there, although the school was noted for its strong academics.

Tony Award winner Brian Dennehy of the Chaminade Class of 1956 has articulated the flavor of the school in the era when he and I were students there. At the same time, he also delivered a crucial message to modern America when he served as the guest speaker at a

Chaminade dinner at the Essex House in New York City forty years after his graduation. Here are excerpts from his remarks then.

But mostly it was the people—your people, your parents, your grandparents, people like Irish, Italian immigrants, first generation, second generation, blue-collared workers, cops, firemen, bus drivers, a couple of accountants and lawyers.

My Dad was a newspaperman. He used to say he was a white-collar worker but his collar was pretty frayed, maybe a little grimy. Chaminade for my brothers and me was a real sacrifice for my father, one I never heard him complain about because he knew Chaminade would help us make better lives for ourselves. And he was right. I'm sure most of us here tonight could tell similar stories (of) parents who sacrificed so our lives would be better—and they are better. Look around you. They're better.

The economic woes of the thirties that so terrified our parents are ancient history to us. And now we're faced with a much more terrifying crisis—a crisis that makes Chaminade's survival and growth ever more important, a crisis for the soul of America.

When you were in high school, could you have imagined that a time would come in your lifetime when abortion would be legal, and school prayer a felony; when political activity and organization would be encouraged for gays and lesbians but regarded as intolerant extremism when practiced by Catholics or other Christians; when the word family—*family!*—would be an epithet spat out with hysterical venom by a whole range of so called progressive activists? A crisis of the American soul.

We're going to need Chaminade, and we're going to need places like Chaminade more than we've ever needed them before, so that our children and our grandchildren will have a chance to learn that man is more than a collection of appetites; and that life is something more than a struggle to satisfy those appetites; and that we remember those sweet, hard-working people who gave us the opportunity to become what we have become, and that we honor their sacrifice and their generosity and their faith.

Named for Father William Joseph Chaminade (1761-1850), who was beatified by Pope John Paul II in Rome on September 3, 2000, the school was founded in 1930 by Father Chaminade's religious order, the Society of Mary, or Marianists (not to be confused with the Marists). Father Chaminade was a French priest who went underground to serve Catholic faithful during the French Revolution. Chaminade High School is staffed by Marianist brothers and priests, as well as lay men and women.

Today Chaminade still holds true to its original mission, that is, to educate Christian young men in "a community of faith" with "a commitment to excellence." As the school's home page indicates, "Students . . . follow a college preparatory liberal arts curriculum in an atmosphere that emphasizes the development of Christian community and education of the heart. Chaminade's goal is to foster the development of well-rounded, faith-filled Catholic men."

Chaminade's rigorous academic program enabled me later to meet the standards of the College of the Holy Cross, then a leading American Jesuit institution in New England. Moreover, its athletic programs, particularly varsity football, gave me the opportunity to test my physical limits at an early age. Both of these prepared me, although I didn't know it at the time, for my service in the Marine Corps. Importantly, I consider Chaminade the cornerstone of my life. To me, both it and the Corps are the greatest of all fraternities.

In his book *Education and Transformation*, subtitled *Marianist Ministries in America Since 1849*, Christopher J. Kaufmann describes Chaminade as a "jewel." Citing a detailed report on the school, he has written:

> . . . with a rigorous academic program, Chaminade had
> an enrollment of thirteen hundred [versus more than 1,600
> today]; it "continues to set the pace in all phases of school life
> by reason of its faculty and select student body . . . Seldom

does a school . . . attract national renown for academic
achievement as Chaminade's modern language department
had done . . ." The science department also excelled.

Kaufmann also addresses the role of Father Philip K. Eichner,
S.M., a 1953 Chaminade alumnus and the school's longest-serving
president (1967-1992):

> Since Chaminade was the most prestigious school in
> the [Marianist] province, Eichner's position as an impassioned
> advocate of Marianist monastic tradition was rooted in an
> institution highly regarded by the Catholic families of Long
> Island as a school of academic excellence, traditional
> Catholicism, and discipline.
> Eichner embodied these qualities.

As I am wont to say, Brother Alexander Ott, S.M. founded
Chaminade in 1930; Bro. John T. Darby, S.M. (Chaminade's
principal from 1945 to 1959) built it; and Fr. Philip put it on the
map to stay. Fr. Philip and I first became acquainted in 1987 during
the planning of my 25-year Chaminade class reunion, which I co-
chaired. We became closer when he invited me to serve as a
development officer (fund-raiser) at Chaminade beginning on
January 2, 1992. Fr. Philip is also chairman of the Catholic League
for Religious and Civil Rights, on whose national board of directors
I have served. He is also president of Kellenberg Memorial High
School in Uniondale, New York, and president emeritus of
Chaminade.
    Father John A. McGrath, S.M. is a Chaminade alumnus and a
classmate of Fr. Philip. Like Fr. Philip, he is a Marianist leader in
the United States and currently a professor in the Humanities
Department at the University of Dayton. Fr. "Jack," as he is called,
is a brilliant scholar and a great friend. He was also a history teacher
of mine in my Chaminade student days. After my graduation,
Jack and I didn't see each other again until 1987 when we
reconnected at my class's 25-year reunion. The occasion was the

catalyst for the rekindling of a strong friendship that will now endure for the rest of our lives.

In 1992 Jack wrote the following "memory" in a letter, and it is something I want to share with my grandchildren, for they have asked what I was like when I was young. Such words are more credible when they come from someone else, albeit a friend:

> Chuck Mansfield was a young, conscientious and handsome student athlete who sat toward the front of the class, pen poised, with a serious and open expression on his face, as if he wanted and expected to learn something. He took good notes in a neat and legible hand, did very well on exams and was often ready to offer an answer and engage in some debate.
>
> It was clear he was brought up to be respectful to his elders (even if they were only 26 years old) and had made part of himself a disciplined, organized and energetic approach to life. You could easily see it in the way he carried himself, the way he spoke, the way he dealt with people and the way he played football. No sitting back and waiting for life to happen for him. You could see that he would tackle life and make something of it, that he cherished things of religious and human value and would pursue them, one such value being Mary Ann Locasto!

Chaminade gave me classmates and teammates who have also become my friends for life. Among them are Frank Biasi, a financial executive; Doug Casey, a commercial real estate executive; Joe Egan, a CPA; Al Groh, University of Virginia head varsity football coach (and former head coach of the New York Jets); Tom Kiley, a law firm administrator; Earl Kirmser, a public relations specialist; Carl LoGalbo, a financial executive and investment banker; Father Garrett Long, Chaminade's chaplain; Gene Maloney, executive vice president and counsel at a large mutual fund complex; Jim Meehan, a sales executive; Cliff Molloy, a real estate executive; Mike Reisert, a stock broker and investment banker; Bill Sellerberg, a railroad accounting executive; Jeff Thomas, a businessman and entrepreneur; and Father John Worthley, a parish priest on Long Island. Joe, Tom, Earl, Gene and John were later my college classmates as well.

Al, Carl, Earl, Tom and I then formed, and still constitute, an especially close band of brothers, and some of us acquired nicknames.

Carl was called "Spunky" and "Lo," which was subsequently upgraded to "The Lo," a title more suited to his background and status.

Today Carl is one of the most articulate people I know but he succumbed once upon a time to two funny linguistic errors, both at lunch in the Chaminade cafeteria. Hungry as he was, he quickly opened his brown lunch bag, and announced with gusto, "I'm vanished!" One of us just couldn't resist saying, "You must be *really* hungry," while another had the nerve to point out that the proper term was, in fact, *famished*. Later, referring to some "hoods" who in those days hung out in a rough section of Queens, New York, with which he was familiar, Carl told us that these guys actually wore their Levi's blue jeans below their "nasal," meaning, of course, *navel*. We all laughed heartily, and then Earl said to Carl, "I hope so; otherwise, they might have trouble breathing!"

To provide additional perspective on his persona, Carl actually referred to himself in the third person as "The Lo"! Now in his late fifties, he still does, although, mercifully, not with the same regularity. In fact, one day at a student Mass in Chaminade's Darby auditorium, he showed me all the references in the missal to "The Lord." He did this to make his case that even "The Lord" could not be spelled without "The Lo." Someone suggested that this might be sacrilegious, but it didn't detract one iota from Carl's assessment.

"Kile" was Tom's handle. Mine was "Mans," which also happens to be my brother's nickname. (The name influenced my choice of e-mail address, which is chuckmans@aol.com.) It was later modified to "The Man," which I happily shared with St. Louis Cardinal slugger Stan Musial, known widely then as "Stan the Man." Kile later translated it into French, that is, "l'homme," which is pronounced *lum*. The etymology, migration and transformation of this name were remarkable, as I shall explain.

By the time we were college classmates, Kile almost always called me l'homme; Earl also used the tag but to a lesser extent. In fact, Kile and The Lo still call me l'homme on occasion. Some fellow students and new friends understandably wondered what this odd-sounding name meant, and sometimes requested and received a correct explanation. Others heard "Lum" and identified the name with a major league baseball coach of that era, whose name was Lum Harris. However, Mr. Harris's proper given name is Luman. Thus, I was also called Luman by some and, in a fusion and confusion of two names, even "Charlie Harris." Later, in a bizarre twist, my college classmates Art Burns and Bob Meikle would even call me *Lumen de lumine* (Light from light), which is from the Latin version of the Nicene Creed.

Enough of that.

Two of the funniest stories from my Chaminade student days come from Jim Meehan and Mike Reisert.

Jim's tale involves a preposterous and hilarious question. He actually raised his hand in E. T. Turner's freshman geography class, was recognized by Mr. Turner, and asked his now infamous question: "If the people in Poland are called Poles, why aren't the people in Holland called Holes?" Like fuel on a fire, laughter erupted from our whole class of thirteen- and fourteen-year-old boys. Jim, I'm afraid, was issued a "gray slip" for a disciplinary infraction. In fact, I believe it was a six-pointer. (Fifteen points in a semester meant expulsion from Chaminade.)

Mike Reisert's classic anecdote likely would have earned him a gray slip too because what he said would almost certainly have been construed by school authorities as disrespectful of the two teachers about whom Mike made his uncommon observation.

These teachers were well liked and respected Catholic gentlemen: Mr. Joseph Fox and Mr. Patrick Stafford, both of whom were completely bald. We are not talking thin hair here; theirs was full-follicle impairment. Anyway, our junior varsity football team was returning one day in sophomore year on the team bus from a scrimmage. Mike, who was even then a master at holding court, observed that, "If Mr. Fox and Mr. Stafford were to put their heads together, they'd make a complete ass of themselves."

Once more, a laughter eruption.

Among the fondest memories of my Chaminade years were the times spent at "Mamma Lo's."

"Mamma Lo" is actually Carl LoGalbo's mother, Florence, a beautiful Italian-American lady. When I first met her in the summer of 1959, she was wearing a pale yellow summer dress in her kitchen, where she was cooking. Carl, who had two brothers (Frankie and Richie, both of whom attended Chaminade), led me through the kitchen and upstairs to his room.

I asked Carl who "the girl in the yellow dress" was because, as I told him, "You didn't tell me you had a sister." He guffawed.

"That's my mother, you idiot," he said, still laughing.

"Why didn't you introduce me?" I asked.

Carl rectified his oversight a few minutes later. She was charming and very young-looking for the mother of three young men.

When we returned to the kitchen, Mrs. LoGalbo was making her own pasta and sauce. No jars of tomato sauce or boxes of macaroni encumbered this lady; she made everything from scratch.

With all appropriate homage and respect to my Mom and my wife, both of whom are gourmet cooks, Mamma Lo may well have been in a class by herself. Her culinary skills became legendary among us Chaminade guys, and we couldn't wait to be invited for Sunday dinner, which typically lasted from one to seven p.m. It was a feast of the best food ever.

Mamma Lo was also exceptionally good-natured, and I believe she loved Tom, Earl, Al and me, well, like her own sons. Even when we showed up for a midnight snack, she seemed thrilled to see—and serve—us. Her kindness and generosity were above and beyond the call of duty. At this writing she is eighty-nine, and I had a lovely visit with her just before Thanksgiving 2001. She allowed as she doesn't cook much anymore, and I said that's probably a good thing for her, given all the work her methods involved.

"I did it because I loved it, and it made you boys happy," she said. What a doll!

A footnote: Carl's brother Frankie was away at college when Carl and I were in high school. Thus, I would sleep in Frankie's bed when I stayed at the LoGalbo home, which was often. Given the reality of six children in the Mansfield house, however, there were no extra beds; so, my parents actually bought one for Carl, who also spent many nights with us.

Virtual brothers, Carl and I actually once had a major row.

One evening he, Tom and I attended a basketball game at Chaminade. Tom drove us there in his 1949 Pontiac, in which the only item that worked properly was the clock. The floor immediately in front of the left rear seat actually had a hole in it through which one could see the road below. (We covered it with a piece of plywood.)

At the basketball game I met and sat with a lovely girl by the name of Dede Williams. Although I had been introduced to her before by mutual friends, this was an unusual opportunity for me inasmuch as she was unescorted; Dede was beautiful and almost always had a date. To be sure, I regarded her as "out of my league," but, as the evening progressed, she seemed to show some interest in me. Our serendipitous meeting significantly enhanced an otherwise agreeable evening.

At the end of the basketball game, Carl appeared. He knew Dede; I think he had even taken her out a few times. It is important to understand that The Lo regarded himself as a ladies' man extraordinaire, which, I must concede, was pretty much the way it was. At the very least, The Lo was a legend in his own mind.

Carl swooped down—I cannot find more suitable language— and swept Dede away without even the slightest acknowledgement of my presence. As for Dede, I had the impression that she considered Carl a better deal than the guy she had just sat with during the basketball game. I sulked for a while as anger toward The Lo built within me.

When Tom, Carl and I rendezvoused later at Tom's Pontiac, I sat in the back seat while Carl joined Tom in front. I remember Carl then launching into a self-congratulatory monologue about Dede and how much he thought she liked him. On hearing this, I became disgusted and angry with The Lo. I told him that his whole approach was conceited and selfish, and that he had no business butting in on my time with Dede. Then he touched a nerve.

"Mansfield, you're unbalanced," he said.

I called Carl on it, insisting that, if he dared say it again, I would clean his clock.

Turning around in the front passenger seat to face me in the rear, he declared, this time pointing his finger at me and with inimitable LoGalbian vocal emphasis, "Mansfield, you're unbalanced!"

I attacked him.

To this day, the images of that moment in my mind are ones of Carl and me pummeling each other as Tom tried to steer the car with his left hand and break up the fight with his right. It was tragicomedy at its highest or, maybe, its lowest, yet another instance of relative extrema.

By the following day, all was forgotten and The Lo and I were friends once more.

⧗

In the spring of 1997, nearly thirty-nine years after we met as freshmen at Chaminade, Al Groh returned to Long Island for a new coaching assignment with the New York Jets, of whom he would become head coach less than three years later. Al's return occasioned a dinner in GC, an evening that would mark a special reunion for him, Tom, Earl, Carl and me. It was a special time that is instructive of just how strong the bond among us remained.

On August 6th of that year, Tom wrote the four of us the following letter:

Dear Al, Earl, Chuck and Carl,

It was a great pleasure seeing each of you at the Newport Grill a few weeks ago. That night brought together for the first time in a long time a group of guys that I have always considered quite extraordinary in so many ways.

As we laughed uproariously at our jokes and stories and the years began to melt away, I could not help but wonder at the strength and continuity of a friendship that has remained constant through all the years, sometimes despite long periods of enforced separation and even silence. Clearly the bonds that we began to forge nearly forty years ago bind us tightly still. Certainly they have proved far more enduring than we could have imagined back in 1958.

Therefore I am pleased to send along to each of you a copy of a picture that was taken on the evening of our reunion. I think it captures a little bit of the spirit and camaraderie of the group as well as some of the affection we still have for each other. It is rare to find such feeling among any group much less one thrown together purely by fate as we were so many years ago.

Although the circumstances that brought us together recently may change sooner or later, it is my hope that our love for each other never will. It is in that spirit of hope and love that I enclose this picture of the Boys of Summer, still young in the autumn of their lives.

Your friend,
Tom

Some of Chaminade's most prominent alumni include Bishop Christopher Cardone '76 (the first of the school's 16,000 alumni to be so elevated); Major General Matthew P. Caulfield, U.S. Marine Corps (Ret.) '54; the aforementioned star of stage, screen and television Brian Dennehy '56; recently retired IBM Corporation chairman and CEO Louis V. Gerstner, Jr. '59; retired RiverBank America chairman, president and CEO Jerome R. McDougal '45; Rear Admiral Paul T. Gillcrist, U.S. Navy (Ret.) '46; NBC chairman and CEO Bob Wright '61; Bill O'Reilly '67 of the Fox News Channel's *The O'Reilly Factor*; former U.S. Senator Alfonse D'Amato '55; and the aforementioned Al Groh and Carl LoGalbo, my '62 classmates.

Several years ago I had lunch in Manhattan with U.S. Senator Ernest "Fritz" Hollings of South Carolina, and happened to sit next to David Rudd, one of the senator's senior aides. Also in attendance were my classmate Terry Mahony, Chris Sweeny '47 and Bob Wright, who hosted the meeting. Subsequently, I received an e-mail from David, in which he wrote: "At various times I have heard eloquent soapbox elocutions on who actually ran the world . . . the Post Office, the Mafia, the Federal Reserve, the Zionist Occupation Government and Bill Gates. These people, however, did not know what I learned in New York yesterday – that a little known Catholic boys school in Mineola, Long Island, was actually in control of our destiny. Based on what I saw yesterday, we are in pretty good hands."

In an interview prior to his 1997 induction into Chaminade's Alumni Hall of Fame, Gen. Matt Caulfield provided interesting, perhaps surprising, perspective on his long and distinguished career as a military officer:

At some time very early in my career, I discovered that, as a Marine officer, I could serve in a way that met my responsibilities as a Christian. The dedication to a cause more important than self; the sacrifice; the taking care of others, indeed, placing others above self; the demands of personal honor and integrity; the sacredness of the term *duty* all combined to make my life as a Marine officer as close as one can come to life in a religious order.

The echo of Matt's words may be heard in the actions of another Chaminade alumnus, who had 'a cause more important than self, who sacrificed, who took care of others and placed them above himself.' George Howard '75 was an officer with the Port Authority of New York and New Jersey's Emergency Services Unit at JFK International Airport. On the day of the catastrophic terrorist attacks on New York's World Trade Center, his day off, he left home and raced to the scene.

"As Howard ran toward the north tower to help people escape," according to *People* magazine, "the building collapsed, burying him under an avalanche of debris."

In an address to the nation on September 20, 2001, President Bush held up George's shield and promised to carry it as a reminder of those who lost their lives, as well as an inspiration in the war on terrorism. George's mother, Arlene, had personally pressed her son's badge into the President's hand. George was posthumously inducted into the Chaminade Alumni Hall of Fame in New York City on March 21, 2002, as was Admiral Paul Gillcrist.

Liz Willen recounted the following for the Bloomberg News Wire:

> Minutes after two hijacked planes crashed into the World Trade Center . . . , the Reverend James C. Williams got on the public address system at Chaminade . . . and urged students to pray. Father James, a 32-year-old Marianist priest, who is president of Chaminade, invited pupils worried about

relatives to his office . . ."Be patient," Father James told the 300 students who gathered. "We are going to get word about all of your dads. There are a lot of you and a lot of confusion in our world. The best we can do is pray." . . . The close-knit school, 22 miles east of Manhattan, where God is part of the everyday fabric and the motto is [Fortes in Unitate] "strength in unity," now finds itself tested in new ways as it copes with insurmountable loss. Immediately after the second plane struck the south tower, Chaminade officials began tracking down the 19 parents who worked in the trade center, crossing off names of those who called in. Father James, a 1987 Chaminade graduate who sometimes plays Frisbee in his cassock, said he found a moment to slip into the school's chapel to ask God for strength. He knew it would take a lot of prayer.

"I had to be the rock," he said. "The Lord is my rock."

"The first thing I tell (our students) is there are no rules about how a young man grieves."

Chaminade lost sixty-two family members, friends and alumni in this enormous tragedy.

The Los Angeles Times Magazine of October 21, 2001 published a story about Chaminade's losses as well. Once more Father James was described as "one of the youngest high school principals in the state of New York" and acquitted himself with distinction. "In eternity, God calls the shots," he said. "There aren't any terrorists in heaven."

The article's author, Janet Reitman, continued: "One year [actually it was two years] after taking the helm of Chaminade, one of Long Island's most selective private schools, he now has to steer his boys through an ocean of grief. In addition to the devastation among families of current students 20 alumni are dead or missing. And fathers of dozens of boys are firefighters, police officers and emergency workers."

"I have boys who come to me and say, 'Father, my dad's never coming home,' and they're talking about the psychological damage . . ." "We have so many kids who are mourning deaths, and others who are mourning a kind of living death. The impact is so huge—I don't think we've even begun to feel the real repercussions of this yet."

Patrick Boland '96 is a New York City firefighter who survived the catastrophe. On October 6, 2001, he e-mailed the following compelling words to Chaminade chaplain Father Garrett Long, my classmate and friend:

> Today is my first day off since 9/11. I was extremely upset to see that Matt Vienna has passed. Unfortunately he is part of a long list of friends that I have lost. There is hardly a day that I don't cry for their loss. It is hard for me to express myself at a time like this. I cannot even begin to speak about what I have seen and have experienced. I feel like my eyes have been burned.
>
> I was happy to see all that Chaminade did to help the relief efforts. Believe me, sometimes the only thing that kept us going were the efforts of all the volunteers, and to see all the citizens of NY and the world unite behind us. God is truly present at Ground Zero. I'm not sure if it made the news or not, but one of the iron workers found a cross buried in the wreckage. Two steel beams in the perfect shape of a cross. It was lifted out by a crane and placed upright on a concrete slab. At the beginning of every shift a group of us remove our hard hats and say a few prayers. The Cross has become one of the few bright spots in the past weeks. At the foot of that cross I left a note that said "Fortes In Unitate." For all of us down there those words have never been more true.
>
> Please pass my sympathy on to all members of the Chaminade family; their loss will not be forgotten. Those who died did not die in vain. Their death has brought together so many people in a way that I never thought possible. I pray that this sense of unity never passes.
>
> It's times like these that we should all remember what's really important in life. It's not about getting the

highest grade, wearing fashionable clothes, or making a team. It's about the people around you. Thank you for all the prayers.

God Bless Chaminade,
Patrick Boland '96

As author Peggy Noonan has so eloquently written, "If you are of a certain cast of mind it is of course meaningful that the cross, which to those of its faith is imperishable, did not disappear. It was not crushed by the millions of tons of concrete that crashed down upon it, did not melt in the furnace. It rose from the rubble, still there, intact.

"For the ignorant, the superstitious and me (and maybe you), the face of the Evil One was revealed, and died; for the ignorant, the superstitious and me (and maybe you), the cross survived. This is how God speaks to us. He is saying, "I am." He is saying, "I am here." He is saying, "And the force of all the evil of all the world will not bury me."

In hoc signo vinces. (In this sign you will conquer.)

General Matt Caulfield visited Chaminade on November 13, 2001 and addressed the student body. Emphasizing that Chaminade men will play important roles in the future, especially in the post-9/11 era, he said: "Chaminade has always been right for all the ages, and the age that we are now in is one that is going to decide our survival as a nation and the ideals we believe in. Now, more than ever, we need the Chaminade man making his mark."

I entered Chaminade as a 13-year old freshman in September

1958. On June 24, 1962 I graduated with honors and served as salutatorian. In between, my football dreams came true: I was a 16-year old starting guard and linebacker on Chaminade's first undefeated and untied varsity football team; we became (New York City, Westchester and Long Island) Catholic High School Football League champions and I received Honorable Mention from the League. My classmates also honored me when they elected me president of the senior class, student body, student council and the school's chapter of the National Honor Society. I also received the American Legion award for "Leadership, Scholarship and Character," the predecessor of today's *Chaminade Man Award*, an honor I still cherish deeply forty years later.

The Village chose me as Chaminade's representative to the "Experiment in International Living," a student exchange program for which Mame was also selected. Indeed, she spent a portion of the summer of 1961 in Germany where she witnessed the initial erection of the Berlin Wall. I decided not to go abroad—because it would have meant missing summer football practice sessions. Some folks thought I had lost my marbles; for me then it was a straightforward matter of priorities. My classmate and friend Jeff Zabler was selected as my alternate and went in my stead.

In the academic realm at Chaminade, I loved Latin, French, English and mathematics.

In my post-graduate years, in addition to being a development officer, I serve as a member of Chaminade's Torch Fund committee, a permanent member of the board of its alumni association, a member of the Golf and Tennis Open executive committee and chairman of class representatives. I also write a regular column in the *Chaminade News*.

On August 25, 2001, the Chaminade Alumni Association surprised and honored me with the *Crimson and Gold Award*, its highest recognition. This was extraordinary to me because I was only its twelfth recipient in Chaminade's seventy-two-year history.

Moreover, it had been presented only four times in the preceding twenty-three years. Here is its inscription:

Charles F. Mansfield, Jr.
has provided the highest level of
personal dedication and distinguished service
to Chaminade High School.
Chuck has served as Alumni Association President,
as a member of the Alumni Board, as chairman
and member of countless committees,
and as Development Officer.
In recognition of his numerous contributions
to the school and in appreciation for
the many thankless jobs that he has performed,
the Chaminade Alumni Association
is proud to honor him with this
Crimson and Gold Award.
June 25, 2001

I learned after the presentation that the award was supposed to have been given to me two months earlier at the dinner following the Chaminade Open, which I did not attend due to illness. As things turned out, the later presentation was, to me, more meaningful inasmuch as Mame, my Mom, and cousin Isabelle ("Issy") Charrot, who was visiting from England, were all in attendance.

Above all, I was honored and touched to be included among the likes of earlier recipients: Brothers John Darby and Albert Kozar, two pioneering principals of Chaminade; Mike Lee, the renowned *Long Island Press* sports columnist; legendary Chaminade coaches Eddie Flynn, Frank "Boiler" Burns and George Toop; Jack Lenz, my fellow Marine and an Iwo Jima veteran; Fr. Philip; Bro. Richard Hartz, my friend with whom I have worked closely since 1988; and Joseph F. Thomas, coach, teacher and one of the true heroes in my life.

Today (President George W.) Bush said that "this conflict is a fight to save the civilized world" from an evil regime that starves its people and supports terrorists who live "on the hunted margin of mankind." He added: "By their hatred they have divorced themselves from the values that define civilization itself."

—David E. Sanger in *The New York Times*
[October 21, 2001]

ODE TO CHAMINADE,
CORNERSTONE AND CLASSIC

I

Fully seventy years have already passed
Since where you stand now potatoes grew last.
Those boys you first welcomed a'way back then
Alas now are either gone or today's old men.

FORTES IN UNITATE your familiar seal doth proclaim.
'Tis so recognizable, there's nary a need for your name.
Its three symbols—the Cross, the torch and the rule—
Convey a clear message that you're no ordinary school.

Fully faithful to your mission have you always been:
Spiritual, intellectual and moral maturity for young men.
You have become and will remain for many years hence
"A community of faith, a commitment to excellence."

Your students are enthusiastic, vibrant and bright.
The Chaminade Man, they learn, will do what is right
Always for the right reason, no matter who looks on.
His moral code endures when ephemeral culture is gone.

Catholic is your tradition (elsewhere confusion abounds)
Thanks to your brothers and priests,
their influence redounds.
Consistency, rigor and excellence underpin your lore,
Evinced in academics, athletics and *esprit de corps*.

Your young men while students may not always get it,
As they wonder sometimes, 'How does Chaminade fit?'
Yet they, when alumni, with warm affection will return,
Drawn by a true depth of feeling, for which they yearn.

II

You teach and develop in context and environment
Character, principles, self-discipline, sound judgment.
Faith, service and values you integrate in daily life
To create happiness from within, nevermind joy or strife.

Your rubric for the Chaminade Man
is about being whole;
One alumnus has called it the 'awakening of his soul."
Another lauds your diligence, once beyond his ken,
In shaping intellectually disciplined and morally
grounded men.

Your sons today number fifteen thousand some,
And year after year many back to you come.
The Marianists you shelter once showed them the way,
With a template for life that thrives to this day.

Down through the decades, to your beliefs did you hold;
After all, that's the significance of your crimson and gold.
You have created the Chaminade Family; yes it is real,
For you still forge a bond all its members deeply feel.

Faith, morals, friendship, ethics, leadership, integrity:
Lo, these are your lasting life-lessons and legacy.
Young men do you challenge, test their mettle you can,
For a boy enters your doors and emerges a man.

Godspeed, Chaminade, as the Lord's work you continue
With all the goodness and grace and spirit within you.
Be courageous and steadfast in Mary's great love,
And long may you serve blest by God above!

.January 2000

*This poem was written by the author on the occasion of
Chaminade High School's seventieth anniversary.*

5

COACH JOE THOMAS:

EXHORTATIONS TO EXCELLENCE

Follow your bliss.

—Joseph F. Thomas

There is a strong link between my experience at Chaminade and that I would gain years later in the Marine Corps. (Conveniently, both institutions have the same colors: crimson and gold.)

I entered Chaminade in September 1958 as a thirteen-year-old freshman. At an even younger age I had arrived at the decision that, if accepted by the school's admissions apparatus, I would enthusiastically attend. I readily admit that part of Chaminade's attraction for me derived from the spirited support that its administration, students and their parents, as well as its neighbors, accorded its football program. For me as a boy, attending Chaminade football games was probably my top priority, at least in the autumn.

Perhaps the most prestigious athletic award given annually at Chaminade goes to the outstanding varsity football player. It is the Terzi Award, named in memory of Marine Corps Captain Joseph Terzi, a 1937 Chaminade alumnus, of whom the eighteenth Marine Corps Commandant, General Alexander Archer Vandegrift, wrote the following on the occasion of a banquet honoring Terzi's memory in 1944:

Three years after our country was treacherously attacked by the enemies against whom he later so gallantly fought, I wish to join you in paying honor to a brave and able officer. As his commanding general during the campaign on Guadalcanal, I take particular pride in his fine record during those difficult months. There he won the Silver Star medal for remaining in an exposed and isolated outpost overrun by an enemy night attack against our lines, eventually directing four of the five men in the outpost to safety when they were surrounded and could no longer hold their isolated position. The day after Christmas last year he received the wound that cost his life while leading his company in a savage frontal assault during the attack on Cape Gloucester, New Britain. His brilliant leadership and great courage on that occasion won him the high honor of the Navy Cross.

When Captain Terzi first entered the Marine Corps we learned from his friends, associates, and teachers that he excelled on the football field no less than in the classroom. Those qualities of grit, determination, intelligence, and leadership which he developed in sports and studies in his community are the qualities that made him a distinguished officer in the Marine Corps. His brother officers and I salute his memory.

Another young military officer, this one a U.S. Army lieutenant who was awarded two Bronze Stars for his courage and leadership in combat in the European theater, was Joseph F. Thomas. Many Long Island readers and sports fans, as well as some in New York City, will still recognize his name. From 1948 to 1988 he distinguished himself as coach and teacher at Chaminade. Indeed, many of the school's alumni and their parents, not to mention fellow coaches, faculty members and competitors, will remember the dedication of this extraordinary Christian gentleman who has become a virtual legend in his own time.

A native of Philadelphia born in 1915, a product of Marianist education both there and at the University of Dayton, and today still a remarkably youthful presence, Coach has given of himself selflessly to many Chaminade men and their families, as well as to many others. To be sure, in the minds of many who know him, he is one of the rarest of men and could well have achieved in coaching the status of, say, a Vince Lombardi, a Don Shula or a Bill Parcells. Coach chose instead to devote his life to the young men of Chaminade, to whom he has imparted the richness of his spirit, as well as memories to last a lifetime.

Now in my late fifties, I remember. These memories—and there are many—are still with me but among the most vivid certainly are those moments of inspiration and exhilaration that always came on autumn Sunday afternoons. It is these memories that were provided, actually created, by Coach Thomas, for his energy and spirit were palpable.

Sometimes, as my mind looks back, I believe I may have taken Coach for granted. In other words, I would ask myself then: Isn't everyone this good? Anyway, my first close-up experience with him came as a fifteen-year-old junior on Chaminade's 1960 varsity football team. His reputation, of course, had preceded him. He was universally said to be a great coach, demanding and hard-driving, as well as a special sort of man. Still, how were my teammates and I to have known that he was in fact any different from other high-school coaches or teachers?

And in truth, I've never known a man worth his salt who in the long run, deep down in his heart, didn't appreciate the grind, the discipline. There is something in good men that really yearns for discipline and the harsh reality of head to head combat.

—Vince Lombardi

Well, we learned; did we ever! Yet, the lessons he taught and the mark he left on us, be it in gym class, on the basketball court, on the football field or on the track, were not fully understood or appreciated by us while we were still Chaminade students. He made us winners while at the same time instilling in us humility when we savored victory. As juniors, we became league champions with a 7-0-1 record. A year later, we went 8-0-0 and became Chaminade's first undefeated and untied varsity football team, as well as league champs for the second consecutive year. This was the first time in Chaminade's history that back-to-back varsity football titles had been won, a feat that wouldn't be repeated at the school until seventeen years later. (A large black and white photograph of that first undefeated and untied team still hangs on the second floor of the west wing of the school just off the main lobby.)

That unforgettable thrill produced a deep and abiding sense of pride, not only in us players but throughout the entire student body (Chaminade's 1962 yearbook theme was "The Year of Champions"). Furthermore, everyone knew and readily acknowledged that the achievement would simply not have been, were it not for Coach's leadership and motivational skills. In the last analysis, regardless of the rigorous conditioning and precision drills he put us through, the key to our success was that he enabled us truly to believe in ourselves.

Coach's pre-game and, particularly, half-time talks with his team were the most compelling motivators I have ever heard or seen. Significantly, it mattered not that we were winning or losing. (Make no mistake; clearly, he preferred the former.) What did matter, and mattered most in his mind, was that there was a game or another half to be played, and played as well as it could be, for the real name of the game called football, as he never failed to communicate to each of his players, is excellence. He has often said to me, "Show me a student's school notebook and I'll tell you if he'll make it on our team." Football or not, academics always came first. And before *and* after every game, win or lose, Coach made sure his team knelt to pray together.

I strongly believe there's another reason Coach's exhortations to excellence were so powerful: Although his coaching responsibilities necessitated his being on the sidelines, he was, in a very real sense, *in* the game. While each of us players was concerned with managing his position and executing his assignments as well as he could for as long as he was in the game, Coach was in there too—intellectually, viscerally and spiritually—on every play at every position—"110% for forty-eight minutes," as he used to say. Not only did he take the game seriously, I believe he took it *personally*. His players knew it, and we all felt it.

> *I don't say these things because I believe in the "brute"*
> *nature of man or that men must be brutalized to be*
> *combative. I believe in God, and I believe in human decency.*
> *But I firmly believe that any man's finest hour—his greatest*
> *fulfillment to all he holds dear—is that moment when he*
> *has to work his heart out in a good cause and he's exhausted*
> *on the field of battle—victorious.*
>
> —Vince Lombardi

Incidentally, among the hundreds who also played football for Coach are Messrs. Dennehy, Gerstner, Groh, Kiley, Kirmser, LoGalbo, Molloy, Reisert and Sellerberg; Sen. D'Amato ran track for Coach.

When I went off to play college football, I wondered and even partially dreaded what it would be like. You see, I had figured that college competition, practices, workouts and the like would be, by definition, more difficult than those in high school. It was not so; they were non-events.

In college we were expected to stay in shape on our own time, and our coach there even told us not to smoke in public! Be that as it may, Coach Thomas's approach to physical conditioning included summer double practice sessions, running through stacks of tires, three-man rolls, bull-in-the-ring and seemingly endless wind sprints, to cite a few of my personal favorites. For me it was to prove a valuable vaccine of experience three years after my Chaminade graduation when I attended my first Marine Corps summer camp, and again a few years later as a Marine lieutenant in Vietnam.

Coach has also been a wonderfully dedicated husband and father; he is also a grandfather and great-grandfather. His wife, the late Mary Kathryn Herrold Thomas, and he met while both were students at the University of Dayton. As unusual as it may seem to some, Coach's love affair with "Kay," as she was called, has never ended, despite the fact that she passed away in 1996. He has told me that every Sunday, as a rule, he visits her final resting place and speaks to her of the week just past and the beautiful life they shared.

Kathy Thomas Cybriwsky, Joseph F. (Jeff) Thomas, Jr. and Michael Thomas are Coach and Kay's children. Already mentioned, Jeff is a Chaminade classmate of mine, and Mike attended both Chaminade and Dayton with my brother Mike. Thanks to his three kids, Coach today delights in his nine grandchildren and three great-grandchildren.

Next to my parents, Coach Joe Thomas, more than any other person, has been the single greatest influence on who I am. He is, in my own view and that of thousands during his forty years at Chaminade who have benefited from his leadership, or even simply known him, the quintessential role model. He was always there in our midst, and we had only to look to him.

"The Chaminade Man" is the moral standard that Chaminade endeavors to inculcate in every student. He does the right thing at the right time for the right reason no matter who may be watching. Ironically, although Coach never attended Chaminade as a student, he was and always will be for many, including me, *the* Chaminade Man. I feel privileged to know him, and it is a badge of honor and pride for me to say: I played football for Joe Thomas.

When we see men of worth, we should think of equaling them.

—Confucius

6

THE COLLEGE OF THE HOLY CROSS

We cannot live our dreams. We are lucky enough if we can give a sample of our best, and if in our hearts we can feel that it has been nobly done.

—Oliver Wendell Holmes

I n August 1962 my parents drove me to the College of the Holy Cross (HC) in Worcester, Massachusetts, where I was then to report for freshman football practice. Despite my relatively small size (5'9" and 200 lbs.), I had a solid football season, starting most games. As at Chaminade, I was a guard and a linebacker.

When I look back, I am nearly incredulous recalling that, when I went there then, it was my first trip to the campus. Once HC accepted me, I had accepted it, sight and site unseen.

It's odd, I suppose, but then it didn't really faze me. I had declined, perhaps unwisely, some football scholarship assistance at Columbia University and Rutgers University but, according to the assistant varsity football coach at HC, who recruited me, there was some football potential for me there. Perhaps more significantly, there was no way, thanks to my parents and the Marianists at Chaminade, that I would attend anything but a Catholic college.

Actually, my decision was strongly influenced by a 1961 magazine article in which then Notre Dame University president Father Theodore Hesburgh was quoted. As I remember it, he proclaimed HC as virtually the top Catholic institution of higher learning in the U.S. Not surprisingly, Father Hesburgh also placed Notre Dame, as well as Georgetown University, right up there but seemed to give the nod to the Cross, citing its small student population, diverse curricula and outstanding faculty, among other attractions. In short, I was impressed. (Having spent two weeks at Notre Dame in August 1960, I have sometimes wondered if Father Hesburgh was familiar, in light of his comments, with the Worcester of the early nineteen-sixties.)

In addition to HC, I applied for admission to Notre Dame and Fordham University, my Dad's alma mater. For me, in the last analysis, Notre Dame, located in South Bend, Indiana, was too far from my GC home, Fordham was too near, and HC, 180 miles distant, was almost perfectly situated. For some inexplicable reason, Georgetown never managed to get into the running.

In September 1963 I made the HC varsity football squad as an 18-year old sophomore. Now, this is significant because the assistant varsity football coach, a cigar-champing, heavy-set fellow called "Hop" Riopel, had recruited me to HC, my first choice among colleges and universities, while I was still a student at Chaminade. Two years earlier he had committed in writing to grant me a football scholarship, provided I had a successful freshman football season *and* made the varsity as a sophomore.

With both of these credentials now in place, and already a couple of weeks into the new season, I approached Coach Riopel to remind him of our agreement. As the eldest of my folks' six children and the first to go to college, I felt considerable pressure—not from my parents but the self-imposed variety—because of the financial burden I knew my HC education clearly represented for them.

Alas, Hop told me, "Sorry, kid, we're out of money." Ergo, no scholarship or, for that matter, any financial aid. His deeply disappointing words, together with the fact that I was not doing very well academically, not to mention getting my brains beaten out during weekday practice sessions by players bigger and stronger than I, led me to a decision to give up football.

One such bigger, stronger player was Jon Morris, a member of the HC class of 1964. He was the team's captain, as well as the starting offensive center and a starting defensive linebacker. At 6'4" and 240 pounds, he was a formidable physical specimen; indeed, he went on to play for the Boston Patriots in the old American Football League, where he was named All Pro. To the point, one day, during an intra-squad scrimmage, I was assigned to play defensive "nose guard" directly opposite Morris. Since I believed there was virtually no chance I could 'beat' him one on one, I decided to "submarine" him, that is, dive between his legs. Incredibly, I pulled it off and managed to trip the quarterback before he could move sufficiently away from his center after the ball was snapped. In the locker room following the scrimmage, Jon made it known that, if I ever did that again, . . . well, never mind. His message was hardly encouraging.

Another football tale involves NFL All Pro Dallas Cowboy quarterback Roger Staubach. In his younger days he was a star quarterback at Navy, and "Skip" Orr, the 1960 Chaminade championship quarterback and my former teammate, was his favorite receiver. In the summer of 1963, mere weeks before my encounter with Jon Morris, Roger was visiting Skip and his family on Long Island. These two Annapolis midshipmen worked out at St. Paul's School field in GC with Al Groh, Tom Kiley, Earl Kirmser, The Lo, a few other guys and me.

Following our workouts we played a game of touch football across the width of the field instead of goal to goal. On one play, Skip ran a down-and-out pattern to the left, and Roger passed the ball in his direction. Somehow, despite Skip's height advantage, I managed to get in front of him, leap, intercept Roger's slightly underthrown pass, and score a touchdown.

Many years later, while watching a televised game between the Cowboys and the New York Giants, I told my young sons Chas and John that their father had once intercepted a Roger Staubach pass. John's eyes lit up as he exclaimed, "But, Dad, you never told us you played pro football!"

Years later still, at a September 1988 testimonial to Coach Joe Thomas, I related the tale of this interception to a group of Chaminade alumni, including Skip Orr, who said tersely, "Prove it!"

In retrospect, my decision to quit the Holy Cross team was emotional and immature. It was also a mistake because, for the rest of my student days, each time I went to a HC football game, I had a strong feeling that I could and should have been on the field, not in the grandstand. For the first time in my life I considered myself weak. It saddened me for a long time, and it is unquestionably one of those things I would do differently if given the chance.

Although I was an honor student at Chaminade and did well in graduate school (New York University, Master of Business Administration in Finance), I was academically mediocre at HC. With the benefit of hindsight, I believe I suffered from a lack of concentration caused by chronic depression, an illness not uncommon in my family. Indeed, many years later I was diagnosed with it, treated and, I thank God, eventually cured.

At the Cross, I joined the Navy R.O.T.C. and served as a midshipman all four years. At the end of my sophomore year, I took the "Marine option." This meant that, upon successful completion of the training program, I would become an officer in the Marine Corps instead of the Navy. I decided to take this step because I disliked life aboard ship. Also, although there was no way to forecast such things, the principal risk for a young Marine officer, looking ahead from May 1964, was that he could be sent on a Mediterranean cruise as part of a U.S. Navy ship's complement of Marines.

When I told my Dad of my decision to join the Marines instead of the Navy, he exclaimed, "Chuck, you're out of your goddam mind! Those guys die!" He was referring, of course, to the terrible losses suffered by the Marines during World War II—his war—in such places as Guadalcanal, Tarawa, Peleliu, Okinawa and Iwo Jima, where, in the words of Navy Admiral Chester Nimitz, "Uncommon valor was a common virtue." Over 23,000 of the 70,000 Marines who participated in the Iwo invasion were killed, wounded or suffered battle fatigue.

Since my Dad's caveat, I have contemplated often, as both a former Marine and a 1945 baby, the Marines' victory that year on the volcanic black sands of that tiny Japanese Pacific island. Fought fifty-four days before my birth, the 36-day battle for Iwo Jima has become the stuff of legend and film. Indeed, it has produced one of the most indelible images of war in the history of the United States: five Marines and one Navy corpsman (the equivalent of an Army "medic") raising the Stars and Stripes atop Mount Suribachi on the now infamous island. On Iwo 6,821 Americans, "most in their teens or early twenties," according to the late author Bill D. Ross, "were killed, died of wounds, or were missing in action." As for the 22,000 Japanese defending this impregnable "eight-and-a-half-square-mile chunk of volcanic ash and stone, 1,083 were taken prisoner and survived."

> *The raising of that flag on Suribachi means a*
> *Marine Corps for the next 500 years.*

> —James Forrestal, Secretary of the Navy

In his 1985 book *Iwo Jima: Legacy of Valor*, Mr. Ross, who served with the Marines on Iwo, has written:

> In the 1,364 days from the Pearl Harbor attack to the Japanese surrender, with millions of Americans fighting on global battlefronts, 353 men received the Congressional Medal of Honor, the nation's highest decoration for valor . . . Of these 27 were for actions at Iwo Jima, thirteen posthumous.

Although Dad's characteristically irreverent words momentarily sobered me, I was nevertheless commissioned a second lieutenant in the U.S. Marine Corps Reserve at my graduation from HC on June 8, 1966. Shortly afterward, I reported to The Basic School (TBS) in Quantico, Virginia, where young Marine officers are still trained as infantry platoon commanders.

☒

A blessing of my days at the College, then an all-male bastion, was the circle of then new but now lifelong friends I made there. Among these great guys are Art Burns, an attorney and a semi-retired business executive; Bob Cipriani, CEO of a printing company; Bill Emswiler, who died tragically with his wife Barbara in a helicopter crash on November 1, 1994; the aforementioned Roger Hunt, a retired postal inspector; Bob Lund, former chief executive of several firms; Bob Meikle, a retired high-school English teacher; Ed Matthews, a New Jersey judge; Dick Morin, who was killed in action in Vietnam; Bill Morrissey, a retired advertising executive now a consultant and a real estate entrepreneur; Steve O'Neill, an insurance executive; and Bill Sheridan, Jim Stokes, Frank Teague and John Webster, attorneys all. Each of these men, except Art, Bill Emswiler, Meik, Bill Morrissey and John, became a Marine Corps officer and served in combat in Vietnam. Art and Meik served in the Army, Bill Emswiler in the Air Force. Dick lost his life when his fighter-jet was shot down, while Ed and Frank were both awarded Purple Heart Medals for wounds sustained in fighting in Vietnam. (The Order of the Purple Heart was established by George Washington and re-established in 1932 for granting decorations to those members of the military services wounded in combat.) Indeed, Frank spent more than a year in a naval hospital convalescing.

While I was a student at HC I also made the acquaintance of Joe Altman, to whom Mame and I would have the pleasure of introducing her sister Camille in October 1971. Also now a close friend, Joe celebrated thirty years of marriage to his bride with her, their son Peter, Mame and me on their anniversary in December of this year.

☒

In the autumn of 1962, after the start of my freshman year, I was privileged to attend a lecture by Robert Frost, who was the most celebrated poet in America in the early twentieth century. He read a selection of his poems to a surprisingly small group of students in HC's Kimball Hall auditorium (which is probably no longer there). After his readings, he addressed us and answered our questions. Perhaps most engaging about him were his personal warmth, firm handshake and piercing eyes. He actually remained with us at the end of the program, just 'hanging out' and chatting with a bunch of us college kids. Despite his eighty-eight years, he was visibly young at heart, and he warmed ours.

In November of that year I had the pleasure of meeting the Rev. Dr. Martin Luther King, Jr., who gave an address at the College one evening. It was raining hard, and Dr. King's car had been delayed afterward. As such, after the field house had emptied following his speech, a small group of us had the good fortune to engage him in conversation for about forty minutes. He impressed me greatly.

In June 1964, President Lyndon Baines Johnson was the guest speaker at the College's commencement exercises. As luck would have it, I was assigned, in my capacity as a Navy R.O.T.C. midshipman, to open the door of the president's black Cadillac limousine and escort him to the canopy under which the speaker's podium was located. As the big man alighted from the car, I saluted him, of course.

LBJ then asked in his Texas drawl, "What's yo' name, boy?"

"Midshipman Mansfield, sir!" I responded, still saluting.

I then completed my escort service.

Many years later I wondered who walked him back to his limo after the graduation ceremony.

Holy Cross is also where I made the acquaintance of Father Charles J. Dunn of the Society of Jesus (S.J.).

Like life itself, HC had its own relative extrema. Still, I left the hill after graduation with a feeling of satisfaction due in no small part to a few words that Fr. Dunn, then Dean of Men and later the College's Director of Estate Planning, shared with me during graduation festivities.

In our freshman year the College assigned roommates to each of us; we had no say in the matter. Mine was a studious, cold-prone fellow named Dave who, during the spring semester that year, became through no fault of his own the victim of a rash of physically harmless and, in the opinions of at least some of those familiar with the situation, very funny pranks. Although I was not involved, directly or indirectly, and did not know who was responsible, I paid the whole episode only limited attention. Well, things changed significantly shortly after I was advised by telephone one evening to appear without delay in Fr. Dunn's office.

By way of background, the situation with Dave admittedly did not get off to a good start. When he first came to Wheeler Hall, room No. 219, the space he and I would share, his father, mother and younger sister accompanied him. Having already been on campus for about two weeks for summer football practice, I recall that I was lying on my bed reading a book when they arrived. It was Saturday, September 8, 1962.

I greeted them and introduced myself, whereupon Dave, his sister and their father went downstairs to resume unpacking the car. Dave's mother, seemingly curious about me and the College, remained in the dorm room and engaged me in conversation. While she chatted and questioned me, she also busied herself putting her son's various garments into his dresser drawers. When he returned she made a point of showing him where she had placed his socks, underwear, shirts, etc. I thought that was a bit much; after all, isn't unpacking his own things something Dave could have done without her involvement? During presumably the rest of her family's last trip downstairs to the car she and I were alone for a few minutes and she said, "You'll take care of my Davey, won't you?" I did not consider her words a good omen.

Classes began on Monday, September 10th. I would later write in a letter to my classmates that this day was characterized by chaos, optimism, pride, fear, pessimism, confusion, nervousness, uncertainty, independence and wonder.

Dave and I had different schedules and different curricula. He was a pre-med student; I was into Latin, Greek, French, English, R.O.T.C. and football. In fact, I wouldn't normally return to the dorm until about 9:30 p.m. after football practice, training table and "chalk talk." Then, in the HC tradition, at least for freshmen, we had "lights out" promptly at eleven o'clock.

Now, the steam heat emanating from the old dormitory's radiators was centrally controlled. Thus, each room was warm—*very* warm—from October through April. For Dave and me, everything went smoothly until the cooler weather inevitably arrived.

Our room would become so stifling, especially at night, that I would perspire, even clad only in undershorts. Unable to sleep in such uncomfortable conditions, I would open the window a few inches for relief from the heat. Later, I would awaken during the night to discover that it had been shut. I would reopen it, only to find it closed again when morning came. And so it went.

I discussed the matter with Dave, who told me that he was subject to colds and that the cold air from the open window bothered him a great deal. I offered and he accepted my blanket; he also agreed to leave the window open. Unfortunately, he still found it necessary to close the window after I would fall asleep. I found myself becoming annoyed.

I suggested to Dave that perhaps the fairest approach would be for each of us to have control over the window on alternating nights. He agreed, and I thought we had solved the problem.

Wrong.

Despite our agreement, Dave continued to close the window, even on those nights when it was my turn to have it open, if I so desired. His recalcitrance became unacceptable. I got angry with him and recall saying, "From now on we do things my way, and if you dare reproach me, I will destroy you." It was hardly my finest hour.

As I walked nervously and quickly from my room to the Dean of Men's office that chilly April evening just before my eighteenth birthday, I wondered what was going to happen. It was my first personal invitation to the Dean's office and, for all I knew then, might have been his custom with freshmen. Yet, I had a distinct and foreboding sense that whatever had precipitated this sudden nocturnal rendezvous was neither about to win me any prizes nor cause me to leave smiling afterwards. I was filled with terror.

Alas, my intuition was right. Suddenly and swiftly I had become deeply and inextricably involved in the Wheeler II nonsense. Owing to Fr. Dunn's extraordinary persuasive capacities, I would soon be giving the episode my undivided attention for, you see, my roommate had evidently reported to Fr. Dunn that these childish games had profoundly disturbed him. Joking aside, the Dean of Men made it perfectly clear that the situation was serious: "I want you to put an end to this immediately. At Holy Cross we are our brother's keeper."

"But, Father," I said lamely, "I've had no hand in this at all and I don't know who's behind it."

Said my Dean, "Mr. Mansfield, he's your roommate and, if this isn't stopped immediately, you may find yourself out of school." Fr. Dunn neither raised his voice nor repeated his message. He didn't have to.

That was in April 1963. The next time I had occasion to speak with Fr. Dunn came in June 1966 when I found myself with Mame, then my fiancée of less than a week, standing next to him at my class's graduation dance. Though a bit uncomfortable, I decided to introduce her to him. After a brief exchange of formalities, Fr. Dunn stunned me with his nonchalance as he said quietly to me: "Thanks for straightening out that situation over in Wheeler." It was as if it had then happened only yesterday, and I think he even smiled a little.

The next time I saw Fr. Dunn was in the autumn of 1981. True to form, a couple of mischiefmakers from the Class of '65, who were there that evening, set me up. Having heard my "Charlie" Dunn story earlier, and knowing Father then better than I did, they related the whole episode to him. Naturally, and once more with that quintessential nonchalance, the former Dean of Men approached me later and asked how my old freshman roommate was doing. Then, seeing the look of astonishment on my face and knowing fully that I was unaware he had been prompted, he burst into laughter.

These days I see Fr. Dunn less than once a year. Nonetheless, he and I have become true and warm friends. To me he is a Jesuit's Jesuit. He also epitomizes the Marine Corps' motto: *Semper fidelis.* *God bless you, Father.*

That autumn 1981 meeting with Father Dunn took place on the occasion of my induction into Holy Cross's President's Council, its association of major benefactors. Ten years later, on the occasion of my 25-year class reunion, Bill Juska, my class chairman and friend, advised me that, of all the members of our class, I was the fourth most generous donor through the years. (I told Bill, "If that's the case, then we're in the deep stuff!") My generosity to the College would eventually dissipate because of some of the misguided directions it would take in the years ahead.

Sadly, I noticed that Holy Cross was beginning to go off the rails in 1994, the year that Fr. John E. Brooks, S.J., retired as president of the College. During his twenty-four year tenure, he repositioned the school from being just one of the outstanding *Catholic* colleges and universities in the U.S. to being more or less consistently ranked among the top thirty colleges and universities in the nation, regardless of religious affiliation. However, there are other alumni who make a strong case that the problems that plague Holy Cross today reflect poor decisions made during the Brooks era.

In July of '94, Fr. Gerard Reedy, S.J., came out of the administration of Fordham University in New York City and succeeded Fr. Brooks as the College's president. (In 2001 Fr. Reedy assumed the presidency of the Marymount Tarrytown campus of Fordham University.) A few months later, I received a telephone call from Marine Corps captain (now major) Hector Marcayda, who was then the Marine Corps Officer Instructor in Holy Cross's Navy R.O.T.C. unit.

Knowing of my ongoing interest in the unit's activities, he informed me that the school's modest funding for the Marines' *Semper Fidelis Society* had been withdrawn. Simultaneously, he reported, a new organization called "Allies" had been formed and funded by the College.

As I wrote in a September 6, 1995 letter to Fr. Reedy, I had, over the preceding ten months, initiated discussions with various members of the HC Community, including students, alumni/ae, administrators, faculty members and others who then worked on the College's campus. My purpose was to enlighten myself regarding the activities of HC's gay and lesbian students and to understand the nature of their special "Allies" group. Some of my discussions took place on campus in December 1994 and February 1995; others were telephone interviews.

At first my interest was focused on the "Chaplains' Office" because I had been told that the College no longer had a chaplain *per se* but rather a ministerial office headed by a "Director of Chaplains." Whereas this struck me as unusual, I was even more surprised when I learned that the director was an alumna, Katherine M. McElaney '76. "Kim" McElaney and I exchanged telephone calls over an extended period in early 1995, but my last few attempts to reach her drew no response.

Based on my discussions, I learned that Allies was a recognized student organization whose purpose was to address "homophobic behavior on the campus." An assistant dean explained to me that Allies was "a compromise organization" that was given somewhat reluctant approval by the administration because of a "state law in Massachusetts regarding discrimination on the basis of sexual orientation." Moreover, I was advised that Allies was "an educational organization" and "low key." The term "support group" was also employed to describe it.

During my conversation with the assistant dean, it was confirmed that Allies, as a recognized student organization, was indeed funded by the College out of student activity fees. (Were a child or children of mine then students at HC, I would have demanded refunding of the portion of the student activity fees allocated for such purpose.) Although he emphasized that the initial funding consisted of a modest budget, it is my view that principle more than finance was the issue. Despite his detailed knowledge of Allies and their activities, he surprised me when he stated that he had never heard of "Courage" or "Dignity," two gay and lesbian groups, only the former of which is affiliated with the Roman Catholic Church.

The Crusader, HC's student newspaper, in a "Special Report" in 1995, announced "some (Allies) upcoming events scheduled for the remainder of February and March." Here they are:

> "a Gay Retreat"
> "The Unity Parade" in Boston
> "A panel discussion led by a group of Holy Cross Alumni."
> The same article also listed "what to look for from Allies in the coming months":
> "student programs in the residence halls"
> "a possible faculty luncheon" (An "Allies faculty/student luncheon" was reportedly held on March 30, 1995.)
> "Allies will examine Catholic teaching on homosexuality."
> "Allies will create a new *Crusader* correspondent."
> "Allies will try to find ways to educate Holy Cross students about the issue of bisexuality."
> "Allies hopes to become involved with the orientation of first year students."
> "Allies will post 'fact' sheets throughout the campus, even in the bathrooms."

Approximately one week before the Allies faculty/student luncheon, a junior named Jeannie Seidler publicly proclaimed her lesbianism at a "Being a Lesbian at Holy Cross" conference in "an overflowing" Hogan Ballroom. In this connection, Michael L. Gannon, then Editor-in-Chief of *The Crusader*, wrote the following week in his "Commentary" that "Holy Cross witnessed an event that is sure to change this institution for the better." "It is sad," he continued, "to think that in an institution that only recently celebrated its sesquicentennial is *(sic)* only now seeing the emergence of a homosexual student .... Our diversity is now out in the open." Incidentally, a fellow alumnus and friend, who also then served on the board of the HC Alumni Association, reported that a video with a title similar to "Being a Lesbian at Holy Cross" was available in the campus bookstore.

In a reply to my letter, Fr. Reedy denied the existence of this video, which I understand the alumni board later procured, evaluated and criticized.

I found this disturbing but then I also read the following in *The Crusader*:

> ➤ At a Mass the preceding winter "Ms. Marybeth Kearns-Barrett, of the Chaplains' Office, spoke in lieu of a homily."
>
> ➤ Ms. Kearns-Barrett also told the congregation that "we need to cooperate on abortion."
>
> ➤ At the same (Sunday) Mass, there was reportedly no recitation of the Nicene Creed. (The Creed is not always recited but this was a Sunday on which the liturgy prescribed its recitation.)
>
> ➤ Renegade priest George Stallings, who at least then headed the African American Catholic Congregation, spoke at the invitation of the College's Black Student Union as part of Kwanzaa. (Kwanzaa is not a religion. According to the official Kwanzaa web site, it is "an African American and Pan-African holiday celebrated by millions throughout the world African community." It was invented by Dr. Maulana Karenga, "The Creator of Kwanzaa.") The BSU's Charter subsequently wrote of Stallings' well documented mockery of the Catholic faith that "we were enlightened by an individual who, with our money provided clear indication that we as African-Americans do not have to accept the twisted

lies and abusive translations of the catholic tradition
that many so-called Catholics provide."

In fairness, Fr. Reedy wrote in his letter to me that, "George
Stallings has, I think, spoken here, though I refused to fund his
appearance last year—if he appeared it was without my knowledge."
With respect to Ms. Kearns-Barrett, Fr. Reedy was "convinced of the
effectiveness of (her) work with our pro-life group which I first heard
detailed as she described her projects to our new bishop, who was also
impressed." He concluded, "We maintain a fine Catholic culture here
of worship, service, and instruction."

Whereas Allies became official, attempts to establish a
traditional Catholic group on campus proved very difficult. In
fact, under the restrictions that were mandated, such an
organization would not have been free to function as an
advocate of the faith, to include criticism of those who may
warrant it, such as the Chaplains' Office.

Allies, as an organization, is apparently still around. On Holy
Cross's website, the group states "Who we are:"

"Allies are:

> ➤ Students, faculty and staff that support all sexual
>   orientations. Many of our members are heterosexual,
>   while others are homosexual or bisexual. It is never
>   necessary to disclose your sexual orientation.
> ➤ A "safe" people to talk with if you are dealing with
>   sexual orientation—either your own or that of a friend,
>   roommate, or family member.
> ➤ Campus community members who provide support,
>   recommend resources, and maintain confidentiality.
> ➤ People who seek to educate the campus community,
>   counter homophobic attitudes, and promote equal
>   respect and treatment for everyone.
> ➤ People who try to make campus activities more inclusive
>   and comfortable for gay, lesbian, and bisexual members
>   of the community."

The "Constitution" of Allies also appears on the website. Here is its beginning:

"The name of the organization is Allies.

Allies is a campus organization dedicated to creating a humane campus environment for all persons regardless of sexual orientation. Members of Allies are committed to educating themselves and the campus community regarding issues related to homosexuality and bisexuality.

Inspired by the Jesuit educational ideal of being men and women for others, Allies seeks to ensure that the climate of Holy Cross fosters human dignity and mutual respect for all persons. Homophobia, defined as an irrational fear and hatred of homosexuals, is inconsistent with the mission of the College of the Holy Cross.

Homophobia, like any form of discrimination, takes a significant toll on the ability of all persons to grow to their full potential."

Next come Allies' "Objectives" and "Membership:"

"Objectives

Allies shall educate themselves and the Holy Cross community by reading and discussing materials on homosexuality and bisexuality, sponsoring speakers and other public presentations, and seeking creative ways to foster heightened awareness of these issues.

Allies recognizes and respects the Catholic teaching on human sexuality, including the distinction made in Catholic teaching between homosexual orientation and homosexual acts. Allies will make a special effort to educate itself and the college

community about the Catholic teaching and other
theological reflections on homosexuality and bisexuality.
Allies seeks to engage the entire community in dialogue
about these matters.

Through education, Allies hopes to make the environment
of Holy Cross safer and more supportive for gay, lesbian,
and bisexual students. In addition, Allies hopes to provide a
voice for those who may be afraid to share their own voice.
Allies hopes to work together with other interested groups.
Allies is a participatory group whose members share their
ideas and concern and work together to fulfill their objectives.

Membership

All Holy Cross students, faculty, staff, administrators and
alumni/ae are elligible *(sic)* for membership

Membership remains open at all times

Allies does not discriminate on any basis

No person will be asked to identify his/her sexual orientation
to the group or any member of the group

Allies encourages that the membership respect the privacy
of its peers"

Since the establishment of Allies in 1994, the Association
of Bisexuals, Gays and Lesbians, "ABiGaLe" for short, has
become the full flower of homosexual rights at Holy Cross,
despite Roman Catholic Church teaching that homosexual
practice is "intrinsically disordered" behavior. Just as disturbing
to me, the purported legitimization of the odious term
"heterosexism" by its inclusion in ABiGaLe's mission statement
has not only demeaned the Creator's natural law; it has also
debased much of what Holy Cross had historically represented.

Its website tells us that "ABiGaLe was first conceived of in the spring of 1997 and after much work, planning, and communication ABiGaLe was recognized by the college in December of 1997!" In fact, the organization recently celebrated its fifth birthday party with a drag-queen contest, photographs from which are accessible on the College's website. All of the pictures are repugnant; some are obscene.

Courtesy of ABiGaLe, here is "Our Mission:" (Letters and words in bold are as they appear in the ABiGaLe statement.)

> **ABiGaLe** was formed to provide a face and a voice for the
> **gay**, bisexual, **lesbian**, and transgendered
> community at Holy Cross.
> Closeted students who live in fear and ISOLATION
> because of homophobia and **heterosexism** now have
> access to a support network of openly gay, lesbian,
> bisexual and transgendered students and peers who are
> working to be seen and be heard as self-affirming men
> and women here on the campus.
> With our collective identity we will allow individuals
> within the community and the entire College community
> to confront their own **fears** and misconceptions and allow
> Holy Cross to continue its example in the tradition of
> justice and freedom.
> We Hope To Instill A Sense of Pride In A Community
> That Has Been Long Overlooked!!!

I recently sent an e-mail to ABiGaLe to request a copy of its constitution. Here's what I received in reply:

> Hey what do you need the constitution for? I'm reluctant to give you a copy of the ABiGaLe constitution without knowing your intentions. I hope they are good . . . but here it is:

> http://college.holycross.edu/studentorgs/abigale/missionmain.htm

Article I: Name

Section 1. The name of the organization is the Association of Bisexuals, Gays and Lesbians (ABiGaLe).

Article II: Purpose

Section 1. To provide a stable community for any bisexual, lesbian and gay students at Holy Cross.

Section 2. To provide a necessary voice and body for the ABiGaLe community and to work toward dismantling oppression in all its forms

Section 3. To provide an opportunity for lesbian, bisexual and gay individuals to develop a positive self concept and to support their coming out process

Section 4. To increase positive awareness of bisexuals, lesbians and gays among the Holy Cross community

Section 5. To provide an environment in which pride can be developed in the bisexual, lesbian and gay community

Section 6. Recognizing the dialogue within the Catholic community about gay, lesbian and bisexual issues, ABiGaLe seeks to participate in and contribute to this dialogue in the context of Holy Cross as a Jesuit liberal arts college

Article III: Membership

Section 1. The membership of ABiGaLe is open to any student member of the Holy Cross community.

Section 2. This organization shall not discriminate against any person wishing to participate in meetings or events.

Article IV: Confidentiality

Section 1. Since meetings are open to the entire campus there is a limit to the level of confidentiality which ABiGaLe can provide.

Section 2. If so desired by the individual, membership will remain unrecorded in the interest of confidentiality.

Section 3. All members must respect comfort levels and privacy of every individual. Additionally, it is the responsibility of each member to inform the group of their own comfort levels.

Section 4. There will be no pressure on any member to reveal their sexual orientation outside of group meetings.

Section 5. Outing will not be tolerated.

Article V: Leadership

Section 1. ABiGaLe is headed by four executive officers including two co-coordinators, a secretary and a treasurer.

Section 2. As bisexual, gay, lesbian individuals, officers are required to be as comfortable with the level of visibility within the Holy Cross community as their positions require.

Section 3. Voting is open to any member present on the day of the publicized elections.

Section 4. Any of the four elected officers may be removed from office by a 2/3 vote of the general assembly.

Article VI: Group Advising

Section 1. ABiGaLe will acquire a faculty advisor such as stipulated by the SGA. He or she will advise ABiGaLe on programming and other activities. The Advisor shall consult with the Director of Student Activities on these matters. The Advisor shall receive a copy of the minutes of each meeting, and the Treasurer shall send to the Advisor a copy of the regular statement of accounts as provided by the officers of the Treasury.

Article VII: Meetings

Section 1. Meetings shall be held once weekly or as deemed necessary by the group.

Article VIII: Amendments

Section 1. This constitution may be amended by a 2/3 vote of ABiGaLe members present.

Section 2. All amendments shall be presented in writing to the co-coordinators.

Section 3. Members shall be informed of proposed
amendments, and notice of the vote on an amendment will
be given one week ahead of time.

I wonder why the sender of the e-mail was "reluctant to give"
me a copy of the constitution but then sent it so readily. Moreover,
why is "outing" not tolerated? After all, one's "coming out process"
would appear to be important since it requires "support." It's a
matter of "pride," isn't it? Logically, I can only conjecture that the
difference lies in whether the individual publicly proclaims himself
or herself gay or lesbian, or someone else does.

With all this as background, I have for years asked myself
the following question: Why is it so important for homosexuals
"to (have) support (for) their coming out process"? I know no
heterosexuals who believe it is in their interest to proclaim their
heterosexuality. One's sexual orientation should be a private
matter and need not concern the general public or, in this case,
the general College community. Indeed, most people just don't
care—except, of course, homosexuals themselves. Make no
mistake: ABiGaLe, its constitution and its mistaken reliance
on *Always Our Children* (a statement of a *committee* of the
National Conference of Catholic Bishops, not of the NCCB
itself) have become attempts at Holy Cross to advocate the
homosexual lifestyle as the moral equivalent of heterosexual
relationships, including marriage. Homosexual sex is no more
a "right" than premarital or extramarital sex.

As for *Always Our Children*, Bishop Fabian Bruskewitz of
Lincoln, Nebraska, made clear that it "was composed without any
input from the majority of the American Catholic bishops, who
were given no opportunity whatsoever to comment on its pastoral
usefulness or . . . contents . . . (I)n this case flawed and defective
procedures, badly in need of correction and reform, resulted in a
very flawed and defective document." In spite of this criticism and
disclaimer, Jacqueline Peterson, then the College's vice president
for student affairs and now Dean of Students, decided nonetheless
to adopt the document as her authority for the College's "flawed
and defective" policy.

For its part, the bishops' letter states that "the Church teaches that homogenital behavior is objectively immoral, while making the important distinction between this behavior and a homosexual orientation, which is not immoral in itself."

According to Susan Fani, a 1995 HC alumna:

> Theology (at Holy Cross) has been replaced by religious studies, which is lavish in its study of other religions but spouts heterodox Catholic teachings as if they were legitimate. Liberation theology, feminism and progressive liberalism are the dominant ideologies at Holy Cross. Alas the Magisterium is no longer regarded as the only authentic voice of the Church; indeed, it is hardly taken into account, as far as one can tell from the weekend "liturgies" on campus.

Instead of Roman Catholicism, political correctness has become the order of the day at HC (as it has on many other so called Catholic campuses). In addition to the aforementioned George Stallings, here are examples of other HC guest speakers whose selection demonstrates how a secular liberalism has prevailed on campus. Indeed, they typically espouse viewpoints that are neither distinctly Catholic nor Jesuit. They include:

> ➤ Sarah Weddington, the lawyer who successfully argued Roe v. Wade

> ➤ Naomi Wolf, pro-abortion feminist author of *The Beauty Myth* and later a consultant to Al Gore's 2000 presidential campaign

> ➤ Stokely Carmichael, 1970s radical leader of the Black Panthers and SNCC (Student Nonviolent Coordinating Committee), who was still a socialist at the time of his speech

> ➤ Brian McNaught, a Catholic gay activist who addressed homophobia at HC

> ➤ Gustavo Gutierrez, a proponent of liberation theology, a theory of Marxism under the guise of Christianity

This sampling shows how radical the choice of speakers was. The speakers made their agenda clear: pro-abortion (or, euphemistically, pro-choice), pro-homosexual, anti-Rome, etc. They came to HC not to reminisce but to advocate. The influence of such people and their on-campus supporters on students is so pervasive that, if a student does not embrace this liberal agenda—which is usually advanced more subtly on campus than by the cited guest speakers—he or she is ostracized.

Although the free exchange of ideas is important, a Catholic college has obligations in terms of the Catholic faith. Alas, while those who challenge Catholic dogma are invited to the campus and sponsored by HC-funded groups, those who champion Catholicism and its traditions are rarely seen or heard. In this connection, having a conservative point of view is anathema to many professors and students at HC.

Not only does the view of Roman Catholicism at HC seem to be a dissident one, it has been audaciously presented as the only enlightened one. Unfortunately, this is precisely the approach of the Chaplains' Office. Perhaps not surprisingly, students are all for it; as long as they promote the shibboleth of "social justice," they can justify rejecting any tenets of the faith they wish, such as those on abortion and premarital sex.

In the September-October 1995 issue of *Crossroads*, HC's erstwhile alumni journal, Professor David O'Brien wrote a feature article entitled "Holy Cross: Is it Catholic?" Susan Fani and I wrote and co-signed the following letter, which was published in the December 1995 edition:

> Professor David O'Brien's piece . . . was really a

transparent offensive crafted to placate concerned alumni. In this it failed, revealing the problems that have emerged at Holy Cross over the past generation.

The idea that 'sexist old men' are the problem is discriminatory and wrong. The campus ministry, dominated by a Chaplain's Office headed by a lay alumna, has a political and religious agenda contrary to the magisterial Church. The assertion that the 'quality of liturgy' is "universally praised" is not true. On the contrary, many students have complained about the failure of the College's liturgies to adhere to Roman Catholic Church teaching. The same is true of 'famously oversubscribed' courses in the Religious Studies department.

There is no point in being a 'Catholic Amherst' if Holy Cross sacrifices Catholicism in the process. Professor O'Brien lists the three characteristics of the College in a telling manner: 'liberal arts, Jesuit, and Catholic.' He states that HC is committed to the study of religion *independent of* Catholic and Jesuit traditions. That is a crucial problem. After all, religion as philosophy could be taught at any non-sectarian college. Holy Cross students need Catholicism as theology taught to them so that they can serve God while in the world. Today's student body's ignorance of doctrine is reprehensible; not only is it not addressed, it is aggravated by the promotion of incorrect teaching.

"For those who care about tradition, the outcome at Holy Cross is promising." This statement is true only if one wishes to continue on the secularizing path that had led HC in recent years away from Christ toward the worldly. A political party could serve the poor without religion; for the Catholic Church to do so would be an abdication of her responsibility. Alas, in following this trend, the College has disappointed many alumni and will continue to disappoint others, pending reform of campus religious life, beginning with the serious and successful implementation of *Ex corde Ecclesiae* [an encyclical by Pope John Paul II].

In a September 2001 letter to the HC classes of "1930 to 1970," "Four Alumni" (William M. Cousins, Jr. '45, Guy C. Bosetti '49, Edgar L. Kelley '49 and Edward P. Kirby '49) expressed their concern "about the secularization of the college, beginning in the 1970's and continuing today."

They also included in their letter "a copy of a student profile written by" Ms. McElaney, who distributed it "to those attending her lecture as part of the Spring 1999 event 'Classroom Revisited,' attended by alumni and alumnae." The profile reads:

Do not go to confession
See very little relationship between
    sex and faith/religion
Do not hold themselves accountable
    to much church teaching
Do not know much of what the Church teaches
Do not have any devotion to the saints
Come from families that do not attend
    mass regularly

Are very active sexually
Seldom experience the Church as healing
Often experience the church as alienating

Do yearn for intimacy
Do yearn for community
Are extremely generous
Do volunteer regularly and
    love it
do cherish group experiences
do crave retreats
are able to make great use of
    silence and reflection time
    when it is offered to them
do pay close attention to
    homilies
do like to talk one-on-one

    with Chaplains and other
    adults
do get involved with liturgy
    when they are invited

Do find God in lots of places:
music, friends, nature, the ocean,
my journal, music, the Bible,
praying, friends, music, family,
the Chapel, Narragansett, music,
boyfriends, girlfriends, candles,
music.

In their letter, the "Four Alumni" quoted Peter Hans Kolvenbach, S.J., the Jesuit Superior General, saying "For some (Jesuit) universities, it is probably too late to restore their Catholic character." HC has, alas, fallen into this group. The "Four" also cited "a few of the many indications of secularization's growth at the college":

> "Half or more of the faculty (which controls curriculum) is non-Catholic, as is the Dean of Students, good people, but symbolic of the change.

> "The new President, able Father Michael McFarland SJ, faces faculty opposition to his hope of re-emphasizing courses in philosophy and religion, establishing a real core of studies for the 95% Catholic student body.

> "The H.C. Magazine (Spring 2001) touts an alumnus' success as a disc jockey for MTV, that the Wall Street Journal (4/21/01) says broadcasts "gross humor, sex and worse to teenagers." The Federal Trade Commission reports that MTV targets children with ads for recordings with "adult lyrics" (Associated Press, by Gina Holland, April 2001).

> "Homosexual and bisexual groups, whose constitutions are not in accord with a letter from Cardinal Ratzinger to the Bishops, are funded by the College while the Campus K of C council receives none. In October, a month the college traditionally dedicated to honoring the Virgin Mary each year the college now observes Gay, Lesbian and Bisexual Week.

> "Former Harvard Law School Professor Harold Berman has said he and his colleagues have been disappointed in their discussions at Catholic universities about moral issues (e.g. assisted suicide), because instead of presenting a Catholic perspective they offer the same opinions heard from Harvard faculty."

In 1996 the president of the HC General Alumni Association wrote in *Crossroads* a piece I read and responded to in the following letter:

If students' spiritual lives are truly to be enriched, a good start would be to appoint *a* Chaplain. Alas, giving the Office of the College Chaplains, which when I last looked was headed by a lay alumna with a radical liberal *political* agenda, responsibility for a student program of religious and spiritual enrichment will, sadly, do virtually nothing to make "what is presently in place . . . even better."

So, Fr. Reedy and Trustees, beware: Such a move will not only *not* return to the College's students its rich spiritual culture of yesteryear when, to quote Mr. Reilly, "our primary responsibility was to save our souls by generously serving Jesus Christ," for students it will likely debase our faith even further.

Separately, in the Holocaust Collection Homepage article, according to library services director James Hogan, " . . . the College wishes to preserve in memory the six million Jews put to death by the Nazis." I hope Mr. Hogan (and Fr. Lapomarda) will also "preserve in memory" the *five million* Gentiles (Poles, Gypsies, Jehova's Witnesses, mental defectives, educators and Catholic priests) also exterminated by the Nazis.

⌛

On June 21, 2000 I wrote to Fr. McFarland to congratulate him on his appointment as HC's new president. I enclosed with my letter certain information that I was confident would convey a sense of why I became troubled with Holy Cross in the first place. His reply was extremely well written but he took the opportunity to tell me that my views on Kim McElaney and her "chaplains" was "unfair and uninformed."

I replied and conceded that my views may have been outdated inasmuch as they were formed from research in 1995. Still, I wrote, "'unfair and uninformed' they are not." Further, I stated:

> Please understand that my opinions in the matter were based on conversations with instructors, an assistant dean,

students, a Jesuit priest—all then active at the College—
recent graduates, members of the Alumni Association board,
and on articles in *The Crusader* and *Crossroads*. Indeed, the
priest told me that the selection of a lay alumna in general
and of Kim McElaney in particular for the Chaplains
directorship was a major mistake of the Brooks
administration. Interestingly, he went on to say that there
was considerable reluctance to remove her from the post,
despite private recommendations for just such action from
members of the community, because of concerns among
others that removal of a woman from such a prominent
position would cause "a political explosion" on campus.

No reply to my letter was received.

While I am on the sensitive subject of the potential removal of a
woman from her position at HC, I am reminded of another letter of
mine, excerpted next, in the composition of which I experienced some
amusement but to which I also received no response:

As an adjunct professor at Hofstra University and an
occasional critic of things multicultural, I was interested to
read about "(Re)Searching Ourselves: A Women's Studies
Conference at Holy Cross" in the February *Crossroads*. The
article piqued my interest inasmuch as I had just recently
read a most compelling article by Michelle Easton . . . that
concludes that "feminist educators . . . are transforming
young women into a cackling brood with little exposure to
the knowledge and skills necessary to assume leadership in
the economic and political arenas." Indeed, my own
daughter (Harvard '96) has often wondered, since there are
women's studies, why there aren't men's studies as well.

Regarding the College's five-year-old women's studies
program, you were quoted in the *Crossroads* piece as hoping
to show "how it pervades all disciplines." If your words
imply that the women's studies program is itself *not* a
discipline, which happens to be my own view, then I am

perplexed as to students' ability truly "to integrate women's issues with their scholarship."

I would be very pleased to learn why you believe the "effects of women's studies . . . have been momentous."

On February 12 and 13, 2002, the latter being Ash Wednesday, which marks the beginning of the holy season of Lent, a student production of "The Vagina Monologues" took the stage at Holy Cross with the approval of the College's administration. Happily, in my opinion, many at the college said that scheduling the play on Ash Wednesday was doubly offensive. They reportedly asked themselves whether there is anything still considered "Holy" at this Jesuit Catholic institution. Believe me, they're not lone. Indeed, a good friend has encouraged me and like-minded alumni to sue Holy Cross to enjoin it from using the word "Holy" in its name. The idea is becoming more attractive as time passes.

The web site for "The Vagina Monologues," which was written by Eve Ensler, advertises it with the following expressions: "An oral history," "Think inside the box," "Envy goes both ways" and "Spread the word." What clever—and lascivious—use of double-entendres! The play has been described as "ground-breaking, eye-opening" with "powerful, hilarious and provocative" monologues.

According to Amy Contrada in an article on the *Massachusetts News* web site, the production clearly states its aim to arouse the audience sexually. "How can I talk about vaginas without talking about them in action? Am I talking about vaginas to arouse people? Is that a bad thing?" The author says she is "in deep worship of vaginas." Using every vulgarity she can come up with, she says, "Saying these words feels naughty, dangerous, too direct, too specific, wrong, intense, in charge, alive."

According to Ms. Contrada,

(T)he performers led the audience to chant "c_nt, c_nt,

c_nt" and "vagina, vagina, vagina." A lesbian seduction of a 16-year-old girl is presented as a positive, liberating experience. The only "value" communicated is, "If it feels it's exciting, do it." The only frame of reference is one's own pleasure, one's own experience—i.e., immature, and narcissistic hedonism.

I suppose that Fr. McFarland and his administration also condone or value the following "woman's story" from the "Monologues" as legitimate fare for the campus stage:

As a lesbian, I need you to start from a lesbian-centered place . . . . For example, I'm having sex with a woman. She's inside me. I'm inside me. F***ing myself together with her. There are four fingers inside me; two are hers, two are mine . . . . How can I talk about vaginas without talking about them in action? . . . As lesbians, we know about vaginas. We touch them. We lick them. We play with them. We tease them. We notice when the clitoris swells. We notice our own . . . . I like to play with the rim of the vagina . . . with fingers, knuckles, toes, tongue. I like to enter it slowly, slowly entering, then thrusting three fingers inside. There's other cavities, other openings; there's the mouth. While I have a free hand, there's fingers in her mouth, fingers in her vagina, both going, all going all at once, her mouth sucking my fingers, her vagina sucking my fingers. Both sucking, both wet.

According to Ms. Contrada, this filth is a typical passage from the play. It goes on and on, but I will stop here because my writing is not intended to be pornographic.

The college was reportedly plastered with about seventy professional looking posters, blaring "Vagina" in bright red lettering— more posters than the usual student event would see. The students assumed there was outside funding. They asked the Dean to investigate whether or not N.O.W. (National Organization for Women, a major pro-abortion group) might be providing funding, since a N.O.W.

sign was prominent at the ticket sale table. This would be against college policy, and the Dean promised to look into it. Another supporter listed on the handbill was Planned Parenthood, another major proponent of abortion.

The Catholic Family Association of America sent an open letter to Fr. McFarland expressing its outrage, which read in part, "That this anti-Catholic garbage should appear on any Catholic campus is blasphemy." It announced plans to initiate "a formal petition to Bishop Reilly (of Worcester) to begin a canonical action towards removing the authorization of the College of the Holy Cross to operate as a Catholic institute of higher learning."

I concur with the Association's decision. This is madness, and enough is enough.

According to Ms. Contrada's account, during the planning stages of the Holy Cross "Vagina Monologues" production, many students received the following e-mail from a Holy Cross resident advisor:

> I know there has been a slight buzz around campus as to the fact that some of the show's proceeds are benefiting the organization "Women of Afghanistan", a group affiliated with Planned Parenthood. I just wanted to let you know up front that a portion of your ticket may contribute to funding birth control or perhaps even abortions for women in Afghanistan. I understand that some people have moral issues with this. However, this . . . program . . . is optional, and you can reserve the right not to attend.

Word quickly circulated within the Holy Cross Students for Life group. A member of the group told *MassNews*:

> I am very much opposed to the VM being performed this Ash Wednesday. The show degrades women and is an unintelligent way of conveying a rather dignified cause.

> Unfortunately, the method by which these women are
> attempting to articulate their position on battered women
> backfires and appeals only to the incompetent faction of the
> campus. Not only does the production desecrate the integrity
> of the beginning of the Church's Holy Season, but originally
> the benefit monies gained from the show were to be sent to
> pro-choice groups that would distribute birth control and
> build 'family planning centers' in the Middle East. Holy
> Cross Students for Life, however, quickly attended to this,
> and the deans are now trying to cover up their original
> approval by redirecting the funds.

Apparently, enough objections were raised that the decision on disbursement of proceeds was changed. According to a later e-mail, the same advisor said: *I just found out that the Dean of Students . . . has arranged a deal so that the proceeds to the Vagina Monologues are now going to a different affiliate of 'Women of Afghanistan,' a group called ROWA which is anti-abortion.*

Several members of Holy Cross Students for Life reportedly met with the Dean of Students, Jacqueline Peterson, the week before the performance. They expressed their objection to the intent to donate part of the proceeds to a group that would provide abortions in Afghanistan. One of the students said he was very discouraged that Peterson did not agree with any of their other concerns: First, that the content of the work was not in accord with Catholic values and teachings and had no place at a Catholic college. Second, that the work is "terribly offensive to the dignity of women, in reducing every woman to a single body part." Third, that while the stated goal of the production is to contribute to ending "violence against women," is pornography the best way to accomplish this?

Dean Peterson also told the students that it was important to let "The Vagina Monologues" go forward, because "it would open objective dialogue, and students are mature enough to make up their own minds." While disappointed at the time that the play would not be cancelled, the students claim one victory in getting the administration to redirect the proceeds, and not give funds to the pro-abortion group. However, the students also charge the administration with an attempt to cover up the original plan.

While Father McFarland reportedly did not have time to speak to *MassNews*, according to Ms. Contrada's account, he has written on the ideals of a Jesuit education. He apparently believes that these principles are not violated by his promotion of "The Vagina Monologues" on campus.

According to Fr. McFarland, a Jesuit education will:

> ➤ Follow St. Ignatius' advice to imagine oneself walking, talking, and laboring with the Lord.

> ➤ "Praise, reverence and serve God: everything that follows builds on that."

> ➤ Follow the motto of the Society of Jesus, "Ad Majorem Dei Gloriam," which means "For the greater glory of God."

> ➤ Follow St. Ignatius in reading "the pagan authors, as long as the passages were not downright immoral."

> ➤ Ask "What have I done for Christ", "What am I doing for Christ", "What should I do for Christ?"

> ➤ Encourage living "by the highest intellectual and ethical standards."

> ➤ Understand that "every engagement with the created world cannot be authentic without a discovery of God."

> ➤ "Never disrupt the *best* [emphasis added] impulses of the culture in which we work."

Pardon me, but there may just be some slight inconsistency between the president's principles and those elucidated in "The Vagina Monologues."

Ms. Contrada reports that Fr. McFarland reminds us that not all products of Jesuit education—Voltaire and the Marquis de Sade, to cite a couple—went on to lead admirable Christian lives. The way things are going at Holy Cross, as *MassNews* has editorialized, the list of infamous Jesuit alumni will surely grow.

Fr. McFarland reportedly told the *Worcester Telegram* that

"I understand that people are objecting to it, but it also has value. That's why we're going ahead with it." Still, many failed to see where it had any value. Moreover, Fr. McFarland also told the *Telegram* he supports the goal of the play, which is said to be to raise consciousness about violence against women and to raise money for Abby's House, a local shelter for battered women. Still, critics believe portraying women as sex objects would increase violence, not decrease it.

How best to explain such an offensive and inappropriate decision by a Catholic college president? I found insight in the words of my friend Bill Donohue, president and chief executive of the Catholic League for Religious and Civil Rights, who also serves on the board of the National Association of Scholars. He has published commentary on the recently released results of an NAS survey on the ethical lessons that colleges are now teaching:

> The most salient finding was that three-fourths of college seniors report being taught that right and wrong depend "on differences in individual values and cultural diversity." Only a quarter of the students reported that their professors adhered to the more traditional understanding of morality, namely, that there are uniform standards of right and wrong.

Perhaps as a gesture of inclusivity toward those who may have missed its first productions, Holy Cross will again present "The Vagina Monologues" on campus on February 11 and 12, 2003. Get your tickets now!

A plethora of relative extrema, today's Holy Cross is hardly Catholic and barely Jesuit. Indeed, "Holy" is wholly inappropriate to its name. This reality saddens me.

Happiness is not something you experience . . .
it's something you remember.

—Oscar Levant

PART II
THE VIETNAM ERA

I have come to know that the tears of a veteran seldom dry and are rarely seen. They teeter precariously on the rims of aging eyes, spilling mostly at the time of remembrance, borne from pride and the responsibility entrusted to them as they made their way through the horrors of combat.

Flashbacks emerge from the simplest stimulants. They are images that aren't remembered until one accidentally brushes up against them, like hitting a forgotten wound that hadn't quite healed. A wound that shouldn't heal. Is there such a thing? A wound that shouldn't heal?

—A Daughter of a Veteran

7

MARINE CORPS OFFICER CANDIDATES SCHOOL

26 JULY–4 SEPTEMBER 1965

*Some people spend an entire lifetime wondering if they made a
difference. The Marines don't have that problem.*

—President Ronald Reagan

An official U.S. government website provides the following
"Background" in a U.S. Naval War College Joint Military
Operations Reserve Officers Operations Course
(ROOPS) seminar on Marine Corps Doctrine and Capabilities.
In essence, it is a definition of the United States Marine Corps
and its mission.

> The Marine Corps is an expeditionary force-in-
> readiness that is manned, trained, and equipped specifically
> to respond quickly to a broad variety of crises and conflicts
> across the full range of military operations anywhere in the
> world. The Marine Corps' philosophy of warfighting is based
> on the tenets of maneuver warfare and is in consonance
> with joint doctrine. Marines provide a unique combat
> capability that combines air, land, and naval forces from the
> sea—the Marine Air-Ground Task Force (MAGTF). The
> key characteristic of these forces is their expeditionary
> mindset. Marines possess the ability to adapt and engage
> upon arrival, and then sustain operational momentum. They

are logistically expeditionary. Marine aviation is another element that characterizes the unique concept of MAGTFs. The primary function of Marine aviation is, and always has been, support of ground troops—focused, versatile, flexible, and responsive to needs on the ground.

It is the Marine Corps ability to deliver a unique blend of ground, air, and service support elements in a responsive and adaptive manner that makes it the Nation's most effective land combat, forcible entry option.

⌛

General Charles C. Krulak, the thirty-first commandant of the Marine Corps, has said: "The Marines really provide only two essential services to our nation: We make Marines; we win battles."

General Carl E. Mundy is "Chuck" Krulak's immediate predecessor as commandant (from 1991–1995). I had the pleasure of meeting him for the first time in Quantico, Virginia, in 1992 at the retirement ceremony of my friend and fellow Chaminade alumnus, Major General Matthew C. Caulfield. General Mundy and I met again after his retirement at a Marine Corps University Foundation luncheon in New York City a few years later. He has written words that are inspirational, whether one has served in the Corps or not.

Being a Marine is a state of mind that comes from an imbedded belief that he or she is, in fact, unique, a cut above. A Marine is, most of all, part of an organization that demands a difference—and delivers excellence beyond others in all it is and does.

Being a Marine comes from the Eagle, Globe, and Anchor that is tattooed indelibly on the innermost being of those privileged to earn the title. It is a searing mark, one that does not fade over time.

Few who have borne the title fail to identify with it throughout their entire lives.

These are words I applaud but then they are from Marines and I confess to a certain pro-Marine bias. Consider what Rear Admiral Paul T. Gillcrist, USN (Ret.), a 1946 Chaminade alumnus, says about the Corps:

> . . . becoming a Marine is probably the best thing that (a) young man could do with his life regardless of how long he stays in (the Corps).
>
> There is simply no other form of discipline that molds a young man's sense of purpose and personal accountability as well as service in the Marine Corps . . . and that from a former Navy man should be viewed as a great compliment. He can't go wrong.

⧗

In the spring of 1965 Lieutenant Colonel Donald McKeon, USMC, was the Marine Corps Officer Instructor at the Navy R.O.T.C. at Holy Cross. In addition to teaching us "Marine Science," he was preparing us for our first true taste of Marine Corps training. I refer to Officer Candidates School (OCS), which is located at the Marine Corps Development and Educational Center (then called Marine Corps Schools or MCS) in Quantico, Virginia, about forty-five minutes by car south of our nation's capital.

Lt. Col. McKeon took pains with us to explain the ins and outs, the dos and don'ts, of OCS. He also recommended that our group of "candidates" travel to Quantico together and, more importantly, report for training in a group, which would virtually guarantee our being in the same platoon for the six weeks of boot camp for would-be officers. It worked.

Those from my Holy Cross class who went to OCS that summer included Roger Hunt, Bob Lund, Ed Matthews, Dick Morin, Steve O'Neill, Bill Sheridan, Jim Stokes, Frank Teague and me. All of us were assigned to OCS's Sixth Platoon under the command of Staff

Sergeant William Surette, Jr., USMC, alias Wild Bill, already a Vietnam veteran. A native of Olean, New York, he was salty (an old hand), much as the vernacular of some of those in his charge would soon become.

The platoon consisted of some forty-two young men, approximately twenty-one years of age, from all over the country. None of us knew what to expect, except that OCS would not be a picnic. And therein lies a story.

President Lyndon B. Johnson was in office. His younger daughter, Luci Baines Johnson (who shared her Dad's initials, along with the rest of the family, Lady Bird, the president's wife, and Lynda Bird, his elder daughter), was dating her future husband, one Patrick Nugent, who was an Air Force enlisted man. The president, however, encouraged her to make the rounds of various military installations as a goodwill ambassadress, if you will, to encourage our men in the military. After all, the conflict in Vietnam was escalating substantially, and many of those in uniform at the time could use a generous helping of encouragement.

Well, one weekend, the young and charming Luci made her way to a picnic that was held in Washington, D.C. Some officer candidates, including our own Ed Matthews, attended—in uniform, of course. An iffy day weatherwise, the sky was overcast and some precipitation appeared likely.

At the very moment Ed shook hands with the president's daughter, he and she felt the first drops of rain. After exchanging pleasantries, Ms. Johnson commented on what a lovely time she was having and how much she appreciated the presence of the Marines at the picnic.

Completely unwittingly, I am convinced, Ed offered the following: "It's nice to be here with you too, Miss. Too bad it had to fuckin' rain."

Her eyes suddenly glazed over like those of a deer caught in headlights, Ms. Johnson quickly let go of Ed's hand and excused herself.

Relative extrema, anyone?

One of the first things that happened at OCS was the ritual of having our heads "shaved." As a former barber, I can say with some confidence that administering this haircut required no tonsorial expertise whatsoever. All that was involved was the application of electric clippers to the entire scalp; it was, in essence, a shearing. Thus, one's hair was cut as close as possible without actually being shaved. Each sitting for this service took approximately forty seconds. Thereafter, we were to keep our haircut "high and tight," although it was permissible to let it grow out on top, which wouldn't be excessive, given OCS's 41-day duration.

Next we candidates had to report to an outdoor area paved with concrete and surrounded by a six-foot-high chain-link fence. Here each of us was given clothing that included summer service uniforms, covers (military hats called "piss cutters"), utilities (fatigues), combat boots, "Mickey Mouse" uniforms and "782 gear."

The Mickey Mouse apparel consisted of a red baseball-type cap with a yellow M stitched on its crown, a bright yellow shirt with the letters USMC emblazoned in red on its front, red gym shorts with a small pocket and a round Marine Corps eagle, globe and anchor insignia patch stitched to the right front, and sneakers.

The 782 gear was decidedly more military: canteens, entrenching tool, ammunition belt, ammo pouches, helmet (both the steel "pot" and the light-weight silver liner worn under it, or by itself), bayonet, and various other items essential to the would-be trained killers we aspired to become.

Gunnery Sergeant Tolson was the "Gunny" for all of OCS, then possibly the senior enlisted Marine in the organization. He was so tough that it was said he held his socks up with thumb tacks. Be that as it may, one of his collateral duties was personally to make a presentation to all officer candidates on the importance of a message that is ubiquitous today: Don't drink and drive. At that time, the military services were losing too many men from drunk driving accidents.

Well, it was apparent from the outset of his talk on this subject that the Gunny was not accustomed to public speaking. Yes, he would generally get his message across but he lacked poise and had a tendency toward malapropisms. Perhaps he was just nervous. Anyway, as his presentation reached its crescendo, his message lost some of its potential impact when he stressed the urgency of "not drinking under the influence."

> *There are two types of people: Marines and*
> *those who wish they were.*

> —Bumper Sticker

Reveille was at 0525 each morning. Precisely at that time our platoon was awakened by Wild Bill Surette, who would switch on the bright overhead lights in our squad bay (living quarters) and shout us out of the rack (bed). From that moment all forty-two of us had five minutes to wake up, don our Mickey Mouse gear, visit the head (bathroom) and be outside in platoon formation for PT (physical training). PT consisted of calisthenics and a run of, say, a mile or two just to get the blood circulating well prior to morning chow and the main work of the day. Ed Matthews dubbed the still sleepy platoon formation "The Symphony," his classic code for the amazing volume of audible flatulence that was forthcoming from the candidates as they waited to be called to attention.

> *It is best for flatulence to pass without noise and breaking,*
> *though it is better for it to pass with noise than to be*
> *intercepted and accumulated internally.*

> —Hippocrates, circa 420 B.C.

Of OCS, Staff Sergeant Joseph Gilkerson, USMC, has written

that "A candidate will be pushed to his maximum potential and will be evaluated every moment of every day, but there is no brutality—except brutal honesty in appraising one's performance." His comment is nowadays presumed true, but there were a few instances at OCS in the summer of 1965 that could have been termed "brutal."

One of Wild Bill's platoon leader peers was a certain Sergeant Puida, a former DI (drill instructor) from the Marine Corps boot camp at Parris Island, South Carolina. (The oldest training center for Marines, which is located there, has the proper name of Marine Corps Recruit Depot Parris Island.) "Puida the Red-Headed Pervert" was his nickname. "Pervert" is probably too strong a term but he *was* brutal to some of those in his platoon, occasionally getting fist-physical with some candidates.

Of Parris Island, General Mundy has written, "Through this gate, and others like it in San Diego, California, and Quantico, Virginia, thousands of young Americans pass to accept the challenge to become a Marine."

"During the weeks in this forge," as Mundy has portrayed it, "young bodies harden, maturity emerges, minds focus, confidence grows, brotherhood takes form, and pride begins to tingle. At their conclusion, 'recruit' or 'candidate' becomes 'Marine' . . . The new Marine knows that he or she has passed through a trial that others have not dared, and has gained acceptance in a storied band of brothers: The few . . . the proud . . . the Marines."

Marines.com, the Corps' web site, has its own inspirational language that, not surprisingly, is focused on recruiting:

> One must first be stripped clean. Freed of all the false notions of self.
>
> It is the Marine Corps that will strip away the façade so easily confused with self. It is the Corps that will offer the pain needed to buy the truth. And at last, each will own the

privilege of looking inside himself to discover what truly resides there.

Unhappiness does not arise from the way things are but rather from a difference in the way things are and the way we believe they should be.

Comfort is an illusion. A false security bred from familiar things and familiar ways. It narrows the mind. Weakens the body. And robs the soul of spirit and determination. Comfort is neither welcome nor tolerated here.

You within yourself. There is no one else to rely on, and when the self is exhausted, no one to lift you up.

But finally we wake to realize there is only one way to get through this, and that is together.

There is only determination. There is only single minded desire. Not one among them is willing to give up. Not one among them would exchange torment for freedom. Finally, they just want to be Marines.

Once you've walked through fire and survived, little else can burn.

But first, a final test will take everything that is left inside. When this is over, those that stand will reach out with dirty, callused hands to claim the Eagle, Globe and Anchor. And the title United States Marine.

We came as orphans. We depart as family.

The training itself might be described as brutal but only by those who don't understand the Marines' mission or discipline. For example, my OCS class underwent training with pugil sticks.

Designed to simulate hand-to-hand combat with a bayonet-fixed M-14 rifle, a pugil stick was approximately four-to-five feet long and had thick padding on each end. Wearing helmets, two candidates of similar size and weight would be selected to fight each other with these improvised weapons until one of them was on the deck (ground), vanquished but definitely not unconscious. In actual combat, the loser invariably would suffer a terminal bayonet thrust, or be captured.

The Marine confronts his enemy as a fierce,
depersonalized warrior.

—*The Marines*, Marine Corps Heritage Foundation

I remember well my own feeling of reluctance—not trepidation—as I went up against a fellow candidate from neighboring Fifth Platoon, a candidate I happened to like and respect. To this day I can still see his face. (I'm quite sure his last name began with a P but that's the best I can do after thirty-seven years.) He and I squared off and, on command, began our interpersonal battle. It didn't last long but, after some initial sparring, we went at it with a vengeance. I managed to strike a solid blow to the left side of his head and knock him down, surprising myself in winning the contest so quickly. I helped him to his feet and we shook hands; I'm confident there were no hard feelings. To me this was our Corps at its finest.

First to fight for right and freedom, and to keep our honor
clean, we are proud to claim the title of United States Marine.

—From *The Marines' Hymn*

Another OCS highlight—if it can be called that—was, unlike the pugil-stick exercise, not directly interpersonal. The Hill Trail, as it was known, is a topographical nightmare, at least in the view of some of those who have experienced its exceptional challenges. Hardly a hill-and-vale environment, it is a series of very steep parallel ridges.

On a wickedly hot and humid August evening, Sgt. Surette led his platoon on a forced march in full combat gear up and down the Hill Trail for miles—I don't recall how many but it was a long, arduous procession in wilderness and unforgiving terrain.

More than a few candidates, some of them vomiting, fell out along the route of march. Others suffering from heat stroke or heat prostration or sheer exhaustion were evacuated to sick bay (the infirmary). Six-bys (Marine troop transport trucks) with corpsmen were situated on the ridge lines with trash cans full of ice to treat the serious heat casualties. In sum, the Hill Trail is so grueling that men have actually died attempting to negotiate it.

Suffice it to say that, when we reached our destination in a clearing on a hilltop in the middle of a wooded Quantico nowhere, I immediately consumed *both* of my canteens of water, a half-gallon, I believe. I did it with ease, and haven't done it before or since. Each of us who completed the Hill Trail was awed by what he had just endured, and elated it was over. In fact, some candidates called it "brutal."

Upon reflection I came to comprehend that this test of one's physical limits was negotiable for me in no small part because of Coach Joe Thomas's football drills at Chaminade. Indeed, they were my first experiences with grueling physical exercise. Thus, Coach had unwittingly prepared me for the Hill Trail four years beforehand.

As for Sgt. Surette, he seemed inexhaustible and unaffected.

⧗

Wild Bill was a comedian, albeit maybe unwittingly. During at least one outdoor rifle inspection, he endowed us with images that are, for those of us who witnessed him in action, indelible. Sgt. Bill Surette's performances were remarkable, and many qualify as excellent examples of relative extrema.

I came to respect and admire the small arms with which we trained as Marines. First it was the M-14 and later the 45-caliber pistol. At The Basic School (TBS), which commenced for us in the summer of 1966, we, mostly newly commissioned second lieutenants, fired both weapons for qualification. The three categories were marksman, sharpshooter and expert, the last being the best. I qualified as a sharpshooter with the rifle, an expert with the pistol.

The semi-automatic 7.62mm M-14 rifle, which was about to be replaced by the Corps with the 5.56mm M-16 fully automatic weapon, was then touted as a Marine's best friend. Thus, even today, every Marine, enlisted or officer, is trained as a rifleman first and foremost, and must qualify annually on the rifle range. As Francis Parkman once wrote, there is "no better companion than the rifle."

A big part of this companionship is the care and maintenance of the rifle itself. The weapon must be regularly disassembled and its parts cleaned and lubricated. The piece's bore (barrel) must also be cleaned, especially after firing, to remove any carbon deposits therein. In the rifling grooves inside the bore, however, minute carbon deposits can become trapped and hidden. Any movement—marching, for example—can dislodge one or more of these tiny particles, which can easily be seen in the light of day, especially against an otherwise clean and shiny bore. To be sure, some guys thought a clean rifle was nigh impossible.

I am certainly not picking on Ed Matthews but I believe it was his rifle that evoked one of Wild Bill's most memorable denunciations. There again on a stifling summer day was our hapless candidate face to face with his drill instructor.

"Pre*sent* arms!" commanded Sgt. Surette. Ed quickly and crisply obliged.

Again on command, Candidate Matthews next presented his rifle to Sgt. Surette for actual inspection, at which, of course, the latter was long accomplished.

With a keen eye Wild Bill examined the bore of Ed's M-14, in which, alas, he spied a speck of carbon.

"*W h o . . . s h i t . . . i n . . . y o u r . . . b o r e*, Mat*thews*?" Wild Bill queried, slowly for effect.

Our platoon sergeant spoke with sufficient volume to enable all of us to hear his question. As you can well imagine, despite the seriousness of a rifle inspection in Marine Corps culture, for us it was difficult in the extreme to keep a straight face in such circumstance. Be that as it may, even a smirk on one's face, let alone laughter, would earn the errant candidate extra duty or outright punishment for his infraction of military discipline. In fact, it was also Marine Corps tradition that, if a candidate or recruit screwed up, the entire platoon would frequently receive group punishment for the misdeed of just one. This could result in the administration of a "blanket party" (a pummeling) while the offending platoon member slept.

Quite possibly on the same day, another candidate in our platoon had a similar run-in with Wild Bill. His name was Carl Houle, whose surname is properly pronounced *hool*. From the beginning of our six weeks at OCS, our illustrious platoon sergeant insisted on calling Carl *hoolee*.

As he eyed the bore of Carl's weapon, Wild Bill saw therein a small insect, whereupon he declared, once more in full voice, "*Hoolee*, there's a *homesteader* in your bore!" I thought Carl was going to convulse.

Once more, all of us almost lost it.

> To err is human, to forgive is divine. However, neither is
> Marine Corps policy.
>
> —Bumper Sticker

Speaking of penalty for violation of Sgt. Surette's or OCS's rules, I had an interesting confrontation with our platoon's supreme leader over, of all things, a loaf of banana bread. Please bear in mind that, until this incident, neither Sgt. Surette nor OCS nor the Marine Corps itself had any proscription against a candidate receiving, or being in possession of, banana bread in any quantity. But all this may have changed since 1965 and my unfortunate receipt then of the offending loaf.

Mame mailed me a banana bread, which she had baked herself at home. It was meant as a loving gesture, which I would, in retrospect, perhaps more fully appreciate under normal conditions, for which Wild Bill Surette's Quantico would simply never qualify. By the way, Mame's banana bread is the best on the planet. On this point Bob Lund has reprimanded me, at least lightly. He maintains that "categorizing the banana bread as the best on the planet raises all kinds of credibility issues. It may well be, but how would you know without the kind of exhaustive research that would probably bankrupt you, unless, of course, you received a grant or something." Incredible.

Late one afternoon, Sixth Platoon had just returned to its squad bay to change uniforms and get ready for evening chow (dinner). During this brief but savored "down" time, I received word that I was to report immediately to Sgt. Surette's office. This instilled in me a sense of foreboding similar to that I had felt upon being summoned to Father Charles Dunn's office two years earlier.

⧗

"I think you have a helluva nerve for not writing in over a week. Just because I called you up, doesn't mean you can stop writing.—Okay, I'm finished. But no kiddin'—why don't you write more often. And also why don't you send me some cookies, crackers or fruitcake . . . !"

Those words were written on Sunday, August 30, 1942 by my Dad while stationed at Camp Gruber, Oklahoma, shortly after he was drafted into the Army, in a letter to his stepmother, Alice Kirkwood Mansfield. Alice obliged—and often, according to other letters my father wrote that summer.

With that as background, I will now compare the Army and the Marine Corps regarding their respective handling of 'fruitcakes' and recipients thereof, albeit some twenty-three years apart.

⧗

Following standard operating procedure, I stood at attention outside Sgt. Surette's open office hatch (door) and "knocked," which, according to Marine Corps protocol, consisted of striking the hatch frame vigorously with the heel of one's right hand. This knock was to be followed by an announcement of one's presence, which meant a virtual shout with intonation rising sharply on the last syllable, also per protocol or tradition or both.

"Candidate Mansfield reporting as ordered, *sir.*"

"I can't *h e a r* you, Mans*field!*" was his rejoinder. His vocal tone and inflection were reminiscent of *All in the Family*'s Archie Bunker addressing his long-suffering wife Edith. Bear in mind that Wild Bill was no more than seven feet from me.

A second time, now pounding the hatch frame much harder, I raised my voice and again advised, "Candidate Mansfield reporting as ordered, *SIR!*"

"I *s t i l l* can't hear you, Mans*field!*" he persisted, slowly stressing every word.

"CANDIDATE   MANSFIELD   REPORTING   AS ORDERED, <u>*SIR!!!*</u>" I bellowed while simultaneously feeling I may have broken my hand.

"Mansfield, get your *ass* in here, and next time don't *knock* so damn loud!"

"Yes, sir," I said, still at attention.

"At *e a s e,*" came the next command from Wild Bill, his chin and lips jutting forward as if barking cadence at close-order drill.

What a performance!

Now we would finally get down to the business at hand.

With a look of maybe mock disgust on his face, Sgt. Surette gestured toward a 4" by 9" package wrapped in brown paper, resting in the middle of his desk blotter.

"What *is* this, *Mansfield?* A *little fucking package* from *Momsey?*" Enunciating and elongating every sound, he resumed the show.

"I don't know, sir."

"Fine; open the *fucking* thing and *find* the *fuck* out!" he ordered, alliteration unintentional, I'm sure.

I read the return address as I began to unwrap the parcel, and I knew it was from Mame. "MAL," her initials, and "24 Locust Street" were clearly and neatly printed in the upper left corner. Whereas I still wonder why Wild Bill didn't pick up on the "L," I surmised it would be best to let him continue thinking this thoughtful treat came from my mother rather than my girlfriend. Otherwise, forget it, his abuse would likely have become unrelenting, and I didn't need that.

Having quickly removed the brown paper, I could see, as could Wild Bill, that there was aluminum foil covering the package's contents.

"*O p e n* it, Mans*field*," he demanded.

The aroma of this recently baked banana bread was delectable.

"A *little fucking fruitcake* from *Mom*sey, eh Mans*field*," he handed down his indictment. I was not about to disabuse him of the fact that it was *not* a fruitcake. Just try to imagine anyone engaging Bill Surette in a discussion of the differences between fruitcake and banana bread.

"I guess so, sir," I responded, not knowing where he might be headed. *Beheaded* indeed.

"Don't you like the *c h o w* here at OCS, Mans*field*?"

"Oh, yes, sir, it's just fine."

"Mans*field, are you h u n g r y*?"

Implying that we were all about to march to the mess hall for evening chow, I innocently replied, "Yes, sir."

"Good, then. How'd you like to eat all of this *little fucking fruitcake right now by yourself*?"

I was tempted to tell him that it would spoil my appetite but I thought better of it.

"No, thank you, sir. I'm not that hungry."

"Now Mans*field*, first I want you to take this here *little fucking fruitcake* into the squad bay, *share* it with your fellow candidates, and have yourselves *a little fucking party!*" His boisterous and emphatic enunciation of the *t*s in the word *little* followed ubiquitously by the f-word was more than mildly amusing. "Then, you will write to *Momsey* and tell her not to send you *any more little fucking fruitcakes*."

"Dis*missed*," growled Wild Bill, adjourning our meeting.

Sgt. Surette led the way from his office to the squad bay; I followed, toting the loaf. As we entered, he called the platoon to attention, and announced that I, in turn, had an announcement to make. Naturally, he declared loudly that "Mansfield has received a *little fucking gift* from Momsey that he would like to share with the rest of you."

At first I wondered if I could communicate to all these guys—without laughing—that they were about to partake of a banana bread snack. After all, this *was* the Marine Corps. My concern quickly vanished as I had only to remember the likelihood of further special treatment from Wild Bill if I failed to do things just right. A bit nervous, I played it straight.

Wild Bill ordered me to cut the banana bread into little pieces. Standing at a small table, I informed my fellow candidates what was going to happen, that is, that I would be sharing and serving them a homemade banana bread. Next, with my bayonet I cut the loaf into dozens of bite-size pieces. Still at attention, I watched these strong, young Marine officer candidates file by, some casting me furtive glances that said *Are you kidding me?*, and daintily help themselves to a morsel of Mame's delicious but troublesome treat. The scene was comical but no one laughed.

The banana bread disappeared quickly, and I was very glad to see it gone.

Wild Bill abstained.

Dave Taylor was a member of our platoon. A student at Brown University, he was a fine young man, who struck me as a gentleman. One evening, standing at the bar with some fellow Marines, Dave said something at which one of the other guys apparently took offense and left. Puzzled, as we all were, Dave lamented the loss of the fellow's company and offered, laconically, "Well, as my grandmother used to say, if he can't take a joke, fuck him!"

And that's the truth, as Lily Tomlin used to say.

Leader of men, teller of tall tales, legend in my own mind, U.S. Marine extraordinaire, stream fordable, air dropable, beer fueled, water cooled, author, lecturer, traveler, bum, philanthropist, occasional hero, semi-pro comedian, freedom fighter and defender of the faith. Wars fought, tigers tamed, revolutions started, bars emptied, alligators castrated, women chased, etc.

—From the Back of a Marine Corps Calling Card

On the night of August 25, 1965, less than ten days from the end of OCS, our platoon was part of a night war games exercise that involved all OCS units, not just Sixth Platoon.

The weather was awful. Despite the time of year, it seemed unusually cold, which was probably due to the torrential rain that came down in sheets for hours that night.

Following a forced march to our defensive position, we dug in for the night. It was impossible to sleep, for we were sitting in foxholes with water up to our chests. To say this was unpleasant is an obvious understatement. It was so bad that we came to refer to the whole experience that night as, you guessed it, "That Night."

Frank Teague, my Holy Cross classmate and friend, had been appointed to serve as company commander for this combat training. He is a leadership-oriented guy and unflappable in virtually any situation. He also possesses a marvelous sense of humor, which, I must say, came in handy in this instance. That night I served as Frank's company sergeant; thus, he was my commanding officer for the duration of the exercise.

At this juncture I invite and encourage you to feel cold, soaked and utterly miserable, as we did at that time. With no doubt whereof I comment, I believe that virtually all of the candidates and the experienced Marines participating that night were both physically uncomfortable and psychologically fed up with an essentially bogus combat exercise that had become mired in, well, mire. I know that I had lost patience, certainly *not* with Frank, but with the seeming lack of any movement at all—and this while bogged down in mud and immersed in pools of cold rain in foxholes in a Virginia forest. Indeed, more than a few of the candidates were sullen but, of course, not mutinous.

After this lull in activity, Frank's voice pierced the audibly slashing rain.

"Sergeant Mansfield," he called out, "file your report!"

My expected role at this point was to give a status report, such as, "All present and accounted for, sir." However, my mood was foul and, against my better judgement, I shouted to Frank at the bottom of the hill, into the side of which we were so annoyingly dug, "Sir, the company sergeant regrettably but respectfully requests that we get the hell out of here!"

What I didn't know at the time was that the Marine colonel who was then the commanding officer (CO) of OCS just happened to be standing next to Frank from the very moment he issued me the order to report, straight through my most un-Marine-like reply.

There is no doubt that I could have been deemed insubordinate for failing, with obvious deliberation, to carry out a direct order. Instead, to the surprise and relief of all of us then in abject misery, the next word passed by Frank was to secure (leave) our positions and move out. We were going back to the base, which meant hot showers and a warm rack. It was sweet and welcome music to the ears of many.

The next morning I was concerned that I might hear from the colonel, who couldn't have been pleased with my performance the night before. Luckily, whereas he could easily have asked Frank who the idiot was who responded the way I did, identified me as the culprit, and meted out suitable punishment, he did not. Much relieved, I was left to conjecture that the colonel was cool, or maybe just wanted to go home like the rest of us that night.

There was also the chance that Wild Bill would wish to sanction me in some way, probably by designating me a "T.U.R.D.," or "Trainee Under Restrictive Discipline." In any case, I was spared the inconvenience of any disciplinary action, and Frank and the rest of us now had the makings of a tale that has now been told on countless occasions over the past thirty-seven years.

For my part, I have made it my practice to call Frank, Roger Hunt and Bob Lund every August 25th to reminisce about "That Night." I know it will bring us all a good laugh, and I look forward to the calls for that reason.

The Marines have developed a reputation as some of toughest fighting men in the U.S. armed forces. Doubters—and there are many, particularly in competing services—scoff that the Marine aura is a triumph of image over reality. The Corps, they argue, is neither heavy enough for sustained ground operations nor light enough for commando raids. It is a source of constant consternation for the other services to see themselves outmaneuvered by the Corps in the battle for congressional support, leading to cracks about how the "Marines are best at storming Capitol Hill." There is no denying that the Marines have devoted a great deal of energy to burnishing their image. They've had to. Ever since the Corps' birth in 1775, it has been the target of attempts to eliminate it. The Marines have responded by cultivating the American people, whether through their famous band (once led by John Philip Sousa) or through movies like "The Sands of Iwo Jima." It will surprise no one familiar with the Corps that the first reporters allowed to accompany U.S. troops into action in Afghanistan were brought in by the Marines.

—Max Boot

With respect to Afghanistan and the Marines' role there, U.S. Army General Tommy R. Franks, who heads the U.S. Central Command, has been quoted saying:

I ended a recent operations briefing for a lot of our folks over there by discussing some of their morale issues. I related to them about a recent meeting and tour I had with the American ambassador when we went around inspecting all of our Marines deployed into their fighting positions.

I reminded all of the assembled officers that Marines live in holes and don't have a house to live in like 'heavy forces.' No tank or lots of tents to sleep in. They carry their 'house' on their back and they live in fighting holes. Although the Marines had just lost a buddy (in a Humvee accident), their spirit was 'uplifting.'

A question posed by the ambassador to a Marine drove this point home. The ambassador asked a young Marine private sitting in his hole, "How is it here in the hole?" The private answered, "Kind of like the beach without water."

The ambassador then asked, "If you could get something, what would you like to have?"

I related to all of our folks assembled there in front of me that most of us would have answered, 'a hot meal,' 'a cot,' 'a shower,' but this Marine private said, "I could use some more ammunition."

The Marine Corps' "most enduring contribution," to quote General Mundy once more, "is that it makes Marines, imbues them with exceptional qualities of confidence, determination, leadership, and a winning spirit that gives strength to our national character." True to this template, when all was said and done, Staff Sergeant William Surette, Jr., USMC, was a Marine's Marine. On January 20, 1970 he was killed in action during his third tour of duty in Vietnam.

Godspeed, Bill Surette.

My stint in the Marines was one of life's best experiences. It's a lean force, takes an interest in the individual, and instills its touchstones—honor, courage and commitment—into each of its charges. Class is its hallmark. Two months after I left active duty, I received a letter from the Commandant, General Vandegrift, wishing me well and thanking me for my services— a thoughtful touch. If you have an appetite for challenge and adventure, the Corps is the place to be. Measuring up breeds both good feeling and the esprit for which the Marines are renowned.

—P. Henry Mueller

8

VIETNAM:

OUR LEAST POPULAR AND

LEAST SUCCESSFUL WAR

In 1955 Marines with the Seventh Fleet assisted in moving three hundred thousand refugees from north to south Viet Nam, a straw in the wind little noticed at the time.

—*The Marines* by Marine Corps Heritage Foundation

The Vietnam War has been called the longest the United States has ever fought and the only one it has ever lost, although many disagree on this point. A total of 58,132 American men and women died in the fighting, from July 8, 1959 to May 15, 1975. According to the Smithsonian Institution, approximately 2.7 million Americans served in the war zone; 300,000 were wounded and approximately 75,000 permanently disabled. Moreover, there are still 2,266 persons listed as missing in action.

In *The Coldest War* former Marine and noted author James Brady reminds us that, "In the three years of Korea nearly as many of us died as in the decade of Vietnam." Also, "Korea might be thought of as the last campaign of World War II; because of the vague way it ended in 1953, as the opening battle for Vietnam."

Situated in southeast Asia (N23° 30', E106° 43'), a region once called French Indo-China, Vietnam stretches more than 900 miles from its northern border with China to the Mekong River Delta in the south. Its narrow "waist" is less than a hundred miles from its western border with Laos to the Gulf of Tonkin, the northwesternmost waters of the South China Sea. To its northwest, Vietnam still borders Laos; in the southwest, it borders Cambodia (also known as Kampuchea).

Vietnam covers approximately 128,065 square miles. Topographically, it is a country of hills and densely forested mountains, with level land covering no more than twenty percent. Mountains account for forty percent, as do hills, with forests covering seventy-five percent. The north consists of highlands and the Red River Delta, whereas the south is divided into coastal lowlands, the central mountains (Giai Truong Son) with high plateaus, and the aforementioned Mekong Delta.

Vietnam's climate is tropical and monsoonal, with a humidity that averages 84% annually. Its yearly rainfall ranges from 47 to 118 inches, and annual temperatures vary between 41°F and 99°F.

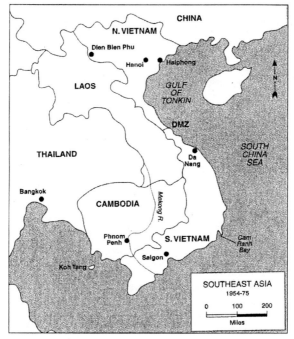

Source: *The Battle History of the U.S. Marines* by Col. Joseph H. Alexander, USMC (Ret.). Map drawn by Mary Craddock Hoffman.

⌛

For the Marines the Vietnam War began arguably in 1965, when the Ninth Marine Expeditionary Brigade (MEB) made a widely publicized landing at Danang on March 8th of that year. Initially, the Ninth MEB assumed a defensive posture around the Danang air base, which was the northernmost of the three jet-capable airfields in South Vietnam. The newly arrived Marines found it difficult to take seriously a war fought against "little guys in black pajamas." Still, the ensuing build up was swift.

In those days, a Marine served a 13-month tour of duty in-country, that is, in Vietnam. After several months in-country, he would begin to count the number of days until his tour ended and he would go back to "The World." (The other American services in Vietnam served a standard 12-month tour of duty there.) Once the half-way point was passed, a Marine considered himself "short," as in short-timer. Going back to The World simply meant going home but the expression implied that, not only was Vietnam foreign and far away from the U.S., it was an environment so detested by Americans serving there that it was not even considered part of planet Earth.

> It cheered us to know we were not forgotten, not lost in this great allied army, that we were not just another infantry division of dogfaces, but that we were, and always would be, amphibious assault troops, that we were marines. I know that sounds corny, but it is how marines think.

> —James Brady in *The Coldest War*

When American veterans returned to The World from Vietnam, as I did in 1969, there were no cheering crowds, as there were after World War II, although there were individual homecoming celebrations. Instead, Vietnam veterans returned to a discomforting silence, as if everybody were ashamed of them. Indeed, I remember once distinctly avoiding the topic of my combat service as a Marine in Vietnam.

According to David Clayton Carrad, a lawyer who served with the U.S. Army in Vietnam in 1968 and 1969, "Although I was proud to have served, I quickly learned the basic survival skill for Vietnam veterans: keep quiet about it, leave it off your resume, turn the other cheek."

"You people ran a number on us. Your guilt, your hang-ups, your uneasiness, made it socially unacceptable to mention the fact that we were Vietnam veterans. Whenever we brought it up, you walked away from the conversation." With these words former Marine Lieutenant Robert Muller rebuked his audience at the opening of Vietnam Veterans' Week in New York City on May 29, 1979, as reported in *The New York Times*.

In its edition of that same day, another major daily editorialized that it had not been established that Vietnam veterans suffer neuroses to any significant extent. However, it had already become clear that Americans in general had not yet come to terms with the war, its purpose or its outcome.

In 1998 Major General Matthew P. Caulfield, USMC (Ret.) wrote me a letter to thank me for a copy of a Vietnam War presentation I had given at Chaminade. In it he also wrote:

> Your presentation also reminded me of my own homecoming. There was only one welcome home party for me. My classmates from Chaminade invited me up to New York, took over a restaurant and we had a hell of a time. Our Chaminade friends never lost faith in us however they might have felt about the war. And when I think about it, neither did Chaminade. We were very well prepared to endure what we had to endure, to serve, and were inculcated with such a deep sense of responsibility for others, that some thirty years later I still feel for those Marines as though it were yesterday.

In writing "I still feel for those Marines," Matt refers to three Marines under his command who were killed during the siege of

Khe Sanh. Sadly, American veterans were, according to *Newsweek,* "obliged to bear an inordinate share of the blame both for having fought at all and for having failed to win." In contrast, a Californian named Roy Rockstrom later wrote in a letter to *U.S. News & World Report* (June 18, 1984) some compelling words about this. "The shame of Vietnam," as he put it, "lies not on those who fought there, but on the politicians who so ably programed *(sic)* our defeat and citizens who sided with the enemy. May we never forget those who died; may we always remember those who came home."

By the time the U.S. military presence reached its peak of 543,000 in early 1969, most Americans had already turned against the war. A Gallup poll reportedly found that a majority of Americans for the first time were persuaded that it all had been a horrendous mistake. Presidential power was transferring from Lyndon Johnson, whose efforts to win the war became his political undoing, to Richard M. Nixon, whose goal was simply to get out of Vietnam without seeming to have lost it.

Here I should like to make clear my belief that the lesson of the Vietnam War for the United States is that never again should we enter a potentially long conflict without the support of the American people. Moreover, we should never enter any conflict unless we have the will to win.

Just the same, the U.S. had an obligation to help defend South Vietnam by virtue of its membership in the Southeast Asia Treaty Organization, or SEATO. In that agreement we promised to support and defend nations in the region in the event of aggression against them. In short, we made a commitment. (Ironically, South Vietnam was not a member of SEATO, at least not initially, but its strategic position made it critically important, especially in light of the "domino theory," which postulated that if one country in a region fell to communist control, so would the others.) Alas, our commitment lasted too long and cost us too dearly.

To personalize this notion of commitment, I believed in 1968 that I had a *duty* to fight in Vietnam, and I went there willingly. Nonetheless, I readily make the distinction that I had little *desire* to go there and fight. Today I juxtapose that lack of desire then to a full willingness to fight against terrorism today and in the years ahead. When I tried to rejoin the Marines in the days following 9/11, I was told by their recruiter in GC that I was, as he put it, too old.

With respect to President John F. Kennedy's role in involving the U.S. in the Vietnam War, Robert L. Bartley, editor of *The Wall Street Journal*, has written:

> My own view of President Kennedy is much more direct: His callowness and amorality got us into Vietnam. Or to be more precise, his blunders turned a limited commitment into an open-ended one. One of the few specific pieces of advice Gen. Eisenhower gave his young successor was to put American troops in Laos, that is, astride what later became the Ho Chi Minh Trail. Instead, Kennedy sent Averell Harriman and Roger Hillsman out to negotiate an agreement on Laos, which of course gave Ho (Chi Minh, the North Vietnamese leader) the access he wanted.
>
> Infiltration and subversion increased in South Vietnam. With Buddhist bonzes [monks] committing self-immolation, the best and brightest argued the problem was the Catholic recalcitrance of our ally, Ngo Dinh Diem.

In an era when Presidents Johnson and Nixon are widely perceived as the "bad guys" responsible for America's phenomenal losses in Vietnam, Mr. Bartley's is a refreshing, if dismaying, perspective.

On November 2, 1963 the United States under President Kennedy engineered the overthrow and assassination of Diem, then South Vietnam's President. Twenty days later Kennedy was himself assassinated in Dallas, and Vice President Johnson was sworn in as president. Just before moving into the White

House, Mr. Johnson reportedly showed Hubert Humphrey a photograph of Diem.

Continued Mr. Bartley,

> "We had a hand in killing him," LBJ said. "Now it's happening here." Johnson of course made his own errors, but the die was already cast. In overthrowing an ally in the name of winning the war, the U.S. had made a commitment from which it could scarcely walk away. Many of Kennedy's admirers later became war protesters, of course, chanting that American society was immoral.

Robert Strange McNamara, who served as Secretary of Defense under both Kennedy and Johnson, has written in his 1995 book *In Retrospect*:

> I think it highly probable that, had President Kennedy lived, he would have pulled us out of Vietnam. He would have concluded that the South Vietnamese were incapable of defending themselves, and that Saigon's grave political weaknesses made it unwise to try to offset the limitations of South Vietnamese forces by sending U.S. combat troops on a large scale.

His assessment notwithstanding, during the first eight months of the Johnson presidency our involvement in Vietnam deepened ever so crucially.

Ironically, President Johnson probably could have obtained a declaration of war in Vietnam when he didn't need it, and when he did need it he couldn't get it. Still, in 1964 he came close, by persuading Congress to authorize him "to take all necessary measures to repel any armed attack against the forces of the United States and to prevent further aggression." This became known as the "Gulf of Tonkin" Resolution, named after the body of water in which a controversial naval encounter between American and North Vietnamese vessels took place earlier that year. The resolution was rescinded by Congress only a few months after the so called Kent State "massacre" in May

1970. (At Kent State University in Ohio, the National Guard was called in to restore order during a student demonstration against the war. Tragically, four students were shot to death by the guardsmen.)

During this time frame, Chaminade alumnus Paul Gillcrist was a Navy fighter pilot who, as a fleet squadron commander, completed three aircraft carrier deployments to the Gulf of Tonkin. He flew 167 combat missions for which he was awarded seventeen combat decorations.

Now an aerospace consultant and a teacher, Rear Admiral Paul T. Gillcrist, USN (Ret.) was one of sixteen American aviation pioneers honored in the PBS documentary *A Gathering of Eagles* for their extraordinary personal contributions to "the history of modern flight" and for "expanding the envelope of aerospace operations."

In addition to being a fighter pilot, Paul served also as a test pilot and a weapons delivery instructor, and actively flew from sixteen carriers for over twenty-seven years. He commanded an F-8 *Crusader* fighter squadron, then a Navy aircraft carrier wing, and finally, as a flag officer, became wing commander for all U.S. Pacific Fleet fighter squadrons.

Throughout his aviation career, Paul flew virtually every airplane in the Navy's inventory. Included in his flight log book are over 6,000 hours flying in seventy-one different types of aircraft from 1952 to 1981. He retired in 1985 as Assistant Deputy Chief of Naval Operations (Air Warfare). He is the author of seven books, including two novels. Among these are *TOMCAT! The Grumman F-14 Story*; *CRUSADER! Last of the Gunfighters*; *Feet Wet: Reflections of a Carrier Pilot*; *Vulture's Row*; *Cobra* and *An Nasher, The Asp*.

Paul was inducted into the Chaminade Alumni Hall of Fame on March 21, 2002.

Nineteen sixty-five was a turning point for Johnson and American policy in Vietnam for two major reasons. First, the president ordered our forces to begin bombing North Vietnam. Second, he also ordered a major escalation of U.S. involvement with the addition of 100,000 combat troops in-country.

In his conduct of the war, I believe Mr. Johnson made six critical mistakes.

> ➤ *Despite his public rhetoric, he did not believe that the U.S. could win the war.* This is well documented by presidential historian Michael R. Beschloss in *Reaching for Glory: The Johnson White House Tapes, 1964–65*, which was published in November 2001. According to these secret recordings, the president actually confided to his wife Lady Bird, Secretary McNamara and Senator Richard Russell, Johnson's former Senate mentor, that the war was unwinnable. His behavior was reprehensible and unforgivable.

The remaining five reasons were offered by Leo K. Thorsness in a letter to *The Wall Street Journal*, which was published on February 1, 1985.

> ➤ *He kept McNamara on as Defense Secretary.* In his own book *In Retrospect*, cited above, McNamara admits that "we could and should have withdrawn from South Vietnam either in late 1963 amid the turmoil following Diem's assassination or in late 1964 or early 1965 in the face of increasing political and military weakness in South Vietnam." Despite this belief, McNamara did not resign from Johnson's cabinet until February 1968, another reprehensible behavior. Had he resigned earlier, or been more courageous in making his case for early American troop

withdrawal from Vietnam, a lot of American lives probably would have been spared.

➤ *He failed to declare war.*

➤ *He did not mobilize U.S. military reserves.*

➤ *He granted students deferments from military service, which automatically split the young generation.*

➤ *He lacked confidence in the military.*

As for this lack of confidence, it's too bad President Johnson didn't know Army First Lieutenant Steve Karopczyc and Marine First Lieutenant Tim Shorten, whose stories come later.

True leadership is the ability to provide continuity and stability in times of rapid and violent shifts.

—Pehr G. Gyllenhammar

9

Bullets Dodged:

Tet and Khe Sanh

Khe Sanh was famous, one of the very few place names in Vietnam that was recognized by the American public. Khe Sanh said "siege," it said "encircled Marines" and "heroic defenders." It could be understood by newspaper readers quickly, it breathed Glory and War and Honored Dead. It seemed to make sense. It was good stuff.

—From *Dispatches* by Michael Herr

When he was eighteen, my son Chas told me he was glad I had made it back from Vietnam. I told him that he well may have been the reason I did. You see, my orders to Vietnam had directed me to be in-country by December 1967 but, thanks to a benevolent Marine Corps personnel policy, I did not have to report for duty in Vietnam until after Mame gave birth, which occurred the following April. As a result, I didn't leave the States for Vietnam until June 1968 and, fortunately (for me), missed two of the most disastrous events of the war: the Tet Offensive and the "siege" of Khe Sanh. Although I was not in-country for either, had the fates behaved differently, I almost certainly would have been. Still, Tet and Khe Sanh provide a backdrop to my service in Vietnam.

While Tet stunned America, President Johnson said of Khe Sanh: "This is a decisive time in Vietnam. The eyes of the nation and the eyes of the entire world—the eyes of all history itself—are on that brave little band of defenders who hold the pass at Khe Sanh."

Tet is the lunar new year, which is celebrated in Vietnam much as it is in China and other Chinese communities around the world. It began on January 27, 1968. The Viet Cong (VC) announced that during Tet they would observe a one-week cease-fire. Instead, they celebrated their cease-fire with rocket attacks up and down South Vietnam; ground attacks followed. On January 30, 1968, the VC, together with the North Vietnamese Army (NVA), launched an all-out assault on American military installations and those of the Army of the Republic of Vietnam, or ARVN, as it was called. It was almost certainly the bloodiest period of the entire war.

Hundreds of towns and villages throughout South Vietnam, in 36 of its 48 provinces, reported large-scale enemy attacks. The ancient imperial capital of Hue (pronounced *whay*) came under an especially heavy attack. It was the cultural center of South Vietnam, seat of a great university, and site of the Citadel, known for its enormous brick walls and moats, which were built in 1802. The battle for Hue would last for twenty-five bloody days.

As for the Marines, they were too few and too light to breach the Citadel, and fell back to await reinforcements. With the American military under attack throughout the country, there were too few ground troops available to recapture Hue. Despite fierce NVA resistance, Hue was later taken but not without 1,000 Marine casualties, including 142 dead.

In the same time frame, the isolated forward base at Khe Sanh in the far northwestern corner of South Vietnam saw U.S. Marines trapped for four months. According to *The Battle History of the U.S. Marines* by Col. Joseph H. Alexander, USMC (Ret.), "Few Marines ever held an exposed outpost longer, under more relentless pounding, than India Company of the 3rd Battalion, 26th Marines, on Hill 881-South." It was to be a "grueling seventy-seven-day battle for the western DMZ," the demilitarized zone that separated North and South Vietnam.

The "siege" began when two companies of the 26th Marine Regiment (some 6,600 strong) inadvertently encountered a well armed NVA battalion while on patrol between Hills 881-South and 881-North on January 20, 1968. (The hills were numerically named for the number of meters they stood above sea level.) The NVA occupied 881-North in force. When these Marine patrols encountered the enemy entrenched in the hills, comparisons were immediately made with Dien Bien Phu, the site of the climactic French defeat in Vietnam in 1954.

General William Westmoreland, America's top soldier in Vietnam, gave two major reasons for the defense of Khe Sanh. The first was to provide a "killing ground" for NVA troops; the second, to prevent an NVA flank attack against Dong Ha and Quang Tri City to the east. In sum, Khe Sanh was the gateway to South Vietnam.

Initially, Gen. Westmoreland recommended that the Marines deploy a battalion to Khe Sanh but the Marines resisted. They argued that the base was too isolated to be supported adequately. According to Brigadier General Lowell English, then assistant commander of the Third Marine Division, "When you're at Khe Sanh, you're not really anywhere. You could lose it, and you really haven't lost a damn thing." "Westy," as he became known, stood firm and the Marines characteristically followed his orders. In early October 1966, the First Battalion of the Third Marine Regiment, "1/3" or "One Three," arrived at Khe Sanh, and the Army's Special Forces camp was relocated to Lang Vei, some seven miles away.

Khe Sanh became the best-known Vietnam battleground of all as Americans at home were treated to daily doses of its horror, both in the newspapers and on evening television news programs. It was there that a young Marine captain named Matt Caulfield received a literal baptism of fire.

I received an aforementioned letter from Matt, dated April 12, 1998, Easter Sunday, in which he wrote:

> I have read a lot of postmortems on Vietnam but nothing so
> comprehensive and personal. I happened to read it today.
> Easter Sunday. It was Easter Sunday 1968 when we finally

broke out of Khesanh by attacking Hill 881N. I planned the attack every day of the seventy-two day siege and it would have been my best day except that we lost three Marines. We came very close to pulling it off without any KIA's. [KIA means killed in action.] Your presentation reminded me of my most vivid memories of that day. Reports from an air observer of the enemy withdrawing from the backside of the hill, a faceless Kilo company Marine shinnying up the stump of a tree and affixing an American flag to it, reports that we had no serious casualties and then when it was almost over, the report that Mike Company had three KIA's. It still tears me up.

According to Michael Herr in his book *Dispatches*, "Khe Sanh's original value to the Americans might be gauged by the fact that in spite of the known infiltration all around it, we held it for years with nothing more than a Special Forces A Team; less than a dozen Americans and around 400 indigenous troops, Vietnamese and Montagnard." (The Montagnards, or mountain people, have been called America's most loyal allies in Vietnam. There are some eighteen Montagnard tribes in Vietnam, to whom the Vietnamese referred as *moi* or savages.)

Americans' biggest concern, as Herr has written, was that "Khe Sanh was vastly outnumbered and entirely surrounded; that, and the knowledge that all ground evacuation routes . . . were completely controlled by the NVA, and that the monsoons had at least six weeks more to run." Therefore, from the American standpoint, the key to defending Khe Sanh was overwhelming airpower.

Hard pressed on my right. My center is yielding. Impossible to maneuver. Situation excellent. I am attacking!

—Ferdinand Foch

According to Col. Alexander's account, "the NVA uncorked a tremendous bombardment of Khe Sanh Combat Base itself (just slightly northeast of Khe Sanh village), raking the compound with mortars, artillery and rockets." His account continues:

> One of the first enemy rounds set off the main ammo dump, causing a chain reaction of fire and explosions that would create havoc for the next forty-eight hours and blow up 90 percent of the Marines' supplies. Pallets of artillery rounds detonated at once, creating powerful shock waves. Clouds of tear gas swept the compound, as did deadly bursts of flêchettes, the tiny steel darts released from exploding Claymores and 106mm "Beehive" antipersonnel shells.

As an aside, one of my Marines, Corporal Dan Schiavietello, a strong young man who introduced me to the Beatles "white" album, managed to take a photograph of the spectacular ammo dump explosion, which he later had made into a Christmas card, thanks to Kodak's service. The greeting he chose to have printed on the card was, perversely, if not predictably, "Peace on Earth."

At one point the Joint Chiefs of Staff were convened by the president and forced to sign a statement "for the public reassurance," insisting that Khe Sanh could and would be held at all costs. In fact, General Westmoreland stated that the Tet Offensive was a smokescreen intended to distract Americans from the real target—Khe Sanh. Regardless, Hanoi had masterfully surprised both American and South Vietnamese forces with its huge offensive of January 30, 1968.

The relief of Khe Sanh commenced on April 1, 1968, the day before my first son, Charles III, now called Chas, was born. It was also the day after President Johnson went on national television to announce that he would neither seek nor accept the Democratic Party's nomination for the presidency, whose next occupant would be determined in the general election the following November when Richard M. Nixon beat Hubert H. Humphrey.

I might have served with Matt Caulfield and the other Marines at Khe Sanh had it not been for that fortuitous birth. I went to Vietnam at age twenty-three; Chas was then just two months old.

That was a "bummer," which, by the way, is a term that came out of the Vietnam era.

Code-named Operation Pegasus, relieving Khe Sanh included over 10,000 Marines and three full battalions of ARVN troops. Soon there was, in Herr's words, "a forward operational base that looked better than most permanent installations in I Corps, complete with a thousand-meter airstrip and deep, ventilated bunkers. They named it LZ Stud and once it was finished Khe Sanh ceased to be the center of its own sector; it became just another objective."

According to *The Vietnam Experience: Nineteen Sixty Eight*, "the men at Khe Sanh endured a sustained attack that ceased to be an event with cause, beginning, and foreseeable end but became a condition of life to which the only alternative was death." Moreover,

> They never got a glimpse of the Big Picture. They were only small pictures, moments of fire, pain and sudden death. Only those who were there can really know what it was like.
>
> Nearly 500 Marines died defending Khe Sanh and perhaps 10,000 North Vietnamese soldiers assaulting the place were killed or wounded . . . Once the fighting was over, the dead of both sides buried, and the wounded removed to where they might be healed, Khe Sanh had no attraction for either side. Gen. Westmoreland ordered the base dismantled.

The siege "officially" ended on April 5 [th] but the shooting and dying went on into early summer when the base was closed on July 5 [th]. I went to Khe Sanh later that year and found it a wasteland.

Although a reported 103,000 tons of bombs were dropped on the enemy during the siege, who actually won what at Khe Sanh remained obscure, for both sides had claimed it as a victory.

Since then, however, former North Vietnamese Army colonel

Bui Tin has offered a different view. Having served on the NVA general staff and received the unconditional surrender of South Vietnam on April 30, 1975, Mr. Tin confirmed an American Tet 1968 military victory. In *Following Ho Chi Minh: Memoirs of a North Vietnamese Colonel*, he wrote that "Our losses were staggering and a complete surprise. [Tin's long-time mentor and the hero of the Battle of Dien Bien Phu, General Vo Nguyen] Giap later told me that Tet had been a military defeat, though we had gained the planned political advantages when Johnson agreed to negotiate and did not run for reelection." He continued:

> The second and third waves in May and September were, in retrospect, mistakes. Our forces in the South were nearly wiped out by all the fighting in 1968. It took us until 1971 to reestablish our presence but we had to use North Vietnamese troops as local guerrillas. If the American forces had not begun to withdraw under Nixon in 1969, they could have punished us severely.
> We suffered badly in 1969 and 1970 as it was.

With respect to strategy, Tin concluded that "If Johnson had granted Westmoreland's requests to enter Laos and block the Ho Chi Minh trail, Hanoi could not have won the war."

⬙

In addition to taking himself out of the presidential race, President Johnson replaced General Westmoreland with his deputy, General Creighton Abrams, and announced the start of peace talks with North Vietnam. On June 10, 1968, Mame's and my first wedding anniversary, "Westy" held a news conference in Saigon at ComUSMACV (Commander, United States Military Assistance Command, Vietnam).

A reporter asked him a final question: "General, can the war be won militarily?"

"Not in a classic sense, because"—the general paused briefly—
"of our national policy of not expanding the war."

Defense Secretary Robert McNamara also resigned. Thus, Tet
and Khe Sanh had combined to unhinge some of the major
American players in the conduct of the war; they had also succeeded
in turning public opinion in the U.S. against it.

There was irony in all this as well, for the only major American
combat base *not* attacked during the Tet Offensive was Khe Sanh.

These events set the stage for my time in-country. They spawned
at least two specific positive outcomes, of which I, along with
countless others, would be a beneficiary. First, the worst fighting
of the Vietnam War was over. Second, Dong Ha and Quang Tri
were more secure than before Tet and Khe Sanh. In terms of relative
extrema, and as one about to pay an extended visit to Quang Tri
Province, I considered myself at least twice blessed.

> *To be sure, Khe Sanh will be a subject of controversy for a*
> *long time, but this much about it is indisputable: It has won*
> *a large place in the history of the Vietnam war as an inspiring*
> *example of American and Allied valor. One day, in fact, the*
> *victory over the siege may be judged a decisive turning*
> *point that finally convinced the enemy he could not win.*

> —*Washington Star*, June 9, 1968

10

LEAVING HOME:

THE PARTY'S OVER

Be strong and of good courage. Do not fear, for the Lord your
God goes with you. He will not leave you or forsake you.

—Deuteronomy 31:6

Nestled on the south shore of eastern Long Island, New York, Westhampton has always been in my blood. Indeed, my mother took me there for the first time when I was two months old, and I make my home there today. My maternal grandparents first frequented the area in 1928 when my Mom was only six. The ocean beaches there are among the most beautiful on earth, and it retains many of its rural qualities, despite substantial development in the post-World War II era. As young children, my brother and I, and also our four younger sisters in pairs, would spend a fortnight with Mimi and Poppa in their cottage at Cedar Beach on shimmering Moriches Bay, part of Great South Bay.

In June 1968 Mame and I took our infant son Chas to Cedar Beach for a few days of vacation before I shoved off for Vietnam. All those wonderful, golden days I had spent there during my then twenty-three years flooded my mind. Fishing and crabbing with my brother Mike, the salt air, the musty scent of the cottage, its coziness, Poppa's *Chuck* boat, the main house where we took our meals—these familiar sensual experiences and physical structures had always been revisited and renewed each year and gave me a generous measure of joy.

With now only Vietnam ahead of me, I wanted to block it and everything else out of my mind, except my beautiful bride, our baby boy and the old-new wonder of Westhampton. I remember only the love I felt and would miss in the as yet unknowable year ahead.

Although the weather was very cool, too cool for the beach, I am sure we found plenty to occupy ourselves; after all, Mame's fertile mind and imagination have never failed in the realm of good ideas. Nonetheless, my memory retains little about those precious days other than my strong desire to remain right there at the little cottage on the bay.

So many significant and, for that matter, insignificant dates are etched in my memory that some people occasionally call me "Rain Man," after the character played by actor Dustin Hoffman in the title role in the film of the same name. Why, then, I do not recall with certainty the date on which I left home for Vietnam, I am at a loss to say. Suffice it to say that it was on or about June 27, 1968.

My orders indicated that I would travel to Norton Air Force Base in San Bernardino, California, "FFT," that is, "for further transfer," to "WestPac Ground Forces." WestPac was a contraction for "Western Pacific" but invariably meant Vietnam, at least at that time.

My journey began at my parents' home in GC. My sister Peggy, then 16, was seated in the living room recliner holding my son Chas, not yet three months of age.

I had no wish to leave but I was as ready to go as I was going to be. Mame and my parents were readying themselves to take me to New York's John F. Kennedy International Airport, about a twenty-minute drive. There I would meet my flight to the West Coast FFT.

The moment had arrived. I walked over to Peggy and the baby, each still comfortable in the big recliner. I kissed her goodbye. When I kissed Chas, I said, "Goodbye, little fella." Well, Peggy, Mom and Mame all began to wail. It was awful. Then I recall Dad saying, "Let's get the hell outta here" but his voice somehow lacked its usual "Now hear this" fanfare.

The ride to JFK was understandably unenjoyable. Dad was driving, and Mom sat next to him in the front seat. Mame and I sat behind them. There was little conversation. The ladies were choking back tears; Dad was characteristically silent, as he had long since relied on the women to do the talking in many social situations. I was hurting but would be damned before I would let on.

Having arrived at the airport, I said goodbye to my folks, and Mame accompanied me to the plane. As there were no security checkpoints in those days, we strolled slowly and directly to the door of the aircraft. There we hugged and kissed, maybe thrice. She was tearful, and I was dying inside. I had to get on that plane, sooner or later, never mind having no remote wish to do so.

We left the comfort of each other's arms, and I turned away and boarded my flight. As much as I wanted to take in the sight of her beautiful face once more, I knew I dare not turn around. I made up my mind that I would walk, face and eyes rigidly forward, straight to my assigned seat on the port side near the front of the plane. Had I looked back, my own tears would surely have flowed. As it was, I sat down, closed my eyes and composed myself. After all, a man goes to war by himself.

As Bob Lund used to say when daunting responsibilities presented themselves, "The party's over."

Once more the pessimist, although I never breathed a word of it to Mame or anyone else, I did not believe I would come home from Vietnam alive. In truth, this pessimist actually thought he would never see his beautiful bride, his son or his homeland again. It was scary.

With greater resolve than ever before, despite my unprecedented and possibly unhealthy state of mind, I told myself it was time to get serious.

The party was over.

Au revoir, mon amour.

At Norton Air Force Base, together with scores of other young servicemen, I boarded a Continental Airlines flight bound for Hawaii. In those days, there were so many military people, virtually all male, being sent to WestPac that the government through the Military Airlift Command contracted with civilian domestic air carriers to transport the troops. Although I hadn't flown commercially more than a few times at that point in my life, it soon became clear that Continental's comforts were far superior to Uncle Sam's.

First stop was Henderson Field, now Henderson Air Force Base, in Hawaii to refuel for the remainder of the flight across the Pacific. I do not recall disembarking; we gassed up and took off again.

Next stop was Okinawa, where Marines had once landed— unopposed at first—and later fought one of World War II's bloodiest battles, which lasted more than seven weeks. Marine Private First Class Eugene B. Sledge, a veteran of the Battle of Okinawa, has written: "You never knew when you were drawing your last breath. You lived in total uncertainty, on the brink of the abyss, day after day. The only thing that kept you going was you just felt you had to live up to the demands of your buddies who were depending on you." Sledge died last year, a victim of cancer.

It was the middle of the night when we arrived on "Oki," also known as "The Rock." We were all tired, some possibly confused. Many of us had never made such a long journey in our lives. Today my mind still etches an image of Okinawa as a desolate, awful place. However, when the sun came up a few hours later, I could see that it was not as bad as I had imagined. Then again, the worst was still ahead for most of us, namely, Vietnam. We Marines were bussed to Camp Hansen, the Corps' main installation on the island. There we trained with the M-16 rifle, some of us for the first time, and were processed FFT to our next duty stations.

One of the bonuses of being on Okinawa then was that my "best buddy" Jim Norwood was stationed there as a Navy communications specialist. We managed to share a meal, and he introduced me to some of his friends. The next day we went to the beach and had a few beers. I would return to Okinawa in October but Jim would by then have finished his stint in the Navy and gone back home to Long Island. Not finding him still there was disappointing since I had hoped to spend more time with him. Nonetheless, I took satisfaction in knowing that he was better off where he was.

On the morning of the next day, the welcome respite ended when I boarded yet another Continental Airlines flight that would take me to Danang, South Vietnam. I would be in-country at last. *Sayonara.*

> *When the cigarette was gone he felt his face go slack. He dug his nails into his neck, but the pain was not enough. The days were too long, the nights too short between, and a few moments of sleep seemed all that mattered in this world. He checked his watch and realized he was not going to make it.*

—Billy Roark in *CW2* by Layne Heath

11

ARRIVING IN-COUNTRY

This is first a political war, second a psychological war,
and third a military war.

—Lt. Gen. Lewis F. Walt, USMC

Aboard the Continental flight from Okinawa to Danang,
all, except members of the crew, were Marines. Home of
the First Marine Air Wing in-country, Danang was a
sprawling American base in the northern part of South Vietnam.

We arrived in darkness on the evening of July 8, 1968. In my
mind's eye, I can still see most of us milling about, waiting to be
assigned a rack and, darkly, for the first "incoming" (artillery round,
mortar fire or rocket). For most of us it was our first night in
Vietnam.

On the next day, a Marine Corps C-130 *Hercules* transport
flew a group of us north to Quang Tri where I officially joined the
Third Marine Division's Headquarters Battalion, which was
abbreviated 3d MarDiv HqBn. From there I would travel about
five miles north to Dong Ha, which Joe Moosbrugger, a fellow
Chaminade alumnus and a Marine Grumman A-6 *Intruder* attack-
jet bombardier-navigator, later dubbed Dung Heap. Dong Ha
would be my duty station for most of the ensuing year.

Quang Tri is the northernmost province in what was then South
Vietnam. It was a Tactical Area of Responsibility (TAOR) in what
was designated I Corps Tactical Zone (ICTZ), and it included
Quang Tri, Khe Sanh, Dong Ha and other perhaps lesser known

outposts. The "I" was actually the Roman numeral for the number one, but this ICTZ was simply called I Corps, which was pronounced *eye core* by the Marines and others stationed there. Some in other services suggested that those of us in the Corps didn't know the difference between the capital letter and the Roman numeral. This is, of course, untrue.

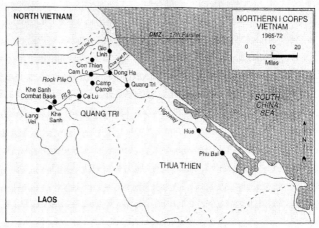

Source: *The Battle History of the U.S. Marines* by Col. Joseph H. Alexander, USMC (Ret.). Map drawn by Mary Craddock Hoffman.

Dong Ha sits about five miles south of the demilitarized zone (DMZ) and was the last major American military installation before North Vietnam. Thus, it was equidistant between Quang Tri City and the "Z". Officially, my "Combat History" would include "Counter-Insurgency Operations" from this day until May 21, 1969; also from this day I would be a participant in "Operation KENTUCKY" until February 28, 1969; and, finally, I would participate in "Defense of Dong Ha Combat Base" from March 1 to May 21, 1969.

Operation Kentucky was a long-term area operation in the vicinity of Con Thien, about five miles northwest of Dong Ha. It kicked off on November 1, 1967 and formally ended on February 28, 1969. During this period, 478 Marines were killed and 2,698 wounded. Enemy casualties were 3,304 killed, and we took sixty-four prisoners. Earlier, Kentucky had been described as a Ninth Marines operation in the vicinity of "Leatherneck Square," which was formed by Gio Linh, Con Thien, Dong Ha and Cam Lo. Actually, the "Square" was an irregular quadrilateral with Dong Ha at the southeast corner, Gio Linh about five miles to the north, Con Thien several miles southwest of Gio Linh, and Cam Lo just a few miles slightly southwest of Con Thien. My responsibilities took me frequently to Con Thien and Cam Lo but I can't recall specifically having been to Gio Linh.

As it appears nowhere else in this essay, the term "Leatherneck," the Marines' oldest and most colorful nickname, deserves comment. The name derives from the characteristic black leather stock worn around the necks of all enlisted Marines, as well as many officers, during the Corps' first century. The device reportedly improved posture on parade, and protected the throat in battle.

Upon arrival at the Dong Ha Combat Base, I met with Colonel Woods, USMC, a "full bird" (a reference to his rank's silver eagle insignia), who offered me an Orange Crush, which I accepted and enjoyed. He told me that several buddies of mine had just arrived the preceding day, among them Merv Benson, Owen Chambers, both first lieutenants, and others whose names now regrettably escape me. At the time, they were leading rifle platoons or companies inasmuch as, the colonel volunteered, there weren't any captains left; they'd all been killed or wounded. Suffice it to say that this was neither appealing information nor a morale booster. To be sure, Marine rifle platoon commanders in Vietnam had a short life expectancy.

Col. Woods did a thorough job of interviewing me and took particular note that I had a young wife and a then three-month old son. He allowed as he could have me "out in the bush" that evening, or, alternatively, we could have a beer and some chow together in the officers' and NCOs' (non-commissioned officers') mess hall at the Dong Ha Combat Base. Despite the quasi-civilized ring to his invitation, if it was one, I felt a strong urge to say, "Colonel, send me out tonight," for I was trained as a "grunt" or infantryman, as are all Marines, each of us "a rifleman first." I also wanted to get what I regarded as inevitable over with.

The colonel also informed me that there was an opening in the Communications Company, of which Major Fred Reisinger, a Fordham University alumnus, was the commanding officer (CO). The major's executive officer (XO) was Captain Keith Carlson, a really cool guy.

At the completion of his Vietnam tour of duty, by which time he had been promoted to lieutenant colonel, Reisinger was succeeded by Major Frank Mullin, a fellow Holy Cross alumnus. Reisinger gave me my only "Fitness Report" in Vietnam. When I failed to be promoted to captain along with my "peers" shortly after he left Dong Ha, I inquired as to why and learned that Lt. Col. Reisinger had inadvertently neglected to file my fitness report on a timely basis with Headquarters Battalion. My promotion was delayed but came through very soon afterward.

Keith Carlson was eventually replaced by a spit-and-polish, by-the-book captain whose first name was Marty. Perhaps I have unconsciously blocked out his surname but he was undoubtedly the biggest misfit I ever met in the Corps. When Marines are trying to get a tough, dirty and typically dangerous job done under often thoroughly adverse conditions, they don't want or need to be nagged by a guy who is constantly insisting that they shine their boots. Alas, Marty was that guy.

For better or worse, thanks to Col. Woods, I opted for beer and food. Thus, my second night in country was spent with not only him but also a couple of old friends: 1st Lt. John Wegl, with whom I attended OCS in 1965 and TBS in the summer and fall of 1966, and 1st Lt. Jerry Miller, who was a classmate at the Marine Corps Communications School in Quantico in early 1968.

Alea iacta est. (The die is cast.)

—Julius Caesar, as he crossed the Rubicon River

12

DONG HA (1968–1969)

I'm skimming across the surface of my own history...

—Tim O'Brien in *The Things They Carried*

John Wegl was my roommate that second night in-country, in a bombed out cantonment building constructed by the French, who had once colonized Vietnam. The building had a corrugated steel roof perforated by so many shrapnel holes that huge old brown mess tents had to be placed on them and secured by sandbags in order to keep out the rain.

I slept on a military-issue cot that first night in Dong Ha, with no linens of course, although that didn't bother me. What did prove a nuisance, however, was not having mosquito netting. I got little sleep, no thanks to frequent outgoing artillery volleys and the infernal mosquitoes, which by morning had produced on my body some sixty-one bloody welts, by John Wegl's count.

"This place is the pits," I thought, but then I acknowledged gratefully in my own mind that I had lived another day, and in comparative comfort to boot. While Dong Ha was hardly a garden spot, I was not "out in the bush," at least not yet.

On the third day I reported to Communications Company's Radio Relay Platoon as assistant platoon commander under a salty first lieutenant by the name of Bob Dusek, who was getting short. His platoon sergeant was Staff Sergeant Larry Slaugh, a hard-drinking, rough sort of man who at times could be uncooperative. To his credit, though, Sgt. Slaugh is the only man up to that time to beat me in an arm-wrestling contest. (I also lost a match to Chas many years later.)

I would later serve a short stint as Radio Platoon commander, also based in Dong Ha, and be reassigned to Radio Relay as platoon commander upon Bob Dusek's return to The World.

Dusek, for his part, was a chain-smoker who also drank heavily, probably just because of where he was stationed at the time. He had a slightly goofy aspect to his demeanor, as well as a twitch that caused him to close his eyes momentarily but longer than a couple of blinks, as if he were trying hard to avoid a stutter. A mustang (an enlisted Marine who later accepted an officer's commission), he was a solid Marine and a good guy to work with. But what I'll never forget is that he carried in his utility cap what he said was a nude photograph of his wife. Happily, he did not show it to me. Perhaps it didn't exist.

This reminds me of another nude-photo story from those days. Indeed, here we're talking the mother lode of nude photographs. The sister of one of the men in our company then worked for a photo development company back in The World. In those days, as it was told to me, it was the policy of most photo developers that any indecent photographs be culled from the others after printing, and destroyed.

Well, apparently our fellow Marine's sister thought it would do her brother and his buddies a great deal of good if she were to forgo destroying the evidence, and send regular batches of hundreds of these photos to the sex-starved boys in Dong Ha. In the last analysis, however, of the pictures I saw, none were what one might call centerfold or, in World War II parlance, pin-up quality. Indeed, these young women so willing to bare all, and be photographed that way, were, in a word, beasts.

Shortly after I arrived in Dong Ha, the enemy had succeeded in getting its attack forces within striking distance of Danang, its main target in I Corps. In fact, August 18th, 1968 is the date used to mark the beginning of North Vietnam's "Third Offensive" of that year. It was a familiar pattern, with mortar and rocket attacks against district and provincial headquarters and military installations. In addition, Viet Cong sappers (enemy commandos with satchel charges of explosives and the like) were employed, including an attempt against Dong Ha that was foiled. The ARVN had intercepted the NVA but the VC were already inside Danang's gates.

Quang Tri Province, especially along the DMZ including Dong Ha, was almost quiet during August. On the 19th, 2/1 (2nd Battalion, 1st Marine Regiment) made a raid into the Z following intensive B-52 strikes, which were known as "Arc Lights" or "Rolling Thunder." There was also fighting the same day approximately three miles south of Con Thien. Concurrently, two companies of the Ninth Marines got into a battle that went on for three days.

Dong Ha was well within range of North Vietnamese artillery. Every evening around six, like clockwork, the shelling would begin. (One might think the NVA would have learned something about the element of surprise.) Having grown accustomed to this shabby treatment, we would already be in bunkers, usually with cans of warm beer in hand, that is, if we could get any. Attentive, to say the least, we could hear the "pop" of the enemy guns about five miles away, and then would count the ten seconds or so before the incoming artillery round impacted. If we heard the impact, at least we knew we hadn't taken a direct hit. Immediately we would toast the enemy's ineptness at missing us yet again.

In September, 3/1 (3rd Battalion, 1st Marine Regiment) was already in Danang on what one Marine has called "old, familiar, dangerous ground," where the battalion had worked in 1966 and 1967.

Thanks to Operation Houston just north of Danang, Highway One, the main north-south road, was kept open and traffic was moving mostly freely between Danang and Hue to its north.

South of Danang the Seventh Marine Regiment continued its operations. In an action on September 20th, an NVA battalion was caught "in a box" by 2/7, 3/7 and other units. Thus trapped in a killing zone, the Communists lost 101 soldiers.

There were other scattered actions also in late September.

In this same time frame, I received a surprise visit in Dong Ha from Marine 1st Lt. C. Craig Mannschreck, a helicopter pilot and friend. I first met Craig (the C. stands for Charles) at TBS in Quantico where he and I were roommates for twenty-one weeks, the length of the program. A native of St. Joseph, Missouri, he was perhaps the most easy-going and clean-cut young man I had ever met. We became fast friends, despite the differences in our backgrounds. Although I don't see him much any more, he sent me a heartwarming and funny letter dated March 6, 1995 in connection with my upcoming fiftieth birthday. Here are excerpts:

> I remember that I was in mourning on 6 November 1994 when I turned 50. I imagine you look great, although without a doubt, I am certain you don't look any prettier. It sounds like your whole family is doing well while putting up with you for all these years. Even though I haven't seen "ya'll" for quite some time, it seems like the proverbial "just yesterday" since I first set eyes on this hulk from the big city. I admittedly was apprehensive about rooming with a New Yorker who was rather quiet, at least initially. As I have told literally hundreds of people, this fellow from New York turned out to be one of the most sincere, caring, and truly good people that I have met in my entire life. A real friend!!

Craig is one of finest men I have had the privilege of knowing. I hope to see him again before long.

Meanwhile, the Third Marine Division was preempting an offensive across the Z by the rejuvenated 320th NVA Division. A "two-pronged spoiling attack" was launched from the Rockpile, about twelve miles west of Dong Ha. Col. Robert H. Barrow's Ninth and Col. Richard L. Michael, Jr.'s Third Marine Regiments secured, respectively, the Nui Tia Pong ridge, five miles west of the Rockpile, and then Mutter's Ridge, three miles to its north. (Col. Barrow later rose to become the twenty-seventh commandant of the Marine Corps, in which capacity he served from July 1, 1979 to June 30, 1983.)

These successes set the stage for a "sweep" by Task Force Hotel under Brig. Gen. William C. Chip between Mutter's Ridge and the Ben Hai River, which flows through the DMZ. This five-battalion effort reportedly yielded over 500 weapons, nearly 5,000 land mines, 20,000 mortar rounds, thirteen tons of explosives and 250,000 rounds of small-arms ammunition. The 320th NVA Division's planned offensive had been totally gutted.

To the Marines' delight, the battleship USS *New Jersey* (BB-62), with its nine 16" "rifles" and 25" guns, arrived on station off the Z on September 29th. The big guns had a 24-mile range. The ship's 2,700-pound armor-piercing and 1,900-pound high-capacity 16" projectiles were eight times the weight of the eight-inch shells fired by heavy cruisers. On the following day twenty-nine 16" and 116 five-inch shells were reportedly delivered on eight targets north of the Z.

October, in general, proved to be a quiet month along the DMZ, probably due to September's successes on the ground, and the *New Jersey*'s arrival offshore. The Fourth and Ninth Marines had almost no contact with the enemy. Indeed, the northeast monsoon hindered the conduct of operations throughout I Corps. On October 14th and 15th, twelve inches of rain fell on Dong Ha, ten on Danang. Talk about relative extrema, I have still never seen rain like that anywhere else in my life.

Then, on Halloween 1968, we got the news that President Johnson had announced a halt to his then three-year-old bombing campaign against North Vietnam, effective November 1st. Consequently, the daily artillery barrages against Dong Ha ceased, and there were thereafter only limited incidents of incoming until May 11, 1969 when all hell broke loose again with a dreadful and spectacular night rocket attack on Dong Ha.

It was said that the intensity of ground combat in the second half of 1968 was about half of what it was in the first half. Accordingly, I have to believe that I was fortunate to have arrived at the beginning of the second half of that year. Nonetheless, taken together, the "Free World Military Forces" in I Corps that year had killed over 100,000 of the enemy and captured nearly 35,000 weapons.

⧗

There was no luxury in Dong Ha (hence its alias Dung Heap) and more than enough surprises.

Showers were crude and cold. Since the temperature was usually warm, the shower was almost refreshing, except for the invariably dirty water we used to wash ourselves. Shaving was arguably worse because cold water just didn't cut it, at least with my beard.

One morning I was awakened by what I thought was a bomb exploding. I was wrong. The crashing sound that caused me to roll instantly off my rack and onto the concrete floor in search of cover was merely that of lightning striking the corrugated steel roof of our hootch (barracks). To say it startled me is an understatement; it was the loudest noise I have ever heard.

Early on another morning in Dung Heap, with the weather much more agreeable, I suddenly awoke to the sight of a foot-long lizard lying on my chest, ostensibly looking me right in the eye. The feeling of the reptile on my bare skin grossed me out but it was fleeting, for I have never moved so quickly in my life. Bolting swiftly upright, I pushed the lizard off me onto the floor. Next, seemingly instinctively, I grabbed one of my boots and hurled it at the animal, which was then about four feet from the door. The heel of the boot struck the critter hard where its tail meets the rest of its body, and severed its tail. Now, the tail was about half the length of the whole animal, thus about six inches. What happened next was amazing and, to some perhaps, disgusting: The lizard ran under the door and out of the room, its tail visibly unconnected from its body. Then, in an incredible and ghastly sight, the severed tail quickly slithered under the door ostensibly following its owner!

Later, somebody told me that the 'flight' nerve impulse had already been transmitted by the lizard's tiny brain to its tail; thus, the tail was simply following orders.

Since I am on the subjects of impulses and tails, I learned in my freshman-year biology class at Chaminade that an amoeba is "a microscopic, one-celled animal found in stagnant water or as a parasite in other animals." Suffice it to say that many amoebae lived in and around Dung Heap, and at least one took up residence inside me. I learned the hard way that some of these microörganisms cause dysentery, which my dictionary defines as "any of various intestinal diseases characterized by inflammation, abdominal pain, toxemia, and diarrhea with bloody, mucous feces." I was afflicted with amoebic dysentery for about six weeks. That written, I wish neither to recount the episode further, nor to relive it.

⧗

In the autumn of 1968 there was scuttlebutt (rumor) that the number of American troops in-country would be cut, and many sent home. Of course this was soothing to most Marines, irrespective of how much of their Vietnam tours of duty they had served.

One significant aspect of troop reduction was embarkation, not only of troops themselves but also of vehicles and other equipment. Just as such instruments of a military campaign were brought into a theater of operations by air or sea, they would have to be taken out in planes or ships.

I was blessed again by being selected as my company's embarkation officer, which meant I would have to fly to Okinawa to attend Embarkation School, a three-week course. I felt I had won an all-expenses-paid vacation out of Vietnam. I couldn't believe it.

While on Oki, I saw a young woman named Claire Santoro from Huntington, New York, whom I had first met in August 1960 when she and I traveled together on a bus from Rockville Centre, Long Island, to Notre Dame University in South Bend, Indiana. She and I were our high schools' representatives to the national convention of the Catholic Students Mission Crusade.

Now she was teaching at the air base at, if memory serves, Naha, Okinawa. Also on that interminable bus ride was John Burke from Manhasset, Long Island, who graduated from Holy Cross in 1965, served as a Marine helicopter pilot in Vietnam and was killed in action there.

My educational excursion to Okinawa reminds me of some of the good times we had at the officers club at the Kadena Air Force base, the official name of which was Kadena Air Base Open Officers' Mess, or KABOOM, for short. Back in Vietnam, the acronym for the Danang Open Officers' Mess was, yes, DOOM.

While on Okinawa I had the opportunity to introduce Claire to Joe Moosbrugger, the same officer who gave "Dung Heap" its unforgettable and appropriate nickname. I am happy to report that the couple later married and I served as an usher in their wedding party. On Oki, Claire had a friend, a teaching colleague, by the name of Barbara Rounds, or "Roundsie," as we called her.

At "embark school," I met a Marine lieutenant named John Benda, a grunt (infantry platoon leader) who served with 1/9 (a.k.a. Walking Dead) and was also a classmate at the school. "Of all the hard luck outfits in Vietnam," Michael Herr has written, 1/9 "was said to be the most doomed, doomed in its Search-and-Destroy days before Khe Sanh, known for a history of ambush and confusion and for a casualty rate which was the highest of any outfit in the entire war."

John and I became good friends in the short time we spent together. I tried to locate him when I returned to The World but to no avail. Happily, his name does *not* appear among those of the missing or killed in action chiseled into "The Wall," the Vietnam Veterans Memorial, in Washington, D.C.

November 10th is the anniversary of the founding of the U.S. Marine Corps in Philadelphia's Tun Tavern on that date in 1775. Without fail, and no matter the circumstances in which they may find themselves, Marines around the globe observe "Marine Corps Birthday" religiously. Celebrations range from the elegant to the plebeian, with the eldest and youngest Marines toasting the Corps and each other.

In 1968, students at the Marines' Embarkation School were

invited to join all other Okinawa-based Marines on November 10th for a gala hosted by a full-bird colonel. Benda and I invited Barbara and Claire, respectively, for what we expected would be a lovely occasion. And indeed it was, but for one minor glitch.

Part of the protocol at a Marine Corps Birthday ball such as this one was the reading of the commandant's message by the commanding officer of the base. During the reading, all Marines in attendance are required to stand at attention, and spouses and civilian guests are expected also to be on their feet for the moment.

Now, a bottle of champagne had been delivered to our table just moments before we were called to attention. As we all listened intently to the words of our esteemed commandant, General Leonard F. Chapman, Jr., rendered by our capable CO, the otherwise pin-drop silence pervading us hundreds of Marines and our guests was shattered by the seemingly deafening sound of the cork exploding from our champagne bottle, precisely at the crescendo of the commandant's message.

Incredibly, the cork's trajectory took it nearly thirty feet and caused it to bounce once, roll and come to rest at last at the colonel's feet. Despite the furtive and ostensibly irate glance he cast in our general direction, the colonel, as lector, completed his reading to the enthusiastic applause of all present. For John Benda and me, as well as Claire, Roundsie and others who witnessed the unintended and untimely cork launch, stifling our laughter was at least as challenging as it was once upon a time for other Marines at one of Wild Bill Surette's rifle inspections.

I am happy to report that the colonel proved a good sport, as there was no inquisition following the embarrassing and awkward moment during his presentation. A lesser man might have had no tolerance for what was, after all, an accident.

During the fall and early winter of 1968–69, American forces throughout Vietnam braced for what some intelligence reports predicted would be a repeat of Tet '68. Now that things had been relatively quiet since President Johnson had ceased bombing the North, this information gave us in Dung Heap tremendous incentive to construct a bunker that would withstand a direct hit by an artillery shell, a rocket or a mortar round. Starting, I would say, in November '68, just after my return from embark school, our officer group decided to build what came to be known as "Super Bunker."

The basic construction material consisted of ordinary sandbags. The ordinary became extraordinary, given the thickness of the stout walls created by a vast multitude of almost certainly a few thousand sandbags. Likewise, pieces of Marston matting (pierced steel planking) were employed. The principal use of this material was to provide an inexpensive but dependable form of steel-surfaced runway that was rapidly deployable. First tested in 1941 in Marston, North Carolina, it was used in World War II to surface forward airfields on soft ground that enabled speedy construction of airfields for early defense fighters, interdiction bombers and close air support of ground Marines. In Dong Ha, some twenty-seven years later we used Marston matting as the 'bread' in protective 'sandwiches' that contained many layers of sandbags.

By the time Super Bunker was completed in early January of '69, its walls were approximately four feet thick. But the real marvel was the roof: A giant hero sandwich of Marston matting and sandbags, it was fully six feet thick.

My only Christmas Day in Vietnam was that of 1968. It was a sad time, for just five days earlier I had received a telephone call from Joe Moosbrugger in Danang, who gave me the tragic news that my Holy Cross classmate and friend Dick Morin, a McDonnell Douglas Marine F-4 *Phantom* radar intercept operator (RIO), had been shot down during a bombing run. Officially, Dick was listed as missing in action (MIA) but his wingman reported first seeing "secondary explosions" from the target but then realized that the "fireball" he witnessed was from the impact of Dick's aircraft in the target area.

In retrospect, I was probably the last of our group of Holy Cross Marines to see Dick alive. As things turned out, he happened to fly to Okinawa in October during my time at Embarkation School. We met at the Officer's Club *Oktoberfest* and enjoyed a few beers and a meal together. On our return to the bachelor officers' quarters (BOQ) following what became an evening of revelry with other Marines, Dick and I, well served to be sure, decided to take a shortcut to our building, which was situated at the base of a hill. Overlooking the BOQ from about a hundred feet above it, we started to walk, then run, shortly after which we lost control of ourselves, fell and rolled the rest of the way down. We made good time, of course, but our uniforms were badly soiled. Dick is survived by his wife Jean, a Marymount classmate of Mame, and a daughter. *Requiescat in pace.*

I was blessed to be able to spend a quiet Christmas Eve with my friends 1st Lt. Bill Raabe, who hailed from Oakland, California, and Master Sgt. Joe King, whose specialty was a touching rendition of *The Irish Soldier Boy*. We ate, drank and sang Christmas carols into the wee hours of Christmas morn. We also consoled each other, for, despite the strong Marine and Christian bonds among us, each of us knew painfully well where he would rather be.

Silent Night. Happily for us, it was.

One Marine in our company was very *un*happy, although few others knew. He had received a "Dear John" letter from his sweetheart back in The World. Such a communication can be devastating, especially in an environment in which one's morale may not always be otherwise on the upswing.

After evening chow, according to his hootchmates, he smoked some marijuana, a chronic problem among the troops in Vietnam. Not long after he hit the rack (went to bed) he put the muzzle of his M-16 in his mouth and blew his brains out.

That poor wasted Marine may have actually done my children some good, for I used his tragic example as a scare-tactic with my kids in our family discussions about the use of illicit drugs, including pot. After all, it was not difficult to understand: The

Marine smoked a joint, went to bed and shot himself. Was there a direct correlation between the use of marijuana and his suicide?

As their father, I led my 'colts' to water; only they could decide to drink or not.

They drank.

In January 1969 Mame and I met in Honolulu, Hawaii, for the six days of my R&R ("rest and recuperation"). She flew from New York to San Francisco, where she visited her Marymount College classmate Mary Kay Schabel, and then on to Honolulu. I traveled aboard a military transport south from Dong Ha to Danang where I caught yet another Continental Airlines flight to Honolulu. Our days there together were blissful but, alas, too few.

Shortly after I got back in-country, I wrote the following poem for her.

REFLECTIONS ON LEAVING YOU AND COMING HOME

The glimpse of your long-loved face
Watching in the Hawaiian night
Lingers.

My memory shivers in the cold
Of that inevitable separation.
But even now
I listen to the warmth of your silence.

In a moment then
The eagle was winging its way
To the dragon once more,
Ending the ecstasy of your tender presence.

Lost in new-old towns,
No one knows their names
Or ours
Or us
For we only know each other.

Loneliness again becomes our captor:
Common and uncompromising.
Him we share
(Tho' we be worlds apart)
And one thing more:
Love!

Nothing good happens fast—
I'll be home in May.
So dismiss the hundreds
That have passed
For now we see our day.

But still we wait.

Where is the order of the days
In which we live?
Sense and nonsense mingle,
And for the lucky ones alone,
Life is filled with mystical insights.

We have the business
Of our days attending
For scarce a hundred more.
So please don't winter in pain;
Button up your overcoat
When the wind is free
For you belong to me.

As for me, my love, my life was never
So precious to me as now—
Because of you.

To live, to care,
To give, to share; to love you:
This is my prayer

All the days of my life.

So until our day in May
Let us bend back the bow
In dreams as we may
To love's dream we shared
Yesterday.

In the spring of 1969 I had the good fortune of membership on a Marine Corps volleyball team that played others in I Corps. Like Embarkation School, it had the potential for getting Marines out of Vietnam, at least for a while. Winning the league competition would have placed us in a WestPac tournament to be played in Hawaii. Our team was victorious through the semi-finals but lost the big one. My teammates and I were presented individual trophies for our performance, and I still have mine.

Earlier in this chapter I referred to "limited incidents of incoming until May 11, 1969 when all hell broke loose again with a dreadful and spectacular night rocket attack on Dong Ha."

It was about three o'clock in the morning of Mother's Day when I was awakened by the sound of explosions all around. Whereas Dong Ha had been accustomed, at least during my time there, to artillery and mortar attacks, on this night, the rocket was the enemy's weapon of choice.

NVA rockets often proved to be errant missiles. They would come in with a ghastly whirring sound and then explode into what often were huge pieces of shrapnel that could easily decapitate or otherwise inflict horrific damage on humans and other targets. Unlike modern ordnance, these rockets had no guidance systems; nor could their firing or launch be easily plotted according to map coordinates, as could artillery's or mortars'.

At least one enemy rocket volley scored a direct hit on highly explosive and incendiary targets about 200 feet from my rack.

Situated there were several huge rubber bladders, each of which contained thousands of gallons of "AvGas," the fuel for the mostly transport aircraft that used Dong Ha's airstrip daily. Once ignited by the rockets, these leviathans, now lethal, erupted into skyscrapers of flame so intensely hot and bright that one could look at them for only the briefest of moments. The image seared in my memory is that of, in a word, hell. The intense heat, the convulsions of fire and the general pandemonium generated by the attack were truly fearsome. These were relative extrema of the worst sort.

All of us knew it was nighttime, and yet the shimmering flames of the towering inferno in our midst gave us the false impression that midday was upon us. Among some who were so suddenly awakened by the explosions were feelings of confusion and even otherworldliness, either long since forgotten or never before experienced.

"This is so weird, man," said one Marine.

I ran the short distance to Super Bunker and joined my fellow Marines who were already inside. Most were in their skivvies (undershorts), and all were studies in pain and misery. Having neglected to dress for the occasion, I was buck naked but nobody noticed or cared; nor did I.

Hell had ended, at least for a while. The attack was soon over, the Dong Ha perimeter was reconnoitered and reinforced, and we got an early start on what was now, in reality, a new day.

I love the smell of jet fuel in the morning.

—Marine Corps Aviation Bumper Sticker

13

CAPTAIN ROBERT ERIC LUND, USMC, A.K.A.
THE ROUND MAN

No matter what the mission, regardless of the weather or what
had happened yesterday, it was impossible to begin a day in a
Huey in low spirits.

—Layne Heath in *CW2*

One of the first things I was told when I checked into
Radio Relay platoon was that a Marine lieutenant with
"a big red mustache" had come by looking for me the
preceding day. This puzzled me because I knew no Marines, except
some I had just met since arriving in-country, who sported
mustaches, let alone a big red one.

I had to travel on one leg of this day trip from Landing Zone
(LZ) Stud (later renamed Vandegrift Combat Base after the World
War II Marine Corps commandant, the aforementioned Lieutenant
General Alexander Archer Vandegrift) up a nearby mountain,
known as Signal Hill, to deliver scrip currency to my men stationed
there. The most efficient way to do this was to wait until a
helicopter, commonly called a "chopper," came by, and simply
hitch a ride to the outpost up the mountain. To return, one simply
reversed the process.

As I climbed aboard the chopper that was to take me back
down the mountain, a UH1E (Huey) "slick" (as opposed to a
gunship), its rotor blades whooshing overhead, the copilot, seated

left-front, instructed me where to sit. Then he turned to his right to survey his passengers, and, despite the obscuring effects of his visor and helmet, I was able to catch a glimpse of his lower face. Some aspects of him were familiar and unmistakable, and his mouth was partially obscured—by a big red mustache.

It was Bob Lund, my classmate and close friend from Holy Cross. We had not only graduated together, we had accompanied each other through virtually every phase of our Marine Corps training. I grabbed his arm so that he would focus on me; we both laughed heartily, took off, returned to LZ Stud and got reacquainted briefly and quickly. Each of us learned that he was based near the other, with Bob's helicopter squadron, VMO-6, flying out of Quang Tri, just five miles down the road from Dong Ha. This proximity was to produce and witness many good and often raucous times. It was comforting to know he was nearby.

Within my first week I had to visit our various radio relay "shots," which were situated at outposts that stretched from the China Sea west roughly along the DMZ. My platoon's shots were located throughout Quang Tri Province at places with names like Cua Viet, Con Thien, Camp Carroll, LZ Stud, the Rockpile and Quang Tri.

Bob Lund came to be called "Round" or, more formally, "The Round Man"—affectionately, I hasten to add, and it had nothing to do with his size or shape. In the summer of 1966 in the Hawkins Room at TBS in Quantico, draft Budweisers were being consumed after a tough, hot day of training. At our table were Bob, Roger Hunt, Steve O'Neill, Frank Teague and myself, Holy Cross classmates all. As we were drinking "rounds," and it was now Bob's turn to buy one, I had intended to say "It's your round, Lund." What came out instead was "It's your Lund, Round." And the rest, as they say, is history. (Since this accidental conferring of a nickname on Bob, I have observed that, had he been a "grunt" instead of a Marine aviator, we could call him "The Ground Round.")

Bob's combat performances were impressive enough to earn him a host of decorations, including the Distinguished Flying Cross, two individual action air medals (the aviation equivalent of the Bronze Star), 28 air medals (each representing twenty strikes or sorties), the Navy and Marine Corps Achievement Medal with Combat "V", the Combat Action Ribbon, and the Vietnamese Cross of Gallantry, as well as various unit citations.

One of the extraordinary stories about Bob is that, while on a "sniffer" mission, his Huey, another slick, crashed in a high-angle-of-bank, low-altitude turn, which was being negotiated in order to avoid small arms fire. Unfortunately, the chopper impacted at a speed sufficient to separate the engine and fuel cell from the aircraft. Improbable as it was for those on board to survive a crash severe enough to separate the helicopter's rotor head and everything aft of the crew compartment, the mishap proved providential. This is because the aircraft's load of JP-4, a refined kerosene used by turbine-powered helicopters, may have otherwise exploded and made toast of Bob and the other Marines on board. As things turned out, Bob was able to extricate himself from the wreckage and help his fellow Marines, some of whom were injured, to safety. With an explosion possibly imminent, this was a heroic act.

That evening, following a celebration at which adult beverages were served, and I wish I had been present, 1st Lt. Lund managed to break his ankle. His fracture was so severe that he had to be medevac-ed (evacuated from the combat zone for medical treatment), first to a hospital ship and subsequently to an American military base on the island of Guam.

Parenthetically, this was surprising inasmuch as Bob and I, as college buddies, were "men of moderation" or would often describe ourselves as such—usually after having consumed more than a few beers. This led me many years later to e-mail him a definition of moderation especially suited to him and me: *The last refuge for the unimaginative*, which I had heard on the radio. (I learned upon subsequent research that it's a knock-off of Oscar Wilde's famous line, "Consistency is the last refuge of the unimaginative.")

It was during his stay on Guam that Bob's wife Patty visited him, and he got to spend several presumably pleasant months convalescing. He then returned to Vietnam with only eight months left to serve. Call it good fortune, call it being blessed; in the last analysis, as the great Jackie Gleason used to say, "How sweet it is!"

During our earlier training at the Naval Air Station in Pensacola, Florida, Bob and I lived in a four-bedroom ranch house for a period of time on Santa Rosa Island with our fellow Marines and Holy Cross classmates, Roger Hunt and Jim Stokes. Jim later moved out and John "Ace" Astle, now a Maryland state senator, moved in.

As the eldest of my parents' six children, I had developed at an early age some rudimentary culinary skills, nothing special, believe me. Accordingly, I agreed to do the cooking, provided I was accompanied each week by one of my housemates to the base commissary to select the food and groceries, the cost of which we all shared. I would serve as chef; the other three would be responsible for clean-up after our meals. In this connection, some twenty-eight years later, at my fiftieth birthday party, Bob eloquently expressed friendship and warm wishes but still managed to refer to this period "as the only testy time in our relationship."

"You see," said he, "Chuck and I had a fundamental philosophical difference as to whether you wash dishes before or after you eat from them!"

It brought the house down.

In 1999 I read a book entitled *The Right Kind of War* by John "Moe" McCormick who served with the Marines' Fourth Raider Battalion in the Pacific from 1942 to 1945. In Moe's wonderful work were some words he wrote for a fellow Marine. I included the same passage in a letter of tribute to Bob in January 2000.

I had then known him for more than thirty-seven years and had finally found language that I thought aptly described both him and my relationship with him: from its humble beginning at Holy Cross in 1962; through our Marine Corps training and service, including Vietnam tours of duty; in our marriages, both begun within a week of each other in June 1967; in the births of our first children on the same April 2nd the following year; and now, after myriad martinis, on the threshold of the Third Millennium. In my letter, using Moe's words, I described Bob as:

A CHARACTER WHO WOULD BE MY CLOSE FRIEND, DAILY ANTAGONIST, CYNICAL ADVISER, AND FREQUENT ALLY IN UNMILITARY ANTICS

No epitaph, Moe's words, now a gift to my friend Bob, are of life well lived, of humor and warmth, of admiration and affection, of friendship and fun. Indeed, when I first read these mere eighteen words, I thought instantly of Bob. Notwithstanding a wish that I had written them myself, I offered them to him "as a modest millennial gift" for they seemed timeless and, well, perfect for him—from my perspective of course.

I wrote in conclusion that "I hope you will enjoy reading them half as much as I did, and experience at least a small smile afterward. *Semper fidelis!*"

Soon after Bob received my letter, I received a reply from him. Here are excerpts:

"Your letter has given me pause for thought. Perhaps an attempt to gain forgiveness for the slight at your fiftieth, I still consider it a great compliment. I guess you could say we've spent the last 37 years proceeding from (characters at Holy Cross) to (our latest grandsons) Kevin and Colin with a number of unmilitary antics 'in amongst them.' It's been a great journey for me and your friendship has been very important. Thanks. *Semper fi.*"

Pilots are plane people with a special air about them.

—Marine Corps Aviation Bumper Sticker

14

CAPTAIN WILLIAM ROGERS HUNT, JR., USMC,

A.K.A. YORK

Anxiety was a luxury, a joke you had no room for once you knew the variety of deaths and mutilations the war offered.

—From *Dispatches* by Michael Herr

As I called to mind suitable stories to share about this truly exceptional man, I was fortunate to have come across a sample of Roger's goodness and humor in a 1992 letter he wrote to Mame and me in connection with our twenty-fifth wedding anniversary. To wit:

> I first met Chuck during our freshman year at Holy Cross. He was a graduate of a prestigious Catholic high school on Long Island and I from a public institution west of Boston. We became friends and he helped me with Catholicism, i.e. explaining the difference between the large and small beads on the Rosary, and also socially, i.e. how to open a can of Budweiser or was it a "Knick"? Chuck was one of those guys you could depend on—a *true* friend. So when he told me he met a girl with whom he was truly in love, I believed him. I wanted to meet this girl, Mary Ann from New York, if only to see personally if she was everything Chuck said she was. Well, . . . I was impressed—pretty and

intelligent! I knew right from the start these two would end up together.

Thanks to the U.S. Marine Corps, our post-graduate careers were parallel. Moving from such exotic bases as Quantico, VA, Pensacola, FL, and "I Corps," Vietnam, Chuck and I would share many great times. We had that "esprit de corps" not limited to just Marines. We laughed and sometimes cried together but in spite of often adverse conditions, there were no "bad" times. I remember seeing Chuck in Dong Ha in early 1969 and asking him how he was coping. He told me the letters from Mary Ann kept him going. I will never forget that.

My wife, Joanne, who has been with me most of the last twenty-five years, has shared most of these memories. Like Chuck, I am indeed a fortunate man. We think of the Mansfields as family. We have seen our children grow old and have a lot to be proud of. I hope we can grow old together as we enter another generation.

"Roge," as Joanne calls him, is the type of person who would do anything to help another. (Most people simply call him Roger, despite his proper middle name, Rogers.) He has never taken advantage of anyone. His motives are always the purest. I have admired him for a long time, and I have no truer friend.

Roge and I did indeed become friends early in college but I believe that our time together in the Marine Corps forged our relationship forever. Yes, we trained and even lived together in the places he mentioned in his letter. Yet, it was in Vietnam where we had a conversation that not only bonded us as friends and Marines; it gave each of us a look into the other's soul.

Roge or "York," as he is still frequently called by his classmates and fellow Marines, was a CH-46 *Sea Knight* helicopter pilot. Unlike the UH1E Bob Lund flew, the "46" had two huge rotors and was designed as a medium transport. As a chopper pilot, Roge had already seen a lot of combat action during his tour of duty in Vietnam by the time he visited me in Dung Heap in the spring of '69.

The mission of the 46 was threefold: transport (for troops, resupply, etc.), medevac and recon (reconnaissance) Marine insert and/or extract. Of these the most dangerous by far was the recon mission, especially the emergency extract of a recon Marine or his whole team, which often involved a "high hover" by the pilot and copilot, and a "ladder extract." This was highly risky business, to say the least.

The Battle History of the U.S. Marines by Col. Joseph H. Alexander, USMC (Ret.) provides compelling commentary on 'the helicopter war' in Vietnam:

> The low-flying, slow-speed birds were fair game to every Viet Cong or North Vietnamese foot soldier with a weapon. Marine helicopter crews who survived an entire tour unscathed led charmed lives. Enemy gunfire downed 1,177 helicopters during the first five years of the war; many others returned to base shot to splinters. Yet every Marine "grunt" in the bush knew full well that his fellow Marines flying those birds would risk hell on earth to evacuate him should he become seriously wounded.

One evening the CO of York's squadron announced that it was his (the CO's) duty to choose one of his pilots to serve as a forward air controller (FAC), a 100-day assignment with Marine grunts. The FAC's job is air-ground coordination, and he is required to call in close air support by attack and/or fighter aircraft to assist and protect Marines on the ground in both offensive and defensive operations. A Marine pilot, like every Marine officer, is first trained as an infantry platoon leader. Thus, this combination of skills was superbly tailored to the FAC's crucial role in supporting the ground troops' mission.

Roge's squadron commander's selection mechanism was the time-honored approach of picking a name out of a hat. Roge said to himself, "Fine with me. I'm the luckiest guy in the world; I'll never get picked."

The name pulled first was his.

Roge's mother Penny had always told him, "Bad luck comes in threes." His selection as a FAC was the first. The second was his orders, which read "1st Battalion, 9th Marines," the infamous 1/9 or "Walking Dead," so described because it had the highest rate of killed and wounded of any unit in the entire Vietnam War. Thirdly, to make matters worse, when Roge reported for duty, his new CO advised him that the battalion would soon depart for an operation on the Laotian border called Dewey Canyon.

The difference between being named a FAC for duty in Vietnam, and being selected for Embarkation School on Okinawa, as I was, in roughly the same time frame is inestimable. Nonetheless, I have a strong hunch that Roge might have preferred Okinawa, although it would not surprise me in the least that his devotion to duty would anchor him willingly to his FAC assignment. It's the nature of the man.

As 1969 began, the enemy was increasing its forces in the Da Krong valley in Quang Tri Province's southwest corner. Known as Base Area 611, it was fed by Route 922 from Laos and, in turn, Route 548 through the A Shau Valley, from which men and supplies could be moved eastward toward Hue or southeastward toward Danang. The NVA and VC probably felt relatively immune to ground attack because not only was 611 remote, the monsoon weather continued to mask their activities.

On January 22nd, General Raymond G. Davis, CO of the Third Marine Division, ordered three battalions of the Ninth Marines into the Da Krong to kickoff Operation Dewey Canyon.

In *The Marines In Vietnam 1954–1973* Brig. Gen. E.H. Simmons, USMC (Ret.), describes Dewey Canyon:

> Colonel Robert H. Barrow's 9th Marines were to be completely dependent upon helicopters for logistic support, a particularly disquieting prospect in view of the always uncertain flying weather. The North Vietnamese, on the other hand, with a tonnage requirement only a fraction of the Marines, had usable trails and roads running back into Laos. The convolutions of the Laotian border protected the

enemy's back and a portion of his flanks from ground attack and he had—something of a rarity for in-country operations—a number of artillery pieces of up to 122mm. caliber. His base area was also well seeded with light antiaircraft weapons.

. . . Enemy resistance began to stiffen on 2 February, with the heaviest fighting taking place between 18 and 22 February, involving the 1st Battalion, 9th Marines, in the center of line. Soon some of the largest caches of the war were being uncovered. By the time the operation ended on 19 March, the base area was cleaned out . . . Enemy dead had been counted at 1,617, and 1,461 weapons and hundreds of tons of ammunition, equipment, and supplies had been taken.

In addition, Operation Dewey Canyon, which lasted fifty-seven days, claimed many Marine casualties: 121 killed and 803 wounded.

Shortly after Dewey Canyon had ended, York requested permission from his CO to visit "a grunt buddy of mine in Dong Ha," namely me. Providing some insight into his respect for his subordinate, the CO proffered his own jeep and driver to take York to Dung Heap so he could visit me. York arranged for the driver, a lance corporal, to be awarded "several beers" to compensate him for the return trip.

Roger Hunt has always been a superbly physically conditioned individual. A "lean and mean Marine," he was and still is, at 57, perfectly fit and well proportioned. Not quite wiry, neither was he bulky like me. About six feet tall, he was and is exceptionally strong despite his lean musculature. I would estimate his normal body weight to be about 170 pounds. A track man in high school, he was also fleet afoot.

When he arrived in Dong Ha that evening in the early spring of 1969, Roge was emaciated; indeed, he had lost fifty pounds during Dewey Canyon—that's 50 pounds in 57 days, or fourteen ounces per day. We talked and drank a few Budweisers, the calories from which York sorely needed.

It did not take me long to recognize that what Roge had just lived through had killed a part of him. He related a harrowing, heart-wrenching tale of carrying a dead Marine up steep hills to a waiting helicopter.

As he continued to describe the seemingly incessant carrying of Marines killed in action, also to waiting choppers frequently under heavy enemy fire, he had trouble speaking. His lips quivered slightly, and the lower crescents of his eyelids filled. It was not difficult to see how deeply his heart hurt. Brutally, the worst of the war's horrors had insinuated themselves into one of the Marines' best.

Roge spoke of physical exhaustion, and conveyed his worry that he might not be able to continue lugging the dead but precious bodies of his comrades. (Whenever possible, Marines retrieve the bodies of their fellow Marines fallen in battle.) He said he knew he must not stop; he simply had to keep going. His expressed fear that the horror would never cease was palpable. I didn't know what to say to console him, or even if I could. Man, it was bad.

> *I don't know how anyone who hasn't been shot at up close in a real firefight can possibly understand how good you feel afterward. Men have been killed and hurt, the fight has been won or lost, but there is only the one truly significant fact: that you are still alive, you have not been killed.*

> —James Brady in *The Coldest War*

The underlying message of Roge's Dewey Canyon experience was, incredibly, not the obvious. To me it was the fact that throughout his moving account, which I believe he then felt he must share, he never spoke of *himself*, or the deadly risks *he* faced. Instead, he focused exclusively on other Marines, whom he simply *had* to help, whether they were dead or, he hoped, only wounded. He made up his mind that for the rest of his life, no matter what, he would never feel sorry for himself.

Despite his mother's maxim about bad luck, Roger says today, "I can't help but think that I made it out—I survived, intact, whereas several of my fellow officers did not. One of my radio operators had his arm blown off by an RPG (rocket-propelled grenade)—I'll never forget it. These guys were the true heroes."

York received forty-one Air Medals for his 820 (!) missions, the Bronze Star, the Vietnamese Cross of Gallantry and the Combat Action Ribbon (for his service with 1/9). In addition, he was awarded a meritorious citation from Boeing/Vertol, manufacturers of the CH-46, for a medevac mission in 1968 and his "superior flying skills."

The total number of "hits" to his aircraft was thirty-eight; he was also shot down near Hill 55 but, in his words, "I was lucky compared to several others in my squadron."

Roger's Bronze Star citation refers to his "heroic achievement in aerial flight . . . in connection with combat operations against the enemy." Moreover, it reads:

> Arriving over the objective, the pilot was informed by his gunship support that the ground unit was heavily engaged with the enemy less than seventy-five meters from the landing zone. Approaching the area and coming under a heavy volume of automatic weapons fire, First Lieutenant Hunt successfully landed the aircraft . . . During the second approach to the beleaguered unit's landing zone, the aircraft received six direct hits. Undaunted by the hostile fire, (he) steadfastly remained in the hazardous area while the Marines and ordnance were being disembarked, and then departed from the landing (zone) with one man who had been seriously wounded.
>
> His bold initiative and superb aeronautical abilities inspired all who observed him and contributed significantly to the accomplishment of his unit's mission. First Lieutenant Hunt's courage, professional airmanship and steadfast devotion to duty in the face of great personal danger were in keeping with the highest traditions of the Marine Corps and of the United States Naval Service.

As I reflect on these words and on York's visit with me in Dong Ha some thirty-three years ago, I know that I came to know from the words he spoke that he is a genuine hero, albeit a quiet one.

> *I've yet to meet a Nam grunt who wouldn't leap to buy a Marine chopper vet a heartfelt drink.*
>
> —Anonymous

15

OFFICERS AND GENTLEMEN

I asked a lithe lady to lie her down: Holy and meek, she cries.

—William Blake

One of the most affable and knowledgeable officers in Dong Ha in my time there was a 38-year-old mustang captain by the name of Donald O'Neill, who happened to live in the same cantonment I did.

The aforementioned Bill Raabe, my Bay Area buddy, introduced me to Don and worked for him in the Dong Ha Communications Center, or "Comm Center," as it was called, which Don ran. Bill was a quiet, soft-spoken, self-effacing young officer who, like me, had left his wife, Jan, at home early in their marriage to spend some undesired time in-country. I still recall that his favorite song was "San Francisco" (the "wear some flowers in your hair" ballad, not the Tony Bennett classic). Bill's sense of humor was dry and I learned as I got to know him that he had admirable interpersonal skills, which led his Marines to respect him as well. I also remember that he and Jan met in Hawaii for R&R at the same time Mame and I did in January 1969.

I learned a tremendous amount from Bill and Don, the latter thanks to his then already twenty years in the Corps. Like Bob Lund and me, he enjoyed an occasional martini, a rarity for junior officers or anyone, for that matter, in our neck of the woods. We trusted each other, enjoyed working together and became friends.

Occasionally the officers in our little corner of Dung Heap would have a barbecue—with real beefsteaks, a delicacy for us. Beer, usually warm Schlitz, was more regularly available. Don, however, had connections through which he was able to procure the occasional bottle of Beefeater gin. To be sure, in the context of the way we lived in those days, this was extraordinary and highly civilized.

A raconteur par excellence, Don was at his most entertaining after he had consumed a couple of martinis, known variously then as loud-mouth soup, silver bullets or, simply, see-throughs. What follows is perhaps his most memorable tale.

In his younger days in the Corps, he had reportedly made the acquaintance of a delicate flower of an American girl back in The World, whom he affectionately called "Trooper Kelly." Whereas I recollect that her surname may in fact have been Kelly, the Trooper part was Don's playful nickname for this young woman he described as lovely; it was a moniker contrived to assign her—get this—a suitable "rank" for taking and following orders from, you guessed it, Don.

"Trooper, attention!" "Trooper, at ease!" And so it went.

I reckon that Trooper was probably somewhat gullible although, in fairness, I still have no trouble imagining that Don could be extremely charming and kind. After all, he was a genuinely good man, a fine Marine and a consummate professional. Suffice it to say that Trooper was adept at executing orders; put perhaps more considerately, and not to convey a wrong impression, she likely was in love with her 'commanding officer.' Well, one warm summer evening Don and his unsuspecting damsel were outdoors at her parents' home "necking and petting," which eventually progressed to more serious lovemaking.

As Don told it, he and Trooper at this point were lying in a flower bed (!) alongside the patio *in flagrante delicto*. The only available light, dim at that, came from the windows of the house. As such, it was difficult to see much of anything, even at close range. As the young couple's amorous activity intensified, neither Don nor Trooper was aware that the patio door had been quietly opened.

Suddenly, Don sensed on his head, neck and back the splashing warm wetness—and the unmistakable odor—of urine. Trooper was not spared either. Somehow her father had stealthily emerged onto the patio and stood directly above the now frantic but frozen fornicators. Could he not have been aware of the presence of the young lovers who lay just below him in his garden?

As Don and Trooper closed their eyes in abject horror while simultaneously filled with fear of discovery, dear old dad, seemingly unfazed, zipped up and presently disappeared into the house.

When the laughter of his small audience of Marines had subsided, Don stated that he always believed Trooper's father actually knew all the time that the two were there in sexual embrace. The old man's chosen treatment was merely an expression of his disapproval. According to Don, the moral of the story, which he insisted was true, is that it's better to be pissed off than pissed on! To me it seemed that such a story simply must have been apochryphal.

⧗

Like Bill Raabe, 1ˢᵗ Lt. Don Fritz worked for Don O'Neill, at least for a while. Fritz was a big man with a high-and-tight silver crew cut. Another mustang, he teamed up with the Dung Heap Marines well into the second half of my tour of duty, and lived in the same cantonment as the rest of us. Judging by my acquired ear for accents, not fully refined in Dong Ha days, I would wager that Fritz hailed from southwestern Pennsylvania.

A gentle giant, Don Fritz gained the respect and admiration of all his fellow Marines in short order. The slightly ungainly aspect of his demeanor was a perception swiftly displaced by his exceptional knowledge and professionalism. I know not how long he had been a Marine but he was salty, and I believe he had also served in Korea. Always optimistic and positive, he gave his colleagues and friends a generous share of his great inner strength and tremendous loyalty. Don was also great fun to be around because of his wonderful and sometimes bawdy sense of humor, plus his infectious laugh. His jokes were simply hilarious. He is a man I am proud to have served with and would love to see again.

Another super guy in Dong Ha was 1st Lt. Henry Notthaft, a graduate of the U.S. Naval Academy. Hank, as he was called, was one of the smartest people I have ever met. He and I were also roommates for a time after John Wegl's return to The World.

Hank was the only person I met in Vietnam who subscribed to *The Wall Street Journal.* This was in the days long before Dow Jones & Company, publisher of the *Journal,* had likely even thought of publishing *The Asian Wall Street Journal.* He possessed worldliness and sophistication, some would say arrogance, that I thought made him unique vis-à-vis most other Marine officers I had come to know. Always impressive, Hank also taught me what a résumé was. Through the years I have often wondered what he did after Vietnam; perhaps he remained in the Corps.

I salute all these good men with a heartfelt *Semper fi!*

Heaven won't take us, and Hell's afraid we'll take over.

—Marine Corps Bumper Sticker

16

An Introduction to Management

Hope and assurance of a successful outcome are
two different things.

—P. Henry Mueller

J im Wilbanks had made corporal at last.

Lance corporal (LCpl) is one rank below corporal, the usual rank of a Marine rifle fire team leader, and one above private first class (PFC).

LCpl Wilbanks was, at least in the minds of some, a good ol' boy from Huntsville, Alabama. Despite a somewhat comic aspect to his bearing and manner of speech, he had, to his credit, a quick mind, and could be counted on when the chips were down. After all, he *was* a Marine. (Enlisted Marines were generally respected by their officers in many cases simply *because* they had made it through Marine boot camp at Parris Island, South Carolina, or San Diego, California.)

A near-chain-smoker, Wilbanks had the habit of often biting on the filter of his cigarette, ostensibly for emphasis when about to address others, including those senior to him in rank. He also bit the butt when he was telling a joke or, at least in his own mind, about to say something humorous. Approximately my age (I was 23 when I arrived in Vietnam in the summer of '68), LCpl Wilbanks made it clear to me at one point that he was full-corporal material. Now, without the benefit of much formal education, Wilbanks was never accused by anyone of being a rocket scientist.

Although this was the case with many enlisted Marines of that era, it is not intended to be a criticism but merely a statement of fact. Still, in fairness, he was largely hard-working, loyal and quick-witted.

Then, in a surprise move, he actually began lobbying me for a promotion. In my experience as a young officer, that was a first. At the outset, I recall thinking, perhaps unfairly, that Wilbanks was, at base, a brazen son of a bitch attempting to curry favor with me because, I believe, he happened to mistake my reputation for fairness and, I dare say, my largely good nature with the troops for something akin to weakness. With such a perception I was more than annoyed, to say the least. Worse, if such a perception were more widely held, I would have been in trouble.

Indeed, I was deeply displeased with such a presumptive approach by Wilbanks with respect to his platoon commander (i.e., myself). After all, was he not essentially a man I perceived as an uncouth and underdeveloped redneck? Still, he was a Marine. After cooling off and consulting with the two most senior staff NCOs in my platoon, I decided to have a serious word, as the British are wont to say, with the ambitious and possibly already overachieving lance corporal so unabashedly "bucking" for corporal.

In the end, I laid out for him a three-month program, at the communication of which he was puzzled, frustrated, angry or all of the above. My deal with Wilbanks was that, if I judged him to be successful in meeting or completing the various elements of the basic self-improvement course I proposed to him, I agreed to recommend him for promotion.

In explaining the nature of the objective to Wilbanks, I focused on the language of a Marine Corps fitness report, which, I must acknowledge, may have been designed for officers rather than enlisted Marines. Regardless of the specific application, the highest acclamation of a Marine's performance was summarized in the words *Especially desire to have*. If a Marine had this line or box checked on his fitness report, he was virtually assured promotion and/or transfer to one of the more highly-ranked duty stations on his "wish list." Thus, I explained what I believed it would take for Wilbanks to be so designated.

Well, talk about incentive working big-time! I never saw a Marine, let alone anyone in my subsequent experience in the American corporate world, take the ball and run with it the way Wilbanks did. At the end of his metamorphosis, I had the pleasure of presenting Wilbanks with his second stripe, and he seemed genuinely thrilled. Not only did his performance continue to improve substantially, the new rank was prestigious to him and served as a positive stimulus for more than a few of the other men in our platoon. In retrospect, I believe it was almost certainly more a corporate-type negotiation than a military one that led to Wilbanks's new rank but I believe it worked to the benefit of all then and there.

To shift gears, as it were, from the sublime to the ridiculous, one of the most hilarious anecdotes from my time in Vietnam involved the same Corporal Wilbanks, although he may still have been a lance corporal at the time.

Now, it must be understood that girly magazines typically made the rounds in most Marine hootches, and our platoon's were no exceptions.

Before progressing with this particular anecdote, some technical background is necessary. The Marine Corps of the nineteen-sixties had a field telephone designated the EE-8, which is spoken as "double-E eight." A double-strand, black-coated wire referred to simply as "slash wire" physically connected field telephones and their typically small networks. For additional perspective, another significant reference point is that the city of Danang is located approximately 95 miles south of Dong Ha.

One day a Marine in our platoon produced a copy of a particular magazine, which he had opened to display the ever-popular centerfold. Next, he opened the full-length photo of the young lovely in her naked glory for all to see. For his part, Wilbanks, now holding the magazine himself, appreciating the young woman's pulchritude and gesturing toward me, excitedly exclaimed in his inimitable southern drawl, "Lieutenant Mansfield, I'd lay slash wire from here to Danang just to hear her fart over a EE-8!"

The Corps doesn't build character. It reveals it.

—Bumper Sticker

17

A TIGER HUNT

There's something happening here,
What it is ain't exactly clear.
There's a man with a gun over there,
Tellin' me I've got to beware.

—The Buffalo Springfield

There were sporadic reports, both in the American forces newspaper *Stars & Stripes* and also through the grapevine, of American military personnel in Vietnam being attacked and/or killed by tigers. In this connection, on one of the monthly occasions when I served as the "Officer of the Day" (OOD), which meant being on duty continuously for twenty-four hours (without sleep), one of the Marines in my platoon raced into the underground bunker where I was stationed for the night. As for the time, it was around two o'clock in the morning.

This Marine, a young Native American corporal by the name of Sharkie, wore the look of stark terror on his face. This notwithstanding, he was a serious and accomplished Marine.

When I recall the moment, I now believe he may have been in shock. Nonetheless, he managed to relate in a voice constricted by fear how he had rolled over on his rack, awakened momentarily and found himself staring a tiger in the face. Sharkie froze and, moments later, the big cat reportedly sauntered out of the hootch, pushing open, and then letting slam, the screen door of the SEA (Southeast Asia) hut in which Sharkie and other members of our platoon lived. Clad only in his skivvies, he then took off for my command post to relate his unprecedented and unwelcome encounter.

I walked with Sharkie the short distance back to where he had been sleeping. On the plywood floor of his hootch were large paw prints, easy to discern inasmuch as their owner had obviously slogged through the ubiquitous mud outside. At once 1st Lt. Vic Fitzgerald, who was my assistant platoon commander and had the perfect handle-bar mustache, and I organized an ad hoc patrol, perhaps too heavily armed, to follow the tiger's trail—and to capture or kill the animal. If you will pardon the expression, we were loaded for bear. I actually had visions of a tiger-skin rug as a trophy! After all, rank has its privileges, *n'est-ce pas*?

We spent about two hours organizing and conducting our tiger patrol. Keep in mind that such a patrol had all the earmarks of a hunt. To be sure, it was not the typical Vietnam combat patrol, to which few of even the best Marines had limited desire to belong, unless it was absolutely essential. Indeed, for most Marines, patrols were the name of the game in much of Vietnam, and they were often invitations to danger. Yet, participation in this 'tiger hunt' was attractive to many who had sufficient interest in a potentially exciting venture in which there was no chance of the 'enemy' shooting back. Just the same, the tiger had the wherewithal to 'ambush' a Marine patrol and do serious bodily harm.

It was a dark, raw, rainy night during the monsoon season, although it had stopped raining when we set out. There was perceptible nervousness among some of the men but this was largely offset by their heightened sense of expectation. As long as we had the tiger's paw prints to follow, the trail was still hot. Excitement was in the night air.

Someone broke the mostly silent tedium, declaring he had heard the big cat's guttural growl. Others chalked this up to imagination or wishful thinking. We trudged on. After about a mile of heavy going through the muddy darkness, our tiger's trail ended abruptly at the edge of a small rain-swollen pond. All were disappointed; the hunt was over.

For weeks thereafter, skeptics chided an otherwise stalwart Sharkie about the tiger episode, for they readily dismissed it as nothing more than a nightmare or hallucination. After all, no one else claimed to have seen the beast. For my part, I believed Sharkie got a bad rap, and I supported him whenever I had the opportunity, which was not infrequent. Besides, I had already judged the paw prints to be genuine.

In the last analysis, I believe it was a good thing, for all on that patrol, that we never found the tiger. Besides, Mame and a tiger skin probably don't go well together.

Only, here and there, an old sailor,
Drunk and asleep in his boots,
Catches tigers
In red weather.

—Wallace Stevens,
Disillusionment of Ten O'Clock [1923]

18

Oh Rats!

Once I ran into a soldier standing by himself in the middle of a small jungle clearing where I'd wandered off to take a leak. We said hello, but he seemed very uptight about my being there. He told me that the guys were all sick of sitting around waiting and that he'd come out to see if he could draw a little (enemy) fire. What a look we gave each other. I backed out of there fast, I didn't want to bother him while he was working.

—From *Dispatches* by Michael Herr

On another tour as OOD, during a nighttime perimeter check, I was inspecting a section of our line that did not have live guards posted. Instead, this sector was "protected" by fences and huge amounts of barbed and razor wire. It was also heavily booby-trapped with "Claymore" anti-personnel mines and conventional land mines, all designed and placed to spoil the day or night of any NVA soldier or Viet Cong (often referred to as "Victor Charlie" or simply "Charlie") or, for that matter, anyone else who wandered into the area.

Nights were the time for air and artillery strikes for they were when the NVA and VC were out and about. At night we could sometimes see the awesome firepower of AC-47 gunship aircraft, each of which had a wing-mounted gunsight and an electrically operated Gatling gun that could shoot 7.62mm NATO rounds at a rate of 6,000 per minute; the three of these door-mounted "miniguns" with which each AC-47 was equipped by 1966 could fire 300 rounds per *second*. Put still another way, these guns could put a round in every square inch of a football field in less than a minute. Later designated "Spooky" or "Puff the Magic Dragon" or simply "Puff," these gunships are amazing—and scary.

In his evocative Vietnam testament, *The Things They Carried*, Tim O'Brien gives extraordinary texture and flavor to night work in Vietnam by capturing brilliantly the fearful eeriness of the enemy presence after dark:

> We called the enemy ghosts. "Bad night," we'd say, "the ghosts are out." To get spooked, in the lingo, meant not only to get scared but to get killed. "Don't get spooked,' we'd say. "Stay cool, stay alive." Or we'd say: "Careful, man, don't give up the ghost." The countryside itself seemed spooky—shadows and tunnels and incense burning in the dark. The land was haunted. We were fighting forces that did not obey the laws of twentieth century science. Late at night, on guard, it seemed that all of Vietnam was alive and shimmering—odd shapes swaying in the paddies, boogiemen in sandals, spirits dancing in old pagodas. It was ghost country, and Charlie Cong was the main ghost. The way he came out at night. How you never really saw him, just thought you did. Almost magical—appearing, disappearing. He could blend in with the land, changing form, becoming trees and grass. He could levitate. He could fly. He could pass through barbed wire and melt away like ice and creep up on you without sound or footsteps. He was scary. In the daylight, maybe, you didn't believe in this stuff. You laughed it off. You made jokes. But at night you turned into a believer: no skeptics in fox holes.

Some nights had no light, neither moon nor stars. Whether one's eyes were open or closed made no difference, for the darkness was the same.

This night had no light, save some early from a new moon and stars barely visible through a thin, dimming cloudcover. As I strode

across an open space of, say, fifty or sixty yards along this unmanned
section of perimeter, I kept my pistol at the ready. I did so because
I freely admit to finding it disconcerting to have to walk along this
stretch of abandoned outpost in the middle of the night. Frequently,
I would have the urge to use my flashlight but decided, prudently
I believe, against it. After all, I would only be highlighting my
own visibility, and I knew I didn't want to be a target shining in
the dark. I also remember wondering if I was alone, or if there
might be some unwanted presence just outside the wire. Was Charlie
there, somewhere? Were that the case, I suppose I might not be
writing these words now.

As I walked the perimeter this particular night, I felt something
bumping against my legs, mostly on my shins but sometimes as
high as my knees. Although my night vision had kicked in, I still
couldn't make out what was going on around me. I was startled
but slowly kept walking, suddenly realizing the "something" was
more than one. Increasingly alarmed and my heart arhythmic, I
stopped and took the risk of spraying my flashlight's beam quickly
around me. To my disgust, I found myself immersed in a veritable
sea of rats. They were huge—about the size of domestic cats—and
numbered in the hundreds at a minimum.

> *I asked myself what I was doing out here, halfway around*
> *the world, hanging my ass out like this, while my college*
> *buddies were selling insurance or practicing law, in the*
> *warm comfort of their secure offices. At that moment I*
> *could think of no good answer to the question.*
>
> —From *Feet Wet: Reflections of a Carrier Pilot* by Rear
> Admiral Paul T. Gillcrist, USN (Ret.)

To be sure, the apparently sudden gathering of these rats was
not even remotely close to the worst that could have happened to
me in this godforsaken place. Yet, I recall thinking for just an
instant how pleasant it would be to find myself someplace else,
like home. At the same time, I must confess that I also felt like a

wimp. After all, they were just rats, and I should have been thankful that no one was shooting at me just then. I also thought, *I should have some guts; I'm a Marine, for God's sake!*

It was then that I decided to do an about face, return quickly to my jeep, and leave my rodent friends, not to mention any "ghosts" in the vicinity, to do whatever they were doing before I so rudely interrupted their nocturnal pursuits. Besides, my mission had been accomplished: the perimeter was secure.

Bonne nuit, mes amis!

> *I think we are in rats' alley*
> *Where the dead men lost their bones.*

—Thomas Stearns Eliot in *The Game of Chess*

19

BODY BAGS

When someone got killed, his body was not really a body, but rather one small bit of waste in the midst of a much wider wastage. I learned that words make a difference. It's easier to cope with a kicked bucket than a corpse; if it isn't human, it doesn't matter much if it's dead.

—Tim O'Brien in *The Things They Carried*

I recall a few quiet evenings in the early spring of 1969 when I had occasion to sit outside my hootch and read a book. These opportunities came during a continuation of the welcome lull that followed President Johnson's order to halt the bombing of North Vietnam, which took effect the preceding November 1st. Of course, there was still fierce fighting out in the bush but Dong Ha itself had been largely spared for months.

Indeed, it was clear that the war still raged, as each evening I would see scores of dark green rubber body bags stacked like cord wood on the edge of the Dong Ha Combat Base airstrip, just a few hundred feet from where I usually sat. It was hard to concentrate on my book, to say the least, for in each of those receptacles were the remains of a U.S. Marine KIA (killed in action), in all likelihood that very day. Body bags' near-blackness, especially at dusk, augmented their stillness and seemed to cast over the surrounding landscape a lugubrious, almost palpable, pall.

Instead of the workhorse Marine Lockheed C-130 *Hercules* cargo planes, C-123 *Providers* would more frequently land at Dong

Ha because of their easier maneuverability and shorter takeoff run and landing rollout. Still, these sizeable aircraft wouldn't stay long; after all, they were targets, just like everything and everyone else in the area. As the pilots and crew waited, perhaps anxiously, young Marines would work quickly to load the day's dead on board for the beginning of the long journey to their final resting places back, wherever, in The World.

The grim reality of witnessing body bags actually fulfilling their intended purpose caused some Marines to cease exhorting younger and typically combat-inexperienced brethren to be sure to pick up a body bag along with the other required equipment that was standard issue to new arrivals in-country. Make no mistake, I personally detested this form of hazing—I don't know what else to call it—from the moment an obviously sullen 19-year-old Marine, brand-new in-country, approached me and, in all seriousness, inquired, "Sir, where can I get my body bag?"

Feeling disgusted but empathetic, I told him it wasn't necessary, that it was merely a sick joke. A soft smile of relief then slowly spread over his handsome, young face.

Requiescant in pace!

> *A dead buddy is some tough shit, but bringing your own*
> *ass out alive can sure help you to get over it.*

—From *Dispatches* by Michael Herr

20

Costs

*Older men declare war. But it is youth that must fight and die.
And it is youth who must inherit the tribulation, the sorrow,
and the triumphs that are the aftermath of war.*

—Herbert Hoover

Despite extraordinary performances like those of many Vietnam combat veterans, the Vietnam War was often militarily perplexing and morally uncertain. Ground objectives captured with great losses of men and materiel were frequently abandoned soon afterward. Moreover, our overwhelming superiority in firepower was often hard to realize.

To be sure, as I have said many times over the years, we felt as if we were fighting with one hand tied behind our back. I remember Marine Lieutenant Tom Satterlee, a Marine Corps Basic School classmate and friend, once telling our company commander, "Let's just bomb the hell out of North Vietnam, make the place a parking lot, and go home." Sadly, Tom was later killed along with our classmates Randy Brundage and Walt Lubbe, whose wife Pat was then pregnant with their third child, in a tragic training flight accident at the Glynco Naval Air Station near Brunswick, Georgia.

Tom's remark reminded me of a similar one made by U.S. Air Force General Curtis E. LeMay: "My solution to the problem would be to tell [the North Vietnamese Communists] . . . they've got to draw in their horns and stop their aggression or we're going to bomb them into the Stone Age."

As insensitive in retrospect as some, especially pacifists, might regard such cracks, they were nonetheless accurate barometers of the frustration Tom, the general and many more of us were then feeling. What's worse is that we didn't always know who the enemy was. For example, the Vietnamese barber who came into our Dong Ha compound regularly to cut Marines' hair turned out to be an NVA-VC sympathizer. He was found out when he made the big-time mistake of taking a straight razor to the throat of a Marine colonel who was alert and strong enough to stop the little man's potentially lethal attack. Sometimes even women and children were the enemy, and friendly Vietnamese villagers appeared ambivalent about who won.

It is probably true that we couldn't really win in Vietnam because of the strategy, tactics and politics of a war that most Americans opposed. Consequently, as President Nixon quickly learned, we lowered our sights from victory to "peace with honor," which, translated, meant his own political survival.

When Saigon, the capital city of the South, finally fell in 1975, two years after the last U.S. forces left, it was the belief of many that the war had been a colossal waste of American human and financial resources. All the North wanted was to reclaim Saigon, which it eventually renamed Ho Chi Minh City after the North Vietnamese leader, whom we Americans irreverently called "Uncle Ho." (Our enemies concocted the taunt, "Ho, Ho, Ho Chi Minh, the Viet Cong is going to win!") In the minds of many, the American sacrifice was just not worth it.

But just what was the nature of the American sacrifice in Vietnam? A few accounts follow.

From 1965 through 1971, nearly half a million Marines served in Vietnam. And after 1971 was long past, some Marines were still at war in that country.

—E.H. Simmons, Brigadier General, USMC (Ret.)

21

GOOD NEWS?

Nobody likes the man who brings bad news.

—Sophocles

In 1967, about a year before I left the U.S. for Vietnam, I was assigned the duty of informing a widowed mother that her son had been wounded in battle in Vietnam. It was a Corps tradition that a Marine officer would go to the home of any Marine who had been wounded or killed in action to tell his family the bad news personally and try to offer consolation.

It was literally a rainy night in Georgia when I went to the young Marine's home. As his mother opened the door and focused on my Marine uniform, her face turned ashen. She then began to sob softly.

"It's John, isn't it?" she said in barely a whisper.

I replied, "Yes, ma'am. He's been wounded but he's aboard a hospital ship and doing fine."

Next she surprised me by saying, "Thank God!" She then explained that she was actually relieved that John was *only* wounded because her elder son, also a Marine, had been killed in Vietnam earlier that same year.

Everything is relative, isn't it?

But they also felt a kind of giddiness, a secret joy, because they were alive, and because even the rain was preferable to being sucked under a shit field, and because it was all a matter of luck and happenstance.

—From *The Things They Carried* by Tim O'Brien

22

First Lieutenant Stephen E. Karopczyc, USA

Imagine being too tired to snap a flak jacket closed, too tired to clean your rifle, too tired to guard a light, too tired to deal with the half-inch margins of safety that moving through the war often demanded, just too tired to give a fuck and then dying behind that exhaustion.

—From *Dispatches* by Michael Herr

About the time I visited the widow's home in Georgia, U.S. Army First Lieutenant Stephen Karopczyc was leading his platoon against an enemy force in South Vietnam's Kontum Province, and noticed that his lead element was engaged in fighting a small enemy unit along his route. Aware of the importance of pushing through to the main enemy force in order to provide relief for another American platoon, he ran through intense enemy fire into the open, and hurled colored smoke grenades to mark the enemy for attack by U.S. helicopter gunships. Taking that risk alone was brave, to say the least.

According to the Army's official citation, here's what happened next. Steve moved among his men to embolden their advance, and guided their attack by marking enemy locations with bursts of fire from his own weapon. His forceful leadership sped the advance, forced an enemy retreat, and allowed his unit to close with the main hostile force.

During this effort, an enemy sniper shot Steve above the heart but he refused aid for his injury, plugging the bleeding bullet wound with his finger instead until it could be properly treated.

Imagine that for just a moment. We Marines were trained to do what Steve did if we received what the military services call a "sucking chest wound," which has been defined as "a wound that penetrates a lung, through which air is forced as the victim breathes." I am confident that being trained to plug a bullet wound with one's finger, and actually having to do it, are situations worlds apart.

Next, as enemy strength increased, Steve ordered his men to organize a defensive position in and around some abandoned bunkers, where he went on to defend against the increasingly strong enemy attacks.

Several hours later, the situation worsened when a North Vietnamese soldier hurled a grenade to within a few feet of Steve and two of his wounded men. Although his position protected him, Steve leaped up to cover the deadly grenade with a steel helmet, which exploded, driving steel fragments into his legs. Steve's response, however, prevented further injury to his two wounded soldiers. Severely weakened, Steve continued, incredibly, to direct his men until he died of his wounds two hours later.

For this, President Nixon awarded 1st Lt. Stephen Karopczyc posthumously the Congressional Medal of Honor for "conspicuous gallantry and intrepidity at the risk of life above and beyond the call of duty." On the medal itself appears the word 'VALOR', which is, according to Mr. Webster, "strength of mind or spirit that enables a man to encounter danger with firmness." I believe you will agree, now that you have read his story, that Steve was a hero. Indeed, I, for one, am reminded of the words ascribed to Jesus Christ in the gospel of John (15:13) that "A man can have no greater love than to lay down his life for his friends."

Who was 1st Lt. Steve Karopczyc? He graduated in 1961 from Chaminade, and in 1994 became the first alumnus inducted into its Alumni Hall of Fame. An exact replica of his Congressional

Medal of Honor was given to Chaminade by President Ronald Reagan and is displayed permanently at the school.

Steve's parents, Ed and Nina, are dear friends and remain great supporters of their son's alma mater.

> *A true war story is never moral. It does not instruct, nor encourage virtue, nor suggest models of proper human behavior, nor restrain men from doing the things men have always done.*

> —From *The Things They Carried* by Tim O'Brien

23

First Lieutenant Timothy J. Shorten, USMCR

*Between what contact did to you and how tired you got, between
the farout things you saw or heard and what you personally lost
out of all that got blown away, the war made a place for you
that was all yours.*

—From *Dispatches* by Michael Herr

Tim Shorten and his brother Greg grew up in my GC neighborhood and were young men the rest of us much admired. Both fine athletes, they were clean-cut, all-American sorts. They preceded me at Chaminade; Greg next went on to Villanova University, Tim to Holy Cross. Later, Tim became a teacher and a coach at a Catholic high school on Long Island. In 1967 I met him one Sunday morning as I was on my way to church, and we walked the last block together. As I hadn't seen him in some time, I asked how and what he was doing. Gesturing to the Marine Corps officer's uniform I wore that morning, he told me, "I'll be wearing one of those soon."

Surprised, I further inquired, only half-jokingly, "Why would you want to do a thing like that?" After all, his teaching position exempted him from military service. Moreover, he and I both knew that, as a Marine officer in those days, he would eventually be headed to only one place, namely, Vietnam. In an instant, I could not then help but recall the decisions other friends and acquaintances had made to quit other, better paying jobs to go into teaching just to avoid military service, or to leave the country altogether. (Interestingly, Tim's two youngest brothers reportedly openly demonstrated against the Vietnam War, and one was even arrested for doing so in Washington, D.C.)

Then Tim answered my question: "It's my duty," he said, "and I want to go there with you and the other guys." As his words hit me, I felt inwardly ashamed. Although I had already worn Marine green for a year and believed firmly I too had a duty to go to Vietnam, I also believe I would not have relinquished my position as a teacher-coach to volunteer for Marine Corps Officer Candidates School and combat duty in Vietnam.

I met Jack Shorten, Tim's father, in Mike Paulino's barbershop shortly before I left for Vietnam. He told me that Tim had been wounded, medevac-ed and later returned to combat duty only to be killed in action on March 31, 1968 during the infamous Tet offensive. To this day his brother Greg says Tim's commitment to his country and Corps was total and unwavering, even as the U.S. political tide was turning.

Thirteen days before he died, 1st Lt. Shorten participated in an attack against NVA units in Quang Tri Province. As the fighting intensified during the attack's early stages, Tim effectively coordinated mortar fire against enemy emplacements and disregarded his own safety as he moved forward to the points of heaviest contact to evaluate the situation and assist in the evacuation of his wounded men. When an adjacent unit began taking enemy sniper fire, he led a Marine squad to the exposed flank of the friendly unit and, both directing effective mortar fire and throwing hand grenades, silenced the sniper fire in the area.

Later the same day, when another Marine squad became separated from the remainder of his company, Tim assumed command of the unit and led his men against several enemy-held bunkers. During the advance, he observed a North Vietnamese sniper positioned in a bunker to the front of his unit and, after organizing a two-squad attack force, commenced an assault against the fortified emplacement. During his unit's advance, two Marines were killed and several others wounded. Immediately employing a flamethrower against the bunker, he then assaulted the emplacement singlehandedly, throwing hand grenades and firing his pistol into the embrasure of the fortification, killing the NVA sniper and enabling his unit to continue its advance.

"For conspicuous gallantry and intrepidity in action" due to "his courage, bold initiative and selfless devotion to duty," Tim Shorten was awarded the Silver Star, our nation's third-highest military honor. His courage and leadership in combat also won him two Purple Hearts for wounds he sustained and the Bronze Star for "heroic achievement" in a battle on October 14, 1967. In this action, ignoring the dangers to himself from the enemy fire, he skillfully directed his unit's suppressive fire until the enemy force was repulsed. Due to his aggressive fighting spirit and calm presence of mind in the face of extreme personal danger, he was an inspiration to his men and instrumental in inflicting heavy casualties against the enemy. He was also cited for his "courage, superb leadership and unwavering devotion to duty."

Nineteen-sixty-seven was also the year in which Guido Farinaro graduated from Chaminade. An immigrant from Italy, he enlisted in the Marine Corps to repay the debt he believed he owed his adopted country. He went to Vietnam, served in combat with the Marines, and was killed in action in August 1968. The preceding month, my friend and Chaminade classmate Bob Kisch, who served as a Marine officer in Vietnam, was reportedly captured by the Viet Cong, who tortured, hanged and "necklaced" him with their bayonets.

Parenthetically, Chaminade honors at its annual Gold Star Mass its fifty-three "Gold Star Alumni," who gave their lives in the service of their country. Of this, in a letter from which I have earlier quoted, Matt Caulfield has written, "And incidentally, I have never forgotten that the faithful celebration of the Gold Star Mass during those years made a statement about us more powerful than all of the dissent . . . How fortunate I was to have Chaminade with me in those days, and today."

It is thanks to our fallen heroes that we
could have reached this day.

—Menachem Begin

24

A Chauffeured Ride In-Country

Damn the torpedoes—full speed ahead!

—David Glasgow Farragut

One of the more amusing, although potentially deadly, incidents during my Vietnam tour of duty occurred shortly before I went back to The World. During most of my time in-country I traveled alone, though well armed (with a 45-caliber pistol, an M-16 automatic rifle and an M-79 grenade launcher), driving a military jeep wherever I had to go. (There were exceptions, though, when I enjoyed the luxury of being shuttled via helicopter piloted by Bob Lund.) Toward the end of my tour of duty, my division commanding officer issued an order requiring every Marine officer to assign himself a driver. Frankly, given the way we lived in those days, especially in Dung Heap and points north, I thought it was a bit highfalutin for me to have a driver. Besides, I enjoyed driving the jeep. Be that as it may, I complied with the general's new order.

One day I had to travel just five miles south of Dong Ha to Quang Tri, where my battalion's administrative offices were located. Reluctantly I pressed into service as my driver a 19-year old lance corporal from California named Schrader who then had only a few days left in-country. When our Marines got "short," or close to returning to The World, we would make every effort to keep them out of harm's way and send them home safe and sound.

As Michael Herr has written in his book *Dispatches,*

> Such odd things happen when tours are almost over.
> It's the Short-Timer Syndrome. In the heads of the men
> who are really in the war for a year, all tours end early. No
> one expects much from a man when he is down to one or
> two weeks. He becomes a luck freak, an evil-omen collector,
> a diviner of every bad sign. If he has the imagination, or the
> experience of war, he will precognize his own death a
> thousand times a day, but he will always have enough left to
> do the one big thing to Get Out.

On a particularly clement morning in May 1969, LCpl Schrader and I set out for Quang Tri, about a twenty-minute ride from Dong Ha. As we approached the gates of the village, the surrounding countryside was the usual mosaic of rice paddies and farms with the local people busy at work. As we left Quang Tri to return to Dong Ha, we faced a completely different scene. All the people had disappeared, and this usually meant just one thing: VC were operating in the area, and an attack of some sort was likely, if not imminent. Now, Schrader and I both had weapons; what's more, we had wheels and presumably could maneuver quickly, although jeeps then couldn't really do more than forty miles per hour. I made the decision to proceed to Dong Ha.

About a quarter mile outside Quang Tri—*CARRUMPP!!!*—a mortar round exploded on the bumpy dirt road not far behind us. Then came a second and a third, perhaps fifteen in all. Believing it too dangerous to stop, turn around and return to Quang Tri, I encouraged Schrader to step on it in an effort to outrun the highly skilled enemy mortarman who was probably in the treeline a couple of hundred yards east of the road we were traveling. Amazingly, the incoming mortar rounds were being *walked* along the road behind us, and one caused minor damage to our vehicle.

Mortars are small, portable artillery pieces. A mortar shell is simply dropped into a mortar tube in the base of which is a steel pin that causes the firing and propelling of the shell out of the tube. Well, I guessed that the enemy was firing 61mm mortars; after all, the larger 82mm version would have been a lot worse and caused greater damage. (Interestingly, Americans had 60mm and 81mm mortar shells. Thus, our enemy could use our slightly smaller shells in their slightly larger tubes, if necessary, but their shells, thousands of which were captured in Vietnam by American and allied forces, were simply too large for our smaller tubes.)

Soon, thankfully, we got beyond the range of this enemy soldier who was trying to kill us, and arrived safely back in Dong Ha. In what was perhaps a lapse of judgment, I joked with my young Marine, thanking him for such an exciting ride.

For his part, a pale and shaken Schrader looked at me and asked, "Sir, the next time you need a ride somewhere, would you please ask someone else to drive you?"

Fair enough, I thought.

⧗

Nearly thirty-one years after this episode, I had the pleasure of dining with an Irishman named Carl O'Sullivan. Having read a piece I had written about the Vietnam War, in which I related the Schrader story, Carl wrote to me as follows: "You certainly captured the mood of the time and I hope that the article will be the first instalment of a more detailed memoir." Then, referring to an upcoming trip Mame and I were to take to his country, he concluded: "Please contact me when you are coming to Ireland and I will try to assist you with your itinerary. Having read your article, however, I certainly would not offer to drive you anywhere."

> *There's nothing so embarrassing as when things*
> *go wrong in a war.*

> —*From* Dispatches *by Michael Herr*

25

A REGRET

And when he goes to heaven
To Saint Peter he will tell:
Another Marine reporting, sir;
I've served my time in hell!

—Epitaph on grave of Private First Class Cameron,
USMC, Guadalcanal [1942]

After a third of a century, I can say with regrettable conviction that I did my Dong Ha Marines (and myself) a disservice when I failed to write down all their names while we were serving together. I should have kept a journal. It saddens me today that, while I can still see the faces of many of them, the intervening years have impaired my memory of some of their names. I honor all those with whom I served in that time and place, but, alas, my recognizing only a few by name here will have to suffice.

The mission of my platoon was to keep radio relay communications circuits up and running in northern I Corps. One half of my time was spent in Dong Ha, the other visiting and working with my men at various outposts, some remote hilltops that we had to defend as well. Perhaps the most important part of my job was to ensure that adequate supplies of food, water, ammunition and equipment—as well as reasonably regular deliveries of adequate supplies of beer, preferably Budweiser (but usually Schlitz)—were available. These perhaps insignificant elements of management of Marines in those places and times were nonetheless key to two important aspects of leadership: Getting commitment and maintaining morale.

The one hundred Marines in my platoon, many of whom were largely demoralized when I arrived, became a cohesive unit, and pulled together as a team, especially when times were toughest. I have never believed that I could take credit for this, but it did happen. Despite all the risks we faced daily, my Marines and I were able to function in an atmosphere of trust and mutual respect, as well as professionalism—but, then, my young Marines were already professionals, more than I, I sometimes believed. Many of these men actually extended their tours of duty under my command—against which I usually advised—for obvious reasons. Still, this was most gratifying.

> You must reflect that it was by courage, sense of duty and a keen feeling of honor in action that men were able to win all this.

—Pericles in his famous *Funeral Oration*

Gunnery Sergeant Don Simpson replaced Sgt. Slaugh and gained the respect and confidence of all in Radio Relay. He was another gentle giant of a man who had also served in Korea. His loyalty and support were the underpinnings of our platoon.

Staff Sergeant, later Gunnery Sergeant, Jimmy Blackstock was a highly professional, super-conscientious, squared away Marine who loved the Corps. After returning from his second tour of duty in Vietnam, he married Joanne Squazzo in the fall of 1969 in the Bay Ridge section of Brooklyn. A genuine Texas Christian gentleman, Jimmy was kind enough to invite Mame and me, as well as Vic Fitzgerald, to his wedding.

That afternoon Joanne's Dad, an elderly Italian-American gent who had served in World War I, showed me his Army medals at the reception in his home; his pride in both his daughter and his military service was palpable. I have also learned since then that he also served under General John Pershing, chasing Pancho Villa in

Mexico, as did my Uncle Martin Meaney. Jimmy and Joanne lived in West Islip, New York, not far from Westhampton, for many years but recently relocated to Stockbridge, Georgia, to be nearer their daughter.

Sergeant George Krentz was another fine Marine who possessed excellent technical proficiency. He was highly reliable and had probably forgotten more than I would have ever known about the various technologies for which *I* was responsible.

Sergeant Sidney Dines was an exceptionally bright but nearly inscrutable young man, who had another perfect mustache. Independent and strong, he probably felt that I didn't pay enough attention to him. He was a self-starter, which I could see, and I was proud to promote him to sergeant, although I suspect that he felt the promotion should have come sooner.

Corporal Ron Sackie, for whom I believe I also approved a third stripe, was a laconic man who did his job exceedingly well but seemed to keep a low profile. However, he was regarded by his fellow Marines as outstanding, knowledgeable and dependable. I remember exchanging addresses with him just before I returned to The World. Maybe it was 1970 when I wrote to him but I don't recall receiving a reply. I wish him the best life has to offer.

Others I remember well include Sergeant Rick Boisselle from Hartford, Connecticut; Sergeant "T" (for Thompson), a technical genius; Corporal Bradshaw, a skinny young African-American who possessed a great sense of humor and was a top performer; Corporal DeFrisco, who had something of a literary bent and chose the inscription on the farewell plaque our platoon presented to me when I returned to The World ("For those who fight for it, life has a flavor the protected never know."); Corporal Dan Schiavietello, the Beatles fan of ammo-dump Christmas card fame; Lance Corporal Harley Washburn; and Corporals Madsen and McCurley, as well as Lance Corporal Henderson, whose first names unfortunately escape me.

LCpl Henderson hated being anywhere but at posts "out in the bush." He was also the antithesis of a garrison Marine; no spit and polish for this guy. But what a worker and what a trooper! He was a Marine's Marine. Although he typically resembled an unmade bed, there was no one more reliable or willing to help, and he always got the job done. I'd take many Hendersons on my team any time.

To all of these "few good men" in whom I still and will always take great pride, Godspeed and *Semper fi!*

> *Marines are about the most peculiar breed of human beings I have ever witnessed. They treat their service as if it were some kind of cult, plastering their emblem on almost everything they own, making themselves up to look like insane fanatics with haircuts ungentlemenly short, worshipping their Commandant almost as if he were a god, and making weird animal noises like a band of savages. They will fight like rabid dogs at the drop of a hat just for the sake of a little action and are the cockiest SOB's I have ever known. Most have the foulest mouths and drink well beyond a man's normal limits. But, their high spirits and sense of brotherhood set them apart and generally speaking the United States Marines I have come in contact with are the most professional soldiers and the finest men I have had the pleasure to meet.*
>
> —Anonymous Canadian Citizen [1969]

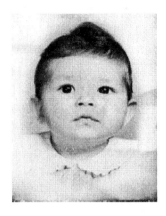

Here I am in 1945 at approximately six months of age. Nice hair.

This picture of Mom and me in the early days in Brooklyn is a favorite of mine.

I thought I was Hopalong Cassidy on April 10, 1949, my fourth birthday. Note the Bugs Bunny-Porky Pig sweater.

At seven I received my First Communion on May 24, 1952. Here I am afterward, flanked by my brother Mike, 5, and sister Pat, not quite 3, at Our Lady Help of Christians School on East 29th Street in the Flatbush section of Brooklyn.

At fourteen I played third base and left field for the Garden City (New York) Babe Ruth League Dodgers, shown here. Front row (left to right): Tom Hipp, name unknown, Tom Schenck and Greg Herbert; second row: Dave Brewer, myself, Bob Wihnyk, Jerry Coyle and Dean Martin; third row: Jim Henderson (a Chaminade High School classmate, now deceased), Edwin "Punky" Booth, Joe Caselli, Ture Dormsjo and Jim Norwood; back row: coaches Jim Norwood, Sr., Nelson Brewer, Sr., Henry Wihnyk, Arthur Herbert, Sr. (manager), name unknown, and Charlie Mansfield, my Dad.

That's me, #63, in pursuit of a Hicksville High School running back on Saturday of Labor Day weekend 1961. I played offensive guard and defensive linebacker. The game was televised, and the announcer was the late, great Marty Glickman. We won 28-7, the Chaminade Flyers varsity's first of eight victories (against no losses or ties) that year.

Here's Chaminade's first undefeated and untied team in the autumn of 1961; it was our second consecutive championship. Some of my best friends also appear in this photograph. In the top row, third from the right is Al Groh, #85; second from the right is Earl Kirmser, #39, co-captain. In the second row on the far left is Bill Sellerberg, #64, co-captain; fifth from the left is Cliff Molloy, #59; sixth is Rod Dwyer, #48; Tom Kiley, #58, is third from the right. Kneeling in front are Carl LoGalbo, #49, fifth from the left; and Frank Biasi, #31, second from the right. I'm in the second row on the far right.

This is Mame as she appeared in the 1962 *Mast*, the Garden City High School yearbook. To me this picture says everything about why I asked her to marry me.

This shot depicts Bernice Bonner Locasto, Mame's mother, Mame and me after Mame's graduation from Marymount College (Tarrytown, N.Y.) on June 1, 1966.

Here is my college yearbook photo as it appeared in the College of the Holy Cross's 1966 *Purple Patcher*. I was twenty when it was taken. I graduated on June 8, 1966.

Here Mame and I are pictured entering the limousine that would take us to our wedding reception. The photo was taken by Denis Murphy's eldest brother Jim, now deceased, shortly after we were married on June 10, 1967 in St. Joseph's Church in Garden City, New York.

Shown here is our wedding party. Left to right: Tom Greene, Denis Murphy, Bernice Locasto (Healy), myself, Mame, my brother Mike (my Best Man), Catherine Locasto (Stovall), Jim Norwood and Larry Hennessy.

Here I am relaxing in Dong Ha, Vietnam, shortly after arriving in-country in July 1968. I'm holding an M-79 grenade launcher in my left hand.

Here I am also in Dong Ha with (left to right) Gunnery Sergeant Don Simpson, Staff Sergeant Jimmy Blackstock and First Lieutenant Bob Dusek (far right). This shot was taken in the autumn of 1968 soon after we had built SEA (Southeast Asia) huts, one of which is seen in the background, to replace the troop tents in which our Marines had been living.

Here's my friend Captain Don O'Neill dancing with a martini at one of our Dong Ha "backyard" barbecues in May 1969.

Marines at ease. A few beers were enjoyed at this party thrown by my platoon. Left to right are Gunny Don Simpson, Corporal McCurley, Sergeant George Krentz, Corporal Jim Wilbanks, Lance Corporal Harley Washburn, myself, and Corporal Madsen, who placed his hat on my head just before the snapshot.

This picture was taken in May 1969 minutes before I shaved off the mustache. Having seen the photo, Mame wrote and asked me to remove the mustache before coming home. She said she was afraid I would scare our then-toddler son Chas, and she was probably right.

Here I am in 1985 in my office at 100 Gold Street in New York City. I served then as chief executive officer of Prudential's international bank.

It was an honor here to present Coach Joe Thomas, who had then retired from Chaminade after forty years, with an album of letters and other memorabilia. The photo was taken at Chaminade on September 11, 1988 during the Joe Thomas Testimonial, which I chaired and at which I served as master of ceremonies. My friend Brother Richard Hartz, S.M., Chaminade's Director of Development and Alumni Relations, appears in the background.

This is one of Mame's and my most cherished pictures of our family. It was taken on October 5, 1989 in Westhampton, and shows (left to right) John, 19, Mame, Chas, 21, Kate, 14, and myself.

Here I am with Mike Paulino in the comfort of The Great Barber's chair. Mike was my tonsorial professional and friend from 1952 to his retirement on September 5, 1992.

Here's the whole clan (as it was then constituted) at my parents' 50th wedding anniversary celebration on Hutchinson Island, Florida, their winter home, on April 27, 1994. Present were (left to right): front row: Tim (10 months), Dawn (his Mom and Chas's wife), my daughter Kate, my mother Mary, my father Charlie, Emily Barnett (my sister Peggy's daughter) and Mame; second row: Chas, Elisabeth, Peggy, John and myself; back row: Tom Phelan, my sister Pat (Tom's wife), my sister Kate, Jim Brumsted (her former husband), Maggie (my brother Mike's wife) and Mike.

On April 8, 2000, the "Boys of Summer" gathered at Earl
Kirmser's home with Coach Joe Thomas to honor Al Groh
on his ascendancy to the head coach's position with the
New York Jets. Standing left to right are Earl, Carl LoGalbo,
Tom Kiley and Al. I'm kneeling next to Coach Thomas,
who is seated.

I love this shot of Mame, which was taken at our son John's
wedding to Elizabeth Van Hook on September 23, 2000 in
Boothbay Harbor, Maine.

This is another recent favorite picture of Mame and me. It was taken in January 2001 at Chaminade's annual Founders Dinner in Woodbury, New York.

I worked for U.S. Senator John McCain of Arizona during his 1999–2000 presidential campaign. Here I am shown with him and Congressman Peter King on April 15, 2000 at a luncheon at the Long Island congressman's home. I was actually elected an Alternate Delegate to the Republican National Convention, held that year in Philadelphia.

"The Gathering" takes place each summer at Mame's and my home in Westhampton. It includes Holy Cross classmates, former Marines and Vietnam veterans Roger Hunt, Frank Teague, myself and Bob Lund, shown here (left to right) in July 2001. Of course, our wives—Joanne Hunt, Dee Teague, Patty Lund and Mame—also participate fully in the festivities. Now an annual tradition, The Gathering has produced some of the most hilarious moments—and photographs—of our lives. *Semper fi!*

Another gathering has traditionally taken place at our Westhampton home each March to celebrate St. Patrick's Day. At our most recent fête on March 9, 2002 Mame took this great shot of Pat, Mike and me.

On April 1, 2002 I visited "The Wall" (the Vietnam Veterans Memorial in Washington, D.C.) for the fourth time. Each visit for me has been a sacred duty and a deeply moving experience.

Here is the next generation of Mansfields: Mame's and my grandchildren. Chas and Dawn's beautiful offspring, Marissa, 4, Tim, 9, and Kevin, 3, surround their newest brother Justin, just shy of his first birthday on August 3, 2002.

26

SOME GOOD IN ALL THIS

For God shall bring every work into judgment, with every secret thing, whether it be good, or whether it be evil.

—Ecclesiastes 12:14

We often hear about Vietnam veterans who are messed up as a result of their service in-country. In fact, there is something called "post-traumatic stress disorder" (PTSD), which in World Wars I and II was called "shell shock" and "combat fatigue," respectively. Researchers tell us the trauma occurs when "a person has experienced, witnessed, or been confronted with a terrible event that is an actual occurrence," or the threat thereof. His or her response to the trauma involves "intense fear, helplessness, and/or horror." Now a part of organized psychiatry, PTSD may include symptoms such as flashbacks, nightmares, rages, alcoholic and/or drug binges, apathy, panics, depression and guilt. Yet, other veterans were strengthened by the war, and came to regard themselves as tough and self-reliant in spite of it. Many of them saw death up close every day, yet they are today married, happy and largely secure in their lives. Indeed, PTSD likely has claimed far fewer victims than previously thought.

In my research I came across a web site named "Vietnam 25," whose "Main Frame Page" bears the headline, "The War Is Over! 25th Anniversary." What really caught my eye, however were two captions on its second and third pages, principally because of their tone. To wit:

> ➤ We also remember the more than 58,000 Americans—almost entirely the sons and daughters of poor and working-class families—who lost their lives, ordered into battle by arrogant men 10,000 miles away.
> ➤ We commit ourselves to continue to oppose U.S. interventionism and foreign policy driven by corporate profits and greed.

So the liberal, aging antiwar crowd is still at it. How I wish they would give us a break. Since that is almost certainly wishful thinking, I will take these extremists to task on some of their *extrema.*

A fellow Marine who led an infantry platoon in Vietnam during the same two years I was there has done some remarkable research that demonstrates that Vietnam veterans are not the victims the liberals and the media would have us believe; nor was Vietnam a "class war," as is commonly claimed.

His name is Mackubin Thomas Owens and he serves as professor of strategy and force planning at the Naval War College in Newport, Rhode Island. He tells us squarely that "The myth of the Vietnam veteran as victim had its genesis in the antiwar left of the 1960s and '70s. Initially vilifying the American soldier as a war criminal, the left eventually bestowed victimhood upon him."

Here are some of his findings about the Vietnam War:

> ➤ 30% of those who died were from the *lowest* income group, but
> ➤ 26% were from the *highest.*
> ➤ 86% of those who died during the war were *white,* and

➤ 12.5% were *black* (in an age group in which blacks comprised 13.1% of the population).

➤ Two thirds of those who served in Vietnam were volunteers, and

➤ Volunteers accounted for 77% of all combat deaths.

As far as PTSD is concerned, it is real but not nearly as widespread as the press would insist. Mr. Owens addresses this too:

> The claim that PTSD continues to affect nearly half of the 3.3 million men who served in Vietnam is implausible, especially given that fewer than 15% of those were assigned to combat units. A more reasonable figure comes from the Centers for Disease Control, whose study reported that 15% of Vietnam veterans experienced symptoms of combat related-PTSD at some time during or after military service, but that only 2.2% exhibited symptoms at the time of the study.

The liberal purveyors of victim status for Vietnam veterans should consult a comprehensive survey commissioned by the Veterans' Administration in 1980. Were they to do so, they would learn that:

➤ Fully 91% of those who had seen combat in Vietnam were "glad they had served their country."

➤ A healthy 80% disagreed with the statement that "the U.S. took advantage of me."

➤ Nearly two thirds said they would go to Vietnam again—even knowing the war's outcome.

In words both balanced and patriotic, "Mack" Owens concludes that "Those who served in Vietnam did so . . . with honor, decency and restraint. Vietnam veterans have fared at least as well as any other generation of warriors."

Perhaps the most eloquent words about the future of Vietnam veterans were written in 1983 by the late Vermont Royster, who earlier served as editor of *The Wall Street Journal*, was a Pulitzer Prize winner and became one of the greatest journalists of the twentieth century. In a Pulitzer-winning column entitled "Those Who Were There," he quoted Shakespeare's *Henry V*: "And gentlemen in England now abed shall think themselves accurs'd they were not here." Mr. Royster then concluded his piece with the following two sentences:

> The day will come, I no longer have any doubt, when those few who were there those years ago will gather with their wives and walking canes, as old soldiers have always done, to talk of how it was.
>
> When that day comes all the others will be excluded from that band of brothers.

At the time Royster wrote his warm and welcome words, which was fifteen years after I had gone to Vietnam, even I had observed the emerging pride of Vietnam veterans. Young people who worked in my organization, as well as others who happened to learn of my Marine Corps service in Vietnam, became inquisitive and friendly, some peculiarly deferential and even admiring. Typically, they wanted to know what Vietnam was all about, why I went there instead of, say, Canada, and how I felt then and now. Like Vermont Royster's column, their desire to know was good, honest, timely, and helped bring us full circle. It made us all once again a "band of brothers."

There is no doubt in my mind that the U.S. made serious errors in judgment and also experienced, at least on occasion, a great deal of bad luck in its conduct of the Vietnam War. Nonetheless, the American purpose was correct and may be more clearly recognized if one considers the landscape and politics of Southeast Asia today, especially in Vietnam, which has been a

Communist state since 1975. Notwithstanding the outcome in Vietnam, the American commitment and effort during the conflict there probably saved both time and integrity for countries from Thailand to Indonesia. Indeed, the post-war successes of many nations on the Pacific Rim would not have transpired were it not for American sacrifices in Vietnam.

Sixteen years after the Vietnam war ended, Congressman Henry Hyde (Republican of Illinois), a man I admire greatly, wrote that "even though Vietnam was conquered, the objective for which we fought—the establishment of a free and independent Vietnam—is still attainable." When I first read these words, I thought Mr. Hyde had flipped. After all, Vietnam *is* a Communist state.

The Congressman went on to say that

> the U.S. was never militarily defeated in Vietnam. When the U.S. entered the war in the early 1960s, the Saigon government's control over the countryside was slim and fading fast, with the Communists dominating . . . When we withdrew in 1973, 80% or more of the territory and population was under government control, and the Communist infrastructure and cadres in the South had been virtually wiped out.
>
> The conquest, when it came two years later, was at the hands of North Vietnamese regulars. This was required because the Viet Cong, which had borne the brunt of the confrontation with the U.S. military over the past decade, had been reduced to tattered remnants.

Mr. Hyde concluded that our military success prior to the North Vietnamese invasion of the South cannot be labeled a defeat, any more than France's surrender to the Germans in World War II could be called a final defeat for the Allies.

Along the same lines, about ten years after I came home from Vietnam, on April 2, 1979, Chas's eleventh birthday, *The Wall Street Journal*, under the rubric "Vietnam Memory: Acts of Good Faith," published a letter from me, part of which follows.

I too believe there remains a "reservoir of feeling" that we, American veterans of the war and the U.S. itself, acted in good faith for a cause that would hopefully serve some ultimate beneficial purpose for the Vietnamese people, many of whom . . . continue "risking their lives en masse to get out on the high seas in small boats." In one fundamental sense the U.S. had an obligation as a member of SEATO to defend then South Vietnam. While this has been acrimoniously debated and treated extensively in the many articles and books written during and since the war, it still relates to other fundamentals like U.S. credibility, decisiveness, and strength—all of which are seriously questioned, if not doubted, every day both here and abroad. In another sense many of us believe that our presence brought some hope and happiness, however temporary, to those poor, devastated people.

The Marine Corps has consistently advocated the principle that the war in South Vietnam can be conclusively won only through convincing the South Vietnamese people in the villages and hamlets that their hope lies with freedom, not with communism. Today while the search for a negotiated settlement to the war continues, this becomes even more important.

—General Leonard F. Chapman, 24th
Marine Corps Commandant [1969]

27

GOING HOME

We gotta get out of this place, if it's the last thing we ever do.

—The Animals

I n early 1969 I received a telex (there were no faxes or e-mails in those days) from Headquarters Marine Corps, which I wish I had saved for its value as a humorous document. Its subject was my "Rotation Tour Date," or RTD. This was the date on which one would leave his duty station in Vietnam and begin the long-awaited trip back to The World, which in official military communications was abbreviated CONUS, for "Continental United States." The telex also addressed my RELAD, or "Release from Active Duty."

After reading this official communication, I could not help but laugh. Here is a reconstruction of its message:

> FROM HQMC TO 1LT C F MANSFIELD JR: RELAD
> SET AT 1 JUN 69 (STOP) ORIGINAL RTD SET AT 27
> JUL 69 (STOP) FOLLOWING OPTIONS NOW
> AVAILABLE: (1) COMPLETE CURRENT WESTPAC
> TOUR OF DUTY AS OF ORIGINAL 27 JUL 69 RTD
> (STOP) (2) EXTEND CURRENT TOUR OF DUTY
> SIX MONTHS OR LONGER (STOP) (3) RETURN
> CONUS 21 MAY 69 FOR RELAD (STOP)

This is another of those relative extrema. Talk about a no-brainer.

When I received word that I would be going home early, I called Bob Lund to tell him my good news. He was now back in Quang Tri with his squadron, VMO-6. I proposed that we get together for a beer and some chow, and he was amenable. First, though, Bob surprised me with an invitation to fly a UH1E (Huey); I don't recall if it was a gunship or a "slick." Of course, he wouldn't even dream of allowing me to take off or land but he did permit me to sit in the copilot's seat and fly the bird once we were aloft. It was late on a sunny afternoon with near-calm winds and a bit of haze in the air. We took off and toured a portion of Quang Tri Province, including, of course, Dong Ha, from which I would soon take my leave. As we headed north, Bob startled me while I was flying the helicopter.

"Holy shit, Charlie, we're in the Z!" he shouted.

The nasty thought of being where we shouldn't, and the attendant risks, flashed through my mind. I could hear the echo of my father saying, "Chuck, for a smart boy, you're an awful dope!"

"Let's get the hell out of here fast," I shouted back.

In fact, there was no reason to be alarmed. Bob had merely reverted to his old college antic of exaggerating a situation, in this case sounding an alarm, when all he wanted to do was dupe someone. Now, my dictionary tells me that "Dupe suggests unwariness in the person deluded and the acceptance of what is false as true." Score one more 'gotcha' for The Round Man.

Before leaving Dong Ha I cleaned out my hootch. This was not difficult since Marines lived in such places with few personal effects. Still, there were some things I decided to discard. In fact, I burned the letters Mame wrote and sent to me during my tour in-country. I still cannot forget that she wrote to me every day, as I did to her. Destroying them was a colossal mistake; as I write now, how I wish I had kept her written words, for they would have added so much to this latter-day account of that time long ago.

I also received letters from family members; I especially recall receiving one from Mimi Charrot every week. My sister Elisabeth, then 12, wrote to me and I reciprocated. (She has given me copies of the letters she received from me, and they are beyond boring.) My Mom, of course, wrote, as did my sister Pat. Receiving mail in Vietnam was wonderful.

There's another mail-related anecdote that deserves telling. When Mame and Chas were living in GC with her parents, my letters from Vietnam would, of course, arrive via the local post office. The letter carrier whose route included 24 Locust Street was known as "Rocky," a true-blue Italian-American man, of whom everyone was fond. On the occasional days when there was no letter from me for Mame, he would always return to the post office at the end of his rounds just to check if a letter from me might have arrived during the day. If so, Rocky would take it upon himself to deliver the letter to Mame on his own time prior to going home at the end of the day. When I returned to GC from Vietnam, I looked up Rocky and thanked him deeply for his service above and beyond the call of duty. Rocky hadn't served in the Marine Corps, but he certainly understood and lived the meaning of the words *Semper fidelis*.

Believe it or not, as much as I could not wait to get back to The World, I was troubled when it came to saying goodbye to my fellow Marines in Dong Ha. My platoon gave me a great sendoff— a steak barbecue with plenty of *cold* Budweiser. Near the end of the party, Gunny Don Simpson presented me a plaque that I display on the wall of my study and cherish to this day. On it is inscribed:

FOR OUTSTANDING LEADERSHIP

TO

1ST LT C MANSFIELD JR

FROM THE MEN OF RADIO RELAY PLT

68-69

FOR THOSE WHO FIGHT FOR IT
LIFE HAS A FLAVOR
THE PROTECTED NEVER KNOW

The next morning, May 21, 1969, I flew aboard a Lockheed Marine C-130 *Hercules* from "Dong Ha International Airport" nonstop to Danang. The flight was uneventful, although personally thrilling, for it was the first leg of my journey back to The World.

In Danang I had to unpack and spruce up my "Summer Service Charlie" uniform, which was required for my return flight to the States. It consisted of lightweight tan trousers, a shortsleeved tan shirt with open collar, the traditional Marine web belt, black shoes and a tan "piss cutter." I hadn't worn 'Charlies' since the preceding November on Okinawa. When I slipped into the trou and zipped them up, they nearly fell down, for I had lost forty pounds, most of it deliberately, going from 210 pounds to 170 in just three months. Because of my new svelte size and appearance, I had to have the pants altered, but this was a good thing.

Also while in Vietnam I gave up my two-pack-a-week smoking habit. I quit primarily because even then I believed that cigarette smoking caused lung cancer. Moreover, the price of a pack of cigarettes in the U.S. had risen to 40¢ whereas I was buying smokes in-country for 10-15¢ a pack. I smoked Camels or Lucky Strikes, unfiltered, of course. If someone gave me a filtered cigarette, I would remove the filter, put the other end in my mouth and light up. Kicking that habit is one of the best things I have ever done for myself.

⧗

While I was in Danang awaiting a flight to Okinawa, I met with several Marine aviator buddies—"airdales," as they were sometimes called—who were stationed there with the First Marine Air Wing (1st MAW).

I was shocked when they told me that another friend with whom I had trained and served, Billy Ryan, had been killed in action in the crash of a Marine F-4 *Phantom*; his was a virtual carbon copy of Dick Morin's tragic death five months earlier. Billy and Dick were both RIOs (radar intercept operators), and I believe they were even in the same squadron.

The two most tragic elements of Billy's death were its timing and circumstances. His wife Judy had already left their infant son with her parents in a Maryland suburb of Washington, D.C., and traveled to New York's JFK airport for the first leg of a trip to Hawaii where she would meet Billy for R&R. Judy and Mame were good friends, having been pregnant with their first children at the same time, and having had the same ob-gyn specialist, a naval officer named Dr. Yon. While Judy was at JFK about to board her flight, she was paged. It was a phone call from her father who conveyed to his daughter the shocking news that her Billy had been killed. The news was heart-rending, and not just for Judy, because there is something especially awful about the thought of a beautiful young mother anticipating a joyful reunion with her husband after a long separation and then instead being pierced by the pain of his sudden loss.

We toasted the memory of both Dick and Billy, but it was not enough.

The only personal consolation I have in this story is that I had dropped out of the F-4 *Phantom* RIO program because, unlike the Air Force's F-4, the Navy-Marine Corps version of the aircraft, as exciting as I found it, did not have flight controls in the back seat, which was the RIO's. There was only a small radar screen there. I left because I didn't want to be at the mercy of a pilot who, for whatever reason, might somehow forget that I was there too, if, for example, it came to ejecting from the aircraft, a time when a split-second might mean the difference between life and death. I have since learned that my concern was unfounded because, in such a situation in the F-4, the back seat goes first, regardless of whether the RIO or the pilot in front initiates the firing of the ejection mechanism.

Gunnery Sergeant Washington was, like me, assigned to Headquarters Battalion, Third Marine Division, in Quang Tri in northern I Corps, although we were both physically stationed elsewhere. Moreover, his tour of duty in Vietnam coincided roughly with mine. I also remember seeing him from time to time during my service in Vietnam, say, every few months.

An African-American, Gunny Washington (sorry to say I don't recall his first name) was a man who commanded, not demanded, respect, for he was a Marine's Marine, one who had served in combat before, namely, in the Korean War. Senior Marine NCOs like him made men like me, as James Brady put it so aptly in *The Coldest War*, "uneasy to be saluted by men of such distinction." Strong but gentle, inspirational and softly spoken, he was, above all, admirable in my eyes. He exuded confidence, maturity, credibility and authority, but he possessed genuine warmth too. To me he was the quintessential Marine, one I could only admire, although I liked him very much as well. Indeed, he was the sort who made others proud to be on the same team as he, an extraordinary man.

As luck would have it, when my day came to leave Vietnam and return to The World, I boarded a flight in Danang chock-a-block filled with fellow Marines. As I walked down the aisle of the Continental Airlines 707 that was to take me on the first part of a journey to Okinawa, California and (finally!) home, I spotted Gunny Washington sitting in a window seat on the starboard side of the aircraft about mid-fuselage. As the seat next to him was empty, I asked if he would mind my sitting there.

Gracious and charming (not all Marine gunnery sergeants could be so described), he recognized me and said, "Lieutenant Mansfield, I would love to have your company on *this* trip."

He and I spoke happily and incessantly until the big bird's take-off roll, when everyone on the plane went silent as it began.

Next, as the large jet's nose wheel rotated upward and we began to lift off, Gunny Washington, his face practically pressed against the window out of which he gazed wistfully, took his last measure of Vietnam.

With near-religious reverence he said quietly, "Adios, *motherfucker.*"

How bizarrely perfect, I thought, as I added, "Amen."

The Gunny then grinned his marvelous grin. He and I quickly and eagerly shook hands; I think we even hugged each other. We then joined in the thunderous applause and hoopla, as he and I felt the tremendous happiness, virtually forgotten during our time in-country, that every Marine on board experienced in that exhilarating moment.

I would not see Vietnam again until November 11, 1982, the Veterans Day on which the Vietnam Veterans Memorial in Washington, D.C., was unveiled and dedicated. That day I was on an airplane headed to Singapore from Hong Kong when the pilot directed passengers' attention to "the coast of Vietnam off the right side of the aircraft." It was a sight I will never forget.

After a stop in Okinawa for a couple of days, we flew on to Hawaii where we refueled. Our next destination was mainland U.S.A., specifically the Marine Corps Air Station at El Toro (Santa Ana), California. We arrived on the afternoon of Sunday, May 25, 1969, and were told that official processing, RELAD in my case, would take at least a week. I remember thinking about, and resenting, being in the U.S. but not actually being able to go home when I wanted to.

So near and yet so far. Hurry up and wait. Typical Marine Corps Mickey Mouse, I thought.

On that Sunday evening many of us headed for the officers' club for drinks and a meal. Despite the reality that we weren't yet where our hearts and treasures were, it was an honor and a pleasure to be in the company of those great Marines, both young and not so young. It was sweet, but we weren't quite home yet, and all of us were anxiously anticipating being with our families after, in most cases, long separations.

On Monday morning, I headed straight for the administration building to begin my processing. There were scores, if not hundreds, who had the same status as I; how could I expect to get home any earlier than the one week of which we were advised?

To my astonishment, Tom Moore, Holy Cross '65 and a Marine captain, was in charge of the administration office. First Lieutenant Gerry Byrne, a classmate from The Basic School and a fellow New Yorker also awaiting RELAD, was with me and exulted, "I can't believe you know this guy!"

Anyway, I spoke with Tom and told him that Gerry and I had been formally advised that it would take at least a week for us to be processed and get back to New York. Unabashedly, I asked Tom, "Is there any way you could get us out of here sooner?"

Citing the horrendous workload of his office, so as not to engender false hope in us, he still managed a smile and promised, "I'll see what I can do." *How sweet it was!*

After that most satisfactory chance meeting with Tom, I had the time to do another friend a favor. Back in Dong Ha I had promised Don Fritz I would look up his wife Betty, a nurse at El Toro. He had given me her office telephone number, so she was easy to find. Betty and I had a brief but pleasant visit, which I found rewarding, for it gave me the opportunity to do something good and tangible for a buddy who was still in-country. While I spoke with her, I recall thinking, *I hope Don's okay.* After all, one never knew.

On the next morning, Tuesday May 27th, I kept an appointment with a Marine Corps lieutenant colonel who, in effect, administered what in corporate America might be called an exit interview, although this one had an unmistakable element of recruitment. Clearly, the lieutenant colonel's primary responsibility was to get me to "re-up," that is, to extend my period of active duty. I must concede that his proposal was not wholly unattractive for there was still a great deal in and about the Marine Corps that I loved.

The initial part of our conversation focused on the success of the Corps' operations in Vietnam, and the importance of having seasoned officers available to lead in the various military occupational specialties (MOSs). Yet, I thought, he can't seriously begin to imagine that I might want to return to Vietnam any time soon. I was right, and this is where the lieutenant colonel employed some fairly savvy marketing. To make the potential seduction even more attractive, I would be given a regular (as opposed to a reserve) commission and promoted to captain virtually immediately. (This was a non-event because I knew I would be promoted very soon anyway, as I was on August 1, 1969.) The other part of the proposal centered on an assignment in the continental United States, one in which I would be living with my wife and son for a minimum of six months. It sounded good—up to a point.

In my own mind I had no technical or differentiating civilian job skills, except reasonable abilities to read, write and speak. Worse, I had no idea what I wanted to do in a post-Marine Corps career, but this unknown did not bother me excessively. What did concern me, however, perhaps more than anything else at the time, was that I wanted to remain with my wife and son indefinitely, to say the least. I also knew that I had no desire to return to Vietnam while the war was still on.

Six months. That's pretty good, I thought. I was a Marine. Being one was my job, the only one I had known since college, and there was so much about being a Marine that seemed to suit me. Still, down deep, my mind and my heart both said the same thing: Go home and take your chances in the non-Marine Corps world.

One question about which the lieutenant colonel was somewhat vague was when, if I re-upped, I might be returned to duty in Vietnam. I understood, of course, that he was not in a position to make commitments of any sort. Nonetheless, I felt I had no realistic choice, for myself or my family, other than to assume that I would go back in-country after the promised six months stateside had passed.

In short, I decided that I'd be a damn fool to re-up. I opted for RELAD, which could not be denied me.

On Wednesday, May 28, 1969 shortly before 9:00 a.m., Gerry Byrne and I boarded a transcontinental flight from Los Angeles International Airport to New York's John F. Kennedy International Airport. Joyful at the prospect of our homecoming, we talked our way across the country; the joy we shared was an unprecedented feeling for both of us. I believe it was the first time in about a year, likely longer, that we had both truly relaxed. We even toasted each other—and the Corps, of course—with glasses of champagne.

Our flight landed in New York on time at 5:30 p.m., and Gerry and I said goodbye. I believe we also hugged each other and verbalized *Semper fi*.

⌛

Mame was at the gate, wearing a green summer jumper. *Mine eyes have seen the glory! I am back in The World!*

Like the reverse-thrusters on the jet engines on the big silver bird that had just brought me safely home, all of the miserable feelings and daunting prospects I took with me on the day I left home for Vietnam the prior year were reversed, and more. Instead, I was experiencing a renewed and vital freedom of mind and spirit, the like of which was novel in my life.

The dream of having Mame in my arms again had at last come true. She and I were together once more, and our life as a married couple, interrupted by a war now a half-world away, had resumed for real in this magic moment. On this bright, beautiful and warm May afternoon, she too was all of those things, as she had always been. She was 'younger than springtime,' as the soaring song from *South Pacific* goes, and, once more, stunning.

My dictionary tells me that joy is "a very glad feeling; happiness; great pleasure; delight." These first moments of renewal with Mame on American soil could also be so defined. But they were so very much more that I do not believe the words exist to describe adequately how I felt. The emotion of happiness was thrilling, and it took my breath away. I cannot imagine what else to say that would adequately convey my feelings.

With my arm around her, Mame led me to American Airlines' Admiral's Club at JFK. As we approached the clear glass doors of the Club, I could see through them my parents and siblings standing inside, awaiting Mame's and my return from the arrival gate.

Then the Club's main door was opened, and my firstborn, Chas, whom I hadn't seen in nearly a year, was turned loose. Seeing his mother, he ran at first, then gradually slowed to a reluctant gait as he approached her and me. Next, with great self-assurance, he peered up at me with those big brown eyes of his that one of his school teachers would later characterize as "chocolate."

The message I got from his look was unmistakable and straightforward: *Who's this ugly bastard with my mother?* Chas is nothing if not straightforward. After all, he could not have remembered me, and I had *my* arm around *his* Mom. In fairness, his look was not necessarily one of dislike, but it did reveal uncertainty. I believe there was also suspicion in his young eyes. He told me without saying a word that, *If you're not home with me, Dad, you're irrelevant.* Maybe that's why he is home with and so close to his own four kids today.

After meeting and greeting the whole clan, I was escorted by my family to the parking lot where we boarded cars for the ride to 62 Fairmount Boulevard, GC, my parents' home. It would be the reverse of the trip I had made the year before.

I believe it was impossible for me to have been happier.

As we drove along Fairmount Boulevard, some of the neighbors, aware of my homecoming, were out on the sidewalk, waving as we passed by. Their shouted greetings were warm and welcome; I was amazed that so many had come out for me.

As we pulled into the driveway at No. 62, I couldn't help but notice a huge sign, made of canvas from an old awning my Dad had saved. Hung from the railing on the house's second storey, the sign was draped over the entire front of the garage. In foot-high block letters, it read: WELCOME HOME, CHUCK! The feeling I had was nearly overwhelming, one I don't think I had experienced before.

At the homecoming party that followed this unprecedented and wonderful welcome, I think every relative, friend and neighbor I had ever known stopped by to welcome me home and visit for a while. It was moving and, at times, unreal. In fact, I had to ponder deliberately the fact that I was finally back in The World.

To my surprise, Mame told me later that she was not happy with the fact that my parents had decided to have such a big party in my honor on my first night home. She believed that immediate family only would have been more appropriate on that special evening. For years she harbored a negative feeling about it, but it's ancient history now. Besides, she and my Mom have long since buried the hatchet and are the closest of friends.

A high point of the evening came near the end of the party. My Dad and I were alone, chatting, when he did something unexpected that I don't remember him doing before—ever. He hugged me, and said audibly, "I love you, and I'm glad you're home." That was all, but it was more than enough.

Mame and I slept in the bedroom that Mike and I had first shared when the family moved from Brooklyn in '52, and later as college students. She and I prefer a larger bed but the room's twin beds were just fine, particularly after such a long separation.

On the morning of May 29th, I was awakened by the unwelcome sound of a "cherry bomb" that some neighborhood kid had set off just outside the bedroom window. Instinctively, upon hearing the explosion, I rolled quickly off the bed and onto the floor, attempting to take cover from the perceived attack. It took me a moment to realize that I was in friendly territory and nobody was actually shooting at me. Mame was at first startled at my unusual and unanticipated behavior but still managed a good laugh, as I did a moment later.

On June 30, 1969 I started a new job as a management trainee at Bankers Trust Company in New York City. A few days later, on Independence Day weekend, my parents, my sisters, Mame, Chas and I spent a long weekend at the home of Aunt Jeanne, my mother's sister and my godmother, and Uncle Bob Peters in Westhampton Beach. Before dinner, Dad and I each enjoyed a martini while watching the television evening news, much of which was about the Vietnam War.

Hearing our discussion about the war and my new position in a major international financial institution, my sister Peggy, then 17, who had just graduated from GC High and considered herself an antiwar protester, denounced me in my Dad's presence as "a war-mongering capitalist pig." I was astonished, for sure, but decidedly not angry. For some reason, I didn't take it personally. After all, she was just a kid, and I guess I couldn't believe she could really intend to direct such invective toward her own brother. As far as I was concerned, this was merely another relative extremum and an example of how the war had affected Americans, even the very young, at home. My father, however, wanted to kill her.

> A warmonger is a person who is invincible in peace and invisible in war. A warmonger is always ready to lay down your life for his country.

> —Q. X. Pham

Vietnam was a benchmark for my life for, when it was time to return to The World, I told myself that, no matter how bad things might ever get for me in the years ahead, they could not, by definition, be as bad as some of my experiences in Vietnam, or just the inability to be with loved ones. At home, regardless of anything else, I would have my wife and family with me.

There are five things that have sustained me and many of us, except that some of us often take them for granted or don't think about them much. I call them the five Fs since each word begins with that letter. They are faith, family, friends, fitness and fortitude, although fortitude likely takes its genesis from the other four.

Aside from the resumption of good times with the family, being back in The World afforded me the opportunity to make good on a vow I had made one day in-country. I had promised God—yes, God—in an especially uncomfortable moment while under attack that, if He brought me home alive, I would attend Mass and receive the Eucharist every day for a full year.

The deal worked—for both of us.

Deo gratias!

> *None of these decorations was for uncommon valor. They were for common valor. The routine, daily stuff—just humping, just enduring—but that was worth something wasn't it? Yes, it was. Worth plenty.*
>
> —Tim O'Brien in *The Things They Carried*

28

THE WAR'S END IN SIGHT

*Vietnam was a dark room full of deadly objects, the VC were
everywhere all at once like spider cancer, and instead of losing
the war in little pieces over years we lost it fast in under a week.*

—From *Dispatches* by Michael Herr

In 1973 President Nixon's Secretary of State and former
National Security Advisor Henry Kissinger, together with
North Vietnamese Politburo member Le Duc Tho, initiated
"The Agreement on Ending the War and Restoring Peace in
Vietnam." Within two and a half years of its signing on January
27, 1973, South Vietnam would collapse in the face of a North
Vietnamese juggernaut, and the Vietnam War would be lost.

As Dr. D.M. Vuckovich of Chicago wrote in 1985, "the
U.S. forfeited any victory in Vietnam by leaving that wretched
country, as a football team might quit at half time. . . . The
failure to win the war was based on our absence of sound
military objectives, the result of sustained interference by the
political short-term planners, not allowing (the) military to
respond in the optimal way which ultimately could have
resulted in a different outcome."

The U.S. Congress reduced its aid to the South and that
was the beginning of the end. Mr. Kissinger, who negotiated
the deal with Le Duc Tho, in the first volume of his work *The
White House Years*, attributed the South Vietnamese failure
to the "collapse of (U.S.) Executive authority as a result of

Watergate," the scandal that led to President Nixon's resignation of the presidency on August 9, 1974.

Lawrence O'Brien, an attorney who served as a U.S. infantry officer in Vietnam, in "The Final Conquest of Vietnam: A Look Back," offered some compelling commentary on the final days of South Vietnam. On January 8, 1975, he wrote, North Vietnam's Central Committee decided to launch a major offensive "to divide the South at its center by means of a west-to-east drive to the sea, much as Grant devised Sherman's march in 1864." The NVA began "(a)ttacking across the waist of South Vietnam on March 4, 1975," and the Southern forces under a leader who failed to believe his intelligence reports withdrew "under pressure." "The ensuing failure . . . and the subsequent collapse of half the country led to (then President Nguyen Van) Thieu's resignation and, ultimately, to surrender." . . . For its part, North Vietnam "had brilliantly played out the 'talk, fight-talk, fight' strategy."

President Thieu, who died in September 2001, was forced to resign in May 1975 shortly after the U.S. pulled out of Vietnam. In resigning, he emotionally asked his countrymen to forgive his mistakes.

Many Americans, including more than a few Vietnam veterans, believe that in Vietnam we lost far more than a war. Some say we lost the soul of our nation. For many, even today, the wounds of Vietnam have never really healed. I prefer a more positive view, such as that espoused by Ronald Reagan when he said, "There is nothing wrong with America that Americans can't fix."

Today, on Vietnam's battlefields, the war's scars have been obscured by time and repairs but some remain. Not long ago I read that still visible are the gaping holes that Marines blasted through the thick walls of the Citadel in the city of Hue when they recaptured the ancient Vietnamese capital in the bloody fighting following the Tet offensive.

On the road north of Hue, according to an old report, the

rusting hulks of destroyed American-supplied tanks dotted fields along the roadside. White-star markings on the vehicles were reportedly kept freshly painted as a reminder of the American role in the war.

The best-known battlefield of all—Matt Caulfield's Khe Sanh—was said to be little more than a weed-covered airstrip surrounded by farms. The Montagnards in the valley around Khe Sanh complained that cultivating the old battlefields sometimes triggered land mines and other ordnance still buried in the soil. Many, including returning veterans on both sides, have attested that after the war there was absolutely nothing left, except the land and bomb craters.

Francis J. (Bing) West, an assistant secretary of defense in the first Reagan administration, served as a Marine grunt in Vietnam and is author of *The Village*. At Christmas 2001 he visited a village 400 miles north of Saigon where he had patrolled decades earlier with a "Combined Action Platoon"—local militiamen combined with a squad of Marines. In an article entitled "Back to Vietnam" written soon after his visit West wrote warmly of how the villagers welcomed him back. He concluded with words that resonated with me: "America has surely praised the generation of World War II. But of their Vietnam progeny, pictures and print have projected a face filled with fear, unworthy of praise. It is left to others in unlikely places to remember the faces that were stalwart."

> *"This whole war," she said, "why was everybody so mad at everybody else?"*
>
> *I shook my head. "They weren't mad, exactly. Some people wanted one thing, other people wanted another thing."*
>
> *"What did you want?"*
>
> *"Nothing," I said. "To stay alive."*

"That's all?"

"Yes."

Kathleen sighed. "Well, I don't get it. I mean, how come you were even here in the first place?"

"I don't know," I said. "Because I had to be."

—Tim O'Brien in *The Things They Carried*

29

Not Fond o' Jane

Nothing in the world is more dangerous than a sincere ignorance and conscientious stupidity.

—Martin Luther King, Jr.

One prominent American who sided with the enemy in Vietnam was the actress Jane Fonda, daughter of legendary American actor Henry Fonda, and former wife of Ted Turner of AOL Time Warner, Turner Broadcasting System and Atlanta Braves fame. In July 1972 Ms. Fonda and Tom Hayden, her husband at the time, actually traveled to North Vietnam to condemn the policy of the United States.

On August 22, 1972 Ms. Fonda gave an address on Radio Hanoi from Hanoi, North Vietnam, in English to American servicemen involved in the war. Here are some excerpts:

> This is Jane Fonda. During my two week visit in the Democratic Republic of Vietnam, I've had the opportunity to visit a great many places and speak to a large number of people from all walks of life—workers, peasants, students, artists and dancers, historians, journalists, film actresses, soldiers, militia girls, members of the women's union, writers.
>
> One thing I have learned beyond a shadow of a doubt . . . is that (then President Richard) Nixon will never be able to break the spirit of these people; he'll never be able

to turn Vietnam . . . into a neo-colony of the United States . . .

(D)espite the bombs, despite the crimes being created— being committed against them by Richard Nixon, . . . the people have taken power into their own hands, and they are controlling their own lives.

. . . I think Richard Nixon would do well to read Vietnamese history, particularly their poetry, and particularly the poetry written by (North Vietnamese leader) Ho Chi Minh.

As if this weren't enough, she made several other broadcasts for the Communist North in which she called American military leaders "war criminals." To Americans' horror, Jane Fonda actually encouraged Viet Cong soldiers to fight "American Imperialists," and sang antiwar songs behind enemy lines. She also had her photograph taken at a Communist anti-aircraft gun emplacement used to shoot down American planes.

Of this episode, North Vietnamese Colonel Bui Tin would write later in his memoirs that

We were elated when Jane Fonda, wearing a red Vietnamese dress, said at a press conference that she was ashamed of American actions in the war and would struggle along with us . . . . (she) represented the conscience of America . . . . part of its war-making capability, and we turning (sic) that power in our favor.

Article III, Section 3 of the Constitution of the United States declares, "Treason against the United States shall consist only in levying war against them, or in adhering to their enemies, giving them aid and comfort." Plainly and blatantly, Jane Fonda committed treason. Even TruthOrFiction.com's website confirms that "There is no dispute that her visit took place, that her words and actions were in support of the enemy, and that her conduct caused harm to the war effort and to some of the prisoners of war."

In sum, I believe Ms. Fonda should have been tried (and executed) for treason.

On her performance and my feelings about it, I would echo enthusiastically the words of former Secretary of the Navy, former Marine and Vietnam veteran James Webb, as told by Robert Timberg in his bestseller *The Nightingale's Song*. When a San Francisco radio talk show host asked Webb what he thought of Ms. Fonda, he replied, "Jane Fonda can kiss my ass. I wouldn't go across the street to watch her slit her wrist."

"Hanoi Jane," as she is known to many Vietnam veterans, has been honored by *Ladies' Home Journal* in "100 Years of Great Women," presumably the twentieth century. Unfortunately, few are aware of how she betrayed not only our country but also specific men who served and sacrificed during the Vietnam War.

Michael Benge, a civilian economic development advisor, was captured by the North Vietnamese in South Vietnam in 1968 and held for five years. He has written that he "spent 27 months in solitary confinement, one year in a cage in Cambodia, and one year in a 'black box' in Hanoi." Here is the rest of his account, according to TruthOrFiction.com:

> My North Vietnamese captors deliberately poisoned and murdered a female missionary, a nurse in a leprosarium in Ban me Thuot, South Vietnam, whom I buried in the jungle near the Cambodian border. [She was Betty Olsen, a Christian Missionary Alliance nurse from New York.] At one time, I weighed approximately 90 lbs. (My normal weight is170 lbs.) We were Jane Fonda's "war criminals." When Jane Fonda visited Hanoi, I was asked by the camp communist political officer if I would be willing to meet with her. I said yes, for I wanted to tell her about the real treatment we POWs were receiving, which was far different from the treatment purported by the North Vietnamese, and parroted by various peace activists as "humane and lenient." After doing so, I spent three days on a rocky floor on my knees with outstretched arms with a piece of steel placed on my hands,

and beaten with a bamboo cane every time my arms dipped. After my release I had the opportunity to meet with Jane Fonda for a couple of hours. I asked her if she would be willing to debate me on TV. She declined to answer me. She does not exemplify someone who should be honored among "100 Years of Great Women."

What goes around comes around—although Hanoi Jane did not suffer any physical torture of which I am aware.

Here is a heartwarming story from Colonel Bob Kielhofer, a retired Marine. He has written, "There are still some people left with pride and a sense of moral fiber. For those of you who have no liking for Jane Fonda ["HJ" or "Hanoi Jane," as he too calls her], I will recount a little story," excerpts from which follow.

> On a movie set, I was acting as the Chief of Staff to the Confederate General who was overall commander of the 6000 troops in the movie Gettysburg, an historical movie of the Civil War. As actors, we volunteered to (TNT) who was making the movie . . .

> Two incidents involve HJ. The first was on the day when Ted Turner made his cameo appearance in the movie. For those who have the movie, he is the white haired officer who dies climbing over the fence in a charge. Now movies, for the uninitiated, are boring to be in unless you are a star. I had brought up a battalion, about 700 men, up on a road in the hot sun to wait the setup of the cameras. HJ and Ted arrived in a helicopter for the take. HJ walked down to about the center of the battalion to see the troops, and accept the adulation she expected her hubby's employees would give her.

> Most of the troops present were North Carolinians, many from Fort Bragg. The Colonel commanding the battalion

reported to me and informed me his troops were nonplused *(sic)* by HJ's presence and asked my permission to make a troop movement to ease their feelings. What then happened, I will never forget. He called his men to attention. HJ, seeing the activity, smiled expecting some show for her benefit, and walked to the front of rightmost company. The Colonel continued his orders and commanded the company in front of which he stood, "B Company! To the rear! By the right— About! Face! Stand at ease!"

ONE HUNDRED MEN PIVOTED AND GAVE THEIR BACKS. Taking the action for what it was, HJ beat a hasty retreat down the line toward the helicopter. The Colonel followed her progress down the battalion with the same disrespectful salute, reversing each company just as she reached the front of the company. Ten minutes later the copter left and we saw her no more that day. I gave the Colonel a written commendation, mentioned in the next day's orders for his innovation, extra rest for his battalion, and first place in the marching order.

The second I'll make brief. One of my sergeants, a former medic in Vietnam, performed meritorious medical duties during the filming. He stabilized half a dozen critically ill and injured troops in several mishaps; probably saving one man's life. During a ceremony at the end of filming, the County and the National Park Service gave him an award. Ted Turner also ceremoniously shook his hand, gave him a large check in thanks, and in front of the throng attending he presented HJ to the proud confederate. She extended her hand to the sergeant, who jerked his hand away as if burned, putting it behind himself, and in a strong voice into the microphones he said, "I mean no disrespect to you Mr. Turner, but I WILL NOT SHAKE THE HAND OF A TRAITOR."

When some of the prisoners of war (POWs) returned to the U.S. and described their mistreatment at the hands of the North Vietnamese, Jane Fonda said that Americans should " . . . not hail the POWs as heroes, because they are hypocrites and liars." What goes around comes around.

God bless America!

To Jane Fonda's credit, during a *20/20* television interview with Barbara Walters sixteen years later, she apologized for going to North Vietnam and allowing herself to be used as a propaganda vehicle. Here is what she said:

> I would like to say something, not just to Vietnam veterans in New England, but to men who were in Vietnam, who I hurt, or whose pain I caused to deepen because of things that I said or did. I was trying to help end the killing and the war, but there were times when I was thoughtless and careless about it and I'm . . . very sorry that I hurt them. And I want to apologize to them and their families.

Some insist that Ms. Fonda actually made no such apology.

In the minds of many of those to whom she addressed her apology, it was too little too late. As Colonel Dana King has written, "I commanded brave men in battle . . . they deserve the recognition and the forgiveness of having to kill or be killed. Jane Fonda deserves nothing. Not even sympathy." I couldn't agree more.

A footnote: In discussions about Ms. Fonda and her activities during the Vietnam War, some people have told me that they are happy that no one holds *them* "accountable for things they may have done in (their) twenties." What a cop-out.

For the record, at the time of her treasonous acts Ms. Fonda was four months shy of her thirty-fifth birthday. Thus, I wonder what then *is* the age of human accountability. Also, I ask myself if "unaccountables" would perhaps modify their view if they had actually known personally one or more of the men who suffered at Hanoi Jane's traitorous hands. After all, but for the grace of God, I could have been one of them.

Oh, yes, I have thrown Ms. Fonda's exercise video, once used by my wife and daughter, into the trash.

> *Do draft dodgers have reunions? If so,*
> *what do they talk about?*

—Marine Corps Bumper Sticker

30

THE WALL

*Considering where you were and what was happening to so
many people, it was a privilege just to be able to feel afraid.*

—From *Dispatches* by Michael Herr

There are several thoughts I would like to share about
something Vietnam veterans simply call "The Wall." Its
proper name is the Vietnam Veterans Memorial and it is
located in Washington, D.C. It is dedicated to the honor and
memory of those who died in the Vietnam War, and, according to
a National Park Service web page about The Wall, "to the sacrifice
of American military personnel during one of this nation's least
popular wars. The purpose of this memorial is to separate the issue
of the sacrifices of the veterans from the U.S. policy in the war,
thereby creating a venue for reconciliation." Some 58,226 names
of the deceased and missing are inscribed on The Wall; of them,
one in four is that of a United States Marine. The memorial also
bears the following inscription:

IN HONOR OF THE MEN AND WOMEN
OF THE ARMED FORCES OF THE
UNITED STATES WHO SERVED IN THE
VIETNAM WAR . . . OUR NATION HONORS
THE COURAGE, SACRIFICE AND
DEVOTION TO DUTY AND COUNTRY
OF ITS VIETNAM VETERANS.

The word Vietnam still stirs strong emotions in a multitude of adult Americans. According to the website of the Smithsonian Institution,

> For many Americans, the mention of places such as Khe Sanh, Ia Drang, A Shau, Saigon, Danang, Quang Tri, Can Tho, or An Loc evokes battles fought and friends lost— brief victories and long-term agonies. For those who served there, the sights, sounds, smells, and heat of Vietnam are indelible. But Vietnam was another world, and episodes in that faraway place were difficult to explain to those at home. Many veterans did not discuss their experiences in Vietnam before the building of the Vietnam Veterans Memorial
>
> Vietnam returnees found America torn by the conflict in Southeast Asia. Few who survived their tour in "Nam" received home-front thanks or respect. [Author's note: Only in recent years have I received expressions of gratitude from friends and family who have actually telephoned or written to thank me for my service in the Marines and in Vietnam. However, even after the third of a century since my return, their words are most welcome.] And few who died were publicly mourned until the creation of the Vietnam Veterans Memorial. For millions, the Memorial has become a healing place. Leaving gifts for the dead, the missing, and all who served has become part of the ritual of grief and recovery.

One of the most poignant testimonials to The Wall comes from Major Q. X. Pham, USMCR. A native of Vietnam, he went to OCS in Quantico in the summer of 1986. Quang or "Q," as he is called, visited the Memorial during his last liberty weekend before graduation.

"It was difficult," wrote Major Pham in a moving article published on Veterans Day in 1998, "to stand before the names of those who gave their lives to fight for my freedom. They were not even from my country." This *Vietnamese-American* patriot continued:

Why didn't they go to Canada? Why didn't they question their orders? Where would I be now if they hadn't fought the Communists? What would their lives be like now had they lived?

At the wall, I realized that I would not be standing there without the sacrifices of those whose names were inscribed. I accepted my commission a year later, after finishing college. I wound up serving seven years on active duty as a Marine helicopter pilot and flew combat and support missions during Operation Desert Storm and in Somalia. The day the Gulf War ended, I felt I had earned my American citizenship and paid back my debt to our great nation.

Earned my American citizenship and paid back my debt to our great nation.

Our great nation.

What compelling words. It's a pity that more native-born Americans don't have such depth of feeling for the land of the free and the home of the brave.

Sadly, The Wall was desecrated on Memorial Day 1993, Bill Clinton's first as president. Veterans from all over the country headed to Washington, D.C., to protest Clinton's presence at The Wall. I supported them, although I could not be there.

Incredibly, the Clinton White House had ordered The Wall enclosed in an "ugly snow fence" that kept veterans about *five hundred yards away*. Hence, the protest rally, which was hastily organized, was kept back behind the fence.

According to one Vietnam veteran, television reporters tried hard to bury—in the word "healing"—the issue of draft-dodger Clinton, who, like Jane Fonda, had actually traveled to a foreign country to denounce the United States. On December 3, 1969 Clinton wrote in a letter to Col. Eugene Holmes, Director of the

R.O.T.C. at the University of Arkansas, that he had gone "to England to organize the Americans here for demonstrations" against America's effort in Vietnam.

Said the vet to the reporter, "Why don't you go down and film the inscription on the Wall and show it on television tonight? That's why we're here, and why Clinton shouldn't be. This Wall was built to honor everyone who served in Vietnam, which most emphatically does not include Mr. Clinton."

Another reporter asked, "Don't you think it took a certain amount of courage for the president to come here today?"

The veteran gave the perfect reply: "If standing around in a suit and tie and getting booed for a couple of minutes, and then going home to the White House is 'courage,' then what's the word for going to Vietnam and getting shot at for 365 days?"

The hundreds of veterans there that day were understandably irate at the highly publicized Clinton letter cited above in which he also wrote of "loathing the military." In addition, Clinton lied to that Arkansas R.O.T.C. program in the same year, and lied again to the American people during the 1992 presidential campaign about exactly what he had said and done while the rest of us were in-country fighting.

As David Clayton Carrad has written of that protest,

> So today was payback (for Clinton), for a lot of things. Our most popular signs were "Vietnam Veterans Loathe Clinton" and "Coward" and "Draft Dodger" and "You Dishonor the Dead by Appearing Here." About 12:45 (p.m.) we fell into a loose formation. We stood on our hillside, kept away from our Wall by the ugly snow fence, until 1:00 when the band played "Hail to the Chief" and we had our first chance to boo.
>
> We came to attention, did a reasonably smart about-face . . . , and turned our backs on him. "Where was Bill?" we chanted, and "Off our Wall," and "Come up here!"—an invitation he did not accept.
>
> We booed our lungs out as Clinton himself rose to

speak, our anger at him mixed with the sheer lighthearted joy of rebellion, and of hearing our strong voices blend together. We came to attention again and turned our backs on him in unison, even more smartly than in our first about-face. We sang "God Bless America" at the tops of our lungs and drowned out his words. We booed him until our throats were hoarse, half angry and half proud of our solidarity and the sheer volume of the noise we made.

I say, God bless those Vietnam veterans.

Tom Brokaw's book *The Greatest Generation* has been referenced earlier in this work. In it he chronicled the commitment and the sacrifice of the generation of Americans who fought and won World War II.

On December 7, 1999, coincidentally the fifty-eighth anniversary of the Japanese attack on Pearl Harbor, Mr. Brokaw was interviewed by Don Imus, a former Marine, on the *Imus in the Morning* radio program, which emanates weekdays from New York City and is broadcast nationwide. At one point, during a discussion of the differences between the World War II and Vietnam generations, Brokaw referred, on the one hand, to those who served in the Vietnam War and, on the other, to "those who followed their conscience and protested it." In that moment I wondered if he himself recognized or understood the bias against Vietnam veterans that his words betrayed.

After all, is it not possible, or even likely, I wrote in a letter to him, that those of us who served our country in Vietnam did so in good conscience, good faith, enthusiasm, devotion to duty and even the confidence that we were serving in the very tradition of our forebears that he so skillfully articulated in his book? Alas, his words seemed instead to imply that those who protested the Vietnam War answered a higher call than we veterans did. This is simply a false premise, and inconsistent with Mr. Brokaw's ostensibly clear understanding of the motivation of those World War II Americans he profiled so poignantly in writing.

In reply to my letter, I received only a form card from Brokaw's NBC office, on which was printed an expression of thanks for having read his book. How very thorough and reassuring.

In the same vein, President Jimmy Carter many years earlier issued a comprehensive and unprecedented pardon of Americans who refused to serve in the military.

The aforementioned James Webb described the pardon for what it was. "Mr. Carter's gesture," he has written, "had the symbolic effect of elevating everyone who had opposed the Vietnam War to the level of moral purist, and by implication insulting those who often had struggled just as deeply with the moral dimensions of the war and had decided, often at great sacrifice, to honor the laws of their country and serve."

I have visited The Wall four times, most recently in April of this year, and I will do so again.

One friend, who has taken his family to it, has told me that he found it to be "a somber place where people did not converse." He said that, even at President Kennedy's grave in Arlington National Cemetery, across the Potomac River from The Wall, folks at least engaged in conversation.

Upon reflection, I believe that the Vietnam Veterans Memorial evokes human feelings that one may not experience elsewhere, even at the grave of a loved one. Faced with the more than 58,000 names cut in stone, which represent all those killed or missing in action, the visitor is inevitably struck by the magnitude of the loss. Then, based on my own experience there, a sense of the spiritual overtakes even the most worldly person, followed by reverence and solemnity, perhaps even, as in my case, tears.

I consulted the directory of those whose names are forever etched into The Wall. It resembles a telephone book, with all the names listed alphabetically with place of birth, military service, rank, date missing or killed and other information. It was also as thick as the telephone directory of a large city.

Having found in the directory the names of those Marines and other servicemen I knew who had made the ultimate sacrifice, I then located the panel and the line on The Wall where each of their names appeared. There were the names of Norm Billipp, a Marine pilot and friend of mine, Guido Farinaro, Steve Karopczyc, Bob Kisch, Dick Morin, Billy Ryan, Tim Shorten and, yes, Bill Surette, among others. I touched each name, moving my fingers across it, feeling each letter, remembering each man, visualizing his face, wishing I could be with him, as sadness and grief engulfed me.

There too is the name of Lance Corporal Michael Alberici, USMC, a friend and classmate of my brother Mike, who was killed in action on August 24, 1968. I also found the names of seven other men I did *not* know, all Mansfields, and I salute them by recording their names here:

> Technical Sergeant Bruce Elwin Mansfield, USAF (East Providence, RI)
>
> Captain Clayton John Mansfield, USA (Fort Bliss, TX)
>
> Private First Class Donald Lewis Mansfield, USMC (Rockland, ME)
>
> Lance Corporal John Michael Mansfield, USMC (Preston, CT)
>
> Private First Class John Montagu Mansfield, USA (New York City)
>
> Corporal Patrick Leroy Mansfield, USA (Tucson, AZ)
>
> Specialist Fourth Class William Granvil Mansfield, USA (Massapequa Park, NY)

Requiescant in pace.

I have visited, with Mame and the kids, the World War II Normandy American Cemetery and Memorial in Colleville-sur-Mer, France. It is situated on a cliff overlooking Omaha Beach and the English Channel. (The cemetery is American territory, having been ceded to the United States in a gesture of international gratitude for Americans' role in liberating France from Nazi occupation.) In this hallowed place are buried 9,386 American military dead, most of whom were killed during the D-Day landings and the ensuing operations of World War II. Their graves are starkly marked by marble crosses or Stars of David. The feeling that washes over a person on first seeing these monuments, row on row, is of the same silent solemnity and reverence he or she feels at The Wall.

In a more recent comparison, the feelings one experiences at The Wall are akin to those felt at the ruins of the former World Trade Center in lower Manhattan. The Wall, however, is a magnificent monument; "Ground Zero," as many now call it, is at this writing, in many ways, nothingness, albeit hallowed ground, like Normandy or The Wall. In another comparison, the number of names on The Wall dwarfs the number of lives lost at Ground Zero by a factor of twenty but, then, of course, Vietnam was a war, not a day at the office.

For those of you who have not visited The Wall, go there when you can. For those of you who have, I am confident that you were moved by its silent black granite beauty and that you will go there again some time, as I have gone. Appropriately, it is a place of reverence and peace, and honors those thousands who died too young.

If you are able, save for them a place inside of you and
save one backward glance when you are leaving for the
places they can no longer go.
Be not ashamed to say you loved them, though you may
or may not have always.
Take what they have taught you with their dying and
keep it with your own.

And in that time when men decide and feel safe to call the war insane, take one moment to embrace those gentle heroes you left behind.

—Major Michael Davis O'Donnell,
USA, a helicopter pilot killed in action on
March 24, 1970
Dak To, Vietnam

PART III
BACK IN THE WORLD

Forsake not an old friend, for the new will not be like to him.

—Ecclesiasticus 9:14

31

MODERN WATERSHEDS:

MAY 4, 1970 AND SEPTEMBER 11, 2001

Patriotism's extraordinary power to expand and constrain the American spirit is hardly new. But it seems novel now because so many people—including many among the huge bulge of population that came of age during and after the Vietnam War—have never lived it themselves.

—Blaine Harden

I f asked, many Americans, especially those of a certain age, would say that the two most memorable dates in their lifetimes were December 7, 1941 and November 22, 1963. The first, "a date which will live in infamy," according to President Franklin Roosevelt, was that on which the U.S. was attacked, as recounted early in the first chapter, at Pearl Harbor in the Pacific by Japanese air and naval forces. The second is the date on which President John F. Kennedy was assassinated in Dallas, Texas. If asked, these same Americans would surely be able to tell you where they were and what they were doing at the time they learned of these events.

I take a different tack. At least as significant and arguably more so are May 4, 1970 and September 11, 2001. The first is actually more significant than the death of a president because of its long-term effects on our culture and politics. As for the second, it dwarfs the Japanese attacks because on it the U.S. mainland was struck and hundreds more people were killed. Moreover, its long-term effects are yet to be fully known or understood.

May 4, 1970

On that day our nation's newspapers carried headlines about President Nixon's ordering of an "incursion" into the "Parrot's Beak" area of Cambodia where the NVA had established significant staging areas for its attacks on South Vietnam. The fact that the president had ordered American forces across the border into neighboring Cambodia was regarded by his administration's opponents, as well as by much of the American public, as not just a further escalation of the conflict but also an unnecessary and outrageous breach of Cambodia's sovereignty.

As a direct result of this intensified military action, demonstrations on college and university campuses increased apace. At Kent State University in Ohio, the National Guard was called in to restore order. In a tragic moment, four students were shot dead by those same guardsmen on that May 4th.

My own college alma mater was not immune from student pressure and demonstrations. In fact, it was perhaps a perfect exemplar of an institution under siege. Its telex to the President at the White House, dated May 5, 1970, reads:

> THE FACULTY ASSEMBLY OF THE COLLEGE OF THE HOLY CROSS AT ITS REGULAR MEETING, MINDAY(*sic*), MAY 4, 1970, IN AN 83-37 VOTE APPROVED THE FOLLOWING MOTION:
> "THAT THE COLLEGE OF THE HOLY CROSS JOIN ITS' *(sic)* SISTER COLLEGES AND UNIVERSITIES IN SUSPENDING ORDINARY ACADEMIC ACTIVITIES UNTIL NEXT MONDAY'S FACULTY MEETING (AT WHICH TIME THE FACULTY WILL DETERMINE WHETHER IT WILL BE FRUITFUL TO CONTINUE CESSATION OF CLASSES DURING THE LAST WEEK OF SCHOOL).

"THAT THE COLLEGE FORMULATE APPROPRIATE ALTERNATE ACTIVITIES INVOLVING THE HOLY CROSS STUDENT BODY AND THE WORCESTER COMMUNITY TO DISCUSS AND DEVELOP PLANS TO BRING AN END TO THE VIETNAM WAR.

"THIS ACTION IS TAKEN WITH A VIEW TO: 1.) CONDEMNING THE RECENT ESCALATION OF AMERICAN MILITARY ACTIVITY IN SOUTHEAST ASIA; 2.) DEMANDING AN IMMEDIATE CESSATION OF AMERICAN MILITARY INVOLVEMENT IN CAMBODIA; 3.) DEMANDING AN END OF AMERICAN BOMBING OF NORTH VIETNAM; 4.) URGING A CLEAR COMMITMENT TO AMERICAN WITHDRAWAL FROM SOUTHEAST ASIA; 5.) SUPPORTING THE FREEING OF ALL POLITICAL PRISONERS BY GOVERNMENT AUTHORITIES; AND 6.) REEXAMING *(sic)* THE COLLEGE'S OWN COMPLICITY IN THE WAR."

FOR THE FACULTY ASSEMBLY

REV. JOHN E. BROOKS, S.J.
VICE PRESIDENT AND DEAN OF THE COLLEGE
COLLEGE OF THE HOLY CROSS
WORCESTER, MASSACHUSETTS

A few months after this communication, Father Brooks was named president of the College.

As for Holy Cross students during this period, they were typically "wacko." To wit: A charter for a "Revolutionary Students Union" was marked "pending approval," in the handwriting of presumably someone in the College administration. It reads in part:

> The Revolutionary Students Union is an organization of young socialists and communists dedicated to the destruction of the international capitalist system, and the creation of a student democracy, free from the evils of white racism, male supremacy, and private property, the three social and economic institutions which form the foundation of contemporary American society.
>
> The R.S.U. disdains to conceal its views and aims. We openly declare that our ends can only be achieved by the forcible overthrow of all existing social conditions. Let the ruling classes tremble at a communistic revolution. The people have nothing to lose but their chains. They have a world to win.

This charter ended with the rallying cry, "*ALL POWER TO THE PEOPLE!*" Tellingly, no names appeared anywhere on the charter, which suggests to me that the students who wrote it weren't as idiotic as their rhetoric.

My view of these protesters aligns closely with that of my fellow Holy Cross alumnus, David Barth, who graduated in 1962 and was quoted in the April 1999 *Holy Cross Magazine*.

"I just thought they were jerks, pot heads, and people afraid to serve," he says. "Later on . . . I thought some are truly against the war and think it's morally wrong. And they're entitled to their opinion, but I didn't agree with them."

Like David's, my time overseas, not just in Vietnam but later in many other countries, has taught me that the U.S. is vastly superior in every way to other nations. As he puts it, "It's worth fighting for. I think it would do a lot of people good to go to Korea, Vietnam, or Mexico and see the freedom we have that other people don't."

Or maybe Afghanistan or Iraq.

In May 1970 I was completing my first year at New York University's Graduate School of Business Administration, now the Leonard N. Stern School of Business, which was then located on Trinity Place in lower Manhattan's financial district, near the nearly completed office tower known as One World Trade Center. At the same time, I was also a full-time employee of Bankers Trust Company where I was working my way through its management training program. I would leave the office around 5:00 p.m. in order to be at school for the 5:30 start of classes, which ended at 9:10 p.m. After school I would usually arrive home just before eleven.

Mame and I then lived in Glen Oaks, Queens, near the New York City line, the boundary with New York's Nassau County. She was pregnant with our second son, John, who was born on May 24th. I commuted to my Park Avenue-based job via city bus and subway.

As I arrived at the business school one evening during this unsettled period, it was clear that neither normalcy nor classes were in session. As usual, I took the elevator and made my way to my classroom, only to find a handwritten notice on the chalkboard to the effect that classes and exams had been cancelled for the remainder of the academic year. The reason: Students and faculty alike were encouraged to participate in the nationwide "strike."

I was really disgusted by what I perceived as a wholesale rush to foolishness but I was otherwise delighted because I was able, as a result of the cancellations, to go home and spend welcome time with my family.

As I was leaving the school building, excited at the prospect of surprising Mame with my early arrival and enjoying the evening with her and Chas, I was accosted in the school's main lobby by two students, a young man and a young woman who was in my class. (By the way, I suppose I was something of an anomaly. I came to school dressed in a business suit whereas most of the other students wore jeans and were largely unkempt. Many men sported long hair and beards and generally appeared scrofulous.) The pair solicited my signature on a petition specifically condemning the

U.S. government's action in Cambodia (which action I happened to support but which view I then thought better of disclosing) and the Vietnam War in general. Hence, I declined to sign.

"Why not?" I was asked.

"I don't sign petitions," I replied politely.

Next, the young woman asked me if I would at least join them at a protest rally at NYU's main campus at Washington Square, not too far north of our location.

I said "No thanks" and "Good evening." Then I turned to leave and started walking toward the lobby's revolving door.

After my first steps away from the couple, the young man shouted at me, "Hey, man, you wanna go to Vietnam?"

Strongly put off by his seemingly angry tone, I walked back to him and, to use the vernacular, got in his face, although I spoke calmly.

"Do I want to go to Vietnam?" I paused deliberately. "No, thanks. I've already been there."

The tension in the air thickened quickly. I thought he was going to hit me but I guess he thought better of it.

During the train ride home I pondered the confrontation. I arrived at an inevitable conclusion: The guy was just another wacko in the Big City.

I don't believe I related the incident to Mame.

According to Professor George Katsiaficas of Boston's Wentworth Institute of Technology, "the largest strike in American history" took place in the wake of the Kent State shootings. Indeed, almost five million American students joined the "strike." Over 500 American colleges and universities were reportedly closed by mid-month; over 900 closed before month's end. Approximately 80% of these institutions experienced protests, and about 175,000 faculty members participated in them.

Five days after the shootings, more than 150,000 protesters, mostly students, descended on Washington, D.C., where President

Nixon, his National Security Advisor (and later Secretary of State) Henry Kissinger and other key figures were kept in the White House protected by military guards armed with machine guns. So bad was the situation that it prompted then Supreme Court Chief Justice Earl Warren to call the aftermath of Kent State the worst crisis in the U.S. since the Civil War. Even Mr. Nixon, in a later memoir, would describe the days after the tragedy as being "among the darkest" of his presidency.

Within days after the shootings, the president limited the U.S.'s Cambodian invasion to 35 kilometers (about 22 miles) inside the country and a two-month maximum duration. Within those two months U.S. troops withdrew from Cambodia.

Outgrowths of this period, according to Professor Katsiaficas, were the "anti-war and counter-cultural movements." In fact, "the first gay-pride week was launched in New York on June 22, 1970, and the Gay Liberation Front sponsored their first national conference in San Francisco in August." Moreover, "radical feminists emerged strongly and the women's movement blossomed in the summer of 1970—their symbol of the clenched fist inside the biological sign for women was created." And "in September, 1970, the Black Panthers sponsored a convention that attracted over 10,000 activists."

It has been my view virtually since 1970 that much of what is wrong with the United States early in the Third Millennium is traceable to these events, with the greatest evils of all being abortion and terrorism; multiculturalism and political correctness are next on my list.

September 11, 2001

At this writing, three weeks have elapsed since Tuesday, September 11, 2001, which some have called the "bloodiest day" in the history of the United States. I refer, of course, to the attacks on the Pentagon in Washington, D.C., and on the World Trade Center in New York City, whose quarter-mile high "Twin Towers," as well as other structures, were destroyed by American airliners that were hijacked and deliberately crashed into the buildings by Islamic terrorists associated with Osama bin Laden.

For perspective, almost as many Americans died on 9/11 as all those killed in action at the Battle of Antietam during the American Civil War. At Antietam in Maryland (called Sharpsburg by the South) on Wednesday, September 17, 1862, 2,100 Union *troops* and 1,550 from the Confederacy were killed in twelve hours of fighting. On September 11, 2001, almost 3,000 *innocent American civilians* were killed in approximately one hundred minutes.

The public reaction to this catastrophic terrorism was an admixture of shock, outrage, anger, fear, sorrow and desire for revenge. Capturing the feelings of many older Americans when it became clear that the attacks were the premeditated murderous acts of terrorists, an incredulous child was quoted as asking, "You mean they did that on purpose?" This reaction also produced perhaps the greatest outpouring of patriotism and the most ubiquitous expositions of the American flag that I have seen in my lifetime. To say it was uplifting, amidst the pervading gloom in the wake of the tragedy, is a huge understatement.

In this connection, *The Wall Street Journal* published on the same day both the extraordinary front-page story of Jenny Traschen, a physics professor at the University of Massachusetts, and a lead editorial that described the anti-patriotic views of other "graying radicals" on our college campuses. This prompted a letter to its editor from me, which appears in part here:

> In fairness to Ms. Traschen, her sickening remark was made the evening before September 11th. Nonetheless, it bears quotation for your readers who may have missed it. Indeed, it is astounding: "What the (American) flag is is a symbol of terrorism and death and fear and destruction and oppression." Virtually echoing her sentiments, according to your editorial, was University of Texas Professor Robert Jensen, who wrote that what was done to America on September 11th "was no more despicable than the massive

acts of terrorism . . . that the U.S. government has committed during my lifetime." Other similar mindsets were also cited.

It is easy to say to such misguided individuals with respect to the U.S., "Love it or leave it," for their comments only exacerbated the daily feelings of anger and near-nausea that I and countless other Americans have experienced since that terrible day. As a former university professor, I am confident I understand what academic freedom is all about. As a former Marine Corps officer and a Vietnam veteran, I am reminded of the words on a plaque that my platoon presented to me when I was leaving Vietnam to come home: "For those who fight for it, life has a flavor the protected never know."

What's wrong with America? Alas, we need look no further than the attitudes and words of more than a few members of our academic community. Happily, as you reported, most students, unlike some of their sorry professors, have "learned something about their obligation to a free if imperfect society" and demonstrated both patriotism and willingness to serve our country.

God bless America!

Just hours after sending this letter, I received the following e-mail from Rev. Michael C. McFarland, S.J., president of the College of the Holy Cross:

October 2, 2001

Dear Friends,

In the past several days there have been news accounts about an incident at Holy Cross involving a sociology professor, the department secretary, and display of an American flag in the department's hallway.

It is most unfortunate that the facts of this incident have

been so mangled that the real issues have been overwhelmed and lost. There was a misunderstanding of the kind that periodically happens in the workplace. There was no disrespect meant for the flag or what it represents. Those involved worked with good will to settle it, and it was settled until the press reported the story in an over-simplified and incomplete manner. When the College gave a statement on the situation most of it was ignored and the rest distorted.

American flags—too numerous to count—are flying and hung across the campus. Students are selling numerous red, white and blue lapel pins (with the proceeds going to one of the many charities established for families of the victims of September 11). The College's NROTC unit on September 21, held a very moving flag-raising ceremony in honor of the victims of the terrorist attacks. We have a continuing respect for the flag and what it symbolizes.

I suggest we all need to step back, cool off and realize that as a nation we are living in a very difficult time and emotions are running high. In our effort to be unified as a nation, we must not trample on our cherished freedoms of speech and thought.

The reaction to this matter by many has been disturbing. Some callers and e-mail users have threatened physical violence and retaliation. This is a dark and extreme side of our national mood. Surely these people do not intend to threaten or commit violence when we have already lost so many to horrible, indefensible acts of terrorism.

September 11 was a horrible day for this nation and, here at Holy Cross, we are certainly feeling the terrible impact. We are mourning the loss of 7 alumni/ae, several parents of current students and countless relatives of members of the

Holy Cross family. Our focus is on helping those who are hurting and on praying for an end to violence.

Holy Cross is a community steeped in a tradition of intellectual inquiry, service, fairness and social responsibility. In these dark and troubling times, we must turn to these core values and beliefs. We have often defined our College as a family. Let us strive, then, to come together as a family and combat intolerance and hatred, rather than striking out at each other. And let us continue to pray for peace and for healing.

Sincerely,

Michael C. McFarland, S.J.
President
College of the Holy Cross

Curiously, Fr. McFarland gives no specifics of the "incident," and advises us that "we all need to step back, cool off." Next he attempts to shift the focus from the sociology professor who in fact took down the flag to what he must have considered, at least from a public-relations standpoint, a more soothing image, namely, that "American flags—too numerous to count—are flying and hung across the campus." These "too numerous" flags were likely being displayed in a triumph of enthusiasm by presumably patriotic Holy Cross students. Would that a certain sociology professor had taken this page from the students' book.

More recently, it has been reported that the secretary who put up the flag did so because she/he had lost a loved one in the catastrophic terrorism rained upon the World Trade Center on 9/11.

The behavior of the sociology professor in removing the American flag was not merely unpatriotic; it was reprehensible and fascist. A fascist, by definition, engages in "forcible suppression of the opposition." The secretary was merely exercising her/his right of free speech guaranteed by the First Amendment to our Constitution. (Let us keep in mind that we also have the protected freedom, courtesy of the United States Supreme Court, to *burn* the American flag if we are so inclined, as the professor might well be.)

Fr. McFarland missed a major opportunity to lead. Indeed, in a defining moment, he failed the leadership test altogether by not taking a strong stand *against* the professor, from whom he should have at a minimum extracted an apology, or, failing that, whom he should have fired. Alternatively, the College's president could simply have walked into the sociology department and rehung the flag where the secretary had initially placed it.

Some maintain that Fr. McFarland was in a no-win situation. Alas, his decision to appear impartial was misguided and backfired. Impartiality is normally important but it can be misapplied, as it was in this instance. I believe Fr. McFarland will regret his decision in the years ahead for its high potential to undermine his presidency.

In this connection, a Marine Corps officer, who is also an HC graduate and wishes to remain anonymous, has written:

> It appears to me that poor leadership has allowed Holy Cross to become mundane and succumb to the same leanings as many other educational institutions where a predominately liberal philosophy is espoused by a self serving faculty base that uses the walls of academia as a shield to protect their "freedom of expression." Unfortunately most of the faculty "protected" by these walls and responsible for mentoring our children have only studied the experiences of others and have not had to sacrifice anything themselves.

My thesis that the academic community is fertile ground for anti-patriotic and anti-military views may be better supported by presenting evidence that is not specifically related to or derived from the Vietnam era or the 9/11 terrorist attacks.

What follow are two letters, each extraordinary in its own right.

The first appeared in the October 4, 1999 issue of *U.S. News & World Report* and was written by Katherine Van Wormer, Professor of Social Work at the University of Northern Iowa in Cedar Falls. The second, a reply to the professor's, is written by Air Force Captain Jonathan Clough, an AWACS (Airborne Warning and Control System) controller then assigned to Air Force Rome Labs in New York State.

Professor Van Wormer wrote:

> How disturbed I was to see your article in the September 6 issue about ROTC scholarships as a means of providing funds for a college education. The education associated with ROTC is a contradiction to the academic freedom enjoyed at university campuses; military training on college campuses, in fact, makes a mockery of education. Far from taking a global view of learning, ROTC encourages narrow patriotism and a philosophy of any means (killing people and polluting environments) to the end. The institutionalized mistreatment of gays and lesbians in the military and sexual harassment of women are par for the course.

Captain Clough replied:

> Dear Professor Van Wormer,
>
> I just finished reading your letter to the editor in U.S. News & World Report magazine (04 Oct) and was compelled to address your shockingly prejudiced, obviously uninformed and frankly laughable viewpoint on ROTC and the military in general. Your unenlightened perspective belies a reckless if not tragic ignorance that brings disrepute upon the institution that employs you. It is a shame you felt obliged to comment on something you apparently know so little about. I wonder if in your extensive research in "Social Work" you ever encountered someone who's actually served in the armed forces? The answer goes without saying. Allow me to be your first.

It troubles me that you must be reminded that the academic freedom you enjoy and cherish so dearly was purchased with the precious lives and blood of many a noble soldier on wretched battlefields here and abroad over the past 223 years. Do you honestly believe freedom of any sort comes without tremendous cost? Are you so willfully naïve to think you'd enjoy the same license if you were a professor in China, Iran, North Korea, or the Sudan?

How many young men and women have you talked to lately who spent their Christmas holiday patrolling some godforsaken minefield like Bosnia, or their 5th wedding anniversary in a row at sea, or the birthday of their first daughter stopping a madman from achieving his goal of ethnic cleansing? Tell me. Do you really think we acknowledge a call to the profession of arms so we can "kill people and pollute environments?" To believe such sophomoric rubbish demands some fairly sophisticated cerebral blinders.

I have served in the U.S. Air Force for 11 years now, flying long hours over countless global hot spots, and I have not once encountered a fellow soldier, sailor, or airman who subscribes to a "narrow patriotism and a philosophy of any means." Not one. Rather, they are ladies and gentlemen of highest caliber, selfless devotion to the cause of freedom, and tireless service to an often-thankless nation. Your mischaracterization is so off base it borders on unforgivable.

It would seem to me that your Department of Social Work would have whole syllabi devoted to the role of the military in the field of social work. I can think of no greater social service than an institution committed to risking the lives of its members to preserve and defend the very citizenry from which it hails. How many oppressed refugees, disaster victims, and starving children have been mercifully delivered from their plight by the military in just the last decade? Need we reflect on the fact that the whole of Western Europe owes its freedom from Nazi fascism to a valiant few in olive drab and khaki? Perhaps you should invite a concentration camp survivor or a Kosovar Albanian to give a guest lecture extolling the magnificent "social services" they've benefited from at the hands of the military.

Finally, I find it humorous that academics like yourselves who indoctrinate our youth with the dogma of "positive tolerance" for every aberrant lifestyle cannot find it within yourselves to tolerate an institution to which you owe your very peace, comfort, and well being. It is an amusing double standard.

My exhortation to you is to get out of the rarified air in your office, walk over to your ROTC detachment in Lang Hall and interact with the men and women in uniform and those aspiring to wear it. Perhaps then you will wake up from your slumber of conscious ignorance, join the ranks of the enlightened, and offer a prayer of thanksgiving to God for the freedoms you take for granted and those who sacrifice daily on your behalf to secure it.

Captain Clough signed his letter, "In Service To You."

Academe can boggle the mind.

My dictionary defines *academic* as "very learned but inexperienced in the world of practical reality." How apt.

Consider the behavior of some *American* Middle Eastern academics in the wake of the terrorist attacks on the United States. According to Martin Kramer, editor of Middle East Quarterly and author of *Ivory Towers on Sand: The Failure of Middle Eastern Studies in America*, the Middle Eastern Studies Association of North America studiously avoids the words "terror," "terrorism" and "terrorist." What happened on September 11, 2001 were merely "violent acts," horrific acts" and "tragic events."

"For years," Mr. Kramer has written, "the academics' response to terrorism has been to act as amplifiers for the 'grievances' behind it. For professors, terrorism was a kind of political protest—and since they sympathized with its supposed motives, they expelled the word "terrorism" from their lexicon. They also refer to the "violent acts" as "crimes," not *acts of war*, and insist, therefore, that the planners and perpetrators be brought to justice in courts of law.

Meanwhile, civil libertarians were in an uproar over President George W. Bush's executive order allowing military tribunals to try accused terrorists. This was the first such action by a U.S. president since World War II. (Incidentally, military tribunals are constitutional, having the sanction of the U.S. Supreme Court.) In this connection, Vice President Dick Cheney, in the autumn of 2001, made it abundantly clear that the foreign terrorists who could be subjected to such tribunals "don't deserve to be treated as prisoners of war." Nor do they "deserve the same guarantees and safeguards we use for an American citizen." This was confirmed by President George W. Bush several months later.

Perhaps the most pithy commentary of all on this subject comes from Justice Jackson's dissent in a case in 1949: "If the Court does not temper its doctrinaire logic with a little practical wisdom, it will convert the constitutional Bill of Rights into a suicide pact."

In September 2002 *The American Enterprise* magazine published an extraordinary article entitled "The Shame of America's One-Party Campuses." In it TAE demonstrated conclusively what many of us have known for decades, that is, that college and university faculty members constitute a significant liberal-leftist voting bloc.

Many professors reportedly registered as members of what TAE described as "an ideologically identifiable political faction." For purposes of its study the magazine classified those registered as Democrats, Greens or Working Families Party members as "Left." Similarly, those who registered in the Republican or Libertarian Party were classified as "Right."

Here is a sampling of the results:

University	Left	Right
Brown University	54	3
Cornell University	166	6
Harvard University	50	2
Penn State University	59	10
San Diego State University	80	11
Stanford University	151	17
State University of New York at Binghamton	35	1
Syracuse University	50	2
University of California at Berkeley	59	7
University of California at Los Angeles	141	9
University of California at San Diego	99	6
University of California at Santa Barbara	72	1
University of Colorado at Boulder	116	5
University of Houston	45	14
University of Maryland	59	10
University of Texas at Austin	94	15
Total	1,330	119

Based on these numbers, 91 percent of professors at the colleges and universities listed above are on the "Left." Those on the "Right" at these schools range between 1.4 and 31.1 percent of the total at their university. Compared to the other schools, the University of Houston at 31.1 percent is a veritable bastion of conservatism. In this connection, the TAE study showed seven of the 21 faculty members in Stanford's Economics Department registered on the "Right," a whopping third of the total!

TAE also cited a poll of 151 professors at Ivy League universities, which was conducted by Frank Luntz Research for the Center for the Study of Popular Culture. Of these, three percent identified themselves as Republicans; 57 percent, Democrats. TAE compared these figures to Americans in general: 37 percent Republicans and 34 percent Democrats.

Thus, American colleges and universities are anything but "diverse." TAE reminds us that "Colleges like to characterize themselves as wide-open places where every thought can be thought, where any opinion can be held, where all ideals and principles may be pursued freely." Alas, "In truth, colleges are now hostile environments for economic and cultural conservatives. Only a comparatively narrow spectrum of views is really welcome on campus." Woe to those who stray from the liberal line.

TAE's study provides another clear example of relative extrema, this time in the American political realm.

Interestingly, a survey of 1,200 undergraduates the following month by the Chronicle of Higher Education indicated that, in sharp contrast to their professors, most are patriotic and pro military. In fact, some 90% considered themselves "very" or "somewhat patriotic," and 70% cited the U.S. military as the government institution they trust the most.

Both during the Vietnam War and now in the wake of the 9/11 atrocities, there were and are Americans who never tire of speaking out against *American* "imperialism, oppression and violence."

One refreshing commentary on these pacifistic views happens to come from a Quaker, Scott Simon, a National Public Radio talk show host and, at least earlier in life, a pacifist. Last year he wrote:

> . . . in the 1990s . . . I confronted the logical flaw (or perhaps I should say the fatal flaw) of non-violent resistance: All the best people can be killed by all the worst ones . . . . About half of all draft age Quakers enlisted in World War II, believing that whatever wisdom pacifism had to give the world, it could not defeat the murderous schemes of Adolf Hitler and his cohorts.

The goal of the United States is not revenge, which some pacifists and liberals, including some misguided members of the clergy and others, insist it is. On the contrary, ours is self-defense, that is, taking steps to protect ourselves in the future from those who have already and ably demonstrated both their desire to kill us and their efficacy in carrying out their murderous missions. Is there anyone who believes that, given the opportunity, Osama bin Laden and his al Qaeda terrorist groups would not hesitate to kill us all? Indeed, on November 6, 2001 President Bush announced to the Warsaw Conference on Controlling Terrorism that, "These terrorist groups seek to destabilize entire nations and regions. They are seeking chemical, biological and nuclear weapons. Given the means, our enemies would be a threat to every nation and, eventually, to civilization itself."

I quote again Mr. Simon:

> Only American (and British) power can stop more killing in the world's skyscrapers, pizza parlors, embassies, bus stations, ships, and airplanes. Pacifists, like most Americans, would like to change their country in a thousand ways. And the blasts of Sept. 11 should remind American pacifists that they live in that one place on the planet where change—in fact, peaceful change—seems most possible. It is better to sacrifice our ideals than to expect others to die for them.

In this realm Thomas Paine, too, has provided food for thought: "Those who expect to reap the blessings of liberty must, like men, undergo the fatigues of supporting it."

> *Anyone who gave (Osama bin Laden) a dime or shared a cup of coffee with him should be placed in fear of his continued existence.*
>
> —Holman W. Jenkins Jr.

I received the following e-mail about two weeks after the events of 9/11. It provides important perspective, which is why I am reprinting it in full.

Subject: FW: Open Letter to America

An academic advisor at the Air Force Academy wrote the following, which I believe everyone should read.

From: Dr. Tony Kern, Lt Col, USAF (Ret)

Recently, I was asked to look at the recent events through the lens of military history. I have joined the cast of thousands who have written an "open letter to Americans."

Dear friends and fellow Americans   24 September 2001

Like everyone else in this great country, I am reeling from last week's attack on our sovereignty. But unlike some, I am not reeling from surprise. As a career soldier and a student and teacher of military history, I have a different perspective and I think you should hear it. This war will be won or lost by the American citizens, not diplomats, politicians or soldiers.

Let me briefly explain.

In spite of what the media, and even our own government is telling us, this act was not committed by a group of mentally deranged fanatics. To dismiss them as such would be among the gravest of mistakes. This attack was committed by a ferocious, intelligent and dedicated adversary. Don't take this the wrong way. I don't admire these men and I deplore their tactics, but I respect their capabilities. The many parallels that have been made with the Japanese attack on Pearl Harbor are apropos. Not only because it was a brilliant sneak attack against a complacent America, but also because we may well be pulling our new adversaries out of caves 30 years after we think this war is over, just like my father's generation had to do with the formidable Japanese in the years following WW II.

These men hate the United States with all of their being, and we must not underestimate the power of their moral commitment. Napoleon, perhaps the world's greatest combination of soldier and statesman, stated "the moral is to the physical as three is to one." Patton thought the Frenchman underestimated its importance and said moral conviction was five times more important in battle than physical strength. Our enemies are willing—better said anxious—to give their lives for their cause.

How committed are we America? And for how long?

In addition to demonstrating great moral conviction, the recent attack demonstrated a mastery of some of the basic fundamentals of warfare taught to most military officers worldwide, namely simplicity, security and surprise. When I first heard rumors that some of these men may have been trained at our own Air Force War College, it made perfect sense to me. This was not a random act of violence, and we can expect the same sort of military competence to be displayed in the battle to come.

This war will escalate, with a good portion of it happening right here in the good ol' U.S. of A.

These men will not go easily into the night. They do not fear us. We must not fear them. In spite of our overwhelming conventional strength as the world's only "superpower" (a truly silly term), we are the underdog in this fight. As you listen to the carefully scripted rhetoric designed to prepare us for the march for war, please realize that America is not equipped or seriously trained for the battle ahead. To be certain, our soldiers are much better than the enemy, and we have some excellent "counter-terrorist" organizations, but they are mostly trained for hostage rescues, airfield seizures, or the occasional "body snatch," (which may come in handy). We will be fighting a war of annihilation, because if their early efforts are any indication, our enemy is ready and willing to die to the last man. Eradicating the enemy will be costly and time consuming. They have already deployed their forces in as many as 20 countries, and are likely living the lives of everyday citizens. Simply put, our soldiers will be tasked with a search and destroy mission on multiple foreign landscapes, and the public must be patient and supportive until the strategy and tactics can be worked out.

For the most part, our military is still in the process of redefining itself and presided over by men and women who grew up with—and were promoted because they excelled in—Cold War doctrine, strategy and tactics. This will not be linear warfare, there will be no clear "centers of gravity" to strike with high technology weapons. Our vast technological edge will certainly be helpful, but it will not be decisive. Perhaps the perfect metaphor for the coming battle was introduced by the terrorists themselves aboard the hijacked aircraft—this will be a knife fight, and it will be won or lost by the ingenuity and will of citizens and soldiers, not by software or smart bombs. We must also be patient with our military leaders.

Unlike Americans who are eager to put this messy time behind us, our adversaries have time on their side, and they will use it. They plan to fight a battle of attrition, hoping to drag the battle out until the American public loses its will to fight. This might be difficult to believe in this euphoric time of flag waving and patriotism, but it is generally acknowledged that America lacks the stomach for a long fight. We need only look as far back as Vietnam, when North Vietnamese General Vo Nguyen Giap (also a military history teacher) defeated the United States of America without ever winning a major tactical battle. American soldiers who marched to war cheered on by flag waving Americans in 1965 were reviled and spat upon less than three years later when they returned. Although we hope that Osama Bin Laden is no Giap, he is certain to understand and employ the concept. We can expect not only large doses of pain like the recent attacks, but also less audacious "sand in the gears" tactics, ranging from livestock infestations to attacks at water supplies and power distribution facilities.

These attacks are designed to hit us in our "comfort zone" forcing the average American to "pay more and play less" and eventually eroding our resolve. But it can only work if we let it. It is clear to me that the will of the American citizenry—you and I—is the center of gravity the enemy has targeted. It will be the fulcrum upon which victory or defeat will turn. He believes us to be soft, impatient, and self-centered. He may be right, but if so, we must change. The Prussian general Carl von Clausewitz, (the most often quoted and least read military theorist in history), says that there is a "remarkable trinity of war" that is composed of the (1) will of the people, (2) the political leadership of the government, and (3) the chance and probability that plays out on the field of battle, in that order. Every American citizen was in the crosshairs of last Tuesday's attack, not just those that were unfortunate enough to be in the World Trade Center or Pentagon. The will of the American people will decide this war. If we are to win, it will be because we have what it takes to persevere through a few more hits, learn from our mistakes, improvise, and adapt. If we can do that, we will eventually prevail.

Everyone I've talked to in the past few days has shared a common frustration, saying in one form or another "I just wish I could do something!" You are already doing it. Just keep faith in America, and continue to support your President and military, and the outcome is certain.

If we fail to do so, the outcome is equally certain.

God Bless America

Dr. Tony Kern, Lt Col, USAF (Ret)
Former Director of Military History, USAF Academy

Since the Vietnam War ended in the spring of 1975, any time the U.S. has become involved in a combat action anywhere in the world, the media and others have admonished whoever occupied the White House at the time, as well as anyone else who might listen: "No more Vietnams!"

I concur to a degree with this sentiment but only in the sense that, as I have written earlier in this essay, "the lesson of the Vietnam War for the United States is that never again should we enter a potentially long conflict without the support of the American people. Moreover, we should never enter any conflict unless we have the will to win."

Max Boot has written that "we would do well to remember the lessons of Vietnam," not to shy away from a particular situation but rather "as a lesson in how to fight successfully."

He points out quite correctly that the enemy America faces today is also a "guerrilla foe—warriors who emerge from the shadows to strike lethal blows, then (blend) in with a civilian population."

"On one level (Osama Bin Laden's) al Qaeda is a much less formidable opponent that the Viet Cong" because it is much smaller in numbers of warriors. "But on another level al Qaeda is . . . more formidable." Whereas the North Vietnamese and the Viet Cong limited their operations to one region, bin Laden's network operates in some fifty countries, including the U.S.

My point here is the U.S. has crack troops available, like the Marines and Army Special Forces, both of whom are formidable in fighting the way soldiers once fought, that is, at close quarters or hand-to-hand combat. Nonetheless, they must now be ready for a different kind of war, one that Mr. Boot says "requires extreme discrimination in the application of force." In this connection, after the first eighteen days of aerial bombardment of al Qaeda training areas and other targets by U.S. and British forces, the effectiveness of such attacks in smoking out and enabling the capture of bin Laden and his men is questionable. All the more reason—and need—to have able U.S. troops on the ground to do what they do best.

It is easy to move from "able U.S. troops on the ground to do what they do best" to retired Marine Corps Lieutenant Colonel Oliver North, another man I have admired and who has addressed eloquently the strategic advantages of pre-emptive military intervention. I received the following e-mail from Christopher J. Suchocki of the Boeing Company; it is entitled "Ollie Knew" and it dates from 1987 when Lt. Col. North was testifying before a Senate panel.

> At a UNC lecture the other day they played a video of Oliver North during the Iran-Contra deals during the Reagan administration. There was Ollie in front of God and Country getting the third degree. But what he said was stunning. He was being drilled by some senator.
>
> "'Did you not recently spend close to $60,000 for a home security system?'"
>
> Oliver replied, "Yes I did sir."
>
> The senator continued, trying to get a laugh out of the audience, "Isn't this a little excessive?"
>
> "'No sir," continued Oliver.
>
> "No. And why not?"
>
> "Because the life of my family and I were threatened?"
>
> "By who?"

"By a terrorist, sir."

"Terrorist? What terrorist could possibly scare you that much?"

"His name is Osama bin Laden."

At this point the senator tried to repeat the name, but couldn't pronounce it, which most people back then probably couldn't. A couple of people laughed at the attempt. Then the senator continued.

"Why are you so afraid of this man?"

"Because sir, he is the most evil person alive that I know of."

"And what do you recommend we do about him?"

"If it were me I would recommend an assassin team be formed to eliminate him and his men from the face of the earth."

Actually, North was referring to Abu Nidal, another international terrorist, who died from multiple gunshot wounds in his Baghdad apartment in August of this year. I have read that the senator was Al Gore.

Of the need to achieve total victory over bin Laden and his network, Senator John McCain (Republican of Arizona) has written:

> War is a miserable business.
>
> However heady the appeal of a call to arms, however just the cause, we should still shed a tear for all that will be lost when war claims its wages from us. Shed a tear, and then get on with the business of killing our enemies as quickly as we can, and as ruthlessly as we must.
>
> We did not cause this war. Our enemies did, and they are to blame for the deprivations and difficulties it occasions. They are to blame for the loss of innocent life. They are to

blame for the geopolitical problems confronting our friends and us. We can help repair the damage of war. But to do so, we must destroy the people who started it.

Veterans of war live forever with the memory of war's merciless nature, of the awful things that had to be done by their hand. They did not recoil from their terrible duty because they knew that the freedom they defended was worth dying and killing for.

War is a miserable business. Let's get on with it.

Amen!

What we should be doing is requiring every adult airline passenger to present a passport or, in the case of a native-born U.S. citizen, an original birth certificate—the same documents that are required for a trip to Canada. If a passenger has a passport from Egypt, Saudi Arabia, etc., he can be given a choice: Take the flight in handcuffs or take the bus. If we do not do this, we are not At War, we are At Patty Cake.

—Gerald Wright

Leaving aside my personal view that Bill Clinton is the most reprehensible and despicable human being ever to hold the American presidency, his role, one of neglect and omission, except, of course, where Monica Lewinsky was concerned, cannot be dismissed as a factor in the attacks on America. In this connection, here are excerpts from a letter written by Barry VanTrees and published in *USA Today*:

➤ After the 1993 World Trade Center bombing, which killed six people and injured approximately 1,000, Clinton promised that those responsible would be hunted down and punished.
➤ After the 1995 bombing in Saudi Arabia, which killed five U.S. military personnel, Clinton promised that

those responsible would be hunted down and punished.

➤ After the 1996 Khobar Towers bombing in Saudi Arabia, which killed 19 and injured 200 U.S. military personnel, Clinton promised that those responsible would be hunted down and punished.

➤ After the 1998 bombing of U.S. embassies in Africa, which killed 224 and injured more than 5,000, Clinton promised that those responsible would be hunted down and punished.

➤ After the 2000 bombing of the *USS Cole*, which killed 17 and injured 39 U.S. sailors, Clinton promised that those responsible would be hunted down and punished.

Perhaps if Clinton had kept his promises, thousands of other innocent people would not have perished as they did on September 11, 2001.

In this vein, Rush Limbaugh, the radio talk show host, has written that President Clinton didn't do enough to stop terrorism. For example,

> Mr. Clinton and his former national security adviser, Sandy Berger, said after Sept. 11 that they had come within an hour of killing bin Laden when they launched cruise missiles against his camps in 1998.
>
> . . . (R)etired [Marine Corps] Gen. Anthony Zinni, who had been U.S. commander in the region . . . revealed it was a "million-to-one-shot."
>
> On Sept. 13, the Associated Press disclosed that "In the waning days of the Clinton presidency, senior officials received specific intelligence about the whereabouts of Osama bin Laden and weighed a military plan to strike the suspected terrorist mastermind's location. The administration opted against an attack." The possible attack was discussed at a meeting last December [2000], which was prompted by

"eyes-only intelligence" about bin Laden's location. A military strike option was presented at the meeting. There was debate about whether the intelligence was reliable. In the end, the president decided against it.

As a Jane's [Intelligence Digest] source put it: "Before the latest catastrophe there was a distinct lack of political will to resolve the bin Laden problem and this had a negative impact on wider intelligence operations."

Granted, Rush is a conservative; so be it. However, consider alternatively the words of Dick Morris, one of Bill Clinton's top political advisors while he was president.

At the White House [in 1996], we held hurried meetings as we watched with worry the growth of terrorism. We polled and speculated about its possible impact on President Clinton's re-election only a few months later.

Advised that his place in history rested on eliminating the deficit, making welfare reform work, and smashing the international network of terrorists militarily and economically, [Clinton] remained unusually passive.

Confronted with one bomb attack after another, [he] seemed strangely uninterested in the war on terrorism.

Bill Clinton revealed himself as a man of the 20th century while Mr. Bush has understood that Sept. 11, 2001, marked the beginning of a new era. In Bill Clinton's epoch, terror was primarily a criminal justice problem which must not be allowed to get in the way of the "real" foreign policy issues . . .

My friend John F. Donato served as an agent in the Central Intelligence Agency from 1955 to 1985. At a lunch meeting on October 18, 2001 he told me that the horrific attacks of September 11th did not surprise him. Calmly but with a tear in his eye, he stated matter-of-factly his reason, namely, that the Agency, as well as the FBI and U.S. military services, had been virtually "gutted" during the eight years of the Clinton administration.

Next, I spoke of today's satellite-borne cameras having sufficient resolution to identify from outer space, say, a fork lying on the ground. This kind of technology has an obvious and major role to play in the gathering of intelligence. Nonetheless, John and I agreed, it is no substitute for an agent 'getting inside the head' of an adversary on a face-to-face basis. Such interpersonal communication is essential, and satellite cameras have no such capability. After all, as Benjamin Franklin put it, "There is no little enemy."

These views are corroborated by another former CIA operative, who has charged that, before the September 11th terrorist acts, the CIA, according to *The New York Times*, "had largely been out of the spy business for years." The only way for the agency to defeat terrorism is, according to Robert Baer in his book *See No Evil*, published in January 2002, "to once again go out and start talking to people—people who can go where it can't, see what it can't and hear what it can't." [The CIA must] "let those who know how to learn secrets perform their jobs, no matter how murky the swamp is."

Another friend, O.J. Betz III, comes from a family with an exceptional tradition of Marine Corps service. "John," as many of his friends call him, served as a Marine sergeant in Vietnam where he was twice wounded in combat. In addition to his two Purple Hearts, he is a recipient of the Navy and Marine Corps Achievement Medal with Combat "V". John's Dad, O.J. Betz Jr., served in the Corps in World War II, and his son, O.J. Betz IV, is a Marine first lieutenant on active duty today.

On September 14, 2001, John wrote a letter to former president Clinton, which begins "Dear Bill," and most of which follows. It is exceptional.

> You and the people who supported you must bear a
> great deal of responsibility for the devastating events that
> took place in New York and Washington on September

11th. The shabby way that you and your administration treated the military and our intelligence agencies has come back to haunt us—and have resulted in the biggest disaster ever to hit our shores.

The many who so openly supported you in the past are now quite conspicuous by their absence. Those of us who fought for our country in Viet Nam, came home to be spat upon by your supporters—the same people who have worked for you and placed the country in a self centered, materialistic mode that will haunt us for years to come.

For this country to remain great, it requires people who are willing to serve their country.

While watching President Bush surveying the rubble around Wall Street today, I was struck by the moment as he walked amidst a sea of policemen, firemen and "hard hats." What a group! True patriots, true Americans—and probably the sons of the men who were our great (and only) supporters during Viet Nam.

How unfortunate that the country has learned in such a violent way that there are factions in this world who hate the United States. Our enemies have watched us and know you cannot be a threat to them if you on the one hand send a computer-operated Scud missile against them, while on the other hand you diddle Monica Lewinsky. You are a disgrace to this country for what you have done to it, and I only hope that you know it. Your legacy is now complete—and because of your lack of leadership for this country it is now bearing a heavy price.

My good friends who know you tell me of your charm, and your ability to control the moment. All wonderful, but sad in that many who voted for you, now wish they had not. But the fact remains that they did and by their votes contributed to the crack in the character of this country and the devastation that this has brought upon us.

I look at the youth of America today and they give us all great joy. They play their sports or wow us with their knowledge and deftness in working the Internet. But they are soft and unprepared for the challenges that face them. This will all change because of the events of September 11th, and in the long run they and their great country will benefit.

Nine years ago when you were first elected President, I wrote (to) my three children. I said to them that, while I am not always right, I am a good judge of character and did not feel that you had the type of character that I would expect the President of the United States to have. I, unfortunately, have been proven right on this, and can only hope that in the future people will not just vote because they want a change. They must be sure that they are voting for someone who has the character, integrity and *unselfish being* so important for someone to be President.

So there it is . . . you will go on with your life, and I hope you are happy. But I know you will live with the fact that under your watch the U.S. became complacent, and will have to work hard to become strong and vigilant once again.

I understand that the former president has received many similar letters. Indeed, even the mainstream (liberal) press has editorially called into question Clinton's stewardship of the military services and the intelligence and law enforcement agencies.

Predictably, the widespread criticism justly meted out to Clinton and his entourage resulted in a media blitz by the former president and many of his former aides to prop up his presidential image and to exercise damage control with respect to his "legacy." Good luck, but I am afraid the damage is not only done, it is far too severe.

I think I have lost all faith in our politicians, so I take the
narrow view and confine it to those around me of like mind,
minds which dictate unselfishness and honor.

—Gene Duncan in *Clint McQuade, USMC:*
The New Beginning

Here is an example of another Clinton administration failure,
the sad result of which was the loss of many American lives on
foreign soil.

In January 2002 a new film named *Black Hawk Down* opened
to rave reviews. It is the story of an American UH-60 *Blackhawk*
attack helicopter that was shot down in Mogadishu, Somalia. I have
seen the film, and there is an aspect of the Pentagon's historical
handling of this situation that deserves serious comment.

On October 3, 1993, U.S. Rangers were helping a Delta Force
commando squadron that was about to descend on a gathering of
Habr Gidr clan leaders in Mogadishu. This clan was led by a
warlord named Mohamed Farrah Aidid who, like Osama bin Laden,
had challenged the U.S. A relief mission, it should have been simple.
By morning eighteen American soldiers had been killed, seventy-
three wounded. Our troops requested help, which they sorely
needed, but it was denied.

Enter Les Aspin, now deceased, Bill Clinton's first Secretary of
Defense. Here is the letter that his inaction compelled me to write
to the president on October 8th:

> As a former Marine Corps officer and Vietnam veteran,
> I can nonetheless only begin to imagine the sense of betrayal
> and outrage our forces on the ground in Somalia must have
> experienced when the likes of Les Aspin, safely ensconced in
> his Pentagon office, denied their request for helicopters and
> armored vehicles when perhaps it slipped the *Defense*
> Secretary's mind that Americans' lives were then being
> threatened—and later, tragically, lost as a result of Aspin's
> outrageous and unforgivable behavior.

Your appointee is resoundingly unfit to hold the office he does. His judgment in this crucial instance was so poor, nay, egregious, that you have an easy decision: *No more Les, and no less!* Not only would dismissing this arrogant loser be the right thing now for a Commander-in-Chief to do, I'm confident that, if you have the moral courage to fire him, you will enjoy the added bonus of popular acclaim here at home. Who knows, maybe such decisive action on your part would even have a beneficial effect on the folks in Mogadishu, both American and Somali.

Give health care a rest for a day, and quell the Aspin outrage.

I have never received a reply.

This year Mr. Clinton was quoted saying, "Now, you know, I didn't blame [President George W. Bush's] father for Somalia when we had that awful day memorialized in 'Black Hawk Down.' I didn't do that."

Yet, in May 1993, just four months into his term and five months *before* the American deaths and injuries in Mogadishu, he gave a speech to link himself with the intervention, which he praised. To wit: "If all of you who served had not gone, it is absolutely certain that tens of thousands would have died by now." Calling it a "successful mission," he added that it "proved yet again that American leadership can help mobilize international action."

This is another example of Clinton's innate and unseemly "spin." Some might call it lying.

> *I sat on January 20ᵗʰ [2001] as did millions of Americans and watched as our government underwent a peaceful transition of power—the "Change of Command." I was proud as George W. Bush took his oath of office. But, I was sad, as I watched Bill Clinton board Air Force One for the final time. It may surprise you to know why the latter made me sad; let me explain. I saw*

21 seasoned U.S. Marines in full dress blues, with rifles, deliver a 21-gun salute to the outgoing president. It was then that I realized the truth about the ready status of America's military: Even the elite of the USMC need more preparation and time on the range with their weapons. Every last one of them missed!

—Military Readiness Alert

32

CORPORATE AMERICA

If talented people are challenged with tough but achievable
goals, and if they are given the leeway to act on their own,
with adequate support, they can, and will, work wonders.

—Rear Admiral Paul T. Gillcrist, USN (Ret.),
in *Feet Wet: Reflections of a Carrier Pilot*

I should begin a chapter with such a title with my own business biography. For better or worse, it will provide some additional insight into my own career and credibility. Before I do, though, I would like to present my philosophy of work. It may be summarized thus: *Ideas are important, risk-takers should be rewarded, and the way to make a difference is to believe in something and fight for it.*

Although I served principally as a commercial bank officer for twenty years after my return from Vietnam in 1969, I am today a management consultant whose areas of expertise include finance, strategic planning, merger and acquisition (M&A) advisory, marketing, business transformation, bank credit policy, investment management and corporate communications. I also serve as an expert witness.

On November 19, 1998 I was elected a director/trustee of the Federated Funds of Federated Investors, Inc., a Pittsburgh-based $195-billion mutual fund complex listed on the New York Stock Exchange; I am also a member of the board's audit committee.

With more than three decades of financial services and

consulting experience in the United States, Britain and France, as well as substantial business travel elsewhere in Europe and in Asia, I am confident that my business perspective reflects broad and long experience in the financial services industry. My clients have included American Express Bank, Campbell Maack & Sessions, Chase Manhattan Bank (now JPMorganChase), China Trust Bank of New York, Citibank, CSC Weston Group, Deloitte Touche Tohmatsu, DVC Group, Inc., Federal Home Loan Bank of Pittsburgh, Ford Credit Europe, General Motors, the former Johnson & Higgins (now part of Marsh & McLennan), KPMG Peat Marwick, the former Mudge Rose Guthrie Alexander & Ferdon, National Westminster Bank USA (now Fleet Bank), State Development Bank of China, Strategic Decisions Group, Thacher Proffitt & Wood, The Limited and others.

I also served a stint as executive vice president of DVC Group, Inc., a marketing, communications and technology company headquartered in Morristown, New Jersey. A key advisor to its chief executive and chief financial officers, I had served the firm earlier as a business strategist, M&A advisor and acting head of human resources. As its liaison with the investment banking and legal communities, I helped position the firm for its sale in 2000 to Chicago-based Lake Capital. Prior to my DVC service, I was employed by Coopers & Lybrand in its New York financial services consulting practice.

Once with Chase Manhattan Bank as CFO of its then $13-billion retail banking sector, I was responsible for the strategic planning, accounting, management information systems (MIS) and treasury functions, and served as a member of its Individual Bank's asset-liability management committee. I joined the bank from Arthur Young (now Ernst & Young) where I was a partner responsible for its New York financial services consulting group. Prior to joining the firm, I was chief executive officer of then Prudential-Bache's international trade bank.

Earlier, I had been recruited by Marine Midland Bank (now HSBC Bank USA) where I was a senior vice president responsible for trade finance and lending to corporations in the commodity-trading and export-import markets with units based in New York, London and Singapore. I also managed the bank's strategic planning for an export trading company, and led its joint-venture negotiations with several major international trading firms. Moreover, I was responsible for Edge Act bank branches in Houston and Los Angeles, served as a director and a member of the executive committee of Marine Midland International Bank, and was appointed by Marine's chief executive to its Credit Management & Policy Committee.

As a vice president at Citibank before joining Marine Midland, I held a succession of posts in New York, London and Paris in corporate lending, credit policy supervision, international banking, correspondent banking and asset-based finance. There I also developed expertise in financial institutions risk analysis and mining project finance. Furthermore, I wrote Citibank's *Credit Policy and Risk Acceptability for International Financial Institutions*, which was disseminated to its branches worldwide.

I have given numerous international banking seminars in New York City and Washington, DC, to a variety of groups, including Russian, Ukrainian, Armenian, Moldovan and Taiwanese bankers, businessmen and economists, as well as professionals from French, German and Swiss banks operating in New York. I have also traveled to Britain, China, Russia and Kazakhstan on various consulting assignments involving credit, foreign exchange and export finance, and served Deloitte Touche Tohmatsu as a consultant at the State Development Bank of China in Beijing.

I was also selected by Hofstra University, where I have served as an assistant professor of banking and finance at the Frank G. Zarb School of Business, to give an international banking seminar to senior Russian bank executives. At Hofstra my course emphasized the credit, interest-rate and liquidity risks of modern banking, including the use of off-balance sheet transactions such as interest-rate swaps and other derivative products.

A public speaker and an author, I have lectured at the Colgate Darden Graduate School of Business Administration and the former Center for International Banking Studies at the University of

Virginia, the University of Dayton, The World Bank, Ohio State University, the American Institute of Banking, Long Island University and, of course, Hofstra. I have also given speeches to major conferences and conventions such as those organized by the Bank Administration Institute (BAI), the National Foreign Trade Council and Robert Morris Associates.

My writings on banking, finance and other topics have been published in various books and periodicals, including *The Wall Street Journal*, *The New York Times*, Dow Jones-Irwin's *The Loan Officer's Handbook*, *The Journal of Commerce*, *The Journal of Commercial Bank Lending*, Robert Morris Associates' *Classics in Commercial Bank Lending*, *The Tablet*, *The Long Island Catholic* and others. I have also appeared on several television programs, including *The Phil Donahue Show* and *The American Family Association Presents*.

One of the more irksome elements that emerged in American corporate culture during the past three decades is the system of quotas that permits certain groups of persons to receive special treatment in both hiring and firing. This system resulted in an insidious double standard. A disturbing case in point caused me to write the following letter to the editor of *The Wall Street Journal*, which was published on June 25, 1997.

> I found your article ("A Promising Career Comes to a Tragic End," page one, May 9) about the career and recent suicide of Duquesne Light's Dianna Green both sad and disturbing—but not so much for the reasons you reported.
>
> Following the headline that "Pittsburgh's Dianna Green Overcame Racial Barriers to Help Lead Big Utility," you quote CEO David Marshall's memo in which he stated that Ms. Green "is leaving the company . . . to begin pursuing other career interests *that she has had for many years*" (emphasis mine). The article continues: "The memo made

no mention of Ms. Green's rise to power—how she had catapulted through the ranks. . . ."

Later, readers learn that, "She was fired after the company learned that she had lied in a sworn deposition and on her resume, falsely claiming she had a master's degree in business administration."

Earl Hord, who "is black and is managing general partner of Pittsburgh-based Keystone Minority Capital Fund," was quoted saying that "if you are black, you have to be twice as good [as white counterparts] to be equal" and that "The same scale is used when you are found to have flaws. You don't get the same kind of soft landing that is given to white male executives."

Flaws? This is outrageous. Ms Green *lied*, for heaven's sake. Is that now merely a flaw? She *should* have been fired—and for *cause*. Indeed, she shouldn't have been hired in the first place. In this connection, had Wesley von Schack, Mr. Marshall's predecessor as CEO, done his homework when he hired Ms. Green some nine years ago, perhaps she would not have received the opportunity he afforded her to "catapult through the ranks." Or did Mr. von Schack hire her anyway, maybe even with the knowledge that Ms. Green lied about having an M.B.A.?

As for the "soft landing" purported by Mr. Hord as being available only to "white male executives," it seems to me that Ms. Green was being positioned by Duquesne Light to receive just that. After all, "The company hired a New York attorney to conclude a severance settlement with her." I wonder how many other people who are fired because they lied receive severance settlements. Alas, even Mr. Marshall seemed a bit disingenuous in the soft tone of his announcement of Ms. Green's departure when he stated that her "other career interests" were ones "that she has had for many years."

Enron, a Houston-based energy-related enterprise, last year became the largest bankruptcy in American history. With many thousands of people—even those outside the business community—the name Enron has become a household word, one that is synonymous with corruption and greed. In July of this year, WorldCom, a huge telecommunications company based in Mississippi, which one friend recently dubbed "the Godzilla of fraud," announced that it had improperly accounted for a reported $7.2 billion in expenses, thereby inflating its earnings. It has since eclipsed Enron by filing for bankruptcy involving some $30 billion in debts, which is twice as large as Enron's. During the same period other companies, including Qwest and Global Crossing, announced accounting irregularities or bankruptcies or both. In early November, WorldCom admitted that its phony profits due to its fraudulent accounting could exceed $9 billion! Then there is the case of Dennis Koslowski, CEO of Tyco International, who essentially looted his company of tens of millions of dollars to feather his own nest.

> *Profit is an opinion, but cash is a fact.*

> —Saying in Accounting

In March of this year Princeton professor of political science Uwe Reinhardt wrote of "the heroic and the pathetic in adult American society" in an article entitled "Can't Executives Be as Honorable As Our Soldiers?" No surprise in the aftermath of 9/11, he cited soldiers, firefighters, policemen and journalists, who take huge risks to keep their fellow citizens informed, as "brave folks." Then he juxtaposes these heroes with some other types:

> Compare (them) with the morally flexible ones whose shenanigans helped fuel the asset bubble in what was supposed to be the most efficient and trustworthy financial market in the world. Picture such executives, and their

> auditors, lawyers, consultants, and bankers, gathered around
> a conference for but one purpose: to devise structures,
> transactions or accounting techniques designed to deceive
> shareholders and prospective investors.

Fortunately, debacles like WorldCom's, Enron's (as well as that of Arthur Andersen LLP, its auditor, now under indictment for obstruction of justice) and Tyco International's don't occur frequently. Nonetheless, the damage inflicted on these companies' employees and ordinary citizens, what with lost pensions and worthless investments, has been unprecedented. The problem is exacerbated by the grand compensation schemes that Enron's and many other senior executives prepared for themselves and from which they benefited handsomely, even as their firms' stock prices were in free fall.

With respect to compensation, many Americans believe that corporate executives in business today are obscenely overcompensated. Although I am a confirmed capitalist, I have arrived at the same conclusion. Even the second most powerful person in the Federal Reserve System has publicly chastised American CEOs for their greed and excess. William McDonough, retiring president of the Federal Reserve Bank of New York and a Holy Cross alumnus, has called upon them to reduce their own compensation packages. For example, Jack Welch, General Electric's recently *retired* chairman and CEO, receives $1.4 million per *month*. Is anyone really worth that much?

Henry Clifford of Wainscott, New York, a former Marine, has provided timely perspective on this issue in the following letter to *The New York Times*, which was published on April 28, 2002.

> The commandant of the Marine Corps receives a base
> salary of $163,000 plus monthly allowances. He manages
> an organization of 172,600 men and women and an annual
> budget of $13.5 billion, comparable to that of a midsize
> public corporation. His total compensation is 11 times that
> of the lowest pay grade in the Marine Corps.

A corporate chief executive paid $10 million is receiving approximately 400 times the compensation of his lowest paid employee for doing roughly the same job as the commandant. They are both chief executives of large enterprises. There is also the matter of accountability, which is considerably more swift and sure in the military than in the corporate world, where executives are often generously rewarded by a friendly and forgiving board of directors even when the performance of the business is poor—and sometimes awful.

While there has always been a compensation gap between the corporate and other sectors, the word unbalanced does not adequately describe the distortions we are seeing today.

The corporate scandals of the past year became fodder for the 2002 election season. Predictably, the Democrats sought to identify Republicans with American corporations and their political and financial support, even going so far as to blame the administration of President George W. Bush for corporate America's ethical problems. In this connection, I received an e-mail that places the issue in amusing perspective.

Enron's chairman did meet with the president and the vice president in the Oval Office. Enron gave $420,000 to the president's party over three years. It donated $100,000 to the president's inauguration festivities. The Enron chairman stayed at the White House 11 times. The corporation had access to the administration at its highest levels and even enlisted the Commerce and State Departments to grease deals for it. The taxpayer-supported Export-Import Bank subsidized Enron for more than $600 million in just one transaction. But the president under whom all this happened wasn't George W. Bush. It was Bill Clinton.

It is clear that Enron chairman Kenneth Lay, WorldCom CEO Bernard Ebbers, Tyco International CEO Dennis Koslowski and their colleagues fostered an environment in which the ethically doubtful could and did thrive. In contrast I consider myself fortunate to have worked for men who were ethically and morally upright, in both business and personal dealings.

Indeed, there were exceptional people in leadership positions during my business career. Still, I can count on fewer than one hand's fingers the number of bosses I have had whom I admire and for whom I would enthusiastically work again, any time, anywhere. The five men, four bosses and a peer, whose brief profiles follow, all possess character, integrity and ability. Each is a success in every sense of the word.

P. Henry Mueller

"Hank" Mueller is the retired chairman of the credit policy committee of Citibank and Citicorp, now Citigroup. He is a consummate Christian gentleman with an extraordinary intellect and a dry sense of humor. Author of countless articles and books, he also served as a Marine Corps officer in World War II. (Quotations from Hank herein appear in the **Preface**, at the beginning of the chapters entitled **Chaminade High School** and **An Introduction to Management**, as well as at the end of the chapter on **Marine Corps Officer Candidates School** and at the beginning of the section entitled **End Papers**.)

Hank began his career at the bank as a page in 1934. While he was attending New York University to gain some college credits, the bank recognized his enormous talent and sent him to Princeton University to complete his education, for which the bank paid the freight.

One of my favorite stories about him is that he was absent only one day in his forty-eight years at Citibank. When I asked him how he explains this blot on his record, he replied modestly, "I was really sick that day." Hank is *the* Renaissance man. I believe I learned more from him during my business career than from any other man, except my father. At 85, he is still my friend and mentor.

Phillip B. Lassiter

A former U.S. Navy officer, Phil joined Citibank in 1968 and was instrumental in hiring me five years later. In 1979, shortly after my return to New York from assignments with the bank in Paris and London, he invited me to join him in a new Citibank venture, the Financial and Information Services Group. Later, we both moved to Citicorp Industrial Credit, the bank's commercial finance arm. After approximately twenty years with Citicorp, and having attained membership on its elite Policy Committee, Phil moved to Ambac Financial Group, a leading holding company providing financial-guarantee insurance and financial services. Headquartered in New York City, Phil serves as its chairman and chief executive officer. Hard-nosed, practical and evenhanded, he always knew when and how to backstop his people. He is a genuine leader.

John W. Hannon, Jr.

John Hannon became president and chief operating officer of Bankers Trust Company in New York City. It is fair to say that he was the most instrumental person in my joining the bank. Perhaps because he and my Dad had worked together at the old Commercial National Bank of New York following their military service during World War II, John always took an interest in me. A graduate of St. Lawrence University and another strong leader with a wonderful sense of humor, he would often stop by my desk and drag me off to lunch, which was invariably great fun. Not only was he a good and able man, he was one of the finest and most loyal people I have ever known. He gave me my first job in the business world, and his early advice to me as a then-twenty-four-year-old was invaluable.

One of the most unforgettable stories of my banking career involved John. In the 1970s, as the bank's president, he would regularly attend the meetings of the Reserve City Bankers Association. Since much of the activity was social, John found himself at a cocktail party one evening being brow-beaten by a junior officer's wife who was singing her husband's praises, and speculating, because of her man's considerable credentials, that he would soon be made a vice president.

Then, not being aware that John was Bankers Trust's president, she asked him, "What do you do?"

"I came to sing bass, and help out with the screwing."

Shocked and outraged, the woman ran to find her husband. Gesturing toward Mr. Hannon, she hastened to ask him, "Do you know what that awful man over there just said to me?"

Already uncomfortable at his realization that it was John to whom she was pointing, the woman's husband inquired, "Now *which* man again said what?" Sure now that it was the bank's president whom his wife would have him reprimand, the young officer decided that discretion was the far better part of valor.

"C'mon, dear, let's get out of here," he said as he ushered his bride from the room.

I am proud to have known and worked for John, who passed away in 2000. He led two generations of once young bankers at Bankers Trust.

Joseph A. Manganello, Jr.

Joe rose to essentially the same position at Bankers Trust as Hank Mueller did at Citibank, and was a close acolyte of John Hannon. Instrumental in hiring me fresh back from Vietnam, and later my department head in the early seventies, Joe had served as an Army Special Forces officer. Furthermore, he debunked the myth that an Italian-American couldn't make it big in the world of New York banking. An alumnus of Cornell University, he is a remarkable profile in courage and one of the most admirable and positive people I have ever met.

Although not tall in stature, Joe possessed a powerful personality that tended to make him larger than life, brilliant communications skills and a not infrequent satirical wit. He did not suffer fools lightly. I recall vividly him describing a man whose powers of intellect were in his estimation insufficient as "the east end of a westbound horse."

Joe was another fine leader who had extraordinary ability to get commitment from those on his team.

Victor D. Brunst

Born in Prague, Czechoslovakia, of Russian parents two days before Hitler invaded Poland, thus igniting World War II, Victor was *not* one of my bosses. Both of us employed by Citibank, he and I met in 1977 in London, where I then lived and worked. Two years later, we were transferred to the bank's head office in New York, and I persuaded him to join me in Phil Lassiter's new organization, into which I preceded him by a few months.

Having emigrated to the U.S. in 1959, he served in the Army and later earned an M.B.A. from Columbia University. After a stint at Mobil Corporation, he joined Citibank, then First National City Bank of New York.

Victor is a tough iconoclast who always got things done, and whom I admire for all he has accomplished. Although Russian is his mother tongue, he is equally fluent in English and German. While spearheading Citibank's business strategy in the former Soviet Union, he opened its first office in Moscow in the 1970s. Having retired from Citibank, he has since been president of a Russian-American business venture and a private investor. I am proud to have him as my colleague and friend.

How do you measure success?
To laugh often and much;
To win the respect of intelligent people and the
affection of children;

*To earn the appreciation of honest critics and endure the
betrayal of false friends;
To appreciate beauty;
To find the best in others;
To leave the world a little better, whether by a healthy child,
a garden patch,
A redeemed social condition, or a job well done;
To know even one other life has breathed easier because you
have lived—
This is to have succeeded.*

—Ralph Waldo Emerson

33

PARIS AND LONDON

*The age of chivalry has gone. That of sophisters, economists, and
calculators has succeeded, and the glory of Europe is extinguished
forever.*

—Edmund Burke

Shortly after the American Bicentennial celebration on July
4, 1976, Mame, the children and I left GC and moved to
Paris, France. Chas was eight, John, six, and Kate, just 19
months. At the time, I was a junior officer with Citibank, which
transferred me to the City of Lights for a planned two-year
assignment at its office at 60 Champs Elysée, once site of the Nazis'
World War II headquarters in Paris. Located on the building's fifth
floor, my office actually had a balcony that overlooked the marvelous
thoroughfare below. To my right I could easily see the Arc de
Triomphe while the obelisk at the center of La Place de la Concorde
stood to my left. Straight ahead, that is, south, the Eiffel Tower
dominated the skyline. It doesn't get much better than that.

We lived in a spacious ground-floor apartment at 40 Avenue
Charles Floquet in Paris's seventh arrondissement on the River
Seine's Left Bank and virtually in the shadow of the Eiffel Tower.
Owned by Monsieur Le Comte Odon de Cassagne, the place had
an ample garden surrounded by a heavy spiked wrought-iron fence
that was so densely covered with ivy that one could see neither in
nor out. I couldn't imagine a more agreeable and private location
in any big city. And, after all, it *was* Paris.

Both Mame and I had some French-speaking ability, thanks to our educational backgrounds and a last minute refresher at the Berlitz language school in New York. Nonetheless, it took us a while to become accustomed to the frustrating rapidity with which many Parisians spoke. I remember watching and listening to Raymond Barre, then France's prime minister under President Valéry Giscard d'Estaing, on television, and being overjoyed at how easy it was for me to understand him. Monsieur Barre spoke with both a clarity and a cadence far more measured than were typically heard on the street or, for that matter, in the office. With Barre as my model, I vowed to broaden my vocabulary and ultimately speak "comme un français." (Years later Monsieur Barre and I literally bumped into each other turning a corner at a luncheon at a hotel in midtown Manhattan. We shook hands and went our respective ways.)

To this end, I insisted that my French colleagues speak only French with me, and correct my errors. This approach proved beneficial to the personal relationships I developed; moreover, it was not one generally taken by most Americans, who typically expected French professionals to speak English in business situations. In this connection, I often wondered what an American would think, or how he or she might react, if a French national came to the U.S. to work and expected us Yanks to speak French.

As things turned out, Mame and I became fluent, and our children also developed strong proficiency in French, which still attends them today.

One of the most disturbing, unforgettable and touching stories from our time in Paris took place the first day Chas and John went to school. Early on that September morning in 1976, Mame put the boys on a city bus that would take them to the American School of Paris, which is actually located outside Paris in Saint Cloud. She kissed our two little guys goodbye and told them to watch for her at the same spot that afternoon when they returned home. Little did she, or they, know what would transpire in the interim.

Mame had a great deal to do during the day, as we were attempting to survive in our new apartment—without furniture. (The French government was holding our goods in a warehouse and would not release any of them until my work permit was finalized. Of course, Citibank stepped in to attempt to expedite the process but the French still adhered to an unswerving *je ne sais quoi* that was unbearably bureaucratic.) Anyway, she spent the day shopping and getting as much done as she could to make our abode habitable. That afternoon, in order to get home in time to meet Chas and John at the bus stop, she procured a taxi and sat in the back seat holding Kate and the little *poussette* (stroller) she had acquired to accommodate our little girl.

During the taxi ride, Kate threw up all over herself, Mame and the back seat of the cab. That's bad enough in and of itself, but the taxi driver then went ballistic and ordered Mame and the baby out of his vehicle. Despite her protestations and insistence that he drive her to her destination, the creep put her and Kate out on the street a long way from both home and the bus stop. I only wish I had been there.

Now the time was at hand when Chas and John's bus would be nearing home and they would be looking for that essential landmark, their mother. For her part, Mame was running fast and hard, with Kate sick and screaming, both mother and daughter still sporting vomit. Mame was actually becoming frantic, deeply worried that the boys would keep riding the bus to who knows where because of her absence from the appointed place at the time they expected to see her.

There were our sons, ages eight and six, in a foreign city on a public bus. As they approached the bus stop, Chas said to John, "I think this is where we should get off." Doubtful, John replied, "But Mom's not here." Thank God Chas persisted and insisted that they both get off the bus then and there. Though anguished and afraid, they did.

Holding their little lunch boxes, Chas and John next just stood forlorn at that bus stop on Avenue Suffren across from the block on which we lived. There was still no sign of their mother. Then at last, Mame came racing around the corner calling to them. According to her, after what seemed like an eternity, on seeing her, both boys burst into tears, as did she. Reunited at last, my little family spent all the time they needed to feel safe and secure in each other's arms. The ordeal was over.

To this day, this episode may be the most unsettling development that has ever befallen any of us because of the obvious potential that our two sons might have become lost. I can only surmise that we were blessed at the outcome.

While working in Paris, I developed a friendship with a Frenchman named Daniel Alfano, who was the chief credit officer of Citibank's Paris branch. Years later, two of his daughters, Isabelle and Cécile, would come to visit us during summers in Westhampton, and our Kate would be the guest of him and his wife Monique at their home in Mareil-Marly outside Paris.

We also managed to visit our Charrot cousins just across the French border in Switzerland in a small village called Charrot, my mother's maiden name. This little farming hamlet was named after Henri Charrot, who founded it in 1458. There we visited with Léon Charrot and his family, all of whom spoke only French.

Whereas my stint in Paris was originally to have been for two years, it proved to be short-lived. In the spring of 1977 I received a telephone call from Hank Mueller in New York, who advised me that my services were required in England. Thus, after just a year, Citibank transferred me to its London operation, where I was put in charge of its European training apparatus and promoted to vice president.

Mame and I genuinely loved Paris, and still return from time to time. We were both at first disappointed to have to leave such a splendid city after such a short stay. Nonetheless, we regarded London as a great tradeoff and our relocation as another opportunity to 'bloom where you're planted.'

It was our wish to live in central London but we couldn't find an adequate apartment (I should say "flat") to suit our timetable. Fortunately, Citibank owned a house in Wimbledon in southwest London not far from the All England Lawn Tennis and Croquet Club, where the international tennis championship matches are played each year.

The house, located at 23 Dunstall Road just off Wimbledon Common, was perfect for us. Indeed, it reminded us of our own home back in GC. Charming and spacious, it contained five bedrooms, each with a fireplace, three and a half baths, a huge family room, a living room, a dining room, an eat-in kitchen, a mud room, a laundry room and an awninged terrace that overlooked a quintessentially English garden. Twenty-three Dunstall is today worth over one million pounds, or approximately $1,550,000.

We moved into our new home in July 1977 and were amazed at the welcome we received from our new neighbors, some of whom would become friends for life. Even as the movers were carrying our furniture and other personal effects into the house, people brought sandwiches, cakes and cookies (properly called "biscuits" in England), as well as tea and soft drinks. To us it was extraordinary, especially since we were never greeted by anyone, except the concièrge, in our apartment building in Paris.

Soon after we moved in, Mike Willis and his wife Monique, who lived directly across the street from us, invited Mame and me, as well as several other neighbors, to their home on a Sunday afternoon for a glass of wine. Everything was delightful and most cordial.

At one point during our conversation Mike queried, "You know whose house you're living in, don't you?"

"Why, no," I said candidly, telling myself silently that it belonged to my employer, Citibank.

"That's Jack Hobbs' house," continued Mike.

I am quite sure that at this point mine eyes glazed over, which Mike noticed readily.

"Let me put it this way," he said, "Jack Hobbs is to our cricket as Babe Ruth is to your baseball."

In *The Cricketer* of November 1986, Alf Glover wrote of Sir Jack Hobbs, "Like all great men he accepted success and adulation with a sense of humility and often said what more could we ask for than to play the game we love and at the same time get paid for it." Sir Jack sounds like my kind of guy.

Of all Dunstall Road's wonderful neighbors who became our friends, Peter and Maggie Street, who lived next door at No. 21, actually became part of our family and vice versa. Sadly, both are recently deceased but they were friends beyond friendship. Even after the Mansfields returned to the U.S. in 1979, they always welcomed us back to Wimbledon whenever we would travel to London on vacation or business. Indeed, they insisted we stay at their home, never at a hotel, and invariably hosted a cocktail party for us and the neighbors in our honor. Peter and Maggie have two adult children, John and Jane, who now have kids of their own.

Constance Hendrie, who lost her beloved husband Herbert, a stained-glass window artist, when she was only 38, also lived in Wimbledon, although not on Dunstall Road. Highly recommended to us by Rosie and Simon Boome, friends and Dunstall denizens, she initially served as a babysitter for our children. Our family's relationship with Connie progressed and became one of the utmost closeness and trust. The children loved her so deeply that I came to refer to her as their third grandmother. She was also a confidante of both Mame and myself, and I will always remember how deftly she handled us and the kids when Mame was hospitalized for breast surgery in 1978. Her quieting hand and inner strength imparted a sense of calm I shall never forget. "We'll get through this, and all will be well," she said, as if it were foreordained. And so it was.

Connie passed away in July 1992. That year I wrote of her:

> Connie Hendrie was, despite her age, failing health and
> difficult economic circumstances, ever beautiful, radiant,
> smiling. I know why her Herbert fell in love with her years

ago for hers was an exquisite combination of innocence, mischief, humor and timing. Even early in our friendship, she would kiss me goodbye with a closely whispered "Now take care, ducky." I don't know why she called me that but I loved it anyway. I also loved her as did Mame and our children, who were privileged to have Connie as their "third grandmother" once upon a time. Agatha Christie's words remind me of Connie: "I like living. I have sometimes been wildly, despairingly, acutely miserable, racked with sorrow, but through it all I still know quite certainly that just to be alive is a grand thing."

Since then we have come to know Connie's only child, Susan Hendrie Taylor, who visited us last year from her home in Galashiels, Scotland. To Connie, Susan was the most special person on earth. Connie also surprised us by converting, after many visits with us to our parish Church of the Sacred Heart in Wimbledon, to Roman Catholicism.

Of perhaps greatest significance is that during our time in England we came to know our Charrot cousins, of whom there are many, mostly in southern England. Since then, we have not only kept in touch but visited each other's homes from time to time.

Kate attended an English nursery school just down the hill from our Wimbledon home. John was a student at the American Community School of London, which was even closer to home. Chas went to Donhead Lodge, a boys' preparatory school administered by the Jesuits and within walking distance of 23 Dunstall. At Donhead the students were academically ranked weekly, a challenge Chas handled with consummate determination. I recall one week when he slipped from first to sixth (of approximately twenty in his class) and told me, "Dad, that's never going to happen again." It didn't.

When the time came for my transfer back to Citibank's headquarters in Manhattan, I did not want to go; nor did Mame and the kids. Yes, we were New Yorkers, and GC was our home. Still, there was something very special about England, about London, about Wimbledon. Dunstall Road had undeniably become home and we were all happy there. It was a feeling, a state of mind, I suppose, more than anything tangible, and it is a warm memory today, lo, some twenty-five years later.

We departed London's Heathrow Airport on January 12, 1979, Kate's fourth birthday, and celebrated the occasion three times: at breakfast with Connie in Wimbledon, in the upstairs lounge aboard the Boeing 747 that took us home to New York, and at my parents' GC home following our arrival. Aboard the aircraft, the pilots, on learning it was Kate's birthday, took her into the cockpit where she sat enthralled and gazed out at the wide Atlantic far below.

There's an amusing little anecdote about the meaning of my parents' GC home that involves Kate's perception and flawless logic as a very little girl. When we would travel to America for summer vacation or Christmas, we would invariably stay at Mom and Dad's. As a result, even after we had returned from England for good, Kate would ask, "When are we going to America again?" To her, my parents' home *was* America.

In the last analysis, our time together as a young family in Paris and London, both wonderful places to live and work, bonded us as never before. The children's ages were such that they had not yet put down deep roots back in GC; in other words, they had not yet established the sorts of friendships and other interpersonal relationships that, had they been older, would have been extremely difficult to interrupt or replace. All things considered, our sojourn abroad, actually less than three years in all, was a remarkable time in our lives that changed us all. We were given an opportunity not afforded to many people, and we have relished it ever since. It was a special time.

One lives but once in the world.

—Johann Wolfgang von Goethe

34

MARATHON MAN

That man is little to be envied whose patriotism would not gain force upon the plain of Marathon, or whose piety would not grow warmer among the ruins of Iona.

—Samuel Johnson

I played football, baseball and somewhat less basketball (due to being personally vertically challenged) from the time I was a young boy. I loved to play these sports, as well as others, and took running for granted; in other words, one had to run in order to play.

By the time I went to Chaminade, running had taken on new meaning. Under Coach Joe Thomas, wind sprints were integral to every football practice, usually at the end thereof, and running a mile was required as part of the physical fitness test that every student had to take twice annually. I found the mile grueling at first, but then came to respect it, recognizing that running a mile was obviously quite different from running sprints.

When I was a member of the Navy R.O.T.C. at Holy Cross, a three-mile run (in full combat gear) was required in the Marines' PRT (Physical Readiness Test). At this stage I was in my late teens or early twenties and probably as strong as I would ever be. Three miles became my standard workout and would remain so for years.

In the late seventies, while living in Wimbledon on the periphery of Wimbledon Common, I began running longer distances; five miles were standard, although I would on occasion run eight. Once more, this became my distance and remained unchanged for years.

Then I learned that a good friend, an American named Gene Sweeney, who was both a Citibank colleague and a Dunstall Road neighbor, was going to run in the New York City Marathon, a "full" marathon of 26.2 miles. I thought this was terribly ambitious since Gene's typical workout, according to him, then consisted of running only two miles every other day. He told me that he had, however, run thirteen miles, or half a marathon, to test himself before the big event. To be sure, he had much more the runner's build than I. I recall that he finished New York in just under five hours.

My attitude, decidedly negative with respect to my own participation therein, was that marathons were for super athletes who had been running long distances in the mountains of Africa for many years. I knew little about training for a 26.2-mile race, and seriously questioned whether I could finish such a grueling event. I also recalled a college classmate named Mike Marnik, a member of the Holy Cross track and/or cross country team(s), who ran in the Boston Marathon and spent the following fortnight on crutches. *If the marathon treats a real runner like that, what might it do to the likes of me?* I thought.

In the autumn of 1980 I decided to train for the *Newsday* Long Island Marathon, which was held on May 6, 1981. Whereas my regular jogging course in GC covered 5.5 miles, which would usually take me about forty-one minutes (at 7.5 minutes per mile), I stepped up the distance to ten miles, twelve and then fifteen. What was most encouraging to me was that I was not only *not losing* efficiency, I was *gaining* it.

My normal five-to-six miles soon became merely a warm-up, and when I hit my stride in the eight-to-ten mile range, I was sailing, almost effortlessly on, I learned from reading some of the late Jim Fixx's books on running, the so called "runner's high."

As another runner has put it, "I've never been fast, but for some reason I seem to be able to keep going for a long time. Distance running, as far as I can tell, is an acquired taste; the thought of it is just miserable to a lot of people. But I'm addicted. Must be the endorphins." (Endorphins are chemicals secreted by the brain that engage after a certain amount of work and distance have been achieved.) This is exactly my experience in running long distances.

At approximately the nineteen-to-twenty mile mark, most runners "hit the wall." My understanding of this phenomenon is that the human body is designed and equipped to go that distance and no more. What happens at this point is that the stores of glycogen, a carbohydrate that is the fuel supply for the body's muscles, become depleted. So I next increased my training distance to twenty-two miles, more than long enough to experience hitting the wall.

For me, hitting the wall was never painful. Instead, my body would almost insidiously transmit to my mind, *Now, it would be so nice to walk to the side of the road, sit down and just relax for a while.* Yet, at this moment, the runner must simply make the tough mental decision to keep putting one foot in front of the other for the final six or seven miles of the race. For me, the lost-productivity effect of hitting the wall was extraordinary: I remember averaging seven minutes per mile for the first twenty miles; then, post-wall, my average mile would take between nine and ten minutes. In other words, my last 6.2 miles would take an hour, whereas my first twenty miles had taken only two and one third hours. It was amazing—and frustrating.

Beginning four months before a marathon, I would run five miles each morning and another five in the evening on weekdays. (This was because running a full ten miles at the beginning or end of a workday would simply take too long.) On weekends, I would usually run fifteen miles on Saturday, and at least twenty on Sunday. I would often *not* run on Mondays in order to give my body a rest. During the week before the marathon itself, Sunday would see me do my last major distance—twenty miles or more. On Monday I would rest. Then, with the big race the following Sunday, I would run eight miles on Tuesday, six on Wednesday, four on Thursday, two on Friday and one on Saturday. On each day of this final week I would engage in "carbohydrate loading," consuming lots of pasta in an effort to mitigate the effects of hitting the wall.

My first marathon completion time was 3:24. I was then thirty-six years old and had finished well within the top ten percent of my age group. I felt good, among other reasons, because my Dad, at dinner the evening before the race, had tried to talk me out of running. He expressed concern that I would be putting my life at risk, and that this was the wrong thing for a family man to be doing. Once more his words sobered me, as they did many years earlier when I told him of my plan to join the Marine Corps.

When Mame dropped me off at the starting line for the 8:00 a.m. race, I asked her to meet me at the finish line at 11:30, having estimated that it would take me three and a half hours to complete the course.

In fact, Mame had made up her own mind that it would take me *four* hours to finish, and planned accordingly. After completing the race, and searching for and not finding her, I decided to run the four miles home; after all, I was certainly loose enough to do a few more miles. When I arrived home, I told the kids about the race and asked where their mother was. They said she had gone to pick me up. Next I parked myself in a hot bath for a good soak; that's when Mame called because she couldn't find me at the finish line. That day I covered more distance than on any other: thirty miles, more or less.

From my perspective, as well as from Mame's and Dad's, all's well that ends well.

Two years later I ran the same race and managed to shave three minutes off my time.

In October 1984 I ran in the New York City Marathon. Although I was arguably in the best physical condition of my life, the weather conditions on race day were literally lethal. I recall that the air temperature was 78°F, and the relative humidity, 96%. A Frenchman who had accompanied me for the early miles of the race *died* later while running, while Australian Rod Dixon, who had won the event the preceding year, walked off the course after about sixteen miles. So did I.

It was a huge disappointment and, alas, the last time I entered such a race.

I have fought the good fight, I have finished the course,
I have kept the faith.

—2 Timothy 7

35

PRESIDENTIAL CAMPAIGNS:

1980 AND 2000

The tools to him that can handle them.

—Thomas Carlyle

Jimmy Carter, a Georgia peanut farmer and a U.S. Naval Academy graduate, was elected president in 1976, to the surprise of many. His campaign slogan was "Gimme Jimmy." Mr. Carter beat Gerald Ford, who had succeeded to the presidency when Richard Nixon resigned the office on August 9, 1974, as a result of the Watergate scandal. Mr. Ford, once a Michigan Congressman, was chosen by Mr. Nixon to serve as vice president after the resignation of Spiro Agnew, also beleaguered by scandal, who had run with Mr. Nixon on the Republican ticket in 1968 and 1972; Agnew is the only U.S. vice president forced to resign.

Living in Paris, France, at the time of the 1976 election, Mame and I voted by absentee ballot and were shocked that Carter beat Ford. As things turned out, President Carter proved to be a good man but his downfall was that he surrounded himself with dishonest and/or incompetent advisors.

Perhaps the death knell of President Carter's administration was sounded on November 4, 1979 when Iranian militants, under the administration of Muslim extremist Ayatollah Ruhollah Khomeini, stormed the United States Embassy in Tehran, Iran, and took approximately seventy Americans captive. This terrorist act triggered the most profound crisis of the Carter presidency and began a personal ordeal for Jimmy Carter and the American people that lasted 444 days.

President Carter committed himself to the safe return of the hostages while protecting America's interests and prestige. He pursued a policy of restraint that put a higher value on the lives of the hostages than on American retaliatory power or protecting his own political future.

The toll of patient diplomacy was great, but President Carter's actions brought freedom for the hostages with America's honor preserved. Nevertheless, his leadership style overall, coupled with a failed military attempt to rescue the hostages, ensured that he would be only a one-term president. Indeed, he was beaten soundly by Ronald Reagan in November 1980.

On January 12, 1979 Mame, the children and I returned to GC from London, where we had lived, and I had worked for Citibank, since 1977. Soon after our return, I went to work for Phil Lassiter at the bank's Manhattan headquarters, and spoke with Bill Spencer, the bank's president, who was serving as chairman of Republican presidential candidate John B. Connally's campaign in New York City. Bill invited me to join the campaign as a vice chairman of its New York finance committee, and I accepted.

John Connally is still remembered by many for the fact that on November 22, 1963, as Texas Governor, he was riding in the same car as President John Kennedy when the latter was assassinated. In fact, he was critically wounded in that attack by a bullet that was said to have passed through the president.

Nominated by President Nixon to be the sixty-first Secretary of the Treasury, John took office on February 11, 1971. He came to Treasury following a distinguished career of achievement in public life and in the private sector. An attorney by profession, he was active in the practice of law and politics in Texas, including three terms as Governor from 1963 to 1968.

As Secretary of the Treasury, John became one of the most influential members of the Cabinet, and was designated chief spokesman of the Nixon Administration in matters relating to the economic program to halt inflation and spur industrial productivity.

A long-time associate of President Johnson, whom he first served as secretary in 1939 in the House of Representatives and later as Administrative Assistant in 1949 in the Senate, John distinguished himself in the Navy during World War II. In 1946 he became president, general manager and attorney for radio station KVET in Austin, Texas.

President Kennedy appointed John Secretary of the Navy on December 27, 1961.

Long active in Democratic Party affairs, John rose above partisan politics to serve on President Nixon's Advisory Council on Executive Organization in 1969–1970, and was appointed by the President to be a member of the Foreign Intelligence Advisory Board in 1970. He subsequently joined the Republican Party.

John married Idanell Brill of Austin with whom he had three children. He passed away on June 15, 1993. Mame and I had the pleasure of meeting and dining with John and "Nellie" during the campaign, and I can say with certainty that we both found them to be two of the finest people we have ever met.

The second presidential candidate for whom I have worked, twenty years after the Connally campaign, is Senator John McCain, Republican of Arizona. From his *Faith of My Fathers*, published in 1999 and an exceptional book well worth reading, as well as from his web site, here is his profile.

The son and grandson of Navy admirals, John learned early the time-honored values of duty, honor, country. In his family, those aren't just words; they're articles of faith. At age seventeen, John followed in his father's and grandfather's footsteps to the

U.S. Naval Academy at Annapolis. There he began a remarkable lifetime of service—and devotion—to America. Graduating in 1958, he was commissioned a naval ensign and trained to become an aircraft carrier pilot. Nearly all the men in the McCain family had made their reputations during wartime, and John wanted to keep faith with them. Thus, as a veteran aircraft carrier pilot, he asked to go to Vietnam.

Lieutenant Commander McCain was assigned to the aircraft carrier USS *Forrestal* off the coast of Vietnam. On July 29, 1967, John, an A-4 *Skyhawk* (attack jet) pilot, was preparing to take off on a bombing mission over North Vietnam, when disaster struck. A missile accidentally fired from a nearby plane aboard the carrier, striking the fuel tanks on his aircraft. In the ensuing explosions and fire, John managed to escape from his jet by crawling onto its nose and diving into the fire on the ship's deck. He turned to help a fellow pilot whose flight suit had ignited, but before John could reach him, more bombs exploded, blowing him back ten feet.

It took twenty-four hours to contain the inferno on the *Forrestal*. By the time it was all over, 134 men had lost their lives, hundreds more were injured, and more than twenty planes were destroyed. It was the worst non-combat-related accident in U.S. naval history.

After the *Forrestal* disaster, John could have returned home. Instead he volunteered for further combat duty aboard the carrier USS *Oriskany*. It proved a fateful decision that would stop the clock on John's life and separate him from his family and country for five and a half years.

Early on the morning of October 26, 1967, just three months after the *Forrestal* tragedy, John took off for his twenty-third bombing mission over North Vietnam. This one was especially risky, for he and his fellow pilots were targeting a power plant in the center of Hanoi, the capital of North Vietnam.

As John was completing his bombing mission, a Soviet-made surface-to-air missile (SAM) struck his plane, shearing off the right wing. John ejected as his plane hurtled toward earth. The force of his ejection knocked him unconscious, and both his arms and one leg were broken. He regained consciousness as he plunged into a lake near his bombing target.

Quickly, an angry mob gathered, seeking retribution for the bombing attack. Dragging John from the lake, they broke his shoulder with a rifle butt and bayoneted him repeatedly. Next, they loaded him into a truck and delivered him to the infamous "Hanoi Hilton" prisoner of war (POW) camp. With no medical treatment for days, John's condition deteriorated so significantly that his fellow POWs, shocked at his appearance, thought he was near death. Still, they were determined that he survive. Thanks to their care, his health gradually improved.

Within a few months of John's capture, his father, Admiral Jack McCain, was appointed commander of all U.S. forces in the Pacific. The North Vietnamese, sensing a propaganda prize, offered the younger McCain early release but he refused, citing the code of conduct that POWs should be released in the order in which they were captured. His captors demanded he accept their offer, but John refused again and again. For his repeated defiance, his communist captors savagely beat him. Before it was over, John would spend five years as a POW, two of them in solitary confinement.

By 1973 the Vietnam War was over. John and some 600 fellow POWs were released and returned to the U.S., ending the longest incarceration in American history. Following extensive physical rehabilitation, John regained flight status and continued his service to his country. Sadly, however, like those of many prisoners of war, his marriage would fail several years later.

Nearing the end of his Navy career, now-Captain McCain's last duty assignment was as the Navy's liaison to the U.S. Senate. It was during this time that he met Cindy Hensley from Phoenix. John and Cindy were married in 1980 and made their home in Arizona. I had the pleasure of meeting them in Manhattan in November 1999 during John's (first) run for the presidency.

By 1982 an Arizona House seat opened up. John, sensing a new opportunity for public service, announced his candidacy. Campaigning door-to-door, he outworked his five opponents and won the Republican primary. He then went on to win the election.

Maintaining a ritual of returning home to Arizona each weekend, John was re-elected overwhelmingly two years later.

By 1986, Barry Goldwater had announced his retirement from the Senate. John was elected to succeed him and continue the elder man's tradition of independence and plain-talk conservatism. Now in his third term in the Senate, John was re-elected in November 1998 with nearly 70% of the vote. In that election, he won 65% of the women's vote, nearly 55% of Hispanics and even 40% of Democrats.

From day one in Washington, Sen. John McCain has been guided by one cause above all others: the fight for freedom. His mission is to make government smaller and taxes lower, so American families have the freedom to chart their own course and small business can create new opportunities. For years he has been on a one-man crusade against wasteful spending in Washington.

John is the nation's foremost leader in national defense and foreign policy matters, and has been quoted for his potent post-9/11 statement earlier in this work. When events in Kosovo unfolded, he was hailed by many for being the *de facto* commander-in-chief (during the Clinton presidency), offering leadership and clarity of purpose. He knows that America has defeated some of the greatest evils ever known to mankind—Nazism, communism, fascism and today's madmen and terrorists—only by staying strong, because weakness or perceived weakness only encourages the enemies of freedom.

Neither John Connally nor John McCain attained the presidency; they were beaten by Ronald Reagan and George W. Bush, respectively. In retrospect, some might say that the better man arguably won. Be that as it may, Senator McCain may have another run for the White House left in him, although he will be sixty-seven at the time of the next presidential election in 2004, and has repeatedly denied that he will run again.

When I had lunch with him on April 15, 2000, he told me that he would definitely not run again for the presidency. Nevertheless, I encouraged him, saying, "Don't paint yourself into a corner."

The senator laughed. In time, we shall know his decision.

> *No one who has not had the responsibility can really understand what it is like to be President, not even his closest aides or members of his immediate family. There is no end to the chain of responsibility that binds him, and he is never allowed to forget that he is President.*
>
> —Harry S. Truman

36

An Unexpected Pleasure:

Marines

Respect was mingled with surprise,
And the stern joy which warriors feel
In foemen worthy of their steel.

—Sir Walter Scott

One afternoon in the spring of 1985 I was preparing to fly out of Washington's Dulles Airport. While walking through the terminal to my flight's assigned gate, I passed a small bar alongside the thoroughfare at which I saw "Marine green." There were three U.S. Marines, a gunnery sergeant and two younger men, one a lance corporal, the other a private first class. Because I was 'running early' and had plenty of time before I had to board my flight, thanks to a cancelled business appointment, I decided to visit with them. There were only the four of us, excluding the bartender.

At the time, I had been out of the Corps some sixteen years and really hadn't had much contact since my service years with more than a few active-duty Marines. Thus, I relished the opportunity to meet some young Marines and get updated.

I introduced myself. To my name I added, simply, "I'm an old Vietnam Marine." That's all.

Next I offered to buy them a drink. Beer was their choice, and I joined them.

"Four beers, please," I requested of the bartender.

I toasted them and the Corps; they reciprocated. We talked for about forty minutes, they about their MOSs (Military Occupational Specialties) and experience, and I about my life as a post-Corps banker in New York City.

Our chat brought to mind many of the things that almost kept me in the Corps so long before this chance meeting. I was refreshed by their youth, enthusiasm and, like thousands of their predecessors and mine in days of yore, devotion to duty. Some things never change, and these few good men reflected the best of those things.

I don't remember their names, but these Marines impressed me, as most have always done.

What I do remember clearly is what happened just after we had shaken hands, said goodbye and recited the customary *Semper fi*. As I was walking away but still within earshot, I heard the Gunny say to his young Marines, "Gentlemen, that's what the Corps is all about."

His words made my day.

The more Marines I have around the better I like it!

—General Mark Clark, U.S. Army

37

CALL ME AL

*I have often thought that the best way to define a man's character
would be to seek out the particular mental or moral attitude in
which . . . he felt himself most deeply and intensely active and
alive. At such moments there is a voice inside which speaks and
says: "This is the real me!"*

—William James

In the spring of 1991, shortly after America's 100-hour Gulf
War with Iraq, I had the pleasure of dining with General Alfred
Mason Gray, Jr., twenty-ninth commandant of the Marine
Corps.

Gen. Gray left college in 1950 to enlist in the Marines, and
attained the rank of sergeant before being commissioned a second
lieutenant two years later. His enlisted experience included
amphibious reconnaissance; he later cross-trained as an officer in
artillery, communications and intelligence. Subsequently, Gen.
Gray extended his tour in Vietnam from the required one year to
three, serving with artillery units and in electronic intelligence.
Following his return to the U.S. in 1968, he took additional trips
to Vietnam on surveillance and intelligence assignments. When
he became a general officer, he commanded successively the 4th
Marine Amphibious Brigade, the 2nd Marine Division and Fleet
Marine Force, Atlantic. As commandant he was determined to
"clean house" and restore the Corps' "warrior image," both of which
he is credited with accomplishing. During his tenure as

commandant, the Persian Gulf witnessed the largest Marine Corps deployment in history. In this connection, his only regret was that, as commandant, he had little or no role to play in direct combat operations.

I sat next to Gen. Gray at a formal dinner at the Waldorf-Astoria in New York City just after the highly successful Operation Desert Storm during the Gulf War and just before he completed his four years as commandant, which concluded on June 30, 1991. He and I had a delightful evening together, engaging each other in conversation and also consuming a few adult beverages. Instinctively, I addressed him as "Sir" and "General" but he soon told me to call him Al. I replied, again as if programmed, "Yes, sir," and we both laughed. He told me: "We're both Marines. I call you Chuck, and you call me Al." And so I did. At the end of the evening we exchanged business cards. His read simply, "Al Gray." Neither his general officer rank nor his title Commandant of the Marine Corps appeared thereon. Printed beneath his name was just one word: Marine.

Consistent with this personal presentation is Gen. Gray's painted portrait, which hangs in Headquarters Marine Corps. Whereas the portraits of his commandant predecessors make some of them appear almost as royalty, Gen. Gray's depicts him in camouflage jungle utilities, sleeves rolled up, hands on his hips and with a background that includes the front end of a tank on what appears to be a Vietnam landscape.

General Al Gray is my kind of guy.

Semper fidelis.

> *A lone Marine standing vigil on a dark night in Kosovo; a Marine Reservist serving as a firefighter or police officer who responds to an emergency in his community; a civilian Marine working alongside his counterparts in uniform who shares the perils and realities of a terrorist attack; and a committed spouse who finds the time to serve as an advocate for family programs in addition to making a home and supporting the family—all are among the heroes of all*

generations. We are indebted to them for their example of strength and their presence of character. They embrace our core values and live them to the fullest. They inspire us to do the same. We admire and appreciate their example as we celebrate the birth of our Corps and our rich heritage. As our motto enjoins us, let us always be faithful, to our God, our country, our Corps and to our families. Let us also resolve to be always faithful to those Marines who have bestowed upon us our proud legacy of sacrifice, courage, and victory against any foe.

—General James L. Jones, USMC
32nd Commandant of the Marine Corps,
November 10, 2001,
the 226th Birthday of the Corps

38

An Imperious, Impetuous Impostor

*An honest man, like the true religion, appeals to the
understanding, or modestly confides in the internal evidence
of his conscience. The impostor employs force instead of
argument, imposes silence where he cannot convince, and
propagates his character by the sword.*

—From *The Letters of Junius, No. 41,* to Lord Mansfield
[November 14, 1770]

In sharp contrast to retired Marine Corps Commandant Al
Gray there are Vietnam veterans who do both Corps and
country deep dishonor. They are among the smallest and most
feckless of men.

B.G. (Jug) Burkett, a former U.S. Army ordnance officer
who served in the infantry in Vietnam, and Glenna Whitley
have written a remarkable book that I wish never had reason to
be published but which I can only accord the highest
commendation. In *Stolen Valor: How the Vietnam Generation
Was Robbed of Its Heroes and Its History* these authors have
provided a valuable service because they, as *VFW Magazine*
has put it, "expose the legion of fake war veterans who have
cropped up over the past two decades. In their perverse quests,
these phonies have belittled the sacrifices of genuine war
veterans." Moreover, the aforementioned James Webb has
written that, "*Stolen Valor* is a tough, courageous book,
overwhelmingly documenting the fraud that has been so

destructive to the true legacy of those who fought in Vietnam. Its central thesis should make American mainstream media cringe in shame from their decades of negligence and collusion in this defamation of those who served with honor."

In his article entitled "Only the Phony," which focuses exclusively on *Stolen Valor* and was published in the March 1999 edition of *VFW*, Al Hemingway cites numerous cases where individual veterans suffer from low self-esteem, seek attention and inflate their own otherwise vacuous and weak personae by spinning outrageous lies. His piece reminded me of a former Marine I know who qualifies as the sort about whom Burkett, Whitley and he have so compellingly written. He is a physically large man to whom some people have accorded deference and respect based solely on his size. Like the big kid in school whom many initially fear, he is eventually taken down by one smaller but tougher than he. Everyone then realizes that he doesn't even know how to fight because he never had to, and that he has no guts.

The individual I know has for years boasted, to anyone who would listen, of being a "combat veteran of Vietnam," a "sniper," a "recon (reconnaissance) Marine," "a rifle platoon commander," et cetera ad nauseam—all in Vietnam. Not only is there a very low probability that the same person could have served in all of these capacities in the same time frame, it turns out that his claims are fanciful fabrications, for he served in none of these posts. It is clear to many who know him that he has always wanted to be a combat hero, and now he has made himself one, but only in his own mind.

In weakness and self-loathing he spends his life striving in utter futility to measure up to, nay, to supersede, those whose true combat experience is the reason for his envy and perceived inferiority. Pretending to be someone whom he presumes he and others would admire, he lives a fantasy of being that other person, for it is his raison d'être. Were his mind not so twisted, he would recognize and acknowledge that not serving in combat is *not* a bad thing and in fact may be the reason he is still alive. Instead of living as a figment of a man whose military experiences he would prefer to call his own, he should be thankful for the opportunities he has enjoyed in his life since the war, ones that were inalterably denied those who were killed in action in it.

His dwindling circle of friends and fellow former Marines has long found his bluster, bombast and—to employ the vernacular—bullshit highly unpalatable, to say the least. Indeed, this phony's major modus operandi is essentially to stomp on any dissent from his views. Striving always to intimidate, he has yet to learn how to win friends and influence people. To him personal loyalty, which for most people has an element of continuance, is a fleeting and foreign concept because he is obscenely utilitarian when it comes to people and institutions. In other words, when they no longer serve his purposes, primary among which is his own aggrandizement, he jettisons them from his life.

Many have been angered by his brash and brazen but ultimately false face. Recently, though, his assertions of having served "thirteen months" in Vietnam and been awarded not one but "two Purple Hearts" have been nothing short of sickening, especially to those genuine combat veterans who are aware of his illusory claims. One written report on this impostor's service record indicates that he actually served less than 90 days in country and has no Purple Heart medals. Indeed, his egregious behavior denigrates, disrespects and desecrates the service, bloodshed and memory of all those who served in Vietnam honorably.

Interestingly, it seems never to have occurred to this bogus belligerent that real veterans rarely talk about their combat experiences; to be sure, true heroes are typically silent about theirs. When someone wears the Marine Corps on his sleeve and constantly broadcasts that he is "a combat veteran," even in writing, the ears of genuine combat veterans become keenly attentive, their eyebrows often raised, although they generally say little.

To most of us who have actually served in a combat environment, that is, been shot at, phonies, especially one like this, are obvious as soon as they open their mouths. In truth, they are invariably and unwittingly the only ones who fail to recognize that everyone who hears their spoken lies recognizes them for what they are. Someday this phony will get his comeuppance when he is exposed for the fraud he is. At that moment of truth, the only appropriate response will be an apology from him. Sadly, the likelihood is that this impostor will continue to persist in his fantasies because, after more than three decades of living innumerable lies, he will be unable to separate fact from fiction. In short, he has become a legend in his own mind, albeit a false one.

In the last analysis, this combat fake is a disgrace to the Marine Corps and to the United States, as well as to everything they stand for. He knows not the meaning of the words *Semper fidelis*; indeed, to him they do not apply.

> *We confide in our strength, without boasting of it;*
> *we respect that of others, without fearing it.*
>
> —Thomas Jefferson [1793]

39

CAPTAIN CANCER

And they shall fight every one against his brother.

—Ecclesiastes 19:2

Mame, Kate and I had just spent a lovely first weekend of spring at Mike and Maggie's home on Tomahawk Lake in Blooming Grove, New York. It was Sunday, March 22, 1992. We had celebrated my brother's forty-fifth birthday on the twentieth.

We returned home perhaps earlier than we might have otherwise because I was committed to meeting my sister Pat and her husband Tom Phelan at New York's John F. Kennedy Airport, and driving them home. They were scheduled to return around five o'clock from Ireland where they had gone to attend Tom's Mom's funeral.

After lunch at Peter Luger's Restaurant in Great Neck, Long Island, I drove my wife and daughter home to GC, and shortly afterward headed for JFK. It was a cold, gray wintry afternoon; indeed, it began to snow. The weather report I heard on the radio en route to the airport called for "three to six inches" of the white stuff.

Thanks to unusually light traffic on the Belt Parkway, I arrived early at JFK's International Arrivals Building. Once inside, I went immediately to the arrivals information monitor to check the progress of the incoming flight. The estimated time of arrival showed it approximately fifteen minutes late.

To kill time I strolled around the interior of the building until, as the number of people awaiting arriving loved ones became a large crowd, I stopped within easy viewing distance of the monitor and simply waited. Regrettably, I had neglected to bring with me a book or a section of the Sunday *Times*.

As I waited and enjoyed, with exceptions, the people-watching, I couldn't help but notice the frequent public service announcements in English and Spanish to the effect that JFK was a smoke-free environment; there were also "No Smoking" and "No Fumar" signs all over the inside of the terminal. I thought momentarily that it was a most civilized policy; I also reflected on the fact that, although I enjoy a good cigar (outdoors) from time to time, I detest cigarette smoke.

Around 4:45 that afternoon a tall young man about 6'1" and in his mid-to-late-twenties appeared and stood next to me. He was dressed in black from head to toe, except for his white shirt. He also wore a black hat and overcoat; I learned later that he was a chauffeur.

He took out a pack of cigarettes, extracted one and lit it. His next action was unpleasant and inexplicable: He turned toward me and blew the smoke from his first drag directly at my face, although from my right side.

A little irritated but not angry, I addressed him politely: "Sir, there is no smoking in this terminal. Would you please put out your cigarette or go outside to smoke it?"

He took another drag, then turned to me and, in his Hispanic accent, blurted: "Who dee fuck are you, Captain Cancer?" His inflammatory utterance no sooner given, he next took a swing at me, a roundhouse punch. Fortunately, I saw the blow coming and managed to move back quickly and sufficiently so that it just missed my face and glanced harmlessly off my right shoulder.

In truth, I hadn't been in a fistfight for some thirty years but now I saw red. Shock and anger exploded within me and I attacked. Fists flying, I became violent and ferocious, surprising even myself and visibly frightening my adversary, of whom I got the better in short order. I connected quickly and knocked the chauffeur to the floor. With the crowd cheering, I knelt astride his thorax and, like a man possessed, continued to pummel him.

Left to my own devices, I might have killed this man, I am ashamed to admit. In the twinkling of an eye, however, another man appeared and forcibly removed me from my position atop the hapless and now dazed chauffeur. Although I was still furious, and the moment was a blur, he showed me a police badge and ordered me to stand behind him. Then, to my amazement, he helped the chauffeur to his feet and angrily placed one handcuff on his right wrist. I was in awe of what I momentarily thought was timely and admirable police service. Then the officer put the other handcuff on my left wrist.

A strong, burly chap, the policeman told us his name was Carter. He was a plainclothesman of the Port Authority of New York and New Jersey. Unceremoniously and ignominiously, Officer Carter then led me and my cuffmate out of the terminal to a waiting unmarked car where another plainclothesman awaited us.

The second police officer, ostensibly Carter's partner, was a typical Irish-American cop. He gestured toward the chauffeur and me, both respectably groomed, and asked Carter, "Where did you get *these* guys?"

Replied Carter curtly in audible disgust, "They were fighting in the terminal." There was no denying that.

Carter positioned himself behind the wheel while the Irish cop attempted to stuff my cuffmate and me into the back seat, which was already partially occupied. Seated next to each other on the left side of the rear seat of the vehicle were two more Hispanics, one an elderly man, the other a boy of, say, 16. They had been arrested for pickpocketing.

The Irish cop began to close the door forcefully on my right hip, which was off the seat and mostly outside the car. I was annoyed at him but managed to keep my cool. When it became evident that two more adult male posteriors would not fit on the back seat, the boy was told to sit on the old man's lap. Now I was comfortable, at least physically.

I asked the policemen where they were taking us; we were

going to "the precinct," which was located inside the JFK complex but, I estimated, at least a mile from where I was supposed to meet my sister and brother-in-law.

From the moment he and I were handcuffed, the chauffeur engaged in multiple mutterings, in Spanish and intermittently in English. His drift was that his boss didn't allow him to smoke in the limousine he drove for a living; thus, "All I wanted to do was have a smoke! Then Captain Cancer here tells me I cannot smoke inside and I must go outside." Occasionally, the chauffeur would tug on the handcuffs, presumably out of frustration and in an effort, I believe, to irk me. My left arm was stronger than his right, as I proved by flexing and locking the muscles of my left arm and simply pulling in the opposite direction when he tried to tug. It was ridiculous but, at that inauspicious moment, it was the only game in town.

After a series of audible outbursts by the chauffeur, Carter stopped the car, turned around and told the chauffeur to shut up. Interestingly, he also suggested that this whole episode was the Hispanic gentleman's fault.

With snow now falling heavily, the Irish cop remarked to Carter that this precipitation was to him a big surprise on this, the second day of spring. Without thinking too much about it, I volunteered the weather forecast I had heard earlier, namely, that between three and six inches of snow were expected.

The chauffeur then gratuitously observed with respect to me and my comment about the snow, "So now he's dee fuckin' weatherman!"

For some reason the chauffeur's crass observation sent Officer Carter, his patience gone, into a rage. He slammed on the brakes and, on the rebound, nearly threw himself into the back seat, lunging at the chauffeur, who now bore the look of stark terror on his face. With his left hand Carter angrily gripped and pulled the chauffeur's tie at the junction with his collar; from the chauffeur's vocal sounds, it crossed my mind that Officer Carter might have been choking him. Then, brandishing a meaty, mighty right fist in front of the chauffeur's eyes, Carter menacingly asserted, "If you say another fuckin' word, this is goin' through your face!"

I was impressed.

More importantly for me, I overheard Carter then share with his partner something to the effect that "We wouldn't be here if it weren't for that asshole." I am confident he meant the chauffeur.

☒

Once inside the precinct I asked to use the telephone to call Mame. Officer Carter agreed and gestured toward a phone on a desk about ten feet from where the chauffeur and I sat, still handcuffed. For his part, my cuffmate continued to mutter and, literally, jerk my chain. Carter glared at him and told him to move to the desk with me—or else.

The chauffeur moved.

When Mame answered the phone, she seemed surprised to hear from me and asked if everything was alright. At first I attempted to assure her that it was. However, as soon as I mentioned that I had been delayed, she became concerned.

"What's the matter, honey?" she inquired, now with urgency in her voice.

"Well," I said, "I've been delayed."

"What *happened*?" she persisted.

"There was an altercation in the terminal and . . . I've . . . been . . . arrested."

"Oh, Kate," I heard Mame say to our then 17-year-old daughter who was at home in the kitchen with her mother, "your father's been arrested."

At the same time, Carter insisted that I had not been arrested, just "detained."

Thinking it might make her feel better, I dutifully communicated that positive news to my bride.

Frustrated, I also told Carter, perhaps unwisely, "Thank you, Officer Carter, I feel much better knowing that I have merely been detained, especially with this handcuff on my wrist." He gave me an uncertain look.

Both the chauffeur and I were issued summonses for "Disorderly conduct," a misdemeanor. Officer Carter then unlocked the handcuffs and advised us that we were free to go. With "Ask and ye shall receive" on my mind, I inquired of Carter if someone could give me a ride back to the International Arrivals Building. Alas, my faith this time was not to be rewarded, as Carter looked at me quizzically. Quoth he: "We don't do that." So I walked out of the precinct into near-blizzard conditions.

Like the 30-year hiatus between my two most recent fistfights, I estimated that it had been just as long since I had last hitch-hiked. Given the weather and the distance to be covered as quickly as possible, I unveiled my thumb. Miraculously, a small yellow school bus appeared and stopped; its door opened. With no passengers, the diminutive Hispanic driver, perhaps a relative of my friend the chauffeur, asked, "Where you go?" To my amazement, when I told him "International Arrivals Building," he said "Get in, I go right by it." The Lord had smiled on me once more in my hour of need.

I was back inside the terminal in no time, and met my sister and her husband almost immediately. Pat had a sort of smirk on her face, having, as I was to learn presently, called Mame to ask my whereabouts.

"Chuck," she said, "I've heard a lot of good excuses for being late but yours takes the cake!"

Tom was later to tell me that, at my funeral, grandchildren and great-grandchildren will be saying of me, "He's the one that got arrested."

On June 3, 1992 I appeared in New York's Queens Criminal Court before Judge Ernest Bianchi. When I arrived in the courtroom I found Officer Carter sitting in the front row waving at me and wearing a wide grin. I shook his hand and sat next to him. My former cuffmate was nowhere in sight.

While I waited, I assessed a basic risk factor in my case: If the judge were a smoker, I was dead meat. If he were not, I had a chance. Judge Bianchi began at 9 a.m. sharp, as advertised. He threw the book at the first defendant, and was lenient with the second. At 9:10 both Carter and I were summoned to the bench.

Dressed in my best blue suit, white shirt and red tie, I stood at attention as the Judge asked Carter to recount the events of March 22nd. I listened attentively to the officer's words. His performance was flawless. More importantly, his account of the story had not changed, and he placed the onus of blame squarely on the chauffeur.

Next, the Judge asked me for my version of the story.

"Your honor, with respect," I said humbly, "I believe I can save the court some time because Officer Carter's testimony is precisely what happened. There is nothing I wish to add or change."

The Judge then appeared to close up a folder in front of him and move it aside. He then leaned forward, and rested his hands and forearms on the bench before which Carter and I stood.

"Mr. Mansfield," the Judge addressed me, "you have provided the people of the City of New York a great public service."

I was elated.

"But," he continued somewhat somberly, "you did so at considerable personal risk. If these people want to smoke, let them smoke; if they want to kill themselves, let them kill themselves; but, please, don't drag us into it!"

I wanted to applaud.

Judge Bianchi then advised me that there was no case against me because I had clearly, in his view, acted in self-defense. He assured me that I would have no police record; the case was being thrown out, as they say.

The Judge's final words were, "The next time one of these miscreants blows smoke in your face, please just walk away."

"Yes, sir," I replied, and I thanked him.

Then the Judge said, "Go in peace, my son!"

I was incredulous. What a great guy!

⌛

Two remarkable aspects of this saga are its popularity and durability. It amazes me how often I am asked to tell the tale at cocktail and dinner parties and the like. Some folks have heard me tell it a half-dozen times, and they are the first to ask me to recount it when there is another opportunity to do so. One thing is certain: the "Captain Cancer" story makes people laugh.

> *There were those in both the Army and the Navy that did not regard Marines as useful. If the Corps was to survive, it would have to prove its worth.*

> —From *The Marines*, Marine Corps Heritage Foundation

THE SENTINEL

by **Craig Middleton**

In a world gone awry, a world devoid of respect for society, a world with no regard for the rules that define civilization, there remain a few valiant individuals who stand sentinel, ever vigilant to protect the rights of all of us.

This is a story of such a sentinel. A man who without regard for personal safety or even personal dignity, risked everything for the greater good of America. The following stands as testimony to the lengths he went. Mocked by friends, denied by family, abandoned by almost all, he stood firm in addressing a wrong and then making certain the world would know that social transgressions would never go unchallenged as long as he and those few like him are around.

Chuck Mansfield is a model for all of us. As friends struggle to find explanations for his courageous act, they have forgotten words like character, bravery and selflessness. They have also forgotten to give thanks for Chuck. As long as a man like him guards the gates, the barbarians will never overrun us.

PART IV

THE WARP AND WOOF OF RELIGION, CULTURE AND POLITICS IN EARLY TWENTY-FIRST CENTURY AMERICA

Conservatism is essentially a discipline of principles while modern liberalism is very often an intervention against principles. Today, for example, conservatives generally want to enforce discipline around the principle of merit, believing that the stricter the discipline the more fairness in society. But today's liberalism, also in the name of fairness, intervenes against merit as a principle that excludes minorities.

—Shelby Steele

40

THE MEDIA AND THE ARTS

Television, movies and the printed word have made evil, aggression and egotism household terms and unconsciously acceptable to the extent of making us immune to displays of evil.

—Mordechai Paldiel

Robert C. Wright, who prefers to be called Bob, is an outstanding and generous person. An alumnus of both Chaminade (1961) and Holy Cross (1965) and an attorney, he is also chairman and chief executive officer of National Broadcasting Company, Inc. (NBC), a vice chairman of General Electric Company, NBC's parent, and an early inductee—a shoo-in actually—into Chaminade's Alumni Hall of Fame in 1995. He is a practicing Roman Catholic, as well. Not a bad profile, to say the least.

Bob and I have been friends since we first met as students at Chaminade in 1958, and I have long admired his many outstanding accomplishments. Still, I cannot help but wonder how and why there are such embedded biases in our television programming and elsewhere across the broad sweep of modern media when men like him are in charge and presumably have some say in what is produced and broadcast.

Perhaps I'm naïve.

In NBC's October 17, 2001 episode of "Law and Order: Criminal Intent," according to the Catholic League for Religious Rights, a church sexton was murdered by a junkie who also works at the same parish. The junkie was then killed by a priest (who is also guilty of embezzling church funds). In addition, the priest tells the police that the junkie was his lover. Later we discover that the priest was lying: the junkie is actually the priest's son. It is now clear that the real motive for killing the junkie was to protect the young boy's mother—the woman the killer priest had an affair with twenty years earlier.

Catholic League president and chief executive officer William A. Donohue had this to say about the show:

> In 1995, there was an episode on "Law and Order" . . . about a devout Catholic woman who kills her baby, confesses her crime to a priest in the confessional, and learns from the priest that it was God's will that she murder her child. Furthermore the sacrament of reconciliation was ridiculed by a detective when he said, 'How many Hail Marys would one be assigned for this crime?'
>
> In 1997, we learned of a 'devout Catholic' mother who, according to her son, 'held a rosary in one hand and beat the crap out of me with the other.' In 1999, we met a 'very orthodox nun' who murders a young woman after a botched exorcism. Another episode that year (this time on 'Law and Order: Special Victims Unit') featured a woman who is raped on a Catholic college campus where all school officials appear weak and disinterested. And last night viewers were introduced to a priest who is guilty of lying, embezzlement, womanizing and the murder of his son.
>
> One wonders what those at 'Law and Order' have been inhaling that alters their thinking. More likely is the possibility that they like anti-Catholicism. All of which is quite revealing. Every day there are reports that in the wake of September 11 (2001), Hollywood is rewriting scripts and changing scenes so as not to rattle the sensibilities of the

public or to show disrespect to Muslims. But when it comes to bashing Catholics, it's business as usual. They never miss a step.

Founded in 1973, the Catholic League for Religious and Civil Rights is the largest Catholic civil rights organization in the United States with more than 350,000 members. The League is analogous to the Anti-Defamation League of B'nai B'rith; indeed, the ADL, as well as the American Civil Liberties Union, is the model for our organization. The League defends the Roman Catholic Church, as well as individual Catholics from anti-Catholic bias and bigotry, be it in government, the media, the arts or elsewhere in society.

Two days after this 'air pollution' from NBC, I wrote a letter to Bob Wright, most of which is excerpted here:

> I have enclosed a news release . . . from the Catholic League . . . of whose national board I am a member. Father Philip Eichner is the League's chairman, and Bill Donohue, whom I had the pleasure of introducing to you at your Chaminade Alumni Hall of Fame induction, is its president and CEO.
>
> Through the years I have often encouraged the Catholic Church to become more involved in, say, boycotting companies that sponsor shows that are offensive to Catholics. (The League has become accomplished at this tactic.) The reticence of the Church to become more aggressive in fighting anti-Catholicism in the media and other sectors of our culture has inadvertently given the League strong new impetus. Indeed, the League has grown from a moribund 11,000 members in 1993 to more than 350,000 today.
>
> NBC's *Law and Order* is a case in point. This program . . . has offended Catholics for years. Moreover, its repetitive shots at the Church disappoint, frustrate and sadden me, especially when I take into account that you are

ultimately responsible for such a show's content. I am confident saying that if blacks or gays or Jews or Muslims were to be portrayed in so obviously biased and distasteful roles, such a script would be discarded without a second thought. Alas, our priests and religious continue to be fair game.

It's a damned shame when Catholics themselves support, directly or indirectly, such forms of Catholic bashing.

I received no reply.

In an article published in *The New York Times* on September 2, 2001, at the traditional beginning of the new television season, Jim Rutenberg wrote:

> Aaron Sorkin, the executive producer of "The West Wing" on NBC, says he hopes to break a longstanding network taboo this coming season: he wants a character to curse in a way that uses the Lord's name in vain.

Just so I don't seem excessively focused on Bob Wright's NBC, I will give equal time to ABC and CBS. Here's what these two networks are up to, according to Mr. Rutenberg:

> Steven Bochco, the executive producer of "Philly," a new legal drama on ABC, has proposed having a character use a scatological reference that has never before been uttered on an ABC series—one considered tougher than the profanities already in use on his police drama, NYPD Blue.
>
> CBS executives say that writers are submitting scripts for programs that include every crude word imaginable, including one considered to be on the furthermost reaches of decorum (let's just say it has to do with the making of stem cells).

I have used offensive language myself, *mea culpa*, as have many folks I know. I don't believe it necessarily makes us bad people. Just the same, it doesn't make the use of vulgarity and obscenity appropriate. Accordingly, to expose our children, as well as other young and possibly impressionable people, to the coarsest side of our culture on a wholesale basis through the medium of television is ignoble, irresponsible and immoral.

Next I will present an example of how the arts—and artists—demonstrate substantial anti-Catholic, or at least anti-Christian, bias. The story is again courtesy of the Catholic League's Bill Donohue.

As of November 7, 2001, the gift shop in the Baltimore Museum of Art was selling souvenir postcards that featured a picture of the Andres Serrano "Piss Christ" artwork, which shows a crucifix submerged in a beaker of the artist's urine.

After 9/11, the very same museum removed a painting by Christopher Wool entitled 'Terrorist' simply because the name of the artwork appeared on the painting. The museum issued a statement saying that the action was taken "out of respect to visitors' sensibilities." Doreen Bolger, the museum's director, went so far as to say, "The work hasn't changed, but our perception of it has."

This is actually amusing, says Donohue. "For years we've been told by the postmodernists that art has no meaning except what people attribute to it. Yet the doyens of our culture now seem to have discovered the precise meaning of Wool's contribution and allow for no diversity of opinion. Why? Because they know what it means and they are offended. Therefore, it must be removed. But when it comes to dunking the holiest Christian symbol in urine, they withdraw their censorial knife. That's because they really don't have respect for the sensibilities of Christians. Nor has their perception changed regarding the Serrano hate art; they like it as much today as they did before September 11th."

Donohue adds that several years ago the same Baltimore Museum of Art featured an attack on Mother Teresa. That was done under the auspices of Arnold Lehman, who has since moved to the other 'BMA'—the Brooklyn Museum of Art—home of dung-laden portraits of Our Blessed Mother and defamatory portrayals of the Last Supper. This is quite a gang. Not even the reality of airplanes flying into tall buildings killing thousands of innocent persons is enough to change their perception of Catholics.

It would be wonderful indeed if we could get the artistic community to treat Catholics the way they do Muslims.

Once more the bias against Catholics is evident.

Here are some insights from the world of today's music.

In January 2001 the rapper Eminem received four Grammy nominations, including best album. Now, to be clear, I believe that rap music and its related genre "hip-hop" represent an affront to humanity, no matter the race of the "artist." (Unlike most rappers in the U.S., who are African-American, Eminem happens to be white.)

Marshall Bruce Mathers III, Eminem's proper name, has long demonstrated his ability to attract adverse publicity. Even his mother sued him for defamation after he labeled her a drug addict. Also, he has been indicted on assault and weapons charges.

Mathers' music includes lyrics that extol the notions of strangling his wife, raping his mother, shooting a bank teller and assaulting gays and lesbians. His poetic genius has given us the eminent lyrics, "But I've still got a lot of growing up to do/I've still got a whole lot of throwing up to spew."

However, many critics have cut him a great deal of slack, too much in my opinion.

To be sure, Eminem, like all Americans, has rights under the First Amendment. Although I condemn the sick lyrics he writes and sings, I support his right to record whatever he wishes, irrespective of how offensive others may find it. Still, when serious and legitimate journalists, such as those at *The New York Times*—the paper of record—judge one of his albums to be among the best made, their judgment must be questioned—seriously and legitimately.

Less than two years after his Grammies, some respected critics have told us that this immoral maggot is entering "mainstream" America's music tastes. In fact, according to Shelby Steele, "80% of rap music is bought by white youth" because "Rap culture essentially markets (essentially thuggish) themes to American youth as an ideal form of adolescent rebellion."

We are into relative extrema again, but this one, to be sure, is a low, not a high. It is another cogent example of how our culture has been and is being debased.

Charlton Heston is one of my favorite people. A Hollywood actor, he has won many awards, including an Oscar for Best Actor in the classic film *Ben Hur*, which I believe is the greatest film ever made. In 1998 he was elected president of the National Rifle Association (NRA), which protects the right to keep and bear arms, which, in turn, is guaranteed by the Second Amendment to the U.S. Constitution. Upon his election the world of political liberals, including some of his "friends," turned against him. Sadly, he was recently diagnosed with symptoms of Alzheimer's disease.

Enter Ice-T, another rapper who not too many years ago was selling a CD called *Cop Killer*, which celebrated ambushing and murdering police officers, and was being marketed by none other than Time/Warner (now AOL Time/Warner), the biggest entertainment conglomerate in the world. Here's what Charlton Heston said—and did:

> Police across the country were outraged. Rightfully so—at least one had been murdered. But Time/Warner was stonewalling because the CD was a cash cow for them, and the media were tiptoeing around it because the rapper was black. I heard Time/Warner had a stockholders meeting

scheduled in Beverly Hills. I owned some shares at the time, so I decided to attend. What I did there was against the advice of my family and colleagues. I asked for the floor. To a hushed room of a thousand average American stockholders, I simply read the full lyrics of "Cop Killer"—every vicious, vulgar, instructional word.

I GOT MY 12 GAUGE SAWED OFF I GOT MY HEADLIGHTS TURNED OFF I'm ABOUT TO BUST SOME SHOTS OFF I'm ABOUT TO DUST SOME COPS OFF . . .

Then I delivered another volley of sick lyric brimming with racist filth, where Ice-T fantasizes about sodomizing two 12-year old nieces of Al and Tipper Gore. 'SHE PUSHED HER BUTT AGAINST MY . . .'
. . . I left the room in echoing silence. When I read the lyrics to the waiting press corps, one of them said 'We can't print that.' 'I know,' I replied, 'but Time/Warner is selling it.'
Two months later, Time/Warner terminated Ice-T's contract. I'll never be offered another film by Warners, or get a good review from Time magazine. But disobedience means you must be willing to act, not just talk.

"Rappers," as Mr. Steele has written, "gain freedom through immunity to feeling. Women are 'bitches' and 'hos,' objects of lust, but not of feeling." He continues,

Everything about rap—the misogynistic lyrics, the heaving swagger, the violent sexuality, the cynical hipness—screams "I'm bad because I don't feel." Nonfeeling is freedom. And it is important to note that this has nothing to do with race. In rap, the (thug) nurtures indifference toward those he is most likely to love.

Steele has added a fitting and accurate summary to his temperate, yes, temperate insights into this cultural phenomenon. Not being musically trained, I accept that rap and hip-hop are regarded by the culture at large as music although to me they represent nothing but further American cultural debasement. I am unabashed in writing that I cannot find more realistic and appropriate words than those in Steele's summary of his view of this genre; indeed, I actually feel a bit better for having read them.

> Conservatives have rightly attacked rap for its misogyny, violence and over-the-top vulgarity. But it is important to remember that this music is a fairly accurate message from a part of society where human connections are fractured and impossible, so fraught with disappointments and pain that only an assault on human feeling itself can assuage. Rap makes the conservative argument about what happens when family life is eroded either by welfare and drugs, or by the stresses and indulgences of middle-class life.

In this context, if "taste is the *only* morality," as John Ruskin has written, then I can only hasten to add the rest of his words: "Tell me what you like, and I'll tell you what you are."

⧖

On another visit to the entertainment world, we find *Corpus Christi*, which in Latin means *Body of Christ*. This *Corpus Christi*, though, is a play about a homosexual Jesus character called Joshua who has sex with his disciples and is crucified as "king of the queers." It was written by Terrence McNally, winner of three Tony awards.

According to John Leo in his *U.S. News & World Report On Society* column,

> In scheduling the play, the Manhattan Theatre Club called it a "spiritual journey," McNally's own unique view of

'the greatest story ever told.' No script has been made public. But McNally has privately circulated several versions of the text, and a copy acquired by the *New York Times* seems to cast doubt on the "spiritual journey" account of what McNally is up to.

Telling readers that the play unfolds "in a manner with potential to offend many people," the *Times* gave this account: "Joshua has a long-running affair with Judas and sexual relations with the other Apostles. Only one sexual encounter, a nonexplicit one with an HIV-positive street hustler, takes place in any form on stage." The draft ends with the frank admission: "If we have offended, so be it. He belongs to us as well as you."

"He belongs to us," of course, doesn't seem to make much sense, artistically or scripturally. It seems more like politicized in-your-face Christian baiting.

Again, people like McNally and their vile work are protected by the First Amendment to the U.S. Constitution but, when their societal contributions are adversely criticized, the critic is vilified.

⧗

Since I am writing today in the month of December 2001, the following situation is noteworthy, especially for Christians. Once again my friend Bill Donohue of the Catholic League has supplied good food for thought:

The principal of the Thomas Jefferson Magnet School of Humanities in Flushing, New York, has issued a memo to teachers encouraging them to bring to school religious symbols that represent the Muslim, Kwanzaa and Jewish religions. No mention of Christianity was made. Indeed, when a Christmas tree was put up in the school, the principal ordered it taken down because it was too large; she said it was too big when compared with the menorah and crescent and star.

The principal issued a memo that is mind-boggling, and, in

so doing, has set her school up for a lawsuit. It would be hard to find a more classic demonstration of discrimination against Christians in a public school anywhere in the nation.

It really doesn't matter if she decides to put back the Christmas tree. The Christmas tree is a secular symbol. If she is going to allow religious symbols such as a menorah and crescent and star, then she must permit the display of a nativity scene. Either that or ban all religious symbols. Otherwise, hers is simply a discriminatory policy and an injustice that must be rectified.

To help make my point and with thanks to the League, which does an incredible job of tracking such behaviors, here's a 'Christmas case' at another school.

According to the *Harvard Crimson*, the campus of Harvard University is dotted with cardboard Santas and menorahs and most of the University Houses have both a menorah and a Christmas tree. But there is no mention of a Nativity scene anywhere on the campus. Indeed, there is considerable controversy over the scheduled placement of a Christmas tree in Leverett House. Some students have said that a Christmas tree is divisive, and one student leader compared the tree to "a Trojan horse." The same student said that by allowing the Christmas tree, Harvard was opening the door to the placement of all other symbols. He cited the swastika as an example.

Now, in my view, Catholic students at Harvard University have a moral obligation to request the placement of a Nativity scene on the campus in the same area where menorahs are placed. (If they are denied, then an organization like the Catholic League is prepared to give Harvard all the publicity it deserves on this issue.)

Just as there are Catholics who are anti-Semitic, there are Jews who are anti-Catholic. Unfortunately, the problem of anti-Catholicism that afflicts some of those in the Jewish community rears its ugly head every December. Not only are Catholics, as well as other Christians, told they cannot have their religious symbol (the Nativity scene) on public property, they are now told that such secular symbols as Santa Claus and Christmas trees must be banned. Yet, such religious symbols as the menorah and the Star of David are just fine.

The latest complaint is that Christmas trees are too big compared to menorahs. Well, not in Central Park. In Central Park Jews will now erect the world's largest menorah. God bless them. We Catholics, thanks to the Catholic League, put our little (by comparison) Nativity scene in the same area every year, thanks to the City of New York. As Bill Donohue has put it, "But unlike anti-Catholic bigots, we will not complain. That's because size doesn't matter to us."

I am proud that the League has the bigots' number big time.

Here's an interesting tale about Christmas cards, or, to be politically correct, 'holiday' cards.

Again, the League has demonstrated that we also face the "dumbing down" of Christmas by makers of holiday greeting cards, who show great unevenness in their handling of Christian, Jewish and Muslim holidays. To be specific, a Catholic League review of the greeting cards available on the home page of Yahoo! revealed the following:

There are over 350 Christmas cards; yet only 25 have a religious content. There are at least eight objectionable cards in the "Humorous" and "Naughty" categories. For example, these categories have cards that show naked buttocks, animals urinating, Santa on the toilet, etc.

Most of the 48 Hanukkah cards show a picture of a menorah or a Star of David. Of the five "Humorous" cards, none was as offensive as any of the Christmas cards in this category. There was no "Naughty" category.

The 66 Ramadan and Eid ul-Fitr cards were all respectful of Islam and most showed a star and crescent. There were no "Humorous" or "Naughty" categories.

All the Kwanzaa cards were respectful and there were no "Humorous" or "Naughty" categories.

There can be no question but that American Greetings is the worst offender of the mainline greeting card producers. By far the most obscene producer is Tomato cards. It had a card this year that mocks the Blessed Virgin Mary.

Once more, this demonstrates that there is contempt for Christianity among our elites in this country that has no rival. Sometimes the bias they sport is subdued and other times it is not. But that it exists is beyond question. Dumbing down Christmas is very important to these people; otherwise they wouldn't be working so hard to get the job done.

⧗

Now here is a tale that is almost unbelievable, except that it has been fully researched and documented by the Catholic League, from whose news releases on the episode I have borrowed liberally.

On the subject of yuletide political correctness, not to mention First Amendment rights, check this one out: The employees of King County, Washington, were warned not to say "Merry Christmas."

A memo was sent to county employees regarding holiday celebrations that required them to use "religion-neutral" language. The memo of November 14, 2001 said it is okay to say "Happy Holidays" and "Holiday Greetings." However, all references to Christmas were regarded as taboo.

Ron Sims, the King County Executive who released the memo, explained that "we at King County want to ensure that any upcoming holiday celebration at the workplace is held in a respectful, inclusive, and sensitive manner that does not favor one religion over the other." The following sentence, however, says that "Particularly in public areas, this means that any holiday recognition or celebration should be religion-neutral." The policy statement ended by saying that "Cultural information sharing about various religious holidays in the name of diversity is allowable when it is done in the context of employee education and is inclusive of various religious celebrations such as Ramadan, Hanukkah, Christmas, etc."

The time had come, as the Catholic League's Bill Donohue put it, for employees in King County, Washington, to be arrested for saying, 'Merry Christmas.' But before this happens, they should contact the local media. What a show this would be—having dozens of Catholics being handcuffed by the cops for uttering what their boss regards as an obscenity. And this business of being allowed to share 'cultural information' about religion is truly Orwellian.

Donohue, who rarely puts the gloves on, never mind take them off, summarizes this episode as follows:

> The champions of diversity are the single greatest proponents of despotism in the United States today. Any expression that violates their crabbed vision of reality is subject to censorship. Indeed, in the name of diversity they promote ideological uniformity. Similarly, in the name of inclusiveness, they exclude people of faith. The diversity despots are both a menace and a national disgrace.

Thanks to the media pressure exerted by the Catholic League, Mr. Sims, a Baptist minister, was forced to reverse himself. His subsequent attempt to say that he was misunderstood failed to convince anyone.

Merry Christmas!

On December 19, 1996 *The Wall Street Journal* ran a short editorial it called **Merry Holiday:**

> Public schools often have a hard time understanding that the First Amendment is not about protecting students *from* religion, but about protecting their religious freedom. The Supreme Court made that a little clearer this week when it allowed a Bible club at a public high school in New York State to require its officers to be Christians. The Court let stand an appeals court decision of last summer that ruled that the after-school club's requirement is not about discrimination, but is protected as a form of free expression

intended "to guarantee that meetings include the desired worship and observance." Whether such a club would benefit from voices representing other religions is a legitimate question. But the issue here is whether it *ought* to do so or should be *forced* to by a court order.

⌛

The feast of Christmas commemorates the birth of Jesus Christ but Easter, the feast of His resurrection, is the holiest day in the Christian liturgical year. Accordingly, I would be remiss were I to fail to highlight the fare that Christian bashers served up for this solemnity in the spring of 2002. Again the Catholic League is the source of this report.

Catholic-bashing events were scheduled for Easter in Washington, D.C., Arlington, Texas, and San Francisco, California. On Easter Sunday, the Source Theatre Company in Washington, D.C., hosted the aforementioned Terrence McNally play "Corpus Christi," which depicts Christ having sex with the apostles. Theatre Arlington in Arlington, Texas, began hosting the play "Do Black Patent Leather Shoes Really Reflect Up" on Good Friday. It was also to run on Easter, for four weeks. The play is advertised as a "Catholic School-Spoofing Musical" and "an irreverent romp."

One of the most egregious decisions was taken at the College of the Holy Cross (Worcester, Massachusetts) well before Easter. On Ash Wednesday, the College ushered in the holy season of Lent with a performance of "The Vagina Monologues," as discussed in Chapter 6.

The Sisters of Perpetual Indulgence, a group of San Francisco homosexuals dressed as nuns, celebrated Easter with an "Indulgence in the Park." They featured a "clown-drag-nun" fundraiser and a "Hunky Jesus" contest. On Good Friday they had a "traditional observance of Very Good Friday" with "scantily clad men."

Easter is simply too irresistible a holiday for anti-Catholics not to bash. This year's targets included Christ, Catholic schools and nuns. While putting these events on at any time of the year is sick, it takes a particularly disturbed individual to celebrate Easter this way. Imagine deriding Jews on Yom Kippur, ridiculing blacks on Martin Luther King Day or mocking homosexuals on Gay Pride Day. There would be hell to pay because of the uproar from these groups themselves, as well as from the media. Yet, Christians, and especially Catholics, remain fair game.

Once more, sad but true.

It is clear that the behavior exhibited by the sick and sickening segments of our culture will be with us indefinitely. Thus, our ability as a society to reinculcate in our children and young adults the values derived from our Judeo-Christian tradition will be crucial to our future as a nation.

> *Look at the Crusades. Look at Galileo. Look at the Scopes trial. Look at the Salem witch trials. Even though about 85% of Americans identify themselves as Christians, most seem unwilling or unable to defend themselves against such diatribes.*
>
> —Charlotte Allen, author of *The Human Christ: The Search for the Historical Jesus*

41

ON DONAHUE

Human beings are perhaps never more frightening than when they are convinced beyond doubt that they are right.

—Laurens Van der Post

In November 1991 my daughter Kate, then 16, and I appeared on NBC's popular and successful *Donahue* television talk show, hosted by Phil Donahue. (The show is no longer on the air, which is a good thing.) The same program was rebroadcast in September 1992. The topic: Should parents allow their teenage daughters to have sex at home?

From the moment I learned what the topic was to be, I was disgusted by the sleaziness of the show, which, by the way, I had never watched. However, because Kate and I had specifically been invited to represent more traditional and conservative viewpoints, we decided that we should and would accept the invitation.

It is precisely because America seems to love sleaze so much that Kate and I decided to go on the show. After all, we felt strongly that someone had to say something reasonable about such an issue. Unfortunately, sleazy fare has only proliferated on television in the decade since our appearance.

Kate and I were pitted against two middle-aged women and their daughters, who had long since been granted home sexual clearance by their mothers. Not counting Phil, Kate and I were thus outnumbered two to one, and yet I believe we fared well, especially because of Kate's performance. The audience we faced consisted of approximately two hundred persons, the capacity of the studio, which was the usual *Donahue* venue. In the end, dozens of people from the audience stopped to congratulate (and even hug) Kate after the show. Consequently, she and I left with the impression that the preponderance of the audience supported our views, which I had insisted were based on Judeo-Christian tradition and values.

As the talk show's host, Phil made it clear early that he had little tolerance for my traditional/conservative views. He knelt on one knee and held the microphone in front of me when it was my turn to speak, the camera on me alone. Then he whispered "Keep it short" while simultaneously making a "cut" motion with his free hand across his throat.

After my opening statement, it became difficult for me to get much more air time. He seemed to avoid me and focus instead on the anything-goes crowd. After all, I dare say that my sleaze factor was considered too low to keep ratings up. In fairness, though, he did give Kate some excellent opportunities to express her views, which she did with credibility and aplomb.

Phil Donahue himself was a sorry case. Yes, financial success was his, big-time, but, for a Notre Dame alumnus, his Catholic faith had apparently gone the way of the dinosaur. If I had to guess, he probably didn't really enjoy being a master of sleaze, but it's what the 'market' wanted, and both NBC and he, perhaps reluctantly, decided to oblige.

And here we go again. In July of this year Phil returned to television with a weeknight program on MSNBC, an NBC cable affiliate.

The medium is the message.

—Marshall McLuhan

42

A Double Standard

Truth lies within a little and certain compass,
but error is immense.

—Henry St. John, Viscount Bolingbroke

M any people believe that Judaism is the only faith that is subjected to religious prejudice in the United States. Yet, Catholic bashing is not only not new, it has been around a long, long time. According to Harvard professor Arthur Schlesinger, Sr., anti-Catholicism is "the deepest bias in the history of the American people."

Just how alive and how well the double standard is for Catholics may be gleaned from the following.

Two days before the 2000 presidential election, *The New York Times*, in its Sunday, November 5, 1999 Long Island edition, published an article entitled "Church, State and Tuesday Converge." It criticized Bishop James McHugh, then head of Long Island's Rockville Centre Diocese and now deceased, for his effort to make abortion the primary factor for Catholic voters. Moreover, it cited yet another tiresome perceived violation of church and state.

I wrote to the *Times*, which published my letter, excerpted here.

Al Gore [who was running for president], Joe Lieberman
[who was running for vice president and his own U.S. Senate
seat in Connecticut] and Hillary Clinton [who was running

for a U.S. Senate seat in New York], among others, have all
many times endorsed specific political candidates from various
pulpits during this campaign year. However, the moment a
Catholic prelate encourages his congregation "to think deeply
on church teachings before pulling a lever for any candidate
who supports abortion," the issue of church and state resounds
shrilly. Never mind that Bishop McHugh did not even endorse
a specific party or candidate. (He) was merely exercising free
speech guaranteed by the First Amendment, one right which
I am confident most people support but also one which others
would deny to Catholic priests.

In the same edition in which the *Times* printed my letter, it
published alongside mine one from my friend Frank Schroeder, an
assistant district attorney in Nassau County, New York. Then
serving as president of the Long Island chapter of the Catholic
League, he wrote:

It is no surprise that Planned Parenthood would get
bent out of shape when a Catholic bishop encourages his
congregation to bring their conscience into the voting booth.
After all, abortion is a multimillion-dollar industry for Planned
Parenthood.

Rose Brown of Planned Parenthood complained that
Bishop McHugh "appeared to be verging on violating the
constitutional principle of separation of church and state."
Which constitution prohibits church leaders from addressing
moral issues that have become contentious political issues?
Would not the entire civil rights movement have been
unconstitutional, considering most of its leading figures were
ministers?

In 1998 *Media Watch*, a newsletter published by the Media
Research Center, published the following:

The murder of Buffalo abortionist Barnett Slepian

topped all the evening news shows on October 26, and ABC and CBS didn't wither from blaming the pro-life movement for inciting the violence with its rhetoric. That didn't happen to liberal environmentalists when all the networks devoted full stories four days earlier to the "Earth Liberation Front" burning buildings in Colorado.

[Author's note: ELF's incendiary activities have since spread to the New York metropolitan area, especially Long Island.]

[CBS News anchor] Dan Rather announced Slepian "was just the latest abortion provider to be targeted by a violent, sometimes murderous, section of the pro-life movement." ABC's John Miller noted: "Activists on the most radical end of the pro-life camp make no apologies for the sniper." . . . But the arson of ski resort buildings in Colorado was reported differently. ABC's Tom Foreman did not place the "Earth Liberation Front" on "the most radical end of the environmental camp." He declared "militant environmental groups such as Earth First say it's fair game to attack property" and suggested sympathetically: "many environmentalists in Vail . . . are afraid their cause will be tainted by the violence."

Double standard, anyone? Relative extrema?

Jim Norwood recently commented to me, "Chuck, I cannot understand how anyone with a brain can say that abortion is not wrong. After all, it's murder."

He's right.

When it comes to the Catholic Church, it always seems to be a different story. When the Catholic League charges that the Church has been defamed, it is expected to provide mountains of evidence. To paraphrase the League's view, our complaint is not that we should be forced to verify our charges;

that's fine. It is simply that there is once more a double standard at work. We Catholics have to pass a rigorous test while others are given a free pass.

> *Blame Christianity first. This is a reflex among the chattering classes [who] twist logic and history for the purpose of characterizing the folks who light candles at St. Patrick's [Cathedral in New York City] as a branch of al Qaeda.*
>
> —Charlotte Allen, author of *The Human Christ: The Search for the Historical Jesus*

The Church, like all organizations under attack, can use allies, and that's what the Catholic League is—an ally of the Church. As lay men and women, we have every right to defend our Church; indeed, we have a moral obligation to do so. We are needed not so much because the clergy can't do the job, but because as lay people we have greater latitude in choosing the right means of redress. Besides, as Bill Donohue has written, "does anyone complain that there should be no Anti-Defamation League for Jews on the grounds that rabbis are sufficient to the task?"

> *There is but one law for all, namely, the law of our Creator, the law of humanity, justice, equity—the law of nature, and of nations.*
>
> —Edmund Burke

43

TAXES AND THOSE WHO TAX

When more of the people's sustenance is exacted through the form of taxation than is necessary to meet the just obligations of government and expenses of its economical administration, such exaction becomes ruthless extortion and a violation of the fundamental principles of a free government.

—Grover Cleveland [December 1886]

I happen to be one of those Americans who believes we are overtaxed. In 2001 and this year the U.S. struggled to break out of a recession that only began to show signs of abatement late this year. Yet, at the same time, we had the majority leader of the U.S. Senate, Senator Thomas Daschle of South Dakota, and Senator Edward M. Kennedy of Massachusetts, liberals both, insisting that, if taxes are now increased, the recession will end sooner and we will, as a nation, be on more solid economic footing. Sen. Kennedy has specifically proposed a tax increase, particularly on "the rich." That is nonsense. (Happily, the November 2002 elections knocked Senator Daschle out of the Senate Majority Leader's role.)

Here are the facts as of 1999 about who pays taxes in the U.S., from no less an authority than the Internal Revenue Service, as published in *The Wall Street Journal*.

Percentiles Ranked by Adjusted Gross Income (AGI)	*Total Share of AGI*	*Percent of Federal Personal Income Tax*
Top 1%	19.5%	36.2%
Top 5%	34.0%	55.5%
Top 10%	44.9%	66.5%
Top 25%	66.5%	83.5%
Top 50%	86.8%	96.0%
Bottom 50%	13.2.%	4.0%

According to these figures, the top 5% of taxpayers pay 55% of the income tax while those in the top half pay 96%, which means the bottom half pays only 4%. This situation is getting worse too.

Moreover, the top 1% of those filing tax returns pay a much higher share of all federal personal income taxes than their adjusted gross income would warrant. Specifically, these folks account for less than 20% of AGI but pay more than 36% of income taxes. In the past two decades, this burden has increased dramatically for the top tier.

There is also multiple taxation in our country. Money earned is taxed; it is taxed again when invested. Next, income from interest and dividends is taxed. (Happily, President Bush has called for an end to taxation of dividends but the cry has predictably arisen that this will only benefit the rich.) Finally, the death tax takes away from life savings left over after this incisive and invasive process. Other complexities of U.S. tax laws also diminish what we earn and save.

A simple way of stating the issue may be found in the following amusing article entitled "The Truth about Taxes & Tax Cuts." It has probably made its way around the world many times via e-mail forwarding, and its author is unknown.

Let's put tax cuts in terms everyone can understand. Suppose that every day, ten men go out for dinner. The bill for all ten comes to $100. If they paid their bill the way we pay our taxes, it would go something like this:

The first four men would pay nothing;
The fifth would pay $1;
The sixth would pay $3;
The seventh $7;
The eighth $12;
The ninth $18.
The tenth man—the richest—would pay $59.

That's what they decided to do. The ten men ate dinner in the restaurant every day and seemed quite happy with the arrangement—until one day, the owner threw them a curve.

"Since you are all such good customers," he said, "I'm going to reduce the cost of your daily meal by $20."

So now the dinner for the ten only cost $80. The group still wanted to pay their bill the way we pay our taxes.

So the first four men were unaffected. They would still eat for free. But what about the other six—the paying customers?

How could they divvy up the $20 windfall so that everyone would get his "fair share"?

The six men realized that $20 divided by six is $3.33. But if they subtracted that from everybody's share, then the fifth man and the sixth man would end up being 'paid' to eat their meal.

So the restaurant owner suggested that it would be fair to reduce each man's bill by roughly the same amount, and he proceeded to work out the amounts each should pay.

And so the fifth man paid nothing, the sixth pitched in $2, the seventh paid $5, the eighth paid $9, the ninth paid $12, leaving the tenth man with a bill of $52 instead of his earlier $59.

Each of the six was better off than before. And the first four continued to eat for free.

But once outside the restaurant, the men began to compare their savings.

"I only got a dollar out of the $20," declared the sixth man.

He pointed to the tenth. "But he got $7!"

"Yeah, that's right," exclaimed the fifth man. "I only saved a dollar too. It's unfair that he got seven times more than me."

"That's true," shouted the seventh man. "Why should he get $7 back when I got only $2? The wealthy get all the breaks!"

"Wait a minute," yelled the first four men in unison. "We didn't get anything at all. The system exploits the poor!"

The nine men surrounded the tenth and beat him up.

The next night he didn't show up for dinner, so the nine sat down and ate without him. But when it came time to pay the bill, they discovered something important. They were $52 short!

And that, boys and girls, journalists and college instructors, is how the tax system works.

The people who pay the highest taxes get the most benefit from a tax reduction.

Tax them too much, attack them for being wealthy, and they just may not show up at the table anymore.

Unfortunately, Liberals cannot grasp this straightforward logic!

In an e-mail from a friend, Michael Wenk, described as "a street smart Louisianian," has offered an appropriate footnote to this story: Since the group came up $52 short, its members told the restaurant owner that they would have to give him an IOU because they didn't have the money. Every day they kept eating and writing the owner IOUs. Think of the owner as the federal government and the IOUs as the national debt, for that's a reasonable explanation of how our system works.

⧖

With people like Senators Daschle and Kennedy still exercising power in Congress, it is less than challenging to understand why we have so many bad laws, one of which is the Endangered Species Act. For decades I have read horror stories about honest, hardworking, successful people who have seen their businesses, and sometimes their lives, ruined by the extraordinary reach of the U.S. government in the name of the environment.

Here is a case in point: The year is 2001; the place is the Klamath Basin that straddles the border of Oregon and California. Thanks to the power of the Environmental Protection Agency (EPA), the federal government (under the auspices of the U.S. Fish & Wildlife Service and the National Marine Fisheries Service) actually shut off water to the region's farmers in order to save the "endangered" suckerfish. "Endangered" is a word that has become common in everyday usage in America because of the disproportionate impact of this federal agency that has unmistakably run amok.

After the water was shut off, researchers from Oregon State University and the University of California found that more than 2,000 jobs and $74 million in revenue were lost by farmers in the basin.

Subsequently, the independent National Academy of Sciences released a report saying the U.S. Fish & Wildlife Service and the National Marine Fisheries Service had "no sound scientific basis" for cutting off water to the farmers on behalf of the "endangered" sucker fish. It has been reported that the real problem here was the fact that these agencies were staffed by the Clinton administration with environmental activists whose priority was stopping development rather than respecting sound scientific findings and conclusions.

How much is the American sucker fish really worth?

Sorry, my mistake. Allow me to rephrase the question: How much are American *people* and their livelihoods really worth?

Happily, in the wake of the NAS report, the federal government decided to restore water to Klamath Basin farmers. Of course, the environmentalists are threatening to sue again, but they will have a tougher go of it this time in light of "no sound scientific basis" last time.

Senator Daschle deserves both singling out and the harshest criticism for playing politics in the wake of 9/11. Bob Lund has said all that needed to be said in the following letter:

> Senator Daschle,
>
> This is my first and last visit to your web site. I am making this visit to express my outrage at your comments on Mr. Bush's conduct of the war. You have raised partisan politics and irresponsibility to a new plateau and given our enemies an additional source of motivation to kill Americans. It appears to me that you did this so you could take a few more self-serving shots at the other party. While trying to weaken the President, you are risking damage to the national resolve and playing with the safety of the American people. I understand your interest in self-promotion and your concern with Mr. Bush's current popularity, but I request that you play your games with less serious issues.
>
> By the way, first and foremost, I consider myself an American, not a Democrat or a Republican. You might want to consider that perspective on this issue. You've got a virtual cornucopia of opportunities to attack the Republicans. I request, for the good of our nation, you exclude this one.
>
> Robert E. Lund
> Plano, Tx

Senator Daschle has announced that he will *not* run for the Democratic Party's 2004 presidential nomination. Good.

Idleness and pride tax with a heavier hand than kings and parliaments. If we can get rid of the former, we may easily bear the latter.

—Benjamin Franklin [1765]

44

Contemporary American Culture:

Politically Correct, Diverse,

Anti-Christian and Thuggish

*North American civilization is one of the ugliest to have emerged
in human history, and it has engulfed the world.... This great,
though disastrous, culture can only change as we begin to stand
off and see... the inveterate materialism which has become the
model for cultures around the globe.*

—Arthur Charles Erickson [1973]

In February 1999 Charlton Heston delivered a speech at Harvard
Law School, which was entitled "Winning The Cultural War."
His focus was on political correctness, which has clear potential
to undermine our nation. It is rampant on college campuses and
virtually throughout our society. Consider the following, excerpted
from his speech:

> ➤ At Antioch college in Ohio, young men seeking intimacy
> with a coed must get verbal permission at each step of
> the process from kissing to petting to final
> copulation . . . all clearly spelled out in a printed college
> directive.
>
> ➤ In New Jersey, despite the death of several patients
> nationwide who had been infected by dentists who

had concealed their AIDS—the state commissioner announced that health providers who are HIV-positive need not . . . need not . . . tell their patients that they are infected.

➤ At [the College of] William and Mary, students tried to change the name of the school team 'The Tribe' because it was supposedly insulting to local Indians, only to learn that authentic Virginia chiefs truly like the name. [Author's note: Some years ago St. John's University in New York City capitulated to similar pressure and changed its teams' name from the *Redmen* to the *Red Storm*.]

➤ In San Francisco, city fathers passed an ordinance protecting the rights of transvestites to cross-dress on the job, and for transsexuals to have separate toilet facilities while undergoing sex change surgery. [Author's note: They later voted to fund sex change operations with public monies.]

➤ In New York City, kids who don't speak a word of Spanish have been placed in bilingual classes to learn their three R's in Spanish solely because their last names sound Hispanic.

➤ At the University of Pennsylvania, in a state where thousands died at Gettysburg opposing slavery, the president of that college officially set up segregated dormitory space for black students.

➤ David Howard, head of the Washington D.C. Office of Public Advocate, used the word 'niggardly' while talking to colleagues about budgetary matters. Of course, 'niggardly' means stingy or scanty. But within days Howard was forced to publicly apologize and resign.

As columnist [now a Fox News Channel anchor] Tony Snow wrote: 'David Howard got fired because some people in public employ were morons who (a) didn't know the meaning of niggardly, (b) didn't know how to use a dictionary to discover the meaning, and (c) actually demanded that he apologize for their ignorance.'

Continued Mr. Heston:

What does all of this mean? It means that telling us what to think has evolved into telling us what to say, so telling us what to do can't be far behind. Before you claim to be a champion of free thought, tell me: Why did political correctness originate on America's campuses? And why do you continue to tolerate it? Why do you, who're supposed to debate ideas, surrender to their suppression?

Let's be honest. Who here thinks your professors can say what they really believe? It scares me to death, and should scare you too, that the superstition of political correctness rules the halls of reason.

Mr. Heston next asked his audience of the best and the brightest what they can do to prevail against this "pervasive social subjugation." "You simply . . . disobey. Peaceably, yes. Respectfully, of course. Nonviolently, absolutely. But when told how to think or what to say or how to behave, we don't. We disobey social protocol that stifles and stigmatizes personal freedom."
Bravo! Give that man another Oscar!

Brother Michael J. McAward, S.M., Chaminade's principal from 1992 to 1999, has written that "a healthy awareness of cultural tendencies is not only necessary, but also critical to personal growth and development, as well as to education, especially if charity and integrity are among the goals of educators." He adds:

One of the challenges we face today is that many of our young people seek their entertainment from shows and personalities that glorify sarcasm, cartoons in which characters say things we would not accept from "real people," sports commercials that demean opponents and promote "trash talk," and music that celebrates violence and anger. We have witnessed the creation of a new verb "to *dis*" which practically elevates the act of disrespect into an art form.

The *Culture of Disrespect* operates from a position of assumed superiority to all. Parker Palmer writes, "In a culture of disrespect, education suffers the worst possible fate—it becomes banal. When nothing is sacred, deemed worthy of respect, banality is the best we can do."

As a footnote to this cultural stimulation, Charles A. Murray, a fellow at the American Enterprise Institute, has written of a phenomenon that has evolved in recent decades. In my view, the affront to humanity known as rap music has its origins in what he calls "thug code."

In essence, thug code's central tenets are: "Take what you want, respond violently to anyone who antagonizes you, gloat when you win, despise courtesy as weakness, treat women as receptacles, take pride in cheating, deceiving, or exploiting successfully." Alas, many of us have witnessed more than our share of such behaviors. Thug code "amounts to the hitherto inarticulate values of underclass males from time immemorial, now made articulate with the collaboration of some of America's best creative and merchandising talent."

Today we are in sore need of strong antidotes to thug code.

What should other people think of parents who claim never to have entered their teenage son's bedroom because they believed it was wrong to 'violate' his space and, therefore, his privacy? Is such behavior genuine parental respect or an abdication of responsibility? (The boy's room, it turns out, was being used as a bomb factory.)

Take it on faith or speak with another who came of age in America during the 1950s or '60s, and I am confident you will soon come to recognize that our culture has been coarsened substantially in the intervening years. Along with this, as I write later in this work, human life has been devalued. Likewise, family life has deteriorated in many homes with parents improperly relegating to schools and teachers their role. In GC I once heard a parent, whose five-year-old was going to kindergarten for the first time, say, "My job's done; it's up to the teachers now. Tennis court, here I come." Alas, many parents have little understanding of the undisciplined institutions their local schools have become, especially at the secondary level.

A few years ago the front pages of many newspapers lamented a deadly spate of American high-school violence. Their coverage included the story of Charles Andrew Williams, a troubled 15-year-old with a history of drug abuse, who shot two classmates to death and wounded thirteen other people at Santana High School in Santee, California. Since then there have been other similar incidents.

We have also read that many of these mass shootings are carried out by highly disturbed, even mentally ill, individuals. Unfortunately, there appear to be no easy solutions to this frightening problem about which so many people, in both public and private venues, have so frequently expressed shock. I would submit that 'thug code' is also a major factor in this problem.

One of the most extraordinary elements in this tragic tale is how it was handled in the media: *The dead aren't victims; the killer is!*

Two young men are dead, we are told, because "Andy" Williams was a victim of bullying. In an interview, Andy's classmate Steve Meincke, 16, said "Andrew was my best friend. He was everybody's little buddy. He was just the kind, caring person that you could rely on. Honestly, he wouldn't hurt a fly . . . He was nice and kind. Seriously, the only way he shot those girls was because of an accident. I know for a fact he'd never shoot a girl. He'd never even hit a girl . . . I could trust him. He never stole off me . . . I don't care that he's done this . . . he made a bad decision, but I still like him . . ." Somewhat more detached, Jenna Bobo, 14, described Andy as having been "in two of my classes last term . . . I knew that he smoked pot and stuff, but I never thought he would do anything like that."

These comments are extraordinary but something doesn't quite add up. Frankly, I was left wondering if these young people had ever had beneficial role models, philosophical ideals and/or—dare I say it?—religious formation of any kind.

As if to reinforce Andy's character, some television interviewers in the immediate aftermath of the shootings, including Katie Couric on NBC's "Today" show, also discussed Andy's goodness and sensitivity, his troubles and his loneliness. "At no point in the interview" (which was with a female classmate of Andy and her mother), wrote Pulitzer-prize winner Dorothy Rabinowitz in *The Wall Street Journal*, "did it occur to the normally inquisitive Ms. Couric to ask if there wasn't something a bit unbalanced, say, in this singularly glowing testimony to Andy, who had just cold-bloodedly mowed down everybody he laid eyes on."

Unbalanced indeed.

Given "the inviolable right to freedom from insult, and from all the slings and arrows that are and always will be part of life's experience," continued Ms. Rabinowitz wryly, "it shouldn't be surprising that a teenager who perceives himself as bullied will absorb the message that he has been the victim of a monstrous crime."

Is this a corollary to thug code?

Let's get real. Bullies have been around forever. In this vein, I have heard it said that even Jesus was bullied from the moment he first stepped out the front door, derided perhaps because of his father's occupation. Unlike Andy, though, Jesus became the innocent Lamb sent to slaughter; alack, Andy became the silencer of other, latter-day innocent lambs. One life glorified, the other ruined. How profoundly sad for the callow Andy and his family.

Prosecutors had asked that Andy be sentenced to 425 years in prison; his actual sentence, handed down in August of this year, was fifty years to life.

> *I believe there are more instances of the abridgement of the freedom of the people by gradual and silent encroachments of those in power than by violent and sudden usurpations.*

> —James Madison

45

THE SELF-RIGHTEOUS BROTHERS:

JESSE AND AL

Jesse Jackson has made important contributions to politics and civil rights; now he looks like a headline-hunting ambulance chaser. Al Sharpton may be shrewd, but this performance, coupled with his past demagoguery, makes it impossible to treat his 2004 presidential run seriously.

—Albert R. Hunt

"No justice, no peace!"

Those words are the mantra and chant of choice of the Reverend Al Sharpton, a resident of New Jersey, who has operated for many years as a civil rights activist in New York City. "The Reverend Al," as many call him, is a consummate demagogue and a blatant racist. His brand of racism is anti-white; he is African-American. He has even gone so far as to fabricate incidents of racial bigotry, as he did in the widely reported 1987 case of Tawana Brawley, an unfortunate black female teenager, who, Sharpton claimed, was raped and smeared with feces by a gang of white men. His assertions in the case were all later proved in a court of law to be lies. Indeed, excess and overreaction are his hallmarks, but they have gained him national attention.

The Reverend Jesse Jackson, who has been on the national stage since Rev. Dr. Martin Luther King, Jr. was assassinated on April 4, 1968, is another African-American who takes the racist tack. He is only slightly less abrasive in his approach than the bombastic, revolting Sharpton.

Both Reverends' brand of civil rights activism has been so offensive to so many for so long that it sometimes surprises me that they continue to command such substantial media coverage. Yet, I'll give them their due for each is skilled in manipulating the media to serve his own often outrageous and self-serving purposes.

John Perazzo addresses this issue in his book *The Myths That Divide Us*, which is subtitled *How Lies Have Poisoned American Race Relations*. The Reverend Al's fundamental position is that black Americans cannot succeed and are treated unfairly because our nation is racist, which unfortunately, no thanks to his demagoguery, is believed by many blacks. Mr. Perazzo addresses a broader reality and puts the lie to Sharpton and his ilk by demonstrating that black-white relations are sabotaged by demagogues like the Reverend Al who mischaracterize the U.S. as racist.

In this connection, Perazzo's book addresses hundreds of remarkable facts. Here is a fascinating sampling gleaned from the book's web site:

> ➤ Countless studies show that fatherlessness, not race, is by far the most accurate predictor that a child will end up in poverty or prison. Today, approximately 70% of black children are born into fatherless homes.

> ➤ Seventy percent of long-term prison inmates, and 70% of juveniles in reform institutions, were raised without a father.

> ➤ Eighty-five percent of all black children living in poverty are raised in single-parent homes.

> ➤ The incomes of fatherless black families are only about one fourth that of two-parent black families. A similar disparity exists among white one- and two-parent families.

> ➤ Ever since 1981, black families with two college-educated, working adults have earned more than similar white families in every age group and in every region of

the U.S. As early as 1970, black two-parent families outside of the South were already earning more than comparable white families.

➤ Black full-time workers today earn slightly more than white workers of the same age, sex and I.Q.

➤ Black defendants are slightly less likely to be prosecuted and convicted of felonies than white defendants charged with similar crimes.

➤ Though blacks commit more than half of our nation's murders, nearly 60% of all Death Row inmates are white.

➤ Ninety-four percent of all black homicide victims are slain by other blacks.

➤ Violent white criminals select black victims for just 3% of their crimes, while black criminals choose white victims for 54% of their crimes. All told, 89% of all interracial violence is black-on-white.

➤ Because of affirmative action, black applicants are much more likely than white applicants to be admitted to the college of their choice, even though whites score about 200 points higher on the Scholastic Aptitude Test (SAT).

➤ Affirmative action has exacerbated racial tensions while doing virtually nothing to improve the economic condition of black Americans. Black economic progress was already well underway and proceeding at a brisk pace well before affirmative action even existed.

➤ Black progress in such areas as income, high-school graduation rates, life-expectancy and home ownership was faster between 1940 and 1970 than after the rise of affirmative action in the early 1970s.

➤ Though significant numbers of blacks surveyed perceive that white society strives to limit their opportunities and civil rights, polls show that racist white attitudes have diminished significantly in recent decades. For example, 93% of eligible whites say they would be willing to vote for a black presidential candidate, and scarcely 1% of whites favor racial discrimination against blacks in the workplace.

Mr. Perazzo also shows that, even beyond America's shores, many who focused world attention on the evils of *apartheid* in South Africa are silent about the far greater atrocities perpetrated by black governments on black victims throughout Africa. Moreover, even under *apartheid*, more blacks actually moved into South Africa than left it, for economic and social conditions in neighboring African countries were worse. Finally, Perazzo challenges the many denouncers of past centuries' white-on-black enslavement who remain silent concerning the black-on-black slavery that pervaded Africa during the same era, and that still exists in several African nations today.

In the last analysis, when it comes to this issue, Americans can be proud that

> ➤ Their country is in fact the least racist white-majority society on the planet,
> ➤ The U.S. provides greater legal protections for minorities that any other society, and
> ➤ Our nation offers more opportunity to a greater number of blacks than any place on earth, including all the nations of Africa combined.

⧗

Early this year, Messrs. Jackson and Sharpton once more made the newspapers in splashy fashion. Their target seemed unlikely: Lawrence Summers, the new president of Harvard University in Cambridge, Massachusetts.

Mr. Summers came under fire from the two black activists for criticism he leveled against Cornel West, who has been described as Harvard's "star professor" of African-American studies. Indeed, West is one of only fourteen people designated "University

Professors" at Harvard. All Mr. Summers, who is white, wanted was excellence from his professor, who is black.

Shelby Steele, a research fellow at the Hoover Institution, in published commentary, described Mr. West as "arguably the most famous professor in the university's well known, if undistinguished, Afro-American Studies Department." "Even on their face," he continued, "the reported charges behind [Mr. Summers'] rebuke seem screamingly true—that Mr. West is an academic lightweight, that his service to Al Sharpton's presidential campaign and his recording of a rap CD embarrass his professorship, and that his uncritical grading practices have contributed to Harvard's serious grade inflation problem." Of course, Mr. West was outraged and, lo, Messrs. Jackson and Sharpton entered the fray on the West side to condemn Harvard as racist.

In his "Politics & People" column, which appears weekly in *The Wall Street Journal*, the respected Albert R. Hunt (to whom some chidingly refer as the *Journal's* resident liberal) wrote that "Mr. Jackson, charging Professor West had been 'violated,' demanded to see Mr. Summers. Mr. Sharpton, claiming that Mr. Summer's *(sic)* chastisement of Mr. West could 'intimidate' African-Americans, threatened to sue Harvard." Both questioned the commitment of the Harvard president, who, incidentally, was a member of Bill Clinton's cabinet, to affirmative action.

In the world of political correctness and ultra-sensitivity, particularly insidious and rampant maladies on American campuses, the racist label would be, as Mr. Steele put it, "a deadly reputation in the academic world." Thus, these two black power brokers had sought to strip Mr. Summers of his moral authority in demanding excellence of West, who with some of his co-stars had relocation discussions with Princeton University, whose president called the professor-turned-rap-artist "eminent." (A few weeks later one member of Harvard's Afro-American Studies Department, K. Anthony Appiah, did bolt to Princeton.) One class act, so to speak, after another.

Kudos to Mr. Hunt for acknowledging that "The message [of Mr. Summers] has merit and it's ridiculous to accuse him of racial insensitivity." Further, to demonstrate just how disingenuous Jesse Jackson was in this situation, Mr. Hunt tells us that "Jackson stormed into Cambridge demanding a meeting with Harvard's president, over the 'insult' he had inflicted on the professor, [although] he had never spoken to Cornel West about the incident."

All this, according to Mr. Hunt, "says much less about Harvard or academic life than it does about the vacuum in national black leadership." To me this is extraordinary; I have believed this for decades, and now I can read it in the written words of a renowned liberal journalist!

In the last analysis, Mr. Hunt demonstrates that he's got the two reverends' numbers:

> This shrill and silly conduct reinforces the political bankruptcy of these national black politicos. Jesse Jackson has made important contributions to politics and civil rights; now he looks like a headline-hunting ambulance chaser. Al Sharpton may be shrewd, but this performance, coupled with his past demagoguery, makes it impossible to treat his 2004 presidential run seriously.

Presidential run? Please God, no.

Recent news of the Reverend Al came in a July 24, 2002 report in which he claimed that the airing of an FBI surveillance videotape, which clearly shows him being offered a share in a drug deal by an undercover agent, is part of a "smear campaign." Undaunted, he still pledged to explore a presidential campaign; indeed, he officially filed the requisite papers and joined the race for the 2004 Democratic presidential nomination. Be that as it may, I believe he is unelectable.

Instead of worrying about black university professors, the two reverends' ever professed concern for black Americans should be focused on the young, if they are sincere about helping their own people. They might start by asking serious questions as to why the average high school non-graduation rate for black students throughout the U.S. is a staggering 45%, according to *Education Week* in its "Quality Counts" annual report.

Mr. Steele has observed that "Everywhere that minorities press institutions today as groups, there is an erosion of excellence." This will sound like a harsh, even racist, assertion to many, but it is patently true. In my thirty-something years in the business world, as well as my five in academia, I can say unequivocally that I have witnessed such erosion time and again. The reason it occurs, Steele says, is not so much the fault of minorities but rather deference (derived from guilt on the part of many whites) to and acceptance of the lowering of standards. This generates mediocrity but, in the minds of many, both white and black, it is far preferable to having a major institution, especially an august place like Harvard (or Princeton), labeled as racist.

Mr. Hunt concludes, almost dismissively, that "Jesse Jackson and Al Sharpton seem often irrelevant, relying chiefly on a press that feeds and stokes the faux conflicts on which they thrive."

As for Mr. Steele, he pulls no punches:

> The mediocrity of Mr. West is visible everywhere across the landscape of black academia, where so much deference corrupts black talent. Nearly every campus has at least one black professor whose special talent is the racial indignation that white guilt loves to reward.

A repulsive situation with relative extrema galore, it is what it is, although I wish it were otherwise.

I received an amusing, if disgusting, e-mail from my friend and fellow Chaminade alumnus Pat Long. It is entitled "Only in America" and reads as follows:

> Jesse Jackson has added former Chicago democratic congressman Mel Reynolds to the Rainbow/PUSH coalition's payroll. Reynolds was among the 176 criminals excused in

President Clinton's last-minute forgiveness spree. Reynolds received a commutation of his six-and-a-half-year Federal sentence for 15 convictions of wire fraud, bank fraud & lies to the Federal Election Commission. He is more notorious, however, for concurrently serving five years for sleeping with an underage campaign volunteer.

This is a first in American politics: An ex-congressman who had sex with a subordinate won clemency from a President who had sex with a subordinate, then was hired by a clergyman who had sex with a subordinate.

His new job? Youth counselor.

Is this country great or what?

Veteran investigative reporter Kenneth R. Timmerman has provided a valuable and refreshing public service by writing *Shakedown*, a new book whose subtitle reads "exposing the real Jesse Jackson." The book's promotional material states that Mr. Timmerman reveals in it how Rev. Jackson:

➤ Elbowed his way into the black leadership, grabbing the fallen mantle of Dr. Martin Luther King, Jr. (who was deeply suspicious of him) to pursue his own fame and fortune;

➤ Profited from "Operation Breadbasket" in Chicago, accepting fees from black businessmen to organize boycotts and demonstrations against white-owned companies—adding muscle to his operation by recruiting members of the notorious Black Stone Rangers, the most violent gang on the south side of Chicago; and

➤ With Bill Clinton's help expanded yet again into the worlds of business and finance, shaking down the likes of Coca-Cola, Texaco, Coors, PepsiCo and Morgan

Stanley, enriching his sons and cronies . . . and living
the high life.

Timmerman also cites certain "lies." Whereas Jackson has
claimed status as a victim of racism and poverty all his life, it seems
his "step-father was a career postal worker and the family lived
comfortably. Jackson's claim that racism denied him the quarterback
position at Illinois is also false. He couldn't beat out the starting
quarterback, Mel Myers—who happened to be black." Then there's
"the lie that Jackson was, in fact, a minister at all."

It may be sheer coincidence or perhaps even merely my own
perception but it seems to me that Rev. Jackson has kept an
uncharacteristically low profile since Mr. Timmerman's book made
the scene.

On August 1, 2002, Don Imus, on his morning radio program,
said of the Rev. Jackson, "There's no bigger phony on the planet."
Amen, I-Man.

*For "diversity" reasons, Brooklyn Borough President Marty
Markowitz has removed the portrait of "old white man"
George Washington from his office. Instead, he'd like a picture
of a black person or a woman, he explains. Other historical
figures are seen as irrelevant too. "We don't know who these
people are," Mr. Markowitz told a New York Post reporter
while viewing the portraits that decorate Borough Hall. If
"Mr. Brooklyn" had a deeper interest in history, he'd have
plenty of Brooklyn heroes to pick from in redecorating his
office. The last time New York was under attack, Nathanael
Greene, Henry Knox, Israel Putnam—all Brooklyn
natives—fought within walking distance of his office under
Washington in the largest military engagement of the
Revolutionary War.*

—"Off the Wall" in *The Wall Street Journal,*
January 21, 2002

46

POPE PIUS XII:

DEFAMATION EVERLASTING

There is an anti-Christian mythology that equates faith in
Jesus Christ with intolerance, capitalist exploitation, hostility
to science, desecration of the environment, oppression of
women, sponsorship of slavery and the slaughter of entire
peoples. . . . (T)he commonly circulated "evidence" against
Christianity falls into the category of urban legend.

—Charlotte Allen, author of *The Human Christ: The*
Search for the Historical Jesus

One gross injustice, born of anti-Catholic bias, is the media's condemnation of Pope Pius XII, who led the Roman Catholic Church during the dark days of World War II. Here is a case in point of the widespread assault on this pope:

On March 19, 2000, *The New York Times* published an article by Deborah Sontag entitled "The Holy Land, in an Edgy Mood, Awaits the Pope's Visit." According to her piece, "The Israeli textbooks' presentation of Catholicism . . . ends with Pope Pius XII's failure to speak out publicly against the Holocaust." Later, we learn that there are "many Israelis who want to hear the (current) pope (John Paul II) apologize more concretely than previously for the church's wartime silence and for its role in fostering the anti-Semitism that fed the Nazi demonization of Jews."

In an op-ed piece entitled "Why Aren't Christians Speaking Out?" in *The Wall Street Journal* of October 30th of the same year, Cynthia Ozick writes compellingly of "Muslim rioting when a Jew walks upon a historic site," and of the absurd Palestinian contention "that the Jewish attachment to Jerusalem is historically and religiously nil." Two paragraphs later, she asks: "Where is the Christian outcry when profound hatred of Jews is once again being unleashed?" Yet, just before this valid and timely question, she notes that, "Half a century ago, when the Jews of Europe were besieged and defenseless, Christian silence was infamous. Since then, some Jews are no longer defenseless, and Christian understanding, conscience, and remorse have expiated that unforgotten and dire omission."

Thus it appears that both Ms. Sontag and Ms. Ozick—strange bedfellows, actually—embrace what seems to have become a new conventional wisdom that Christians were silent during the Holocaust and somehow bear the burden of blame for it and anti-Semitism in general. In short, it's Christians' fault all over again. Whereas Ms. Ozick does not refer explicitly to Pope Pius XII, Ms. Sontag specifically writes of his "failure to speak out publicly against the Holocaust." Nonetheless, the "silence" cited by each in her writing remains, for me, a gnawing concern.

Indeed, it frustrates and saddens me, a life-long Roman Catholic, that such blame is now so ubiquitously and matter-of-factly transferred to Christians in general and to the leadership of the Catholic Church in particular. This is especially vexing when there is a wealth of evidence of Catholic and other Christian successes, at both institutional and grass-roots levels, in not only speaking out but also protecting and saving Jews from Nazi terror and death.

Some readers may find it noteworthy that even *The New York Times*, no friend to the Church in recent times, in 1941 and 1942—on Christmas Day in both of those war years—published editorials that praised Pope Pius XII precisely *for* speaking out publicly and clearly against the Nazi evil at a time when virtually all other voices on the Continent remained silent. Indeed, Hitler

biographer John Toland wrote of this situation: "The Church, under
the Pope's guidance, had already saved the lives of more Jews than
all other Churches, religious institutions and rescue organizations
combined, and was presently hiding thousands of Jews in
monasteries, convents and Vatican City itself." In this connection,
Jewish sources have put this figure at 860,000.

Consider what Rabbi David Dalin, Ph.D., has written in this
regard:

> For Jewish leaders of a previous generation, this harsh
> portrayal of Pope Pius XII, and the campaign of vilification
> against him, would have been a source of profound shock
> and sadness. From the end of World War II until at least
> five years after his death, Pope Pius enjoyed an enviable
> reputation amongst Christians and Jews alike. At the
> end of the war, Pius XII was hailed as "the inspired moral
> prophet of victory," and "enjoyed near-universal acclaim
> for aiding European Jews." Numerous Jewish leaders,
> including Albert Einstein, Israeli Prime Ministers Golda
> Meir and Moshe Sharett, and Chief Rabbi Isaac Herzog,
> expressed their public gratitude to Pius XII, praising
> him as a "righteous gentile," who had saved thousands of
> Jews during the Holocaust.

Perhaps the words of Rabbi Daniel Lapin, writing in the May/
June 1999 edition of *The American Enterprise*, would resonate
with critics of Christians' role during the Holocaust, as well as
with consumers of such critics' misinformation. To wit: "Hitler
saw Judaism and the Christian church on the same side of the
battle—opposite him. He manipulated the deep well-springs of
anti-Semitism . . . but he was not an agent of Christianity."
Furthermore, "Today's Jewish schoolchildren," he emphasized,
"should be inculcated with gratitude toward those Christians who
suffered during the Holocaust to save Jewish lives. Yet the selfless
role of these Christians is largely ignored." As the Rabbi wrote

elsewhere in his article, this "does a disservice to those many Christians who saved Jews specifically *because* of their faith."

Would that authors, journalists and other commentators in our mainstream media, also recognize that the Church's present leadership, in the person of Pope John Paul II, once himself targeted by the Nazis for execution, has demonstrated, according to the Anti-Defamation League, "his solidarity with victims of the Holocaust in his speeches and sermons on numerous occasions, and has denounced anti-Semitism as a sin."

Elie Wiesel, a survivor of the Auschwitz concentration camp and the 1986 winner of the Nobel Peace Prize, has noted that, in the Holocaust, "All Jews were victims but not all victims were Jews." In this connection, it is important to understand that the incalculable suffering and loss of six million Jews at the hands of the Nazis was not the full extent of the Holocaust. Indeed, there were genocides in Germany and elsewhere in Europe of virtually as many other human beings. The truth is that there were five million "others" who were killed, most of them Catholic, the rest other Christians. That is why it is so regrettable that some blame Christianity for the atrocities committed in the same places during World War II.

In the last analysis, it is not unusual for wrongheaded notions to gain adherents even among the elite. Alas, it is increasingly unusual for such adherents to examine the record more rigorously and perhaps give truth a chance.

A full exploration of Pope Pius's conduct is needed. . . . It now falls to John Paul (II) and his successors to take the next step toward full acceptance of the Vatican's failure to stand squarely against the evil that swept across Europe.

—Editorial, *The New York Times*, March 18, 1998

The voice of Pius XII is a lonely voice in the silence and darkness

*enveloping Europe this Christmas. . . . He is about the only ruler
left on the Continent of Europe who dares to raise his voice at all.*

—Editorial, *The New York Times*, December 25, 1941

Could there be greater contrast between these two editorial
excerpts?

⧗

According to the Catholic League, *New Republic* editor Martin
Peretz was quoted in the January 13, 2002 *Sunday Times of
London* as saying Pope Pius XII was "an evil man." His charge is
based on a piece by Daniel Goldhagen in the January 27th edition
of the magazine that blames Catholicism for the Holocaust.

The Catholic League replied to both men: "Ask any American
who were the evil men of the last 100 years and the names of
Hitler, Stalin, Pol Pot, Mao and bin Laden roll off their lips. Ask
Martin Peretz and he answers Pope Pius XII. Never mind that this
pope has been credited by Jews all over the world (e.g. Pinchas
Lapide, Golda Meir, Albert Einstein, as well as dozens of Jewish
organizations) with saving more Jews than any other person. Peretz,
following Goldhagen, is convinced he was 'evil.' Could it be that
he came to this conclusion because he is riddled with guilt? After
all, he inherited a magazine that bowed to Hitler."

The League also reported that Dorothy Wickenden, a writer who
previously worked for Peretz, has written that "The *New Republic*
counseled fatalism and restraint in the face of Hitler, Mussolini, and
Franco." Now, had the magazine's editors followed the lead of the
Catholic Church, perhaps more Jews would have been saved. As for
Goldhagen, he finds incredible the idea that without anti-Judaism in
the Church, Nazism would never have existed. This shows his naiveté:
the pseudo-scientific racism and exterminationist policies of Hitler
were born of a particular set of historical conditions having nothing to
do with Catholicism. But to those engaged in witch-hunts, a careful
examination of these factors is nothing but a distraction.

Catholic League president and CEO Bill Donohue summarized this situation as follows:

> Goldhagen likes his history black and white. His previous work, one that was widely discredited by serious scholars, sought a wholesale indictment of the entire German nation. His new scapegoat is the Catholic Church. But what separates him from the cottage industry of Pius' critics is his thinly veiled hatred of Catholicism from top to bottom. Indeed, his enfeebled attack on the Catholic Catechism demonstrates that it is the theology he despises most, which is why Goldhagen is nothing more than a Jewish version of Bob Jones.

It is a sad commentary that, in a time of supposed inclusiveness, sensitivity, diversity and religious tolerance, Pope Pius XII and the Roman Catholic Church at large are relegated to the status of targets for bigots of virtually all stripes.

> *O Lord, support us all the day long, until the shadows lengthen and the evening comes, and the busy world is hushed, and the fever of life is over, and our work is done. Then in thy mercy grant us a safe lodging, and a holy rest, and peace at last.*
>
> —John Henry Cardinal Newman [1834]

47

MULTICULTURALISM, FEMINISM AND

THE INVALIDATION OF WESTERN CULTURE

Important principles may and must be inflexible.

—Abraham Lincoln [1865]

S ome individuals and groups will undoubtedly consider my
message counter-cultural, given the prevailing winds of
American culture today. Nonetheless, I share a perspective
that has its roots in the anti-Vietnam War era of the sixties and
early seventies, its blossoms in the emergence of feminist ideology
and openly gay and lesbian lifestyles, and its full foliage in
multiculturalism and the often depraved culture of new-
millennium America, recently and aptly personified by Bill and
Hillary Clinton and their entourages.

Consider for a moment the following *"Message of Allegience"*
(*sic*) published in the autumn of 1995 in *The Crusader*, the student
newspaper at the College of the Holy Cross. It is amazingly reminiscent
of a similar manifesto issued by the "Revolutionary Students Union"
at Holy Cross twenty-five years earlier, as discussed in Chapter 6.

> We, the leadership of [the gay students group, the Asian
> students group], the Black Student Union, [the
> multicultural society, the Latin American Students
> Organization], and the Women's Forum have decided to
> issue this statement of solidarity . . .

> While the interrelatedness of the organizations is integral to the struggle against discrimination, the wonderful diversity of the groups must also be heralded . . . Each organization is important in its own right and . . . we must focus on one aspect of oppression . . . While respecting each other's agendas, we have resolved to support one another as organizations, with the recognition that we may not always agree . . .
>
> Racism, sexism, classism, and heterosexism are all rooted in ignorance and violence . . .
>
> We will not be silenced, and we invite others to bring their voices, their minds, and their hearts into this struggle so that we can work for change. When you support one of these groups, you network with them all to dismantle systems of oppression.

It has become clear that multicultural demands in American schools do not develop in a vacuum. Indeed, there is considerable written evidence of a conviction that Western culture is constituted and defined by "a virtually uninterrupted series of crimes visited upon other groups, namely, blacks, women, homosexuals, and natives of the Third World."

Oh, really?

David Sacks and Peter Thiel have produced a work entitled *Multiculturalism and the Decline of Stanford*. In their sometimes amusing but no less deeply disturbing article, they chronicle Stanford University's 1989 creation of the Office for Multicultural Development, the purpose of which is "to integrate multiculturalism in" all university programs. (This was arguably anticlimactic since Stanford had already eliminated the study of Western Culture just two years before.)

On Stanford's decision, former Education Secretary, best-selling author of *The Book of Virtues*, and Roman Catholic William

Bennett commented that "a great university was brought low by the very forces which modern universities came into being to oppose—ignorance, irrationality, and intimidation." Alas, at this once great western university, "Western Culture" was eliminated as a course of study, and a new multicultural curriculum requirement called "Cultures, Ideas, and Values" was created.

Allow me to share with you, courtesy of Messrs. Sacks and Thiel, just a few examples of the extremes of this multicultural curriculum:

> ➤ The class "19th Century American History," taught by Professor Estelle Freedman, devoted one-half of class time to a study of women, as they had constituted one-half of the U.S. population during this time. As a result, the class did not have enough time to learn about the War of 1812.

> ➤ Religious Studies 8, entitled "Religions in America," is a course that can be counted toward three different graduation requirements. It devoted entire lectures to shamanism, the Peyote Cult, and the Kodiak sect, but none to the Catholic Church. When discussed at all, Christianity was viewed from a feminist or gay "perspective" through such works as "Jesus Acted Up: A Gay and Lesbian Manifesto," "A Second Coming Out," and "Beyond the Father: Towards a Philosophy of Women's Liberation."

> ➤ History 267, "The History of Rights in the United States," never even studied the Declaration of Independence or the Constitution but instead centered on a vigorous argument for special minority privileges.

It should be emphasized that these classes were not on the fringes of an otherwise stellar Stanford education. While there was no graduation requirement in American history, students were required to take at least one course on feminism, one on race theory, and one on Third World cultures.

In summary, most students spent close to half of their four years at Stanford (at approximately $30,000 per year) studying thoroughly politicized multicultural requirements. The new multiculturalists think they can reduce the world to a few simple variables. Indeed, their methodology is based on what Sacks and Thiel call a "multicultural paradigm (that) always takes precedence over the evidence, and ensures that the desired conclusion will be reached."

More extrema, to be sure.

As cited earlier in this work, one of Harvard University president Lawrence Summers's 'disappointments' with Cornel West was the latter's contributions to the epidemic of grade inflation on that university's campus. At the time of this episode, Mr. Summers and at least some of his colleagues were considering what to do about it.

Enter my long lost cousin, Harvey Mansfield, a professor of government at Harvard, who has told it like it is. About Harvard's grade inflation, he has written:

> . . . we might pause to reflect on how Harvard got into this mess. We could begin with who is responsible. The answer, without hesitation, is America's liberals: Our liberals own our universities. To be a conservative professor in America—and especially at the most prestigious universities—is a lonely life spent fighting down your indignation, perfecting your sarcasm, and whistling in the wind. Liberals are so much in charge that they hardly know it.
>
> Liberal policies . . . have transferred authority from professor to student. More and more, the university curriculum offers choice to students, implying that they are sovereign consumers free to pick what they want. Even core requirements can be fulfilled in several ways. In keeping

> with the philosophy of multiculturalism it is thought wrong
> to "privilege" courses on Western civilization by requiring
> them, despite the fact that it is our civilization, and that,
> because it is the only self-critical civilization, it is better than
> the others.

Professor Mansfield is referring, of course, to universities like Stanford where the course "Western Culture" was eliminated from the curriculum in order "to integrate multiculturalism" into all university programs, as addressed above.

⧗

Here's one of my own real-life experiences with political correctness and feminism.

From 1991 to 1995 I was an assistant professor of banking at Hofstra University's business school in Hempstead, New York. During this period, the University's administration decided to rename the business school in honor of Frank G. Zarb, an alumnus and a prominent Wall Street executive, now retired.

To commemorate the occasion, a large bronze plaque was struck and mounted on the wall near the entrance to Weller Hall, the "home" of Hofstra's business school. The wording on the plaque contained a reference to Mr. Zarb as "Chairman" of one of the University's earlier fundraising campaigns. Naturally, I suppose, the "sexist" and politically incorrect title "Chairman" touched the nerves of some female faculty members. These "feminazis," as radio talk-show host Rush Limbaugh might call them, insisted that "Chairman" be changed to "Chairperson" or, simply, "Chair;" never mind that "Chairman" was in fact Mr. Zarb's actual title. These women raised such a furor over this perceived injustice obviously derived from male hegemony that the University's administration eventually capitulated, removed the plaque and had it restruck to meet the demands of these strident ladies.

Despite my position as a faculty member, I protested in a letter to then-Hofstra president James Shuart, a former Marine, but was advised in a letter from him that the recasting of the plaque would be financed by private monies, as if that were the only issue. While it would surely have been an egregious misuse of the University's funds for Hofstra to have paid for this fiasco of political correctness run amok, Jim, a good man in my view, missed the point and an important principle, as well as an opportunity to exercise firm leadership.

⏳

Fresh from the foibles of Hofstra's female faculty, I now turn to Clare Booth Luce Policy Institute founder and president Michelle Easton, who has provided some keen insight into how 'feminazis' get that way.

In a March 28, 1996 article entitled *The Finishing School of the '90s,* Ms. Easton critiqued women's studies programs at prestigious American colleges and universities. At Columbia, for example, one of the "Approved Women's Studies Courses" was "The Invisible Woman in Literature: The Lesbian Literary Tradition." In Dartmouth's course entitled "Women and Religion: New Explorations": "Study will be given to . . . the documentation of sexism and androcentrism in the canonical writings and institutional forms of Judaism and Christianity." These course descriptions are reportedly typical of some 619 offerings across the nation in women's studies programs listed in 1990 by the National Women's Studies Association.

According to Ms. Easton, most of these courses explicitly "endorse a political and social ideology rather than explore an intellectual discipline. Most include courses that commend lesbianism, abortion and sexual freedom. Most are antireligious, antiestablishment, anti-male. Most call for a radical reconstruction of society. And most are intellectually superficial and slovenly."

Continued Ms. Easton:

Instead of preparing for specific careers, those who have

majored in feminist studies have spent four years doing little else than blathering about gender and feeling their way around in the discrete world of feminist ideology. They don't have to "know" anything to complete the program. They simply have to "feel" right about the agenda of the National Abortion Rights Action League [NARAL] and the National Organization for Women [NOW].

Ms. Easton concludes that "Instead of preparing their graduates to wrest control of the nation's destiny from the hands of an oppressive patriarchy, feminist educators . . . are transforming young women into a cackling brood with little exposure to the knowledge and skills necessary to assume leadership in the economic and political arenas."

This is so obvious to so many that I cannot help but wonder why so few, to whom it should matter so much, continuously fail to appreciate what is happening to them.

Some readers may recall the national history assessment in the mid-eighties that revealed that two-thirds of the nation's 17-year-olds could not place the American Civil War in the correct half-century. Even more recently a young American woman was asked in which war George Washington fought; without hesitation she answered: World War I. This led the first Bush administration in 1992 to award a contract to the University of California at Los Angeles (UCLA) to develop voluntary national standards for what students should know about American and world history. The release of the standards two years later ignited a firestorm of controversy. Today, quite properly, these original standards have been revised and improved.

According to Diane Ravitch of New York University and Pulitzer Prize-winner Arthur Schlesinger, Jr., "Some critics were originally concerned that students might regard Europeans as the only people who ever engaged in the slave trade. The revised standards now refer to the varieties of slavery practiced by Africans and their role in delivering slaves to the Atlantic passage."

Continued Ravitch and Schlesinger, "The Westward movement in American history, previously ascribed to the greed and rapacity of 'restless white Americans,' is now undertaken by Americans animated not only by land hunger and 'the ideology of Manifest Destiny,' but by 'the optimism that anything was possible with imagination, hard work, and the maximum freedom of the individual.' There is no glossing over the Mexican-American War or the brutal treatment of American Indians, but the overall picture raises fair questions instead of offering questionable moral judgments."

According to John Leo in his *On Society* column in the April 15, 1996 edition of *U.S. News & World Report*, "In the multicultural wars, one of the clever moves by the multiculturalists was simply to add an 's' to the term 'American people.' This apparently harmless plural effortlessly removed the (word) *unum* from *e pluribus unum* in the state history standards of Colorado and in the first and very controversial version of the national history standards."

As John Fonte of the American Enterprise Institute has said, this was a "revolutionary" step, implying that America is a loose multinational confederation of separate peoples, something like the former Yugoslavia. In the much improved national standards, all the "American peoples" have been changed back to "American people."

In his 1995 book *The End of Racism: Principles for a Multiracial Society*, Dinesh D'Souza, a research scholar at the American Enterprise Institute, tells us that Western culture is perceived (by liberals) to be historically defined by racism, sexism, heterosexism, colonialism and imperialism. This is the reason that American multiculturalists look to other cultures to find some alternative to the "oppressive institutions of the white man."

However, when scholars seriously examine the cultures of Asia,

Africa and Latin America, they cannot help but notice that, as Mr. D'Souza put it, "these cultures are rudely inhospitable to the moral and political hopes of their Western admirers."

Interestingly, non-Western cultures do not include traditions of equality, which is, of course, a foundation of multiculturalist philosophy. For example, in India there is a long-standing caste system that has enjoyed the full blessing of Hinduism. Also, slavery was practiced in most societies for literally thousands of years without indication of local opposition.

Women, according to D'Souza, are treated very badly in many non-Western cultures. Here are some examples:

> The Chinese practiced female foot-binding for hundreds of years.
> In an old Indian practice called *sati*, wives were urged to ascend the burning funeral pyres of their dead husbands.
> Polygamy is still common in many parts of the world.
> In Islamic societies today, women are denied the rights of men.
> Genital mutilation of women is commonplace in parts of Africa and the Arab world.
> Finally, homosexuality is a crime or an illness, as defined in the legal and medical literature of some Third World countries.

Just as multiculturalism often misrepresents other peoples, the emphasis in the West on the equality of all cultures results in imbalance and distortion. Thus, in practice, multiculturalism frequently misrepresents both American and world history. In the last analysis, America's future will almost certainly be racially diverse but culturally Western. In other words, America can or may have already become a *multiracial* society but it is unlikely to become a *multicultural* society.

If we cannot end now our differences, at least we can help make the world safe for diversity.

—John F. Kennedy [1963]

On a related topic, namely, diversity, which has attained godlike status in the politically correct crowd, I have longstanding reservations, which arise because diversity for diversity's sake trashes the concept of merit. After all, diversity begets just another form of discrimination, that is, reverse discrimination. (A case involving the liberal and unfair "affirmative action" policies of the University of Michigan is to be considered by the Supreme Court.)

In this connection, I find the words of Wendy McElroy, editor of *Ifeminists.com* strongly on point. "Government," she writes, "should get out of the diversity business. Employers should determine their own employment practices and be left to pay the high economic cost of discrimination." She concludes:

> Personally, I hope employers who discriminate on the basis of anything but merit go bankrupt. I am willing to picket and write articles to hurry that process along. But I am not willing to use the law to pry open their doors of business. Destroying the right of non-association sets too dangerous a precedent. It means I may someday have to invite those employers into my own home or business. And I value highly the right not to associate with bigots.

I couldn't agree more. The truth today is that many of those in our country who claim to oppose bigotry of any sort are in fact themselves bigots.

Relative extrema are once more abundant.

Therefore I am content with weakness, with mistreatment, with distress, with persecutions and difficulties for the sake of Christ; for when I am powerless, it is then that I am strong.

—2 Corinthians 12:10

48

GAY DOESN'T MEAN MERRY ANY MORE

*The placement of a homosexual couple in a position of counselor
to teenage children is . . . an arrogant challenge to the Judeo-
Christian principles that underlay the foundation of [Exeter]
Academy at its birth. It is breathtaking in its audacity as,
indeed, is the request that the school's alumni should finance the
downward progress of its moral instruction.*

—Charles H. Morin, Esq.

ere I will share my views on perhaps the most prominent and outspoken multicultural segment in our society today: the gay and lesbian movement. It is such that many young people, as well as others, have come to regard homosexuality as a legitimate analogue of heterosexuality, that is, an acceptable lifestyle. After all, aren't gay men and lesbians born that way?

In March 1996 in San Francisco, according to *The New York Times*, "By the power invested in him by this bastion of liberal politics, Mayor Willie L. Brown, Jr. pronounced dozens of gay and lesbian couples virtual spouses in the first such mass mock nuptials held by an American city."

One may surmise that the mayor must have strongly believed that this "domestic partnership ceremony," as it was called, was appropriate despite a minor detail that California law, not to mention that of the other forty-nine states, does not recognize marriages between homosexuals. In this connection, even if one does not read or subscribe to the authority of the Scriptures, we humans *were* created male and female, and I would submit that that was and still is for a purpose.

Recent court rulings and political developments would appear to make the legalization of homosexual marriage very likely (at least in the states of Hawaii, Massachusetts and Vermont). Much like the issue of gays in the U.S. military, government recognition of "same-sex marriage" may become reality before many Americans have an opportunity to consider fully its adverse consequences. To be sure, we are already seeing gay marriages depicted on television, notably on the NBC popular sitcom *Friends*. (It may be of interest too that the term homosexual marriage has been replaced, according to John Leo, with the "more abstract and perhaps more soothing," as well as politically correct, same-sex marriage.) In keeping with these developments, *The New York Times* announced in August of this year that it would begin announcing same-sex marriages in its wedding pages. My only question is, what took it so long?

I would like to share with you a new euphemism. "To the amazement of everyone," writes Mr. Leo, "pedophiles and some sex researchers now refer to adult sex with children as 'intergenerational intimacy.'" It would be interesting to speculate "how the rest of the perversions could be brightened up with spiffy new language. Perhaps necrophilia would emerge as 'post-terminal intimacy.'"

Alternatively, *The Advocate*, which bills itself as "the national gay & lesbian newsmagazine," has published this:

> (A)s gay men and lesbians have discovered the delights of sex, we have created a different agreement among ourselves . . . that every form of sexual conduct anywhere and at any time is good; sex is like a glass of water to drink whenever one is thirsty. . . . The conflict of [the Judeo-Christian versus 'gay liberation'] cultural agreements creates confusion in the minds of many gay people as to what is

'right'. I submit that *there is no right and wrong about sex,* only problems about self esteem and community survival.

I have a question for *The Advocate*: Do its editors genuinely believe that "there is no right or wrong about sex"? If so, then these people are intrinsically disordered. Such remarkable declarations notwithstanding, my principal concern in matters gay and lesbian is *not* sexual preference *per se* but rather that the gay and lesbian agenda in this country is fundamentally radical, and often militant, much like that of other so called 'oppressed' groups. Moreover, I, together with the vast preponderance of Americans and, probably, people of other nations too, am confident that there are legitimate issues of right and wrong when it comes to human sexual relationships.

"The Gay Manifesto," which first appeared in February 1987 in *Gay Community News*, now defunct, was read into *The Congressional Record* in 1989. It was written by Michael Swift at the request of *Gay Community News* and has been cited since by gay groups as a misrepresentation, even a "lie," by "The Conservative Religious Right." Specifically, these groups cite the omission in reprints of an "opening disclaimer" that they maintain preceded the body of the "Manifesto." For the record and to be fair, this disclaimer states that "This essay is an outré, madness, a tragic, cruel fantasy, an eruption of inner rage, on how the oppressed desperately dream of being the oppressor."

Here are excerpts from "The Gay Manifesto":

> We shall sodomize your sons, emblems of your feeble masculinity, of your shallow dreams and vulgar lies. We shall seduce them in your schools, in your dormitories, in your gymnasiums, in your locker rooms, in your sports arenas, in your seminaries, in your youth groups, in your movie theater bathrooms, in your army bunkhouses, in your truck stops, in your all-male clubs, in your houses of Congress, wherever men are with men together. Your sons shall become our minions and do our bidding. They

will be recast in our image. They will come to crave and adore us.

. . .

All laws banning homosexual activity will be revoked. Instead, legislation shall be passed which engenders love between men.

All homosexuals must stand together as brothers; we must be united artistically, philosophically, socially, politically and financially. We will triumph only when we present a common face to the vicious heterosexual enemy.

. . .

The family unit—spawning ground of lies, betrayals, mediocrity, hypocrisy and violence—will be abolished. The family unit, which only dampens imagination and curbs free will, must be eliminated.

All churches who condemn us will be closed. Our only gods are handsome young men. We adhere to a cult of beauty, moral and esthetic. All that is ugly and vulgar and banal will be annihilated. Since we are alienated from middle-class heterosexual conventions, we are free to live our lives according to the dictates of the pure imagination. For us too much is not enough.

. . .

We shall rewrite history, history filled and debased with your heterosexual lies and distortions.

We shall be victorious because we are fueled with the ferocious bitterness of the oppressed . . . We too are capable of firing guns and manning the barricades of the ultimate revolution.

Tremble, hetero swine, when we appear before you without our masks.

Gay manifesto? "Gay" used to be synonymous with "merry." Why, this "eruption of inner rage" is nothing short of a declaration of sexual terrorism.

⧗

What about so called pedophile priests? The answer is simple and straightforward. Get rid of them, and with all due dispatch. Yes, get them out of the priesthood, out of the parishes and away from young people without delay. There is no room for sexually abusive priests, or other abusers, anywhere in the Church or, for that matter, in society at large. Out, *now*! The same goes for those Church prelates who permitted the abusers to continue their 'ministries' by transferring them from one parish to another. As far as I am concerned, those Church leaders who were enablers of abusers continuing their ministries should be in jail.

One of the underpinnings of this crisis is the fact that the Church knowingly ordained gay men to the priesthood. Some of these individuals saw the seminary and the priesthood as safe havens for their sexual disorder. Indeed, some even regarded a life of celibacy as appropriate to their situation. Tragically, in more than a few cases, their homosexual tendencies surfaced and their targets, in the overwhelming majority of cases, were post-pubescent males. Already physically and sexually mature, these young men were vulnerable to the overtures of sexually predatory homosexual males who happened to be priests. They became victims of abuse because they were not yet emotionally or psychologically mature enough to deal with overt sexual situations, especially with a man. Moreover, in all likelihood, they knew and trusted the abusive priest prior to the sexual abuse.

Again the Catholic League's Bill Donohue provides valuable perspective:

> The sex abuse scandal in the Catholic Church has provoked a torrent of criticism, much of it fair and deserved. There are also reports of priests being under siege in the wake of the sex abuse scandal in the Catholic Church. Once again the few miscreants who have caused this problem are just that, few in number. Virtually all the priests I know are angry and saddened by the scandal. Moreover, they are

good men who would neither commit nor countenance evil
acts against children or adolescents.

At the same time there was an explosion of bigotry, some of
which came from the ranks of radical feminists.
According to the Catholic League, on March 20, 2002,
Maureen Dowd of *The New York Times* went ballistic putting the
Catholic Church in the same camp with the Taliban and al Qaeda.
Two days later syndicated gossip columnist Liz Smith said that
Dowd deserved a Pulitzer Prize for her remarks. Smith added that
Dowd's "stunning column may have done more for the cause of
women than the entire feminist attitude in the world."

In the March 25th edition of *The Nation*, Margaret Spillane
accused the Boston hierarchy of "treating women as contaminants
and children as invisible," maintaining that the "real goal" of Boston
Archbishop Bernard Cardinal Law is to "make a permanent move
to Rome as the first American Pope."

Wrote Donohue: "Even in the asylum such voices would not
be heard. Still, the fact that they are coming from mainstream
journalists is revealing."

He continued:

> Radical feminists have long hated the Catholic Church.
> Their agenda has never been the interests of housewives or
> working mothers. Instead, it has always been a lust for power
> coupled with an embrace of the most libertine conceptions
> of sexuality. Angry with nature and with nature's God, they
> see the Catholic Church as the last bastion of traditional
> morality. Therefore, the Church must fall.
>
> The Catholic Church has weathered many storms in
> two millennia. Some of its wounds have been self-inflicted
> and some have been the result of unrelieved bigotry. Dowd,
> Smith and Spillane are wrong, however, in thinking that
> they will end up on the winning side. Lay Catholics have
> got their number. In one sense they've done us a favor:
> they've cleared the battlefield of all camouflage.

For my part, the Church will certainly weather this storm for I believe what Jesus said to his apostles two millennia ago: "I am with you always, even to the end of time."

As a footnote to all of this, noted author and counselor Father Benedict Groeschel commented at a breakfast I attended on April 7, 2002 that there are seventy-nine members of the clergy behind bars in the U.S. for sexual abuse of minors. Of these, he said, forty-nine are ministers from various Protestant denominations and most of them are married. The remaining thirty are comprised of Catholic priests, Jewish rabbis and Islamic clerics.

Another footnote: As of October 2002, *two-thirds of one percent* of Catholic priests have stepped aside this year pending *accusations* against them. This is a miniscule percentage that is less than that of sex offenders in the population at large—and I am referring to *accusations*, not firm findings or admissions of guilt. Even *The New York Times* has reported that less than two percent of priests ordained between 1950 and 2001 have been *accused* of sexual abuse. Furthermore, it has cited studies that today more priests and seminarians identify themselves as gay than in decades past.

Yes, offenders should be punished to the full extent of the law, but those accused priests who are in fact innocent should have complete access to the presumption of innocence until proven guilty. Unfortunately, this due process has become in many instances a rush to judgment against them.

In the last analysis, it is incontrovertible that the admission of gay men into Catholic seminaries, and their eventual ordination to the priesthood, have been major factors in the sexual abuse crisis facing the Church.

⌛

Charles H. Morin, Esq., the distinguished senior partner of the lawfirm of Dickstein Shapiro Morin & Oshinsky LLP in Washington, D.C., wrote on October 3, 2000 a letter to William H. Connelly of the Heritage Circle at Phillips Exeter Academy in

Exeter, New Hampshire. Once a student there, Mr. Morin first credited Exeter for having "influenced enormously my progress through the years that followed." Then he addressed his main issue:

> Now, the governing body of the school has apparently concluded that a homosexual couple is to assume the position of guidance and advice to young boys and girls ranging in age from fourteen to nineteen that is, teenagers at a critical stage of judgmental development. I am sure the couple will be charming, intelligent, caring and everything else that's good. They will also be a conspicuous example that the homosexual life style is a perfectly normal and acceptable alternative to traditional marriage of a man and woman.
>
> I happen to be Catholic as, I am sure are many of our alumni. Many are also Jewish or members of other Christian churches, all of whose guiding moral and spiritual beliefs are founded upon the Bible—the Old and/or New Testaments. My own Catechism (and I would guess yours) teaches me that, basing itself on Sacred Scripture, tradition has declared that homosexuality is intrinsically disordered and cannot be approved under any circumstances. Protestant and Jewish teaching is the same. We are also taught that homosexuals must be accepted with respect, compassion and sensitivity, and that, I am sure, Exeter has traditionally done. But Exeter has apparently decided to go beyond this teaching and notoriously approve the relationship as one to be admired and emulated.
>
> So what I am saying is that this latest activity of the Academy which, I note, bore the unanimous approval of the Trustees, is a flagrant insult to Christian and Jew alike. I guess these people are trying to make a statement: that Exeter is all-inclusive, welcoming all to come to her arms. But that statement has long since been made and exemplified.
>
> The placement of a homosexual couple in a position of counselor to teenage children is not a statement at all—it is, rather, an arrogant challenge to the Judeo-Christian

principles that underlay the foundation of the Academy at its birth. It is breathtaking in its audacity as, indeed, is the request that the school's alumni should finance the downward progress of its moral instruction.

So no, Bill, I can't join the Heritage Circle, or even gnaw at its circumference—even though I do admire your personal efforts to do what must be a very difficult job. I could only wish that the circumstances were different.

Thus did Exeter manage to lose at least one substantial benefactor. I wonder how many others might react similarly and, by the way, appropriately.

Another prominent voice that has weighed in on the issue of homosexuality is that of Chuck Colson, Charlie Morin's best friend. A non-Catholic but a deeply religious Christian, he is a friend and former Marine who once worked for President Nixon. He has written:

> *Why does homosexuality, of all issues, arouse such outrage? Why can't Christians just live and let live?* secular critics ask. Though gay groups and liberal clerics have tried to find ways to justify it (like claiming the apostle Paul was gay), the Bible condemns homosexual behavior. But so does it condemn lying, murder, disobedience to parents, and unethical business practices. The Scriptures don't grade sins on the curve: *all* sins, from little "white" lies to murder, are cosmic treason.
>
> Homosexual sin cuts to the heart of the creation covenant. In the Genesis account, God speaks the world into creation. He shapes man in His own image, anticipates his loneliness, creates a wife exactly suited to him. And God is no Victorian killjoy when it comes to sex. He invented it.
>
> The pattern is clear: One man cleaving to one woman, bearing children, raising them up in the fear of the Lord. It is a morality so biblically and biologically based as to be the self-evident foundation of civilization.

Next I come to an episode that was, in a word, disgraceful. Again I cobble together valuable descriptive material from the archives of the Catholic League.

If there were one event in which activist organizations engaged that was particularly offensive to Catholics, not to mention other ordinary and decent citizens, it would be the illegal march by homosexuals that took place up New York City's Fifth Avenue on June 26th, 1994. The so called "Gay Pride Parade," this obscene spectacle has been held every year since 1970. Pride? Why pride? What pride? I am heterosexual. It has nothing to do with pride; it is simply a matter of fact.

Then-New York City Mayor Rudolph Giuliani, who is a Catholic and a graduate of two Catholic schools on Long Island, succeeded in getting a court order to stop the march. Nevertheless, when the homosexual group decided to march anyway, the mayor not only permitted it to proceed with impunity, he ordered the New York Police Department to escort the criminals along the avenue. Yet, it is not what happened *on* Fifth Avenue that angered Catholics most of all.

The radical homosexual contingent that marched up Fifth Avenue did so for one reason: so they could participate in an anti-Catholic demonstration in front of St. Patrick's Cathedral. When these marchers reached the Cathedral, they yelled—in unison—four-letter epithets and made obscene gestures at the people on the steps of the Church. Some of these protesters were dressed as Cardinals, others as nuns and priests, and many wore nothing at all. They sat down in the street, did satanic dances and generally showed as much disrespect as they could. Some even masturbated. No one was arrested.

What is particularly odious about this case was the refusal in the New York media to brand the marchers as anti-Catholic bigots. Yet, had this happened in front of a Jewish synagogue or a Black Baptist Church, the charges of bigotry would have been swift and decisive. Indeed, it is doubtful that the mayor would have authorized such a parade in the first place. If we keep in mind that former Mayor Giuliani *is* a Catholic, he not only allowed the march to take place, he also never condemned it for what it was—a vile, public exhibition of anti-Catholic bigotry. (In fairness to Mr. Giuliani, however, he did put out the word that the police would not tolerate the kind of behavior the following year that was tolerated in 1994.)

Now permit a contrast of this with bigotry suffered by other segments of our society. The terms racist, sexist and homophobic are bandied about so recklessly that those who ask for proof are often regarded as part of the problem. It is as though mere declarations of bigotry are evidence enough. After all, just consider how many people thought, during the years of the Clinton administration, which included the Whitewater and Monica Lewinsky scandals, as well as Vince Foster's "suicide," that merely *asking* Hillary Rodham Clinton to testify before a grand jury was proof positive that there is sexism in the land.

As Bill Donohue has written, "If multiculturalism is taken seriously, then today's educators [and, I would add, political leaders] must begin to address the problem of anti-Catholicism in such programs. If those in the workforce are interested in promoting greater sensitivity to workers of various cultural backgrounds, then they should show more concern for the sensibilities of Roman Catholics. Those in the media for whom tolerance is a mantra will similarly have to question whether their work contributes to tolerance, or intolerance, of Catholics. And government officials for whom bigotry is the world's greatest sin will find a new source of evil" in today's ubiquitous anti-Catholicism.

With attribution again to the Catholic League, here's a real beauty: In November 2001 a gay activist actually equated the Pope with Osama bin Laden!

"Flash! This just in: All the while that Afghanistan's ruling Taliban has been protecting Osama bin Laden, Italy has been harboring another omnipotent religious zealot, one who condemns

us Western sinners and incites violence with his incendiary rhetoric."
So wrote Bill Donohue in a League news release.

That is how Michelangelo Signorile begins his article, "The
Gay-Bashing Pope," in the November 21-27, 2001 edition of the
alternative weekly newspaper, *The New York Press.*

The pope, according to Signorile, is guilty of "inspiring
thugs across the globe who commit hate crimes against
homosexuals, a form of terrorism if ever there were one." The
writer, who is the father of "outing" (the practice of making
public a gay man's or lesbian's sexual preference), is upset with
the Church's teaching that holds homosexuality to be
"intrinsically disordered," a view with which I wholly agree.
Put somewhat less delicately, this means that the human rectum
was not designed by our Creator for penetration. Or, as Don Imus
once declared to his homosexual friends on his morning radio
program, "Guys, it doesn't go there."

Many Catholics and other Christians are disappointed with
Mich. After all, as Donohue quipped, "we never thought that
anyone who has had as much practice turning the other cheek
would ever write such an intrinsically disordered article."

I have written earlier of my friend Joe Moosbrugger, a 1961
Chaminade alumnus, a former Marine and a Vietnam veteran. A
few years ago he took issue with a David Carpenter, a student at
Bucknell University over an article in *The Bucknellian*, the campus
newspaper. Specifically, in a piece entitled "Getting Out of the
Bucknell Closet: A Personal Narrative," Mr. Carpenter went into
considerable detail explaining his sexual orientation and imploring
other gays and lesbians to "come out" at Bucknell.

As Joe wrote in a letter to *The Bucknellian*,

> As a Bucknell Parent, . . . I do not feel one's sexual
> preferences are of any concern to the general public or in
> this case the general university community. Sexual orientation

should be a private matter and need not become public unless one's civil rights are being threatened. Basically, most of us just don't care.

Whereas Joe's words echo some views I have already expressed herein, it seems that Mr. Carpenter crossed another line, and Joe properly cut him no slack. His letter continues:

> (A)s a former U.S. Marine Corps Captain and as a Veteran having served in Vietnam in 1968–1969, I take serious issue with David Carpenter paraphrasing a Marine Corps slogan to bring focus to his homosexuality ("The Few, The Proud, The Homosexual").
>
> It is his affair, to which he has every right, as long as other's *(sic)* rights are equally respected. But, PLEASE, David should not feel he is advancing his cause by trying to ride along with one of the finest, most respected military organizations in the world, and one which I feel we should all respect more than he recently did.

Shortly after publication of his letter Joe was targeted in *The Bucknellian*'s "Letters to the Editor" section for 'missing the student's point' and for 'criticizing, not respecting' the student. In the end, Joe wrote to me, "They wore me out! I got to a point where I had said my piece & didn't care to contest or argue their (youthful) view of the world, because I'm certain that my thoughts would only be met by their aggressive intransigence."

It is certainly not surprising that Joe's letter attracted such reactions, given not only the embedded opposition to the military on America's college campuses but also the pro-homosexual atmosphere engendered there by the politically correct crowd in their undying quest for diversity. Still, I wish Joe had written at least one more letter.

An interesting perspective on gay rights (and abortion) comes from Don Feder, writing in *The Weekly Standard*:

> An Associated Press story on a school prayer case before the Supreme Court begins, "Prayer in public schools, for 40 years a divisive and politically charged issue, split the Supreme Court anew as the justices heard arguments yesterday over letting students lead stadium crowds in invocations at high school football games."
>
> Only your average reporter would describe an issue on which upwards of 75 percent of the American people agree as "divisive and politically charged." By the way, you will never see abortion or gay marriage characterized in most newspapers as "divisive and politically charged," even though the public is genuinely divided on the first and overwhelmingly opposed to the second. When the media say an issue is "divisive," they mean it divides majority opinion from their opinion.

Sad but true.

Another insight, this one perhaps startling to some, comes from a young man who has been a friend of my family for more than a decade. Several years ago he wrote a letter to Mame and me initially thanking us for the many good times he shared with us at our GC home. A few paragraphs later he informed us that he was a gay man, which did not come as a surprise.

What was surprising, however, was the expressed unhappiness, even torment, that he was experiencing in his life because of his sexual "preference," to use the politically correct euphemism. Indeed, in his case, it was no preference at all, inasmuch as he stated in writing that, if there were a pill that would change him from homosexual to heterosexual, he "would be first in line" to buy it. Our friend is not alone, for there are many male homosexuals who, according to Paul Popper, Ph.D., want "to leave the lifestyle, increase their male identification, and change the orientation of their sexual-object choice."

Through church programs and his own private practice, Dr. Popper has written that he became involved in this work "(b)ecause I saw the pain of these men and because I thought I could help." This is precisely why I have often questioned—and strongly doubted—the notion of so called "Gay Pride." In other words, if gays and lesbians are so insistent on expostulating "Gay Pride," why don't heterosexuals behave similarly and extol "Straight Pride"? Once again, sexual orientation is, or should be, a private matter and not one of constant public proclamation.

Alas, Dr. Popper has also encountered "the cultural, political and professional forces" working to denigrate and eliminate his important psychotherapeutic work with gay men. These forces are unswerving in their profoundly flawed insistence that gay lifestyles are not only acceptable but the equivalent of heterosexual relationships. What is offensive—indeed, anathema—to them is the plain truth that their sexual behavior is intrinsically disordered and potentially lethal. They know it but, in their arrogance and self-loathing, will deny it, in many tragic cases, to the death.

> *Cases of clerical misconduct with minors appear regularly in virtually every denomination and faith-tradition. . . . This is not a celibacy problem with frustrated priests being driven to perversion and molestation.*

> —Philip Jenkins

49

WILL WE SAVE THE BABY HUMANS?

Nowadays the reward is for those who make right appear wrong.

—Terence [circa 161 B.C.]

Whatever the world's greatest sin may be, I offer here my views on what is arguably the consummate evil and the deepest depravity in our society today.

With capital punishment acceptable, let's devise a modern method of execution for especially evil persons—say, Osama bin Laden, if he is brought to account for the terrorist atrocities of 9/11. "Why not stick a catheter in his brain and suck it out until his skull collapses?"

These are words taken from the lead editorial in *The Wall Street Journal* of April 25, 1996. Having entitled the piece "Who Are the Extremists?," the newspaper's editors later made clear that they were not truly serious about such an extreme method of execution. Quite correct, they reasoned that no one would ever think of doing such a thing to another human being—not even Osama bin Laden.

Yet, the editorial continued, "the President of the United States stands up foursquare for doing it to babies still in the womb but nearing birth, vetoing Congress' attempt to ban this procedure in late term abortions." Perhaps not surprisingly, the president at the time was Bill Clinton.

Now, let's be clear about the procedure. Washington, D.C.'s former Cardinal James Hickey described "partial birth abortion (as) three-fourths infanticide, one-fourth abortion." In his May 1,

1996 *Respect Life* column in *The Long Island Catholic*, entitled *Embracing infanticide*, my friend Monsignor James Lisante was more graphic. Here are his words:

> The baby which is killed is almost completely out of the birth canal. Only its head remains inside its mother's body. The child is still alive and able to feel pain. And then, with a nearly born child, the doctor provides the death blow using a scissors inserted into the base of the skull.

Mr. Clinton, the Monsignor continued, "finds no overwhelming condemnation for this newest form of depravity. He goes blithely on his way, still publicly proclaiming that he finds abortion to be 'wrong,' while still doing everything he can to expand the right to kill."

"Mr. Clinton calls this 'sad but necessary.' In that too, he lies. Even the author of this procedure in text and on tape admits that in over 80 percent of partial birth abortions, the procedure is elective. Not necessary but elective." *Elective*, for God's sake!

True to form in trying to escape responsibility for and 'spin' this butchery of humankind, Mr. Clinton maintained that his veto of a Congressional ban on partial birth abortion was required by a constitutional obligation to enforce Roe vs. Wade, the 1973 Supreme Court decision that made abortion legal. This Clinton lie was quickly disproved by Boston's Cardinal Bernard Law, recently resigned, who stated that, "as the President and everyone familiar with abortion law knows, neither the Roe (Supreme) court nor any other has ever ruled on the constitutionality of a law against killing a child during the process of being born."

Regarding the old Clinton line that partial birth abortion is necessary to save the life of the mother, Cardinal Hickey concluded that "Medical experts do not maintain that this procedure saves the life of the mother nor does she derive any other medical benefit. What we do know is that partial birth abortion takes the life of a fully formed infant about to take its first breath." Once more, 80% of partial-birth abortions are *elective*.

For his position and his veto, Bill Clinton received not

condemnation but *praise*, as the *Journal* put it, "from all those most eager to brand the Christian right and other abortion foes as 'extremists.' . . . (F)or all his posturing President Clinton remains the captive of his party's own . . . extremists. . . . Why else would [he] end up in favor of doing to the most innocent humans what no one would do to the most diabolical?"

> *Life is so much more than having "things"—bearing life from love can make that love grow into immeasurable proportions if you let it. Raising children is not easy; but, again, nothing worth much is.*

> —Mary Ann Mansfield

At the time of the election of November 6, 2001, according to the Catholic League, Americans United for Separation of Church and State accused the bishops of New Jersey of interfering in the electoral process simply because they voiced an opinion on abortion that the radical group abhors. The bishops in the Garden State had urged Catholics to "use their voting privilege to reflect a choice of candidates who respect and sustain the dignity of all human life." This was enough for Americans United to say that the pro-life candidate for governor, Bret Schundler, benefited from an "implicit endorsement."

Americans United took specific aim at Archbishop John Myers. They said the new archbishop "is well known in the Catholic Church for his hardline to politics." They mention that while serving as bishop in Peoria, Illinois, Myers issued a pastoral letter saying it is "morally illicit" for Catholics to vote for pro-abortion candidates.

This outburst by Americans United for Separation of Church and State shows how little respect it has for the Constitution of the United States and how downright hypocritical it is. Catholic bishops do not check their First Amendment right to freedom of speech at the church door. Indeed, they have every right to address any public issue they want.

Americans United is led by Rev. Barry Lynn, a minister in the

United Church of Christ. His religion teaches him the value of abortion. Since 1970, his religion has maintained a strong pro-abortion position. Indeed, he himself has boldly proclaimed in public his support for abortion rights. Now, according to the principle by which he judges New Jersey bishops, he and his religion are in violation of the Constitution. Of course, there is no principle involved, just politics as usual. The Catholic League expressed delight that Americans United was upset with Archbishop Myers. That's a good sign and another reason why the new archbishop won the League's support and mine as well.

Consider for a moment the Herculean efforts our society undertakes to save premature babies, even ones afflicted by their mothers with alcohol abuse, crack cocaine or AIDS. Can it be that our society truly believes that fetuses of the same stage of development and same prospects for viability are not deserving of some degree of respect and protection as fellow humans? At least liberal extremists think so.

Our Federal government has extensive rules and regulations on the humane treatment of animals in biomedical research. These regulations mandate "avoidance of minimization of discomfort, distress, and pain," and specify that "Surgical or other painful procedures should not be performed on unanesthetized animals paralyzed by chemical agents."

Late at night on July 18th of this year the U.S. Senate passed the Born-Alive Infants Protection Act, which President Bush signed on August 5th. According to my friend Bill Donohue in an article entitled "The Rediscovery of Evil Since 9-11,"

> The Democrats insisted on a voice vote so there would
> be no record of their decision. The bill, considered highly
> controversial by some Democrats, allows doctors to treat
> children who survive an abortion. That's right. It has long
> been legal in this country to allow a baby that survives an
> abortion to die on an operating table while doctors and
> nurses do nothing. Other forms of infanticide, such as partial-

birth abortion, persist: it is still legal to stick a scissors into an infant's head when he's 80 percent born. This way there's little chance he won't be dead on arrival.

An irony in all of this is that those who are "pro-choice" (i.e., liberals) support permitting a woman to kill her unborn baby, while many, if not most, of the same people oppose choice for that same woman to choose her child's school. Conservatives believe the exact opposite.

God help us!

⌛

On the cover of Rabbi Daniel Lapin's book *America's Real War* is a subtitle that reads, "An Orthodox rabbi insists that Judeo-Christian values are vital for our nation's survival." His strong words are both appropriate and well timed.

A web site for the book tells us that "There is a tug of war going on for the future of America. At one end of the rope are those who think America is a secular nation; at the other end are those who believe religion is at the root of our country's foundation." We are experiencing, as award-winning actor Brian Dennehy once put it, "a crisis for the soul of America."

A classic example of relative extrema, this tug of war may well not be played out in my lifetime. Nevertheless, the necessity to revitalize the nation's spiritual vitality and to reemphasize genuine moral principles has never been more urgent. It is a message that is crucial for today, if tomorrow's outcomes are to be peaceful and favorable for all, both born and unborn.

> *Many American Jews instinctively oppose any public expression of Christianity. This opposition has had a corrosive effect on American life . . . . American Jews must stop devaluing the Judeo-Christian basis of America.*

—Dennis Prager, Jewish commentator

Part V
End Papers

I wrote you a long letter because I didn't have time to write a short one.

—P. Henry Mueller

50

A MARINE HERO OF YORE NAMED MANSFIELD

From the halls of Montezuma
To the shores of Tripoli,
We fight our country's battles
On the land as on the sea.

—From *The Marines' Hymn* [1847]

Born in Albany, New York, in February 1773, Duncan Mansfield enlisted in the Marine Corps in Philadelphia on August 11, 1798. He served until 1805 and attained the rank of sergeant. Alas, I have not been able to establish a link to Duncan as a likely ancestor.

In those days, according to author Paul Johnson, "the rulers of Algiers, Tunis and Tripoli," known collectively as the Barbary States, "had become notorious for harboring pirates and themselves engaging in piracy and the slave-trade in whites (chiefly captured seamen). European states found it convenient to ransom these unfortunates rather than go to war."

Admiral Nelson, who then commanded the British Mediterranean Fleet and was forbidden to carry out reprisals, wrote "My blood boils that I cannot chastise these pirates." The U.S., however, was determined to do something about them. Indeed, pirates were the main reason Congress established a navy in 1794. "In 1805," according to Mr. Johnson, "American marines marched across the desert from Egypt, forcing . . . Tripoli to . . . surrender all American captives." This performance is recalled to the present day in the Marines' Hymn with the lyrics, "From the halls of Montezuma to the shores of Tripoli."

While serving aboard the schooner *Enterprise* during the war with Tripoli, Sgt. Mansfield volunteered for the "cutting-out" expedition led by Lieutenant Stephen Decatur, Jr. on February 16, 1804. Lt. Decatur and his 84-man crew sailed the ketch *Intrepid*, disguised as an Arab ship, into Tripoli Harbor to destroy the recently captured U.S. frigate *Philadelphia* and prevent her use against the U.S. Lord Nelson, the former Admiral, called the action "the most bold and daring act of the age."

These exploits were reinforced in 1815 when Commodores Stephen Decatur and William Bainbridge conducted successful operations against all three of the Barbary States.

In light of modern-day terrorism originating in the Middle East and Africa, it is not a stretch to suggest that the roots thereof may be found in the methods of the Barbary pirates. Similarly, the 19th-century wars on piracy and the ensuing colonialism, according to Mr. Johnson, suggest that perhaps the only way to suppress criminal states is for the West to impose political control on them. Of course, such imposition would be politically incorrect, to say the least, according to those who today condemn Western culture as a primary source of evil in the world.

A U.S. Navy destroyer (DD-728) was named *Mansfield* in honor of Sgt. Duncan Mansfield. It was launched on January 29, 1944, and commissioned that same year on April 14th, thirteen days before my parents were married. *Mansfield* served throughout the Pacific theater in the war against Japan and also provided gunfire support in both the Korean and Vietnam Wars. Furthermore, she received five battle stars for World War II service, and three for Korean.

Of greatest interest to me is the fact that, of all the ships in the U.S. Navy, only destroyers are named for war heroes.

I seen my duty and I done it.

—Anonymous [19th Century]

51

CHARLES FRANCIS MANSFIELD

(OCTOBER 26, 1921–JULY 26, 1999)

If any of you ever visit my grave,
you're out of your goddam minds.

—Charles F. Mansfield
[October 9, 1980]

Make no mistake; my father was an original.
I have always admired him for what he accomplished.
Born in Manhattan, raised in the Bronx, and later a
resident of Brooklyn where the first four of his and my Mom's six
kids were born, he graduated from Brooklyn Prep, had his Fordham
University education interrupted by World War II Army Air Corps
service in the South Pacific campaign against Japan, and went on
to serve as president and chief executive officer of Marine Midland
Bank of New York and later as chairman and CEO of Continental
Copper and Steel Industries, now known as CCX Corporation.

By any contemporary measure, Dad was obviously a successful
public man. But I can tell you from the heart that he was a great
father. He enjoyed the important things of this world—his family,
his homes (in GC and Hutchinson Island, Florida) and his friends.
Although, in the tradition of men of Irish heritage, he rarely showed
his emotions, he was a man of deep and abiding love. Moreover, he
left this world with a clear heart and a clean soul.

At the time of his death, friends and family alike made some remarkable statements about my father. One recurring theme is that it seemed unimaginable that he could be dead, for he was such a strong, even intimidating figure. One of his friends affectionately called him "The Bear" and, and upon learning of his passing, told me that my Dad "really had the brass ones." I believe such characterizations may be common but, as many of those who knew him well also understood, much of his persona was a self-defense built in his early youth when both his natural parents died prematurely. Their deaths inevitably scarred him for life; they are the reasons he avoided hospitals and funeral parlors, unless he absolutely had to be there.

⧗

One of the great and characteristic stories about Dad involved his grandson, my son Chas, telling his grandfather that his wife Dawn was pregnant with Dad's first great-grandchild.

"Grandpa," asked Chas, "how do you feel about becoming a great-grandpa?"

There to witness the exchange between the two, I could see Dad's mental wheels turning.

"Chas," the old man asserted while lightly poking his index finger on Chas's chest, "I don't want any of this great-grandpa shit. You tell that kid I'm 'Uncle Charlie.'" That was vintage Charlie Mansfield, direct and earthy.

⧗

Another tale of Dad involves the dry martini—gin, not vodka—of which he was once an aficionado.

It was Thanksgiving weekend of 1962, and I had returned home from college for family holiday festivities. On that Friday evening Dad offered me a martini. Now, it should be understood that I was only seventeen and a half at the time (the legal age in New York was 18), and my consumption of alcoholic beverages had included a few beers only. Still, big college man that I must have fancied myself, I said, "Sure, Dad, why not?"

My father mixed a small pitcher of martinis, which he brought into the living room, where I awaited him and my first cocktail. He poured the libation, we toasted one another, and I tasted the icy, unusual concoction.

"Well, what do you think?" Dad asked.

"I love it," I said foolishly, not really knowing whether I did or not.

Dad then got serious. "Most people have to acquire a taste for martinis," he advised. "If you are going to drink them, you must remember this: A martini is like a woman's breast; one is too few, two are just right, and three are too many."

This proved to be sage advice.

Dad, as my mother, his wife of fifty-five years, knows better than anyone, was gentle and kind inside. For her he was even docile, not necessarily because she had him well trained but rather because he loved her. Indeed, he loved her more than anyone on earth.

On the evening before Dad passed away, he told Mom, "Mary, I'm going to tell you again now that I love you because I won't be here in the morning." At the moment of his unexpected passing early the next day, I was with my Mom as she held his hand and said, "I love you, Charlie, and I want to thank you for the wonderful life you have made for me."

A great man is one who reminds us of no one else. In giving Dad's eulogy on July 29, 1999, I asked the congregation of more than five hundred in St. Anne's Church in GC, "Have you ever heard anyone say, 'Charlie Mansfield reminds me of so and so' or 'So and so reminds me of Charlie Mansfield'?" In my then fifty-four years I hadn't.

There is so much I learned from my father. He taught me long ago to ride a bike, throw a ball, paint a house, cut a lawn and, most importantly, that life is too short to spend time doing things that are less than fulfilling. I learned from him never to give up on myself. Indeed, many times in my life when things got tough I had the courage and faith to keep going. I know my Dad was the original architect of those qualities in me, and I am deeply grateful to him for that. He gave good advice—and fewer orders, as the years passed.

His gifts to us include words of both wisdom and, often, incredibly zany humor. Many of his expressions will live on in the family lexicon as long as the rest of us do, and perpetuate his memory.

In a very real sense, Dad and I grew up together and became closer with each passing year. Yes, we occasionally butted heads, but how did he usually know what was right? More than once, for example, he told me, "Love and put your faith in God, live as a Christian and love your family." He often said that there were times in his life when all he could do was get on his knees at night and give his problem, whatever it was, to God.

Today, I believe I can take some solace from the hope that he knew how I still feel about him, for I still love him deeply. Dad was more than my father; he was my friend. It hurts now that he is gone.

In 1996, for my Dad's seventy-fifth birthday I wrote a poem for him, a few verses of which I repeat here:

> I have memories to last a lifetime, but here just a few:
> Seeing at Ebbets Field my first Dodger game with you;
> With Michael, Uncle Johnny and you summer fishing;
> And having your paternal support—never for it wishing.
>
> Now, your humility I must mention and then put aside

For you have precious little; so freely I chide.
Your personal strength and self-confidence
always stand out;
Though sometimes mistaken, you're never in doubt!

You are also a man who his own counsel keeps,
And year in and year out a rich harvest reaps;
Yet, the richness I mean here mere money transcends
For you truly care for your family and friends.

Husband, father, grandfather and great-grandfather all—
These have been your roles, and I hope you've had a ball!
Your family above all and, yes, your friends true,
For all you have given us deeply thank you.

Our lives are enriched by your goodness and love.
Now, long may you live blest by God above!

All of my Dad's family and friends will miss him for a long time to come. His children thank God for making him our father and allowing all six of us to know him for more than forty years.

The candle has burned down and gone out but it will warm us all the days of our lives.

Thank you, Dad.

Requiescat in pace.

> *Love for his wife as mother of their children and love for the children themselves are for the man the natural way of understanding and fulfilling his own fatherhood.*

> —From *The Christian Family in the Modern World, 25*
> by Pope John Paul II

Monday Mourning

For My Father

Monday morning
is transformed:
no longer
a beginning,
a new start,
nor a fresh breath.

No, Monday morning
brings sad memory now:
the darkness of early day,
the shrillness of a telephone
tearing me from dreams,
the careless washing, dressing,
locking the house,
night's lights still burning,
the dazed driving to your bedside.

And there you were, dear Dad,
still as stone,
eyes unseeing,
the last battle done,
your new journey under way.

I clasped your quiet hand,
And grief grasped me.

It holds me yet.

—*Patricia Mansfield Phelan*
October 1999

52

MARY ELIZABETH CHARROT MANSFIELD
(BORN DECEMBER 15, 1921)

*The womb (is) that space we are born out of, into this world,
where the soft iambics of our mother's heart become the first sure
verses of our being.*

—Thomas Lynch in *Bodies in Motion and
at Rest: On Metaphor and Mortality*

A s her eldest child, especially one who has now lived for more than seven tenths of *her* life, I believe my mother and I share a great deal beyond a wonderful family.

Yes, she is my natural mother, a mere biological fact, but she is so much more to me. Since she brought me into the world, some fifty-seven years ago, she has been an inspiration to me, and to others, in more ways than she can know. Together with my Dad she made me what I am, thanks to a marvelous family life, the way she reared me, and her unconditional love and support.

Her life as a young woman growing up in Brooklyn was remarkable. Her multiple and manifest talents, leadership, scholarship, character and integrity were, and are, of the highest order. The values on which Mom has built her life are desired by many but attained by few. She has lived the Christian life to its fullest, and all who know her have been witnesses to this.

Her life lessons have been well learned by me; at least I hope so. As a mother, she has been an exemplar of goodness and a tower of strength for all six of her children. More than anything else, her profound love for all of us, no matter our shortcomings, failures and mistakes, is her essence and perhaps that quality by which everyone who knows her recognizes the extraordinary person she is. Mom has never failed to forgive, no matter the pain or suffering she may have experienced. She has never held a grudge.

In this connection, when I was in my thirties I came to a realization that some of my male friends reject and resent. It is that women in general are better human beings than men in general. Of course, there are exceptions on both sides. I arrived at this view after having observed the behaviors and communications skills of the ladies in my life, who include Mame, my mother, my grandmothers Angelica Stewart Charrot and Alice Kirkwood Mansfield, my mother-in-law Bernice Bonner Locasto, my daughter Kate, my sister Pat and others. For example, too many men see a problem or challenge as a nail; thus, their only tool is a hammer, if you get my drift. In sum, I am confident that, while I still have much to learn in the realm of successful interpersonal communications, women are the ones who seem often to possess an intuitive ability to deal with others forthrightly and correctly, as well as with charm, style and grace. Thus, I said to myself, I can and will learn from them.

For me personally, Mom's epic faith in Our Lord Jesus Christ has strengthened my own. I have heard her say countless times, "It's the Lord's will." Even in the face of adversity, she has always held fast to that belief, accepting completely whatever obstacle she may confront, and looked ahead, always believing that something good would eventually happen as a result. "Everything happens for a reason," Mom is fond of saying. And then she would let it be known that the resulting good was an answer to prayers—another demonstration of "the power of prayer," as she calls it.

I witnessed this incredible faith when I was with her and my sister Pat at the moment my Dad died. As his heart monitor finally "flatlined," Mom immediately began praying the *Memorare*. It begins, "Remember, O Most Gracious Virgin Mary, that never was it known that anyone who fled to thy protection, implored thy help, or sought thy intercession was left unaided." When I asked her a short while afterward why she prayed as she did, she looked at me as if I should have known better than to ask such a question, and then quietly rejoined, "What else could I do?" Enough said.

She is dynamic and energetic, even at age four score and one. Still walking two miles every day, she puts many younger folks to shame! I will always have images of her, even as the mother of six, doing cartwheels and standing on her head in her backyard. I have observed her staying youthful too, even as she has aged.

Mom is generous to a fault. She consistently thinks of the other person first, never herself. She seeks always to give, never to receive. She never criticizes, even when I have merited criticism. She is a peacemaker, and blessed is she for that. Above all, she has taught and lived the selflessness of true, abiding love. She is a messenger to us all, and I, for one, have gotten and am grateful for her message.

In so many ways my mother is a person whose approach to life has been patterned along the lines of George Sand's advice, quoted earlier in the Preface to this essay: "Try to keep your soul young and quivering right up to old age, and to imagine right up to the brink of death that life is only beginning. I think that is the only way to keep adding to one's talent, and one's inner happiness." In my experience, as a witness to Mom's life, I believe she lives it very much that way.

(Incidentally,—and I think this is funny—George Sand is actually the pseudonym of a woman whose real name is—are you ready?—Amandine Aurore Lucie Dupin, Baronne Dudevant! She lived from 1804 to 1876. Anyway, I find her words inspiring and spiritually uplifting.)

As a man who has been married to the love of his life for more than thirty-five years, I have learned how blessed I am with God's gift of Mame. So, in a personal communication like this, I want to tell Mom and the world once more some of the words I spoke three years ago at my Dad's Mass of the Resurrection: "Dad, I am confident you are listening and I say to your bride: Mom, you made a wonderful, indeed a beautiful, life for Dad and we all thank you for that." I know he loved her more than anyone on earth and, as her son and his, and as a husband myself, I am deeply grateful for the happiness that she brought him, for it made all the difference.

Mom's personal strength and resiliency have been exceptional. In the months following Dad's passing, many people were justifiably concerned about her, and some suggested that she might succumb to a deep depression because of the loss of her husband of fifty-five years. Indeed, this has been true of many who have lost their spouses after a lifetime together.

In those days my siblings and I, all of whom love Mom deeply, observed her carefully—perhaps excessively, with our daily telephone calls and what not. In the last analysis, none of our worries played themselves out, for, day after day, week after week, month after month, Mom moved forward with her life. To be sure, she never ceased to think about, pray for and even talk to her husband, whom, I have no doubt, she still dearly misses. My point is that she has consistently exhibited uncommon strength. I also have communicated to Mom that she certainly impressed me with her mastery—in short order—of the many business aspects of life, most of which, of course, my Dad used to handle.

More recently—this year to be precise, Mom suffered a severe compression fracture of the lower spine in a backward fall at the beach near her Florida home. Seven months later, after enduring excruciating pain and virtual immobility for many weeks, she recovered fully. Why? Because her positive outlook, basic optimism, determination, perseverance and, of course, prayer saw her through. In fact, she returned from Florida to her GC home in July of this year and is back to her normal routine.

In 1986 I wrote a poem for Mom, in which there is a refrain: "Oh, sweet Mary, how you thrive!" I remember reading it to her and the other dinner guests who came to Mame's and my home at 54 Pine Street in GC to celebrate her sixty-fifth birthday. After listening to the poem, Dad told me, "I'm so happy someone finally wrote such beautiful words about your mother." I was touched by his compliment, and I thanked him. More importantly, I was happy to express in the presence of our family and friends what Mom meant to me then.

As for today, my love for her has only grown, and I am thrilled that she is still thriving these many years later. Mine is actually a feeling of great joy because we all have her with us, and last December celebrated her four score years; joy, indeed, especially in light of having almost lost her due to grave illness in August 1998.

As I said in my toast to her on her eightieth birthday, "For at least six of us, you have given us life itself. For all of us you have enriched it by your goodness and love. Long may you live, long may you enjoy the harvest your life has yielded, and may God continue to bless you always."

Thank you, Mom, for all you have given me and so many others. I love you.

> *A mother holds her children's hands for a while . . .*
> *their hearts forever.*

—Anonymous

53

BERNICE MARY BONNER LOCASTO
(JULY 27, 1917–AUGUST 7, 2001)

The reason angels fly is that they take themselves so lightly.

—Gilbert Keith Chesterton

Antonio Porchia has written that "One lives in hope of becoming a memory." Bernice Mary Bonner Locasto has done it, except that she has also provided warm and wonderful memories to countless people whose lives she touched with beauty and grace.

My mother-in-law and, despite that much maligned title, one of my closest friends, Bernice was a phenomenal human being. She was a stalwart traveler and adventuress, even to her life's end. Her family members often speak of her zest for life, her insatiable curiosity (decidedly *not* nosiness) and her thirst for knowledge, especially in the medical field and of other cultures. A voracious reader, she had an extraordinary book collection, built over many years. She is remembered by her five daughters, fourteen grandchildren and hundreds of friends as a tower of strength, an indomitable spirit, and a person of virtually unlimited love and compassion.

Because it conveys the wonderful essence of Bernice's personality and life, I am reprinting here with permission the eulogy given for her on September 29, 2001 by her granddaughter, my daughter Kate.

Dear Grandma,

We are all shocked and saddened—not the typical words for an 84-year-old's passing. By the time she's 84, her children and grandchildren usually find her a dear, but passive presence, perhaps a joy to have around—or maybe a burden requiring too much time and effort. The end of a great-grandparent's life on earth is never a happy occasion, but it's usually not such a surprise.

But losing you is a shock. You dance, you sing (with that beautiful voice), you listen intently, you give us strength, you help your friends and community, you procrastinate, you recycle left-overs, you snore with gusto, and provide a sense and direction and inspiration when we cannot find it. You never faded to become less of a presence in any of our lives. So let us celebrate your life, your extraordinarily full, beloved life. Let's put aside our grief and revel in who you are and the good fortune we had to share your lifetime.

What a remarkable woman. You are my hero, and I'm not alone. James Altman made sure you got public recognition—you met the students at his school as "Person of the Year" more than 10 years ago! You are a hero in many ways—first, in your practical nature. You and your family knew how to make the best of things. How often have we relished tales of the Bonners digging up the front lawn to plant potatoes to feed everyone? You sewed your own dresses; you mended everything; you knitted us beautiful afghans— we all cherish the image of your precious hands knitting peacefully, hands that had given care to so many patients.

But your practical nature is only a small piece of your heroism. Your love of life and your courage inspire us all. In your 70's and 80's you traveled the world, making friends of all ages everywhere you went. The "Friendship Force" might have been named after you. You appreciated the little joys (and ignored the little pains) each day had to hold, despite—or maybe because of—the hardships you had to endure. You cared for and loved your husband passionately, and we trust that you two are having a delightful reunion. Even after the terrible time he went through, when most people would have given up, you charged back into life. You nursed, trained nurses, and became a senior staff member at Hempstead General [Hospital]. You were an energetic and involved grandmother, having us over (to) your apartment to play "lion" and do exercises to that record ("close flip, close flip, this is how you build your grip"). You took the boys as little Santa's helpers to deliver presents at the hospital. You came to our baptisms, communions, confirmations, graduations and weddings. But importantly, you found and shared joy every day, not just on special occasions. You relished so many memories of your life, keeping them fresh by recounting them to us in stories and in letters.

You were an exceptionally intelligent person, although you never made anyone feel like they lacked intelligence. You were high school valedictorian. You devoured so many books, contemplated so many ideas—life and death, love, relationships, world religions and cultures . . . actually, trying to make a list would belittle the incredibly multi-dimensional nature of your intellect and your curiosity.

You are generous and supportive—as parent, friend, grandparent, great-grandparent. You give of all that you have. You forgive us our trespasses and give boundless love. When we need help, strength, a voice of reason, we turn to you.

You are serene. When we all yelled at each other about a game of Scattergories, you knew how to set us straight. When bad news comes your way, you accept the things you cannot change. When we need peace and calm and perspective, we turn to you. You listen, ask the right questions, help us find answers, make every person feel special, see and bring out the best in us.

There's some greeting card cliché about some people lighting the world because their own lights burn so brightly, and some lighting the world by reflecting the light of others. You stand, as my hero, as both a brilliant, burning flame and as a reflector of so many others.

But suddenly we are all unable to turn to you in person for the day-to-day practical solutions, for the mending of shirts and hearts, for your insight and intellect, for that lust for life that lit your wonderful blue eyes and your giggle, for your giving nature, for your serenity. So how do we proceed?

We all have choices on this one, and of course we'll each choose a unique path—but maybe we could each pick out one of those amazing qualities of yours and take it as our own to keep your spirit a constant presence in our lives. I, for one, have already adopted procrastination and penchant for clutter! Maybe someone can learn to knit, someone else pick up the secrets to left-over anything. Maybe we can learn to be as flexible as you, as willing to face and overcome the hurdles. Maybe we can do more to appreciate the wonders of the life we have. We can keep our minds open and intellectually curious. We can listen patiently and try to help each other discover our own answers. We can try to take down the boundaries that keep us from loving or forgiving fully. We can embrace serenity, not just as something to admire or pray for, but as a way of life.

If each of us takes the littlest step toward even one of these goals, you will have helped us, once again, by your example. The fact that all of these qualities defined one woman, Bernice Locasto, leaves me in awe. So let us go and perpetuate her character in little ways in our own lives. Grandma, Mommy, Bernice, Bonga, you are nothing short of inspiration. Forever and ever, Amen.

Requiescat in pace!

"On Dec. 27, 1944 I fell in love with the gift given to me through you. I loved you and cherished you from the moment I held you in my arms (actually many months before that) and that love has never ceased to grow.

I love you—have in the past, in the present, and will continue to do so forever.

Love cannot be measured."

Mother

These words were written by Bernice Bonner Locasto in a birthday card to her daughter Mary Ann. It was dated December 27, 1999, Mame's fifty-fifth birthday.

54

KID STUFF

Sometimes you don't have no control over the way things go.
Hail ruins the crops or fire burns you out. And then you're given
just so much to work with in a life and you have to do the best
you can with what you've got.

—Mary White in *The Quilters*

Since 9/11, a date that will now be published and defined in dictionaries, the United States in particular and, probably to a lesser extent, the world in general, have come to understand as never before that evil exists and can manifest itself in atrocious and terrifying ways. To be sure, all people have recognized anew the fragility of life and the suddenness with which it can be taken from them. Nine-eleven has become the Pearl Harbor of the Baby Boomers and Generation X.

Still, there are often valuable lessons to be learned from difficulties, even when they are cowardly acts of terror that take thousands of innocent human lives. In this connection, Joan Breton Connelly has given us an example arising from the total destruction of the Acropolis in Athens in 480 B.C. To wit:

> The long view from history is an invaluable source of
> hope. It was following tragedy that the Greeks achieved
> their finest moment. Along with the Parthenon [which was
> built to replace the temples that had preceded it] came a full
> flourishing of art, literature, theater, philosophy, religion

and politics, culminating in the development of the democratic system of government. The Athenians responded to outside threat by forging the new and utterly revolutionary concept of self-sacrifice for the common good. From this newly hewn bond of altruism, a strong communal identity was born, one of unity in the face of adversity.

Instant gratification has afflicted many Americans for a long, long time. Some people who don't get what they want immediately go into a funk, sometimes into a bona fide depression. Some say we Americans are "soft." I believe this condition mostly afflicts some of those born after World War II who have had it so good for so long, that is, virtually all their lives, that they frequently find it difficult to deal with adversity, or even reality. I am reminded of the old Dutch proverb, "In prosperity, caution; in adversity, patience."

The realization that dawns with some modicum of maturity impresses upon most of us, sooner or later, that whatever we wish to attain or acquire will necessitate some investment of ourselves. This is the ultimate reality check; in short, it is a four-letter word some people avoid as much as possible: work.

To anyone with kids of any age, or anyone who has ever been a kid, here is some excellent reality-based advice from the book *Dumbing Down Our Kids: Why American Children Feel Good About Themselves, but Can't Read, Write, or Add.* Indicting America's public schools, author Charles J. Sykes, a research fellow at the Hoover Institution, writes refreshingly of how feel-good politically correct teachings have produced a generation of youth with little or no concept of reality, and how this conceptual shortcoming has set them up for failure in the real world. Here are the eleven rules that Mr. Sykes's readers did not, or will not, learn in school.

> *Rule 1*: Life is not fair—get used to it.
>
> *Rule 2*: The world won't care about your self-esteem. The world will expect you to accomplish something BEFORE you feel good about yourself.

Rule 3: You will NOT make 40 thousand dollars a year right out of high school. You won't be a vice president with a car phone, until you earn both.

Rule 4: If you think your teacher is tough, wait till you get a boss. He doesn't have tenure.

Rule 5: Flipping burgers is not beneath your dignity. Your grandparents had a different word for burger flipping—they called it Opportunity.

Rule 6: If you mess up, it's not your parents' fault, so don't whine about your mistakes, learn from them.

Rule 7: Before you were born, your parents weren't as boring as they are now. They got that way from paying your bills, cleaning your clothes and listening to you talk about how cool you are. So before you save the rain forest from the parasites of your parents' generation, try delousing the closet in your own room.

Rule 8: Your school may have done away with winners and losers but life has not. In some schools they have abolished failing grades and they'll give you as many times as you want to get the right answer. This doesn't bear the slightest resemblance to ANYTHING in real life.

Rule 9: Life is not divided into semesters. You don't get summers off, and very few employers are interested in helping you find yourself. Do that on your own time.

Rule 10: Television is NOT real life. In real life people actually have to leave the coffee shop and go to jobs.

Rule 11: Be nice to nerds. Chances are you'll end up working for one.

With respect to Mr. Sykes's Rule 8 on winners and losers, I found in 1999 the following words of wisdom written on a sheet of plain paper tacked to a bulletin board at American Express Bank, my client at the time. No attribution was given.

> A winner says, "Let's find out." A loser says, "Nobody knows."
> A winner makes commitments. A loser makes promises.
> A winner says, "I'm good, but not as good as I ought to be." A loser says, "I'm not as bad as a lot of other people."
> A winner credits "good luck" for winning—even though it wasn't good luck. A loser blames "bad luck" for losing—even though it wasn't bad luck.
> A winner listens. A loser just waits for a turn to talk.
> A winner respects those who are superior and tries to learn from them. A loser resents the superiority of others and tries to find chinks in their armor.
> A winner does more than the job requires. A loser says, "I only work here."
> A winner says, "I fell." A loser says, "Somebody pushed me."

This is nourishing food for thought for all of us, parent and child, old and young.

⧗

There is a particularly poignant, recent and disastrous example of the cost of American parental ignorance and/or non-implementation of core values. It is that of California native John Walker Lindh, the first American Taliban, who fought against the U.S. in Afghanistan and actually said he supported the 9/11 attacks on America.

In a brilliant article entitled "The Road to Treason," Jeff Jacoby wrote that, for Lindh's parents, "There were no absolutes, no fixed truths, no mandatory behavior, no thou-shalt-nots. If they had one conviction, it was that all convictions are worthy, that nothing is intolerable except intolerance."

Without early absolutes, fixed truths, behavioral requirements and even religious proscriptions, our young cannot begin to learn and grow with the benefit of moral and societal benchmarks that will enable them to become judgmental. That's right, *judgmental*. Of course, being *non*judgmental is today regarded by many as the only proper way to function in American society or in life, for that matter. However, I firmly believe that, if we fail to exercise appropriate value judgments, based on sound moral principles, then we and our children will ultimately lose. Some of us may even lose our children as Frank Lindh and Marilyn Walker lost their son.

Like all young people, John Walker Lindh "craved standards and discipline," according to Mr. Jacoby. Sadly, to his ruin and his parents' presumed regret, "Mom and Dad didn't offer any. The Taliban did."

Admittedly, John Walker Lindh is a relatively extreme example. Still, how he ended up as he did is certainly not incomprehensible. His chosen path was destructive of his American countrymen, for which he will be held accountable, and of himself.

In July 2002 Lindh pleaded guilty to charges that he conspired to kill his fellow Americans in Afghanistan. Three months later he was sentenced to twenty years in prison.

In his 1990 book *The New Freedom* my friend Bill Donohue writes compellingly in a chapter entitled "Children's Rights" of liberationists' association of freedom with rights, which was the disastrous miscalculation of John Walker Lindh's parents:

> To make the point more plainly, consider two children, Frank and John. Frank is under strict adult supervision, both at home and at school. He is told when to go to school, what clothes to wear, when to speak in class, when to study, when to play, when to come home, when to go to bed, and so forth. John chooses if and when to go to school, wears whatever he wants when he goes, does exactly as he pleases in class, decides if and when to study, stays out late, and generally sets his own standards. Who is freer, Frank or John?
>
> If the lack of constraints is what counts, John is freer. Now ask yourself who will be freer when he's twenty-one, John or Frank? Frank, of course. But why?

Because while John at twenty-one will be hostage to his passions, Frank will more than likely have developed his resources to at least a satisfactory level, leaving him freer to choose among society's options. His freedom is a function of the constraints placed on him while growing up, limitations imposed on him by responsible adults. Freedom, then, is not anathema to discipline. Rather, freedom is conditioned on discipline.

To discipline a child is not to tyrannize him; it is to enable him to become what he is capable of becoming. Success in any field, whether it be music, athletics, science, or whatever, is dependent on the ability of the individual to practice self-restraint. Self-restraint alone doesn't insure anything, but its absence guarantees failure.

The structured nature of Frank's early life became the platform for his freedom in later years. The disciplines in the approach of those who provided the structure are key, for they never fail.

I am confident, though not proud, that I have learned much more from my children than they have learned from me. As I have often said, "They have their mother's brains." They are my pride, as already noted in this work's dedication.

Since this writing has been in large measure *for* my kids and their progeny, I suppose it ought not be *about* them, at least not in any substantial way. To be sure, Chas, John and Kate are mentioned from time to time herein. Still, I have wondered a ridiculous number of times if I ought to have been serving, to a greater degree, as their biographer. For better or worse, my decision has been not to so serve.

Despite this conclusion, there are important messages I wish to affirm, not only for my grandchildren and, if any, great-grandchildren but also for Chas, John and Kate themselves.

Parents can only give [their children] good advice or put them on the right paths, but the final forming of a person's character lies in their own hands.

—Anne Frank in *Anne Frank: The Diary of a Young Girl*

Although today a plethora of how-to books is easily available on how to be a good parent, the vaccine of experience is still, always has been and likely always will be the best and most authentic teacher. I know I was not always a good parent but I hope I was less frequently a bad one. My role model for fatherhood was a tough but good man—my Dad, who lost his father at thirteen when he arguably needed him most. Dad's Dad's death may have been for my father doubly traumatic since he had lost his mother when he was only eight. In sum, Dad parented me and my five siblings without the opportunity or benefit of long, continuous observation of his parents parenting him; in contrast, I had both my parents in my life for more than fifty-four years.

When does a parent stop being a parent? Some say never.

When do children no longer need their parents? Earlier than their parents arrive at that conclusion, I would say. To be candid, I believe that my children no longer *need* me, but I take comfort in another belief that they probably still *want* me, as well as their mother, in their lives. As all three are independent and successful young adults, I would characterize their parents' wish today as being able to 'be there *for* them,' if and when necessary or appropriate.

I also believe that Chas, John and Kate somehow learned self-reliance early in their lives; precisely how they were taught this, I do not know. Be that as it may, there is no question at least in my own mind that, after each left our household, he or she chose a path, took it, not always knowing where it would lead, and made good things happen for himself, herself and others along the way.

⧗

Chas and his wife Dawn-Marie (Chiaramonte) and their four children (Timothy, Marissa, Kevin and Justin) live in Charlotte, North Carolina, where Chas is a vice president at Bank of America. They first made their home there in 1996, and have since become welcome members of a warm and friendly community. While there's little chance they would ever *choose* to return to New York, they do visit us a few times each year, and vice versa.

In my estimation, Chas and Dawn are extraordinary, not merely good, parents, and I admire them immensely for that. I am also happy for them as they have celebrated their tenth wedding anniversary this year.

Chas has been a self-starter ever since he was a little boy. The challenges in his life are now enormous, but he seems to take them in stride.

He is a 1990 alumnus of the Massachusetts Institute of Technology (MIT), where he belonged to Sigma Phi Epsilon, the fraternity.

Today I often have the feeling that Chas and Dawn must somehow build me up, thus misrepresenting me, to their children as some sort of super hero. If this is not the case, then I cannot comprehend why my grandchildren seem to revere their "Poppa" so. It's amazing and sometimes embarrassing. I honestly wonder what I have done to deserve such apparent adulation, because nothing significant comes to mind. Maybe that's just the way it is for grandfathers, and, if so, it is beautiful. That said, I increasingly suspect that Tim, my eldest grandson, nine, has already gained many insights into his grandfather's myriad shortcomings. By the way, Tim, an exceptionally bright young lad and an A-student, is already an outstanding athlete; I am proud of Chas for all he has done for and with Tim and, of course, the younger three.

John has made it clear—in a reading from Robert Frost rendered stirringly by his sister Kate at his wedding ceremony—that "Two roads diverged in a wood, and I—/ I took the one less traveled by,/ And that has made all the difference."

Of maybe thousands of memories of John, one of my fondest is of a day during his years at Vermont's Middlebury College, from which he graduated *cum laude* in 1992. At his behest, just he and I walked the Robert Frost Trail on the side of a mountain, I know not which, stopping along the way to sample the great man's poetry, which was inscribed on various weather-proof markers under the open sky.

A fine athlete with incredible agility and ability to control his body *in the air*, he has excelled at diving, pole vaulting, skiing and, nowadays, snowboarding. He was also once a bunji jumping fanatic, and is still an avid surfer.

One of John's great attributes is his proven ability to overcome adversity, and I admire this in him. We all get knocked down; the important thing is to get up and keep going.

John is married and still lives in Vermont with his wife Elizabeth (Van Hook). He is employed by Controlled Energy Corporation, and Liz is a marketing representative. In addition, they own a residential-retail building and deal in antiques and other collectibles. They have also purchased some 107 acres of additional land in Vermont, and have recently shown us the plans for the home they will build on the parcel soon.

⧗

To me Kate has always seemed to know where she was going, although I don't recall her saying, 'I plan to do this, or I want to be that.' Her inner compass has guided her well, at least from where I sit. I recall traveling with her in North Carolina many years ago, having just visited Duke University, to which she was considering applying for admission. In a somewhat offhanded way, I suggested that she apply to Harvard University in Cambridge, Massachusetts.

Without hesitation, Kate answered, with seeming but uncharacteristic impatience in her tone, "Dad, Harvard's a place for the Edward Joneses of the world; I wouldn't get in."

Taken aback by what I perceived as this never-before-heard lack of self-confidence, I challenged her.

"Kate, I'll bet you fifty bucks (said he who was out of work at the time) that if you apply to Harvard, not only will you be accepted, you'll be granted early admission."

"Dad, I love you, but you're crazy," she said.

As I had foretold, she was accepted and admitted early by Harvard. (Edward Jones, the fictitious name of the brilliant Chaminade student who happened to be a good friend of Kate, was not.)

In 1996 Kate graduated *magna cum laude* and joined the investment management division of Goldman Sachs & Company in New York City. She was promoted to vice president at age twenty-six, and at this writing lives and works in London.

On September 8, 2001 Kate arrived in the U.S. for three weeks that would include time at Goldman Sachs's offices in New York City, family visits and the interment of her Grandma Locasto's cremains, or ashes. By irony of fate, three days later she would find herself working in lower Manhattan just a few short blocks from the World Trade Center at the moment of the terrorist attacks.

For hours on that horrific morning I could not reach her, either by landline or by cell phone. Then, having gone on line, I found and read an e-mail from one of Kate's colleagues in London, whom Kate had asked to assure Mame and me that she was safe and well. I learned later in a never-more-welcome telephone call from Kate that, after a harrowing flight on foot during which she heard one of the towers collapse, she managed to make her way to a friend's apartment and, later, to catch a train to the home of other friends in Connecticut. As she told it, "Dad, the earth shook and I thought a bomb was going off."

On Sunday, September 30 th, I drove Kate to JFK airport for her return trip to London. The following e-mails were exchanged the next day.

Kate wrote:

Don't worry about me. I actually felt a sense of relief when I got back here. It is helping me to be around my usual colleagues, familiar scenes, etc. London is much less concentrated than NY, and that is a comfort. I am going to walk to work tomorrow, and see how I feel from there.

Everyone here seems to feel that the world is changed, but not as viscerally as we feel. I wish you could be here with me; it is helpful to have people around who don't feel the weight of what we've been feeling in NY.

I love you and I think we just need to keep chipping away at the fear. Elisabeth [my sister] sent me a wonderful quote last week: "You can gain strength, courage and confidence by every experience in which you really stop to look fear in the face . . . You must do the thing which you think you cannot do."—Eleanor Roosevelt

Although we're all at the point where we're questioning the value of strength, courage and confidence somewhat at the moment, we have built our lives on them and have to continue to build.

Love you and miss you already,
Katie

I replied to Kate:

Thank you for writing; Mom and I are happy and relieved that you are back, safe and sound.

I told Mom when I got home from JFK yesterday afternoon that saying goodbye to you there was very hard for me. I actually told her that the only goodbye more difficult in my life was when I left her and Chas to go to Vietnam in '68.

Yesterday I didn't want you to go. I almost asked you not to go. I was so worried about losing you. My inner voice told me on the one hand, that you wouldn't be going if you really didn't want to; after all, it was your decision. On the other hand, I knew I couldn't live with myself if something happened to you, especially aboard your flight yesterday.

This thing has gotten to us all, I'm afraid.

I love you deeply, and I miss you already.

God bless you!

Kate is very much in the mold of her mother and both of her grandmothers, Bernice Locasto and Mary Mansfield. Translated, this means that her human gifts are abundant. I once said that she could be president of the United States, that is, if she wants the job. I still believe it.

⧗

A learned man once told me that life is a series of accidents, and there is truth in what he said. The key is how we address each accident and what we make of it. If you prefer, substitute *opportunity* for accident. The message then becomes a little clearer, I suppose, for opportunity probably sounds more positive and implies choice.

What are the choices we make each day? How do those choices we have made over the course of our lives appear in retrospect? How do we judge ourselves vis-à-vis our performance in dealing with those opportunities and choices? Where did the choices made for us by our parents, and the guidance provided by them, leave us when it came time to seek our own opportunities and make our own choices? Were we prepared or not?

America's children are her hope for the future. Each of us has countless opportunities throughout our lives to influence, for good or ill, many children, be they our own or those entrusted to us by others. In many cases, today's kids are being shortchanged because of the lack of discipline, values and even basic morality that pervades our culture.

Many people, including friends and family members, often assert that the world has changed to such an extent that the core values of yesteryear are no longer applicable in today's society. To those who hold such a view, I certainly would not deny that the world has changed since the 1950s and 1960s, when I came of age. Nonetheless, the lessons to be learned today can and should draw on the solid foundations on which many of today's parents and grandparents have built happy, steadfast and successful lives. In other words, the rules of basic morality and human decency need not be rewritten.

True, life isn't fair, and Charles Sykes wasn't the first person to make this observation. Indeed, it may have been Adam or Eve. God's blessings and even plain old good luck are always welcome. In the last analysis, though, life is what we make it.

If I live to the age of 85, more than two-thirds of my life is already behind me. There are many things I have accomplished, and many I would still like to accomplish. More than anything in my life, though, I now look to and hope for my children, for I recognize that the world is now in their hands, at least somewhat more than it is now in mine. Each of them has set a course and is moving in line with his or her goals and happiness. All three have surpassed in many ways, except one, what their parents have accomplished. That one yet to come will amalgamate for them the pride, the joy and the satisfaction of having witnessed the best come forth from the best.

These three young adults—Chas, John and Kate—are the best I have ever known. Easy to say, yes, and I concede that I'm hardly objective. Still, as I consider all the people I have met, worked with and come to know, even the hundreds in years past, I am struck by what my kids have been and have become. I have long watched them grow and mature. Now, as a spectator on the sidelines of their life performances, I see and experience their profound goodness, their inner strength and their unconditional love. I am blessed to be able to call them my children, and I thank God for sending them my way.

May they and theirs be as blessed as I have been.

Deo gratias!

> *Grown-ups never understand anything for themselves, and it is tiresome for children to be always and forever explaining things to them.*

> —Antoine de Saint-Exupéry in *The Little Prince*

For the Record
My Kids' Dates and Places of Birth
Charles Francis Mansfield, III—April 2, 1968
(Quantico, Virginia)
John Camillo Mansfield—May 24, 1970
(Mineola, New York)
Kathryn Mary Mansfield—January 12, 1975
(Mineola, New York)

Epilogue

Now hollow fires burn out to black,
And lights are guttering low:
Square your shoulders, lift your pack,
And leave your friends and go.

—Alfred Edward Housman

In the preface to this work I expressed hope that some day my children and grandchildren would read it. Since I began writing it I have said to many that, if my offspring do choose to read it, they may say to themselves, "So that's what the old man was all about."

To some others who pick up this offering, there will be only a few surprises. Indeed, "The book is all Chuck," as Mame has described it. She's right, and my writing derives principally from the defining time I spent in Vietnam, which I believe enlightened and matured me. In this connection, shortly after I returned to The World, Mame told me I was a different person than the young man who had gone there the preceding year. Right again.

In the last analysis, a man, especially one who is a father and a grandfather, typically leaves behind as traces of his life such tangible items as photographs and other memorabilia. Then there are intangibles too—mostly memories, stories and even a few remembered spoken words—all of which fade and eventually disappear, as do the generations before and after. For me the written word is my legacy, for words on a printed page usually last longer.

It is finished.

—John 19:30

487

CREDITS

Grateful acknowledgement is owed and offered to the following friends, authors, contributors, publishers and institutions:

Acuff-Rose Music, Inc.: Lyric from "('Til) I Kissed You." Words and music by Don Everly. Copyright © 1959 (renewed 1987) by Acuff-Rose Music, Inc. All rights reserved. Used by permission.

The Advocate: Excerpt used with permission of Michael W. Elkins, Director of Editorial Operations, Liberation Publications, Inc., Los Angeles, 2002.

Charlotte Allen: Excerpts from "God Knows Why, Lies About Religion Are Taken as the Gospel Truth" published December 19, 2001. Reprinted with the author's permission from *The Wall Street Journal* © 2001 Dow Jones & Company, Inc. All rights reserved.

David Barth

Basic Books (A Member of the Perseus Books Group): Excerpt from *The Savage Wars of Peace: Small Wars and the Rise of American Power* by Max Boot. Copyright © 2002. Used with permission of the author.

Dr. William J. Bennett

O. J. Betz III

Big Sky Music: Excerpts from "Lay Lady Lay" by Bob Dylan. Copyright © 1969 by Big Sky Music. All rights reserved. International copyright secured. Reprinted by permission.

Bloomberg News Wire: Excerpts from "Chaminade High School Relies on God, Unity to Cope with Losses" by Liz Willen. Copyright 2001 Bloomberg LP. Reprinted with permission. All rights reserved. Visit *www.Bloomberg.com*.

Patrick Boland

Dr. Tony Kern, Lieutenant Colonel, USAF (Ret.), "Open Letter to America," September 24, 2001.

Colonel Bob Kielhofer, USMCR (Ret.) (from his website)

Colonel Dana King

Earl P. Kirmser, Jr.

Martin Kramer: Excerpts from "Terrorism? What Terrorism?" published November 15, 2001. Reprinted with the author's permission from *The Wall Street Journal* © 2001 Dow Jones & Company, Inc. All rights reserved.

Rabbi Daniel Lapin

Rush Limbaugh: Excerpts from "Clinton Didn't Do Enough to Stop Terrorists" published October 4, 2001. Reprinted with the author's permission from *The Wall Street Journal* © 2001 Dow Jones & Company, Inc. All rights reserved.

Patrick K. Long

Los Angeles Times Magazine: Excerpts from "Waiting for the Real Repercussions" by Janet Reitman published October 21, 2001. Copyright © 2001, Los Angeles Times. Reprinted with permission.

Judy Lutz, *Naples Daily News*

Harvey Mansfield: Excerpts from "To B or Not to B?" published December 20, 2001. Reprinted with the author's permission from *The Wall Street Journal* © 2001 Dow Jones & Company, Inc. All rights reserved.

Massachusetts News: Excerpts from "Students in 'Vagina Monologues' Divide Holy Cross Community" by Amy Contrada published February 15, 2002. Copyright © 2002. Used by permission.

Bro. Michael J. McAward, S.M.

Senator John McCain: Excerpts from "There Is No Substitute for Victory" published October 26, 2001. Reprinted with the author's permission from *The Wall Street Journal* © 2001 Dow Jones & Company, Inc. All rights reserved.

Wendy McElroy: Excerpts from "Government Should Not Dictate Diversity," January 1, 2002. Reprinted with the author's permission.

Media Research Center: Excerpt from *Media Watch*. Copyright © 1998. All rights reserved. Used by permission.

Joseph C. Moosbrugger, Jr.

Charles H. Morin, Esq.

Dick Morris: Excerpts from "While Clinton Fiddled" published February 5,

ABOUT THE AUTHOR

A Brooklyn native, Chuck Mansfield graduated from Chaminade High School (Mineola, N.Y.) in 1962. Upon graduation four years later from the College of the Holy Cross (Worcester, Mass.), he was commissioned a second lieutenant in the United States Marine Corps Reserve. Later, he received an M.B.A. in finance from New York University, which he earned by attending evening classes.

In June 1968 he was assigned to WestPac Ground Forces in Vietnam where he served as a platoon commander with the Third Marine Division's Headquarters Battalion Communications Company. Based in Dong Ha approximately five miles south of the demilitarized zone, or DMZ, which then divided North and South Vietnam, he was responsible for approximately 100 Marines, half of whom were situated in Dong Ha; the rest were assigned to various outposts along the DMZ, as well as elsewhere in the northern I Corps Tactical Area of Responsibility.

Chuck served in Vietnam in 1968 and 1969, the two bloodiest years of the war for both sides. Promoted to captain in 1969, he was awarded the Navy and Marine Corps Achievement Medal with Combat "V", the Combat Action Ribbon, the Vietnam Campaign Medal, the Vietnam Service Medal and the National Defense Service Medal.

A former banker and a management consultant, he has lived and/or worked in Belgium, Britain, Canada, China, Colombia, France, Italy, Japan, Kazakhstan, Luxembourg, the Netherlands, the Philippines, Russia, Singapore and South Korea.

He is a director/trustee of the Federated Funds of Federated Investors, Inc., a $195-billion mutual fund complex headquartered in Pittsburgh and listed on the New York Stock Exchange.

Chuck and his wife Mame have three adult children, and live in Mineola and Westhampton, New York.